SHEFFIELD STEEL AND AMERICA:
A CENTURY OF COMMERCIAL AND
TECHNOLOGICAL INTERDEPENDENCE,
1830–1930

SHEFFIELD STEEL AND AMERICA:

A CENTURY OF COMMERCIAL AND TECHNOLOGICAL INTERDEPENDENCE,

1830–1930

GEOFFREY TWEEDALE

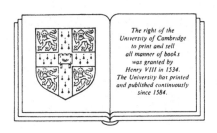

The right of the
University of Cambridge
to print and sell
all manner of books
was granted by
Henry VIII in 1534.
The University has printed
and published continuously
since 1584.

CAMBRIDGE UNIVERSITY PRESS

CAMBRIDGE

LONDON   NEW YORK   NEW ROCHELLE
MELBOURNE   SYDNEY

CAMBRIDGE UNIVERSITY PRESS
Cambridge, New York, Melbourne, Madrid, Cape Town, Singapore, São Paulo, Delhi

Cambridge University Press
The Edinburgh Building, Cambridge CB2 8RU, UK

Published in the United States of America by Cambridge University Press, New York

www.cambridge.org
Information on this title: www.cambridge.org/9780521109758

First published 1987
This digitally printed version 2009

A catalogue record for this publication is available from the British Library

Library of Congress Cataloguing in Publication data
Tweedale, Geoffrey.
Sheffield steel and America.
Bibliography.
Includes index.
1. Steel industry and trade – England – Sheffield –
History.   2. Steel industry and trade – United States –
History.   I. Title.
TS304.G7T84   1987   338.7′6272′0942821   86–26433

ISBN 978-0-521-33458-7 hardback
ISBN 978-0-521-10975-8 paperback

For my parents

CONTENTS

TABLES AND MAP

PREFACE

In an analysis of the early nineteenth-century Atlantic economy, Jim Potter has written: 'The development of separate industries [in Britain and the US], especially from a technological point of view, needs to be examined in both countries with a view to discovering to what extent, for example, the lines of development were competitive and to what extent complementary. There are of course many excellent studies of the growth of separate industries on both sides of the Atlantic, but these generally provide only partial explanations of the trends.'* In this book I have attempted to provide such a transatlantic study for the Sheffield steel industry's and allied trades' commercial and technological relationship with America during the period 1830–1930.

When I began my research in 1978 a survey of the published literature soon showed that there was plenty of room for such a work. Not only has very little been written on Sheffield's American connection, but also the history of the world's most famous steelmaking centre has been surprisingly neglected. For most economic historians the age of steelmaking dates from the activities of Sir Henry Bessemer and Andrew Carnegie, and reference to most of the standard texts on the steel industry would lead to the conclusion that very little steel was made before the arrival of Bessemer's converter. This viewpoint seems to stem from a fascination with the personalities involved and quantitative measurements of steel production. The Bessemer process, spouting showers of sparks and flames and producing prodigious tonnages of steel, was far more spectacular than Sheffield's crucible, and its achievements were fully advertised (with some exaggeration) by its illustrious inventor and the American entrepreneurs who made it work so successfully. The advance of crucible steelmaking, though equally hard won, was altogether less dramatic, being achieved over a century or more with almost no publicity. Economic historians'

* The Potter article and the other works cited here are fully referenced in the endnotes and the bibliography

concerns with quantification and growth have done little to correct this imbalance. The steel industry has been a firm favourite in debates over comparative Anglo-American growth, but in the work of Birch, Burn, Burnham and Hoskins, Habakkuk, McCloskey, and Warren, relatively little or no consideration has been given to Sheffield special steel. American authorities, such as Temin and Hogan, have also given high-grade steelmaking only a passing mention. The neglect, apparently, reflects a widely held view, shared by Temin, that crucible steel was of only 'limited' economic importance. Business historians have done little to revise this verdict. Of the published monographs on Sheffield steel firms, including those by Andrews and Brunner, Grant, Scott, and Trebilcock, only Pollard's study of Marsh Bros has focused on crucible steelmaking. Although an excellent unpublished study by J. G. Timmins exists, only very recently has the first full-length treatment of the Sheffield steel industry been published – the work of K. C. Barraclough, a trained metallurgist rather than a professional historian.

In terms of tonnage, few would argue with crucible steel's minor ranking: at the end of the nineteenth century when crucible steel was facing severe competition from both the Bessemer and open-hearth processes its share of total production in both England and America was a mere 1–2 percent. However, once it is accepted that most bulk steel was useless without tougher steel to machine it, and that crucible steel was never surpassed in the nineteenth century for the cutting edge of tools and the critical parts in machinery, then it becomes evident that the importance of special steel has never been properly appreciated. Certainly the technology of special steel manufacture has received far less attention than it deserves. Although a few historians, such as Rosenberg, have stressed the importance of special steels and their 'interdependence' to the general level of technological and inventive activity, as yet no attempt has been made to assess in detail the impact of such steels on the American economy.

Nor in the light trades of cutlery, saw, and file manufacture has any really detailed work appeared since the study by G. I. H. Lloyd. Again, much of the best research is unpublished and, although some of it relates to the US market, there has been no systematic attempt to analyse the interaction of the Sheffield and American industries.

By bringing together material from a diverse range of sources – including business records (some of which are used here for the first time), technical journals and newspapers, company histories, scholarly monographs, and official publications – this study seeks to redress the balance. After an introduction which outlines the origins of Sheffield's

American trade, the crucible steel sector of the steel industry is considered both in Sheffield and American centres such as Pittsburgh. A second section discusses the development of special steels – manganese, silicon, vanadium, tool, and stainless – in which Sheffield played such a notable part. Finally, the involvement of Sheffield steelmakers and toolmakers in the US is extensively documented and the Sheffield entrepreneur's approach to the American market and his attitudes to advertising and selling are investigated. In summary, the light and heavy steel trades are contrasted and the conclusions are set against current historical debates concerning English and American technology diffusion. It will be evident from the material presented here that, although the American economy became increasingly independent in the late nineteenth century, especially in the hardware trades, this did not bring technological autonomy. In fact, the evolution of special steels shows the Atlantic economy operating far beyond its recognised confines, so that Sheffield continued to provide vital technological inputs for American industry even in the twentieth century.

ACKNOWLEDGEMENTS

This is a revised and expanded version of a thesis which was accepted for the degree of Doctor of Philosophy at London University in January 1984.

The study began in 1974–75 when I was introduced to the subject of American economic history by Mr Jim Potter and Professor Charlotte J. Erickson at the London School of Economics. Mr Potter welcomed my return to the LSE in 1978 and secured for me a two-year Social Science Research Council award (supplemented by an American travel grant in 1980), which enabled me to complete the first part of the research. Professor Erickson supervised me for a further year and gave me the benefit of her own expertise on the Sheffield steel industry and on immigration. She also found part-time employment for me with the University of Massachusetts – an invaluable support when SSRC funding ceased. Professor Leslie Hannah and Dr David Jeremy, in the Business History Unit at LSE, were also helpful in providing extra sources of income in the final stages of my work. Dr Jeremy, whose own study on textile technologies was a source of inspiration for this book, gave me many helpful suggestions and first directed me to the materials at the Eleutherian Mills Historical Library. Finally, a grant from the Central Research Fund of London University allowed me to complete my work in the US in 1982.

I am indebted to a number of libraries and research institutions on both sides of the Atlantic. The following deserve a special mention: the British Library of Political and Economic Science (especially Inter-Library Loans); the Institute of Metals (Miss Wendy Todd); Baker Libary, Harvard University; Butler Library, Columbia University; the Carnegie Library of Pittsburgh; the Historical Society of Pennsylvania; and the National Archives, Washington, DC. Much of the work was conducted in Sheffield Central Library's superb local studies collection, where Richard Childs, Dr David Postles and the members of the Library staff were invariably courteous and helpful. In Delaware my research opportunities were further extended by the marvellous resources of the Eleutherian

Mills Historical Library (now the Hagley Museum and Library) in Wilmington. At EMHL Dr Richmond D. Williams, who secured a grant-in-aid for my visit in 1982, Betty-Bright Low, Carol Hallman, and Marjorie McNinch greatly facilitated my quest for manuscripts and books.

Assistance and information was also provided by: Dr Kenneth C. Barraclough; Professor Roy Church; Professor Robert B. Gordon; D. Hodgkinson of Hadfields Ltd; W. G. Ibberson, OBE; Ron Kley; Sir Eric Mensforth; Lord Riverdale; Dr Bruce Seely; Dennis Wragg of Johnson Firth Brown plc; and Richard Wright. Dennis and Marilyn Siebold provided friendship and support during my stay in Wilmington. Keith Matthews gave indispensable technical help by patiently familiarising me with the latest micro-computer technology. Above all, my parents provided the congenial surroundings without which it would have been impossible to write this study.

Hinckley, Leicestershire, July 1986

ABBREVIATIONS

ACAB   *Appleton's Cyclopaedia of American Biography*
AGM   *Annual General Meeting*
BAISA   *Bulletin of the American Iron and Steel Association*
BL   Baker Library, Harvard University, Boston, Mass.
BLCU   Butler Library, Columbia University, New York City
CEAIA   *Chronicle of the Early American Industries Association*
DAB   *Dictionary of American Biography*
DBB   *Dictionary of Business Biography*
DNB   *Dictionary of National Biography*
EMHL   Eleutherian Mills Historical Library
HSP   Historical Society of Pennsylvania, Philadelphia, Pa.
ICTR   *Iron and Coal Trades Review*
JISI   *Journal of the Iron and Steel Institute*
MPICE   *Minutes of the Proceedings of the Institution of Civil Engineers*
NCAB   *National Cyclopaedia of American Biography*
NFISM   National Federation of Iron and Steel Manufacturers
PASTM   *Proceedings of the American Society for Testing Materials*
PIME   *Proceedings of the Institution of Mechanical Engineers*
PP   *Parliamentary Papers*
PRO   Public Record Office, Kew
RC   Royal Commission
SC   Special Committee
SCL   Sheffield City Library, Archives Division
SUA   Sheffield University Archives
TAES   *Transactions of the American Electrochemical Society*
TASCE   *Transactions of the American Society of Civil Engineers*
TASME   *Transactions of the American Society of Mechanical Engineers*
TASST   *Transactions of the American Society for Steel Treating*
USNA   United States National Archives, Washington, DC

INTRODUCTION: SHEFFIELD AND THE GENESIS OF THE AMERICAN TRADE

> Nothing can account for the sustained prosperity of Sheffield, and the very large increase of its population from 1821 to 1831 ... except the American demand.
> A. Gatty, *Sheffield: Past and Present* (Sheffield, 1873), p. 213.

In England the name 'Sheffield' has long been synonymous with fine-quality steel, no more so than in the early nineteenth century when the town, though seeming to possess few advantages for the manufacture of steel, virtually monopolised the industry in Europe. In contrast, the United States before 1860 was still in the age of wood and iron, relying almost exclusively on England for supplies of cast steel. No better example illustrates the Anglo-American relationship termed the Atlantic economy.[1]

Sheffield's technical mastery of steel manufacture involved the crucible or cast steel process – an invention generally attributed to Benjamin Huntsman (1704–76), the Quaker clockmaker from Doncaster, who, in 1742, hit upon the idea of melting pieces of carburised bar iron in a clay pot. Until Huntsman's discovery the only type of steel commercially available was 'blister' or 'cemented' steel, produced by baking or 'converting' wrought iron in charcoal until it absorbed the necessary carbon. The uniformity of blister steel (so called because of the appearance of numerous swellings on the surface of the bars) could be improved greatly by forging, making it into 'shear' steel, the material of choice for Sheffield's famous cutlery; but it was far from ideal for other uses. By melting blister steel, however, Huntsman not only thoroughly diffused the carbon, so improving the steel's working properties – which could be enhanced by the addition of various 'physics' – but he also had the chance to pour the molten metal into a mould. So was produced Europe's first steel ingot.[2] Huntsman's commercial exploitation of his process began in the 1750s and by 1830, Sheffield, the town where he began manufacture, had firmly established itself as the world's steelmaking capital – a town 'as completely the metropolis of steel as Manchester is of cotton or Leeds of woollens'.[3]

Not only was Sheffield the world leader in steelmaking (it has been estimated that by 1850 the town was producing 90 percent of all British steel and 50 percent of all European), it was also a major European centre for cutlery and edge tool, saw, and file manufacture. Also, while Huntsman was revolutionising steelmaking, Thomas Boulsover had discovered a type of imitation silver ('Sheffield Plate') by fusing copper and silver. Shortly afterwards, another Sheffield metalworker, James Vickers, began producing Britannia metal, from tin, copper, and antimony, which rapidly superseded pewter as the poor man's silver. In 1830 there seemed to be nothing associated with steel manufacture that Sheffielders could not do better than anyone else. No other British industrial town – not even Manchester or Birmingham – could match Sheffield's inventiveness and diversity in metal manufactures.[4]

This diversity reflected the high degree of specialisation that had created minute divisions amongst the local trades, each with its own trade society, its own piece-rates and its own traditions, and each producing innumerable patterns and qualities. In about 1830 this was seen as the great strength of the Sheffield trades. One visitor discovered that 'the perfection of the Sheffield manufactures arises from the judicious division of labour. I saw knives, razors ... produced in a few minutes from the raw material. I saw dinner knives made from the steel bar, and all the process of hammering it into form, welding the tang of the handle to the steel of the blade, hardening the metal by cooling it in water, and tempering it by decarbonizing it in the fire, with a rapidity and facility that were astonishing.'[5] In short, it was mass-production by traditional methods. Manual skill was the main industrial factor and consequently most firms remained fairly small, since the idea of a self-contained factory where each operation was subject to the control of a single guiding hand was alien to the Sheffield trades. Mechanisation had yet made little impact, as much for social as technological reasons. The trade unions dominated the local specialised crafts, ensuring by various sanctions, often involving violence or 'trade outrages', that the skills of the craftsmen were never supplanted by machinery.[6]

Nearly all of the Sheffield trades involved hardship. Burns and gruesome injuries were suffered by the steelmakers; the file cutters risked lead poisoning from their cutting blocks and often ended their days permanently bow-legged and stooped; and the grinders faced the twin hazards of shattering grindstones and 'grinders' disease', a debilitating condition caused by the inhalation of sandstone and steel particles which ensured that they rarely reached the age of forty. In compensation, wages for these crafts were relatively high, a fact frequently mentioned by contemporaries, though it was also noted that the higher earnings were almost invariably spent on the Sheffield workman's favourite pastime – drinking. Such pursuits were not only an escape from working but also living conditions, which for the majority were cramped and insanitary. Sheffield in the early nineteenth century had yet to come to terms with a massive increase in population from 31,000 to nearly 135,000 between 1800 and 1850.

Nevertheless, other industrialising nations regarded Sheffield as an example to be emulated. Foreign visitors toured its crucible steel furnaces hoping to learn the secrets of the processes as they watched the melters tip the gleaming metal into the moulds. Later in the century Americans would be critical of Sheffield's archaic methods and its drunken workmen, but in the 1820s and 1830s, when Sheffield manufacturing techniques represented the state of the art, they too had nothing but praise for its industries.[7] Zachariah Allen, the famous Rhode Island textile manufacturer, visited the town at about this time, and recorded his awed impressions of a visit to the showrooms of Joseph Rodgers (the only such establishment in the world), where he saw displayed scissors large enough to walk beneath and knives with over two thousand blades 'like the horrid quills on a porcupine's back'.[8] Such firms had little to fear from US competition at this time and the emerging American cutlery and edge tool industry was scarcely given a second thought by Sheffield manufacturers.[9] America in 1830 was the town's biggest customer, not its rival.

Sheffield's American connection was an old one that had first flourished with the eighteenth-century trade in cutlery and edge tools.[10] In the words of one Sheffield worthy:

The [American] settler needed his axe to fell the primeval forest, his spade to break the hitherto untilled ground, his saw, and chisel, and file, and scythe, and shears for constant use in building and agriculture, as well as the necessary domestic utensils in setting up a new home. These and the like were the very things which Sheffield could at once supply, and it did so to a very large extent – insomuch that some few houses of business in Sheffield had established their agents at New York before the commencement of the present century, and the result was that its prosperity became most closely linked with the fortunes of America.[11]

The beginnings of the town's American trade cannot be dated precisely. But it was the cutlery and edge tool trade with the US which was largely responsible for the burst of activity and the 'immense earnings' of Sheffield manufacturers, noted by Arthur Young on his tour through the district in about 1769.[12] A little later the trade was of such importance that the American War of Independence 'created much alarm in the town, particularly amongst the several merchants and factors who during the last fifteen years had opened a trade to Philadelphia, Boston, and other places'.[13] The growth of the trade was reflected in the American preference for Sheffield planes, saws and files by makers such as Spear, Greaves, Butcher and Ibbotson,[14] whilst the cutlery marks of Joseph Rodgers and George Wostenholm became as prestigious in the US as they were in England.

Shortly after 1800 it was estimated that a third of Sheffield's working population of 18,000 was engaged in the American trade, which consumed a third of the town's manufactured goods. Moreover, eighteen 'export houses' dealt with the American market (compared with nine to other foreign countries), and firms such as Naylor Sanderson sent almost the whole of their goods to the US.[15] Though the accuracy of some of these figures may be disputed, it is clear that about this time the transatlantic trade was beginning to rival Sheffield's Continental trade. The movement gathered pace enormously after 1815, when:

From seven to ten Sheffield firms at once embarked largely in direct trade with America; some of these sent vast quantities of goods on sale, some took orders on very long terms of credit: 'there was', says an active witness of the period, 'a mad rush for goods'; the *cornu copia* was freely poured into the lap of the ready customer, and then came a glut, dismay, and disaster. 'Many American houses suffered, some so seriously as to disappear from among us. Few emerged from this crisis without heavy losses, all arising from a financial collapse in America growing out of the transition from war to peace.' Some few houses of high character had remained comparatively unscathed during this season of trial, and the competition being lessened by the adversities of those who had suffered, it was not difficult to establish a new basis of commercial engagements, – that of cutting down long credits to the American dealers, to terms almost equivalent to cash payments on the delivery of the goods. This has been considered the first great cause of all the fortunes subsequently made in the American trade.[16]

By the late 1820s the demand was so great that Sheffield had difficulty in meeting orders. William Cobbett, observing that in the scythe trade America was 'still a part of old England', waxed complacent about edge tool manufacture: 'No fear of rivalship in this trade. The Americans may lay on their tariff, and double it and triple it; but as long as they continue to cut their victuals, from Sheffield they must have the things to *cut* it with.'[17] Though Cobbett's optimism was misplaced – the tool trade peaked in the 1830s and 1840s – the increasing self-sufficiency of Americans simply meant, in the absence of domestic cast steelmakers, a greater demand for Sheffield steel, ensuring that from 1820 to 1850 the 'rise of fresh applicants for American orders continued unceasing'.[18] So closely did Sheffield and America become tied that it seemed to one observer as 'if the fortunes of the town rose and fell with the temperature of the American demands'.[19]

Other factors contributed to Sheffield's success. The opening of the canal in 1819 and the Sheffield–Rotherham railway in 1838 gave better access to both American and Baltic markets.[20] Sheffield was an entrepôt in the Atlantic economy, converting Swedish iron into steel for subsequent shipment to the US and also monopolising the sale of Swedish bar iron in America through its own agents.[21] Nevertheless, it seems to have been the American market which fuelled Sheffield's growth. By the 1820s and 1830s several crucible steel firms such as Sanderson Bros, William Greaves, William & Samuel Butcher, and Jessop's had outgrown their 'back-yard' and small-scale origins.[22] All these enterprises traded chiefly with America. By 1850 the number of men who had made large fortunes in the American trade included all the great captains of Sheffield steel: William Butcher, Charles Cammell, Mark Firth, Thomas Jessop, Frederick T. Mappin, Edward Sanderson and Edward Vickers.[23] Such men, alongside many less famous Sheffielders, gained much of their early business experience in America. These were the 'good old days' of the US trade when firms such as Jessop's were 'heaping up their riches in as easy and quiet a way as ever wealth was put together';[24] and when the American trade enabled Greaves to erect the famous Sheaf Works in 1823 at a total cost of £50,000.

Probably very little Sheffield crucible steel was exported to America before 1800, since at that time the American industries that were to become the town's biggest customers were either in their infancy or non-existent. The expense of cast steel (about a third as much again as shear steel) precluded its widespread use, and the needs of colonial craftsmen could be met, to a certain extent, by imports of Sheffield shear steel or domestic blister steel.[25] Crucible steel, however, competed successfully with blister steel and iron: it was free from inclusions of slag, making it far more homogeneous and reliable; it could take and hold a hard cutting edge; it was resistant to the percussion and abrasion endured by sledge-hammers, files, and axes; and its toughness and durability made it ideal for the wearing parts of machines and engines. Above all, the plasticity of the material under heat allowed it to be worked and manipulated to cut other metals.[26] These factors ensured that crucible carbon steel gradually replaced iron and low-grade steel in America in the first half of the nineteenth century.

Sheffield crucible steel, shipped through the town's resident agents in Boston, New York, and Philadelphia, improved the American economy's cutting edge in the drive to exploit the country's huge resources of wood.

By 1860, an American using a high-quality domestic axe, saw, chisel, or plane, invariably wielded a piece of Sheffield steel. In the 1820s and 1830s the imported product became the basis for several New England and Pennsylvanian attempts to overcome the prejudice against home-produced woodworking tools.[27] In New York, Richard Hoe & Co pioneered the production of circular saws with steel from Sanderson Bros of Sheffield.[28] Henry Disston, of Philadelphia, relied upon English steel in founding what was to become the world's largest saw manufactory.[29] Other American sawmakers – Charles Griffiths, Abel Simonds, and Josiah Bakewell – also had the same source of supply.

Sheffield steel likewise became indispensable for American axemakers. In 1825 Daniel Simmons, founder of the Weed & Becker Manufacturing Co, in Cohoes, New York, began using it after a way was found of welding thin strips to the head of the traditional iron axe.[30] Cast steel came into general use for axes sometime after 1830, the composite axe eventually being superseded by one with a completely steel blade.[31] The Douglas Axe Co, of East Douglas, Massachusetts, was another committed user of English steel.[32] The Collins Co, a Connecticut axemaking firm that was to acquire a world-wide reputation, built its early success on Sheffield steel from Naylor & Sanderson, later transferring its business to Sanderson's. In 1842, the superintendent of Collins, Elisha K. Root, was sent to Sheffield to 'pick up information' so that the firm could begin manufacture itself. But shortly afterwards, recorded Samuel Collins, a member of Firth's of Sheffield visited Collinsville and 'made such representations and named terms that induced us to give them our business and we used their steel exclusively for about twenty years'.[33]

American makers had also begun to supply the domestic market with wood-finishing tools. In 1800, New York, for example, had almost no mass-produced tools; but by 1860 the reverse was true, and a wide variety of American woodworking tools were available, typically with a well-advertised edge of 'superior English cast steel'.[34] Throughout the nineteenth century, American planemakers imported Sheffield cast steel for cutting irons from firms such as Butcher, Newbould, Sorby, and Ibbotson.[35]

As American population expanded westwards, steel found new uses. In the 1820s and 1830s the American Fur Co, in Mackinac, Michigan, imported crucible steel for the steel traps and flint steel of the trapper and fur trader.[36] Heavy-duty hacking and hunting knives were also in demand, supplied by cutlery makers in the East, using English steel.[37]

More significantly, the expansion and mechanisation of American agriculture opened up a vast new market.[38] At the time of the American Revolution, most farm tools differed little from the ones which had been used for two thousand years. Grain was cut almost universally with a sickle, and it was not until about the time of the Revolution that the scythe came into use. Several inventors experimented with the plough, but the early designs by Charles Newbold and Jethro Wood were constructed of cast iron, which did not cope well with the sticky soils of the prairies. In 1833, John Lane, an Illinois blacksmith, began experimenting with steel-bladed ploughs, an idea fully developed by John Deere in 1837, who utilised strips of Sheffield steel from discarded saw plates. Deere's success eventually brought him into contact with Naylor & Co's agency in New York, and soon the American was importing regular shipments of Sheffield steel at $300 per ton.[39]

The mechanical reaper also appeared on the scene between 1830 and 1860, the work of Obed Hussey and Cyrus H. McCormick. By the 1820s a corn cultivator and a hay and grain rake were available to farmers. In 1837 John and Hiram A. Pitts patented a commercially successful mechanical thresher. Other machines marketed before the Civil War included mowers, grain drills, corn shellers, hay bailing presses and cultivators of various types. Most of these machines were constructed of cast iron and wood: however, the critical cutting, ploughing, and reaping sections offered a market for cast steel.

Sheffield steel was involved in an area that many historians have identified as the cradle of the so-called 'American System of Manufactures' – armsmaking and toolmaking enterprises in the Connecticut Valley. These included Eli Whitney's New Haven factory, the Collins Axe Co, the Springfield Armory, the Works of Robbins and Lawrence in Windsor, Vermont, and the Ames Co in Chicopee, Massachusetts. In the early nineteenth century the dependence of these factories on imported steel was almost total, a reflection of the poor quality of the small amounts of domestic steel. Most of the steel used, however, was of the blister or shear variety imported chiefly from England and, to a lesser extent, Germany, for sword and bayonet blades. Cast steel had not been generally adopted for rifle barrels, and the armories relied upon local bar iron. The Salisbury District in northwestern Connecticut was the principal source of iron of the requisite quality, and Salisbury iron became the standard material used in the Connecticut Valley manufactories.[40] By the 1840s, however, contemporaries began to complain, it now seems with some justification, of a decline in the quality of Salisbury iron.[41] Firms such as Ames and Colt instead turned their attention to cast steel because of its durability, elasticity and lower failure rate.[42] The material was apparently first considered for barrel manufacture on a large scale in 1845, when the Navy forced a reluctant Nathan Ames to try the new material. Ames' misgivings, however, were offset by the advocacy of men such as Eli Whitney Jr, who in 1848 convinced an Ordnance Board of the superiority of steel barrels.[43] By 1845 cast steel, usually imported from England, was driving out iron as a material for rifle barrels, though iron still held a share of the market.[44] The armories boosted the custom that Sheffield already enjoyed from American cutlery firms in the Connecticut Valley, located in New Haven, Meriden and New Britain.[45]

Carefully heated and then quenched, carbon steel could be used in the shaping of softer metals, especially in the cutting of wheels, gears and axles. As America's engineering works came into existence after 1825, Sheffield began to build a reputation that would make its name synonymous with tool steel in the latter half of the nineteenth century.[46] The blacksmiths who prepared tools for the engineer also benefited from the introduction of cast steel. In 1847 Mark Fisher began welding cast steel to anvils to increase their wearing qualities and manufacture began under his patents.[47] Blacksmiths' tools in the pre-1850 period were also made increasingly from cast steel.[48]

Sheffield steel was imported by wiremaking firms such as Washburn & Moen, for the speciality manufactures of pianos and scientific devices.[49] This foreshadowed the later demand for Sheffield-made wire for steel ribs in umbrellas and crinoline wire for skirts. Sheffield steel could also be found in a myriad of other uses: clock springs and clockmakers' tools;[50] surgical instruments; pen nibs;[51] mint dies; engraving plates;[52] magnets; textile machine parts;[53] skates; and whaling lances and cutting spades.[54] The small amount of crucible steel used in these industries should neither obscure its tremendous impact on the American economy nor its great importance for Sheffield.

In 1850, four hundred American cutlery and edge tool establishments, well over a thousand for the manufacture of agricultural implements, as well as numerous machine shops and blacksmiths' concerns, offered an enormous potential market.[55] The Sheffield crucible steel industry expanded accordingly, and by 1854 growth hit a peak, with new furnaces appearing at the rate of one every two weeks.[56] Sheffield's American steel trade now reached a climax as exports to the US reached 21,998 tons in 1860 – about a third or more of the town's total output! This was a period when Greaves' Sheaf Works styled themselves as 'American Merchants' and when Biggin's 'America Works', Brookes & Crookes' 'Atlantic Works', Alfred Beckett's 'Brooklyn Works', Butcher's 'Philadelphia Works', and Wostenholm's 'Washington Works' proudly proclaimed the town's chief trading interest. Across the Atlantic, Sheffield merchants dominated the selling of hardware in areas such as New York's lower Manhattan district, so that some makers 'became a stranger in their own land and infinitely better known in Broadway [than in Sheffield]'.[57]

Sheffield had the American market completely at its mercy, since competition in the US was virtually non-existent before 1860. Despite optimistic pronouncements to the contrary, the earliest American attempts at crucible steel manufacture were largely unsuccessful and short-lived ventures. The outlook did not appear very promising. Though the US had abundant supplies of natural ores, they were an unknown quantity compared with the well-tested uniformity of Swedish irons. Nor was it known whether another pre-requisite of the crucible steelmaker, the clay for the pots, could measure up to its English equivalent. In the late 1850s, producing only a few hundred tons of cast steel each year, and relying on annual imports valued at over £650,000, America was remarkably dependent on Sheffield. Concluded the *Scientific American*: 'This is a subject to which our people should direct their attention.'[58]

For Americans eager to compete with Sheffield manufactures, though, the prospects were not entirely unfavourable. The 1850s had seen the heyday of the Atlantic economy, fostered not only by the remarkable economic expansion of the US, but also by the relatively low level of American tariffs. But there were some ominous portents. In a situation in which Sheffield was 'indebted to the United States for the greater part of the activity that prevails in the trade of the town',[59] economic and political events left the Sheffielders vulnerable. In 1857 an American banking and financial panic once more plunged the steelmakers into crisis,[60] and, though trade swiftly recovered, worse was to follow with the outbreak of the American Civil War. Heavy orders for steel rifle barrels and tools for fortifications could not prevent severe disruption in the cutlery and tool firms, which began seeking orders elsewhere in China, India and South America.[61] This trend was strengthened when, in 1861, the US Congress passed the Morrill Act, one of the most important of a long series of tariffs levying progressively higher taxes on steel and hardware imports.

Even more disturbing for Sheffield manufacturers were reports of increasing American proficiency in the town's traditional crafts. The heavy edge tool trade to the US had been largely lost by the early 1850s, since the American artisan was 'ever willing to adapt his handicrafts to the exact wants of his customers'.[62] In New York American table knives were 'about the *same price* and *better finished* than the Sheffield article',[63] so that the English, who were also unable to match American delivery times, were reduced to trading in the more common lines. Yet Sheffield houses were said to be 'content with the business they are quietly doing, and only laugh at what seems to them a good joke, knowing full well that their name and influence are known and felt throughout the whole civilised world, and some of these firms will not even stoop to decorate their goods by "labels, inscriptions and devices", for the purpose of "tickling the vanity of even Brother Jonathan"'.[64]

Moreover, in crucible steel manufacture the upsurge in demand had not been without its effect in America, where, by the 1850s, pioneer attempts had been made to cast steel in New York State, often with the help of Sheffield managers.[65] In Pittsburgh capital had also been invested in crucible steel ventures, steps had been taken to attract skilled labour, and efforts had been made to overcome native deficiencies in natural resources. The admonishment of the *Scientific American* elicited pointed rebukes from Pittsburgh entrepreneurs.[66] Disquietingly for English makers, one Sheffielder in Pennsylvania forecast in 1856 that America would be 'setting down, a year from hence, at the door of Sheffield manufacturers, a steel superior to any now manufactured in Sheffield, at a considerably less price'.[67]

Thus the 1850s, that golden age of Sheffield–American commerce, had ended by posing a number of questions: could the US succeed in manufacturing satisfactory crucible steel?; could Sheffield's cutlery and edge tool-makers recapture lost ground in the American market against domestic (and German) producers?; could the town modify its alleged complacency and conservatism and adapt to new technologies and products? To find the answer to these questions we must turn to the history of the American crucible steel industry and examine the involvement of Sheffielders with the US market.

Part one

SPECIAL STEEL TECHNOLOGY

1

THE BIRTH OF THE AMERICAN CRUCIBLE STEEL INDUSTRY

> Consumers of steel who three years ago denied most positively that they used, or could use, American steel, and published that they used English steel exclusively, now do not hesitate to own that they use American steel ... It is to the energy and courage of a few men, principally in Pittsburgh, that this result is due. Works were built at a large expense, costly experiments undertaken, skilled labor brought here by offers of large wages, and, after years of trial and the expenditure of millions of dollars, our steel makers solved the mystery, and made the fabrication of steel in America an assured success.
>
> 'American Steel at the Centennial', *Iron Age* 18 (17 August 1876), p. 5.

Few of the Americans who witnessed the country's success in crucible steel manufacture at the Centennial Exhibition in Philadelphia in 1876 would have foretold such rapid strides a quarter of a century earlier, when the industry lagged so far behind its European rivals.[1] Early American attempts to manufacture cast steel merely underscored the technical problems to be overcome.

The first important crucible steel enterprise appears to have been inaugurated in 1818 by what was later to become the Alan Wood Steel Co at Valley Forge, Pennsylvania. Built to supply plates for the firm's saw manufactory, the furnace was worked by two Englishmen, John Parkins and his son, John Parkins, Jr. Though it was reported to have made some excellent steel the project was soon abandoned.[2]

In 1831 the Convention of the Friends of Domestic Industry met in New York to survey the American iron and steel industry and consider its future prospects.[3] It admitted that England continued to provide America with the finer qualities of steel – blister, shear and cast – but believed that this dependence could be reduced with the Juniata ores of New York and

Connecticut and the domestic equivalent of English Stourbridge clay.

Despite such optimism, the American crucible steel industry made little progress before 1860.[4] Even though some encouragement was offered by organisations such as the Franklin Institute, only a handful of attempts had been made to manufacture the finer grades of crucible steel.[5] Of these the most successful had been the Garrard brothers, who settled in America from Suffolk, and began the production of crucible steel in Cincinnati, Ohio, in 1832. The first crucibles used by Dr William Garrard, the principal architect of the enterprise, made of 'German plumbago', were failures, but experiments were continued until he finally chose a mixture of clay from New Cumberland in 'Western Virginia' and burnt material from old crucibles. For best cast steel, he used Swedish iron and later Tennessee and Missouri charcoal iron. Nevertheless, the product was unable to compete with Sheffield imports and the business foundered in the financial panic of 1837.[6]

More successful was the Adirondack Iron & Steel Co of Jersey City, which, in 1848, began the manufacture of blister steel from its own bar iron puddled at Adirondack, Essex County, New York.[7] It was the fond hope of the directors of the firm that American ores, especially Adirondack ores, could be converted into steel. Remarked one of the proprietors: 'I will be very much mistaken if the Adirondack does not make as good steel as the best of the Swedish brands', and added: 'We really should put up a cementing furnace at Adirondack which is a simple affair.'

In 1840 the firm made efforts to attract English capital by involving one of the Sanderson brothers of Sheffield.[8] About four years later, another Sheffield manufacturer, a Mr Pickslay, whose son lived in America, expressed an interest in Adirondack ore for conversion into steel.[9] The Americans favoured a direct process of converting pig iron into steel and Pickslay wished to explore this technique. Samples were sent to Sheffield and, though the direct process did not work well, Pickslay succeeded in producing cast steel from Adirondack bar iron, which he made into razors and penknives. After further trials the Englishman wrote in 1846 that he was well satisfied with American iron and towards the end of the year arrived in America with detailed plans for the construction of a steel works to utilise the direct process. Pickslay held the key to the success of the venture, but one of the directors had doubts:

Pickslay has now ascertained ... 'that Adirondack iron is fully equal and in some respects superior to that of Dannemora'. This is very encouraging for us. He believes, moreover, that he had succeeded in producing first rate cast steel from the Adirondac [sic] cast metal. But still, as I believe, some doubts exist on this head.

He has, no doubt made such, and can make it again, but will he be able to make it uniformily and constantly, or only occasionally.

These fears proved well-founded. Batches of axes from Pickslay soon showed that he had not solved the riddle of producing cast steel direct from pig iron, using charcoal, and by 1848 it was apparent that he was unwilling to be involved with the future of the company. Meanwhile, the proprietors had hedged their bets by coming to an arrangement with Joseph Dixon of Jersey City for the manufacture of cast steel.

Joseph Dixon (1799–1869), of Marblehead, Massachusetts, had already pioneered the manufacture of graphite crucibles, which were to have such a far-reaching influence on the American steel industry, and had also patented a new method for the production of cast steel.[10] Under his direction the Adirondack Co successfully embarked upon the production of steel in Jersey City.[11] Fortunately, finding enough skilled workers never seems to have been a problem. An English melter and his son from Pittsburgh applied for work; two English hammermen were hired, both good workers; and the firm also received a letter from a Sheffield teemer who worked for Pickslay in Sheffield, had heard about the works from him, and wanted a job.[12]

By 1850 the company was receiving adequate testimonials of the excellence of its steel.[13] But some found the steel indifferent and Jessop's in New York gave the steel only qualified approval. Hence James Swank's comment that 'while good cast steel was made from 1849 at the works of the Adirondack Iron and Steel Company, the product was not for many years of uniform excellence'.[14] One of the firm's founders noted that initially about half of the output had to be broken up and remelted and problems with consistency hurt the firm's reputation, especially in comparison with the uniformity of English steel. On the other hand, Swank attributed the failure to 'the prejudice existing against American cast steel'.[15] However, although the owners made no profit from the venture and sold the works, production continued until 1885, and the enterprise left an important legacy of skilled workers and business experience to the emerging American crucible steel industry.

Despite the great strides in mass-production engineering by 1850, steel manufacture in the US was still in its infancy at mid-century, with an annual production of about 6,078 tons, only 44 tons of which were cast steel.[16] It was Pittsburgh which was to remedy this and become the centre of the American crucible steel industry.[17]

Between 1830 and 1860 several attempts had been made to produce blister and crucible steel in Pittsburgh, with varying degrees of success.

The first endeavour to cast steel in Pittsburgh by Simon Broadmeadow, an Englishman, was a failure, although he and his son made acceptable blister steel as early as 1830.[18] In 1833 the firm of G. & J. H. Schoenberger began blister steel manufacture, and in 1840 constructed several crucible melting holes, bringing over an Englishman, Edward Dunn, to superintend the first operations of this type in Pittsburgh.[19] The enterprise was abandoned in a year or two, apparently because 'the firm was so confident that no iron could be found ... that could in any respect excel the Juniata iron that, when the article failed to produce steel equal to that of Sheffield, they gave up the manufacture of crucible steel'.[20] Other firms followed. In 1852 McKelvey & Blair of Pittsburgh, filemakers, pioneered the large-scale production of cast steel. Manufacture at the company ceased after two years, mainly because of labour problems and the difficulty of finding suitable ores, and it was later bought by Hussey, Wells & Co. Singer, Nimick & Co, and Isaac Jones' Pittsburgh Steel Works, also succeeded in casting steel in 1853 and 1855, respectively.

Pittsburgh, though, was still very much 'Iron City'. According to a contemporary source in the 1850s, the city produced 76,749 tons of iron and only 10,850 tons of blister and cast steel.[21] But in the 1860s this state of affairs was completely reversed as Hussey, Wells & Co, Smith, Sutton & Co, and Miller, Metcalf & Parkin & Co succeeded in making crucible steel of uniform quality as a regular product. By 1867 the *Pittsburgh Gazette* observed that 'the manufacture of cast steel has become one of the largest and most important of the industries of Pittsburgh, and [the city] is likely to be the Sheffield of this continent in this particular'.[22] To Swank: 'It met a want that had long been felt, and dissipated the long standing belief that this country possessed neither the iron nor the skill required to make good cast steel.'[23]

To what extent did Sheffield contribute to these developments? Unfortunately, a series of disastrous Pittsburgh floods and the usual depredations of time and fire have ensured that the relevant business correspondence has been totally lost, but it is clear from several sources that Sheffield men were influential in the early stages of production. In 1880, J. Stephen Jeans, the British ironmaster, commented: 'A large number of the skilled workmen in the steel works at Pittsburgh are from Sheffield, [and] many native workmen have now been trained in the manufacture of cast steel, and their children have also been trained to that industry.'[24]

The Pittsburgh manuscript Census provides some confirmation for Jeans' assertion. It shows a large number of English-born steel workers resident in Pittsburgh and Allegheny City by 1870, reflecting the sudden

Table 1.1 *Pittsburgh crucible steelworks*

Founded	Name of firm
1829	Wayne Iron & Steel Works
*1845	Pittsburgh Steel Works, Anderson & Co
*1848	Singer, Nimick & Co
*1859	Hussey, Howe & Co
*1862	Black Diamond Steel Works, Park, Brother & Co
1862	Fort Pitt Iron & Steel Works, Graff, Bennett & Co
*1863	La Belle Steel Works, Smith, Sutton & Co
*1867	Crescent Steel Works, Miller, Metcalf & Parkin
1870	Nellis's Agricultural Works, Nellis, Shriver & Co
1871	Pittsburgh Steel Casting Co
1875	Hussey, Binns & Co
*1878	Read & Thaw

Source: American Iron and Steel Association, *Directory* (1880), p. 162. Asterisks indicate those firms with production above 5,000 tons per year of crucible steel.

growth of the industry in the 1860s (Table 1: 1).[25] Seventy men were enumerated, including eight steel melters and one apprentice steel melter, one steel refiner, and numerous hammermen and workers. Evidently, some of the immigrants arrived to take up supervisory posts, since the English contingent included two foremen, two managers, and one manufacturer. Economic incentives appear to have been the main motivation for the newcomers, and there are several references in contemporary sources to the high wages offered by Pittsburgh entrepreneurs in the industry's early days. In two days work in a Pittsburgh furnace, a Sheffield melter could earn as much as his English counterpart earned in a week.[26] Among those firms which can be positively identified as having employed such highly paid Sheffield labour were Hussey, Howe and the Fort Pitt Works of Graff, Bennett.[27]

Not surprisingly, the Sheffield methods were copied fairly exactly in the beginning. At the Pittsburgh Steel Works of Anderson, Cook, for example, conversion and melting were done in the traditional way.[28] Four 36-ton converting furnaces, capable of cementing approximately 60 tons each month, a 62-hole crucible furnace, and a Sheffield-made Davy's steam hammer were described as the main features.[29] As in Sheffield, the managers were 'determined that nothing but the very best quality of steel shall be turned out of their establishment, and will save neither labor nor expense to carry out this end'.

Other Pittsburgh crucible steel works were laid out on Sheffield lines. The Crescent Steel Works, with its pot-room, coke-melting holes, and converting furnaces, differed little from a Sheffield works. At Crescent the

Sheffield methods were followed closely, 'merit being claimed for careful and exact working'.[30] Similarly, Black Diamond Works was originally built with six 30-ton converting furnaces, a crucible room which could accommodate 2,000 pots, and a large melting house.[31] By 1876, at least 30 converting furnaces were in use in Pittsburgh, and only Hussey, Howe appear to have dispensed entirely with the established techniques, favouring instead a direct method of melting.[32] Appropriately, the Pittsburgh enterprise of Singer, Nimick was even called the Sheffield Works!

American dependence on Sheffield, though, must not be exaggerated. Along with their skills, some immigrants arrived with less desirable qualities. McKelvey & Blair, for example, in their pioneering attempt at crucible steelmaking 'sent to Sheffield and brought out several skilled workmen ... but the abominable English system, imported along with the skilled labor, of "working to fool the master", [was] too much for the financial strength of the firm, and in 1854 they were forced to drop the enterprise'.[33] English visitors to the New York Industrial Exhibition in 1854 also commented on the intractability of Sheffield labour in Pittsburgh.[34]

Some Sheffielders complained bitterly of working conditions in Pittsburgh. Henry Walker, formerly manager of the Butcher Steel Works in Sheffield, in 1865, urged his fellow-countrymen to avoid 'the temptations and villainous inducements' held out to them.[35] He believed that he and his compatriots in Pittsburgh were very unreasonably treated and shackled by unfair restrictions. Although wages were good, working hours were often arbitrarily reduced and 'the greater part of the workmen here, through certain inducements held out to them by their employers, are teaching a great number of men ... the [steel] trade ... and in a very short time the services of the Englishman will be no further required'.

Insufficient documentation on the Pittsburgh crucible steel industry makes it impossible to tell whether these experiences were typical, though they do highlight factors which could have hindered the integration of Sheffield men and techniques. Sheffield steelmakers with their well-attested capacity for beer, their custom of not working on Mondays, and their tendency to unionise, shocked Americans.[36] As a Sheffield edge tool-maker in the US put it, in reply to Walker: 'The habitual drinker and the never-satisfied class of men will be more at home in Sheffield, for the American employer is not partial to such; and the man who goes "rolling home" is not regarded very favourably by any one in this country'.[37] Sheffielders' disaffection with a country where 'there is no beer fit to drink, where a man is rung in and out of the factory like a tame bear, where there are no holidays, pastimes, or the thousand-and-one delights which make home sweet [and] where rent, living, and clothing are at least twice as dear', may have been a factor in bringing some of them back to their native town in the 1880s.[38]

Nor in the long-term, did Sheffield technologies prove to be entirely appropriate for American conditions. By the late 1870s a revolution was underway in the design of American crucible steel works. As late as 1874, out of a total of 51 works listed making crucible steel, only three of note (Crescent, the Pittsburgh Steel Casting Co, and Singer, Nimick) had Siemens gas furnaces, all the others using the traditional Sheffield methods. By 1880, however, nearly all the steelmaking districts, especially Pittsburgh (where only one-third of the firms had coke-holes), had switched to gas melting and by 1890 the coke-hole had been almost universally discarded.[39]

The revolution reflected the influence of two factors. Firstly, there was the exploitation of Pittsburgh's abundant resources of natural gas. By the 1880s Pittsburgh and Allegheny City, sited conveniently above several gas belts or fields, had sunk a score of producing wells and made the supply of cheap gas 'an assured fact, beyond the possibility of doubt'.[40] Secondly, there was the prompt utilisation of European technology, notably Sir Charles William Siemens' work on the cast steel regenerative furnace, the results of which had been made known in 1868.[41] While Sheffield steelmakers pondered the suitability of gas melting for crucible steel, the Americans found Siemens' furnace, when combined with cheap gas and graphite pots, an irresistible attraction. By November 1867 Anderson & Woods of Pittsburgh had obtained a licence for a Siemens regenerative gas furnace and by the spring of 1868 it had been erected under the guidance of William Durfee.[42] Firing night and day, the gas furnace not only allowed the Americans to increase output with greater economy, but also gave them the opportunity to introduce several labour-saving ideas.[43]

The Pittsburgh steelmakers also differed from Sheffielders in their utilisation of native ores. Perhaps because of the cheapness of American ores and their ready availability, the Americans never shared the typical Sheffield melter's reverence for Swedish iron.[44] The pioneering ventures of the Adirondack Co and McKelvey & Blair had been notable for their adherence to domestic ore. In the late 1860s the Pittsburgh Steel Co used 'Peru' iron from the northern part of New York State.[45] In 1866 the *Pittsburgh Gazette* claimed that the best steel was wrought from the 'spathic' ore found in the Housatonic Valley of Connecticut and Massachusetts; most of Pittsburgh's ores coming from outside the state.[46] Hussey, Wells used 'none but the best American iron'.[47] As the industry developed, American makers reserved Swedish irons for only the highest grades, and the imported product was never in such widespread use as in Sheffield. When Henry Seebohm, one of Sheffield's most distinguished steelmakers, visited Pittsburgh in 1879 he was chagrined to find that the American manager he met was already fully conversant with the analyses of Swedish and other irons.[48] At Crescent the managers soon secured for themselves a leading brand of Dannemora iron, but by 1875 were busily engaged in experiments to furnish an exclusively American tool steel from charcoal-hammered irons.[49] A year later, the *Iron Age* proclaimed: 'Today in our common steels, in which little or no Swedish iron is used, American steel is confessedly superior to all others.'[50] American independence was reflected in the decline of Swedish iron imports during the 1870s,[51] a decline which also meant less business for Sheffield interests involved in the export of Swedish iron to the US.[52]

Sheffield labour and technology, cheap fuel, domestic irons, and a superb location at a natural gateway to the American West (see map) gave Pittsburgh substantial advantages over its rivals in the production of crucible steel.[53] Further economic reasons dictated the location of the industry in the city.

The first related to the availability of capital, since erecting a steel works in America in the mid-nineteenth century, especially with costly foreign labour, was extremely risky and expensive. Curtis G. Hussey is said to have spent up to $400,000 in making his direct process of melting a success, and by 1870 his venture had absorbed over a million dollars.[54] James Park at Black Diamond also encountered serious losses in the firm's early days.[55] These costs were met by Pittsburgh entrepreneurs themselves whose previous business successes ensured that the city's crucible steel industry, unlike its early iron works, did not suffer from a lack of working capital.[56]

Curtis G. Hussey (1802–93) was born on a farm near York, Pennsylvania, and built up a lucrative medical practice using the accumulated capital of several thousand dollars to purchase general stores.[57] Eventually, he devoted his whole time to their management, gradually moving into pork dealing, and later, in 1840, re-locating in Pittsburgh to supervise his marketing operations. His interest developed in the rich copper deposits around Lake Superior and he organised the Pittsburgh & Boston Mining Co, which opened the first of the Lake Superior Copper Mines (the famous Cliff Mine). The Cliff Mine is reputed to have returned profits of $2,280,000 on an original investment of $110,000, a dividend sufficient for Hussey and his partner, Thomas M. Howe,[58] in 1849, to begin manu-

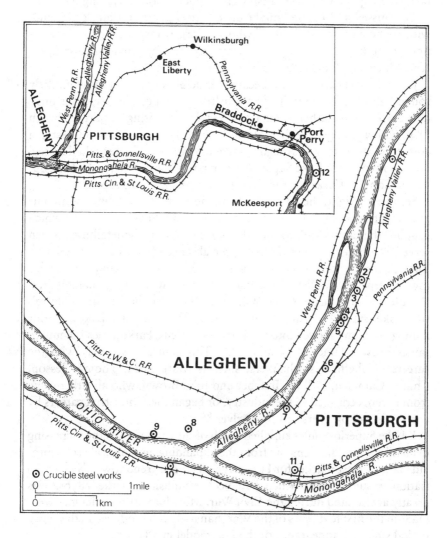

Map of Pittsburgh showing crucible steelworks

1. Crescent (Miller, Metcalf & Parkin)
2. Fort Pitt (John Graff)
3. Black Diamond (Park, Bro & Co)
4. Pittsburgh Steel Casting Co
5. Hussey, Binns & Co
6. Hussey, Howe & Co
7. Wayne (Brown & Co)
8. Nellis Agricultural (A. J. Nellis)
9. La Belle (Smith, Sutton & Co)
10. Sheffield (Singer, Nimick & Co)
11. Pittsburgh (Anderson & Co)
12. Pitt (Isaac Jones)

Source: Iron Age 23 (8 May 1879), p. 1.

facturing copper with the Pittsburgh Copper & Brass Rolling Mills. In 1859, Hussey and Howe bought the old steel plant of Blair & Co, and, with the help of Calvin Wells,[59] who was largely responsible for the erection of the furnaces, began manufacturing steel by Hussey's direct process, which supplanted the older cementation method.

James Park (1820–83) also became a crucible steelmaker by an unlikely, route.[60] Born in Pittsburgh of Scotch-Irish parentage, he began his business career in his father's china and metal store, rising to partnership in 1840 with a younger brother, David E. Park. He acquired an interest in a cotton goods factory in Allegheny, Pennsylvania, and later, like Hussey, became involved in Lake Superior mining, founding in 1857, the Lake Superior Copper Works for the manufacture of sheathing copper.

Seen in this light, the Pittsburgh steel industry can be viewed as an outgrowth of economic developments in the Lake Superior region, which supplied the capital and the introduction to nonferrous metallurgy, which served as a basis for the industry in the absence of first-hand experience. Though some entrepreneurs made their fortunes by starting small edge tool enterprises (William Coleman, William Woods) or making iron (Matthew Graff, Jacob Reese, William K. Nimick), the typical Pittsburgh steelmaker started as a merchant or wholesaler, invested in Lake Superior mining, and later moved into steel (Hussey, Wells, Park, James I. Bennett, James Brown, James W. Hailman).[61] This contrasts strongly with the careers of Sheffield steelmakers, such as Mark Firth, Thomas Jessop, Charles Cammell, William Butcher and John Brown, who all either came from parents engaged in the industry, or began their industrial careers by entering small partnerships themselves.[62]

If Lake Superior mines supplied much of the capital, then the increasing demand for steel implements from the expanding agricultural sector provided the biggest market for Pittsburgh steel. The trend towards mechanisation in agriculture, which had been established in the 1850s, was greatly accelerated during the Civil War. More harvesting machines were made in the first few years of the War than had been produced in the entire period since the appearance of the first model in 1833.[63]

Hussey, Wells in 1860 produced mostly agricultural steels, including 'tool steel, axe steel, nail machine steel, chisel steel etc., with shovel steel, spring steel, reaper steel, saw plates of every description, etc'.[64] Singer, Nimick made a speciality of, and gave pride of place in their advertisements to, steel for saw plates. The output of the Pittsburgh Steel Co, which had been favoured with the first American order for plough steel from John Deere in 1846, was also geared to cater for the agricultural demand.[65] The Crescent steel owners found their best customers in

Pennsylvania and the West, so they did not bother to solicit the Eastern trade to any great extent.[66] At the Centennial the *Iron Age* described the use of the domestic product in section knives for reapers and mowers as 'one of the great triumphs of American tool steel'.[67] Like the early iron industry, it appears, the nascent Pittsburgh steel industry supplied the needs of the westward-moving migrant; demand from the East and the engineering industries came later.

The success of the Americans was duly noted by Sheffielders. In 1858 an agent for the Sheffield firm of Marsh Bros, a cutlery and steelmaking enterprise, had noticed that some American firms were beginning to use domestic steels. He remarked that the Louisiana Rolling Mill 'have a very large stock of steel on hand, are rich, and do all their [cast steel] business with Naylor [Sheffield], spring steel with Earl Smith & Co [Sheffield] and plough steel with domestic houses in Pittsburgh'.[68] Later, in 1865, the Sheffielders observed: 'The Pittsburgh makers are progressing wonderfully and with $50.40 duty they have a good chance'.[69] The following year they reported: 'We observe that the common square edge steel especially the large sizes are selling off slowly and suppose that the domestic steel makers have now got hold of this trade in which they would have little difficulty to produce a satisfactory article'. Best-quality cast steel could still be offered advantageously to any competitor, but 'file steel seems fast to be going entirely to the home makers and the sooner it is realised at low price the better as probably the domestic will decline ere long: machinery [steel] we suppose is now chiefly monopolized by Pittsburgh and our stock of it will probably depreciate, and the same may be said of Mill and Muley saw plates'.[70] By the mid-1860s the Pittsburgh makers, aided by the tariff, which Marsh Bros called a 'very crude and unreasonable production',[71] were able to compete with Sheffield houses. The Americans could often undercut English prices by several cents per pound (see Table 1:2), though they could not yet offer such a wide range of high-quality steels.[72]

It was to be some time before the American crucible steel industry could supply the domestic demand for high-grade steel. Annual production was below 20,000 tons for most of the 1860s. Nor did the quality of American steel recommend itself to many customers. A buyer in Newark, New Jersey, complained that American steel was 'red short' when worked and lacked uniformity; and other users complained of the home-product's temper.[73] American locomotive builders, such as Baldwin's in Philadelphia, favoured the Pittsburgh makers with orders for the common grades of steel in the 1860s, but still bought their tool steel from Sheffield. 'Can you not give us an order for Tool Steel?', begged Curtis G. Hussey, in a letter

Table 1.2 *Sheffield and Pittsburgh crucible steel prices 1863*

	Cents per lb		
	Sanderson Bros New York	Singer, Nimick Sheffield Works	Jones, Boyd Pittsburgh Works
Best cast steel	22	21	20–21
Extra cast steel	23		
Round Machinery	14	13–15	13–16
Swage cast steel	25		
Best double shear steel	22		
Best single shear steel	19		
Blister first quality	17½		
Blister second quality	15½	} 8–12	
Blister third quality	12½		
German steel best	15½		
German steel Eagle	12½	} 9–12	} 9–11
German steel third quality	11½		
Sheet cast steel 1st quality	22		
Sheet cast steel 2nd quality	18	} 15–21	} 15–23
Sheet cast steel 3rd quality	16		
Shovel steel best	14½		
Shovel steel common	13½		
Sheet cast steel for hoes	14½	11½	11½
Mill saw steel	15½	14	14
Billet web steel	17½		
Cross-cut saw steel	17½	18	18
Best cast steel for circulars to 46 in.	25	23	23
Toe corking best	10	9¾	9¾
Spring steel best	11		
Spring steel 2nd quality	10	} 9–10¾	} 9–10¾
Spring steel 3rd quality	8¼		

Source: SCL Marsh Bros. 249/24, 28–9.

to Baldwin's in 1865, 'We do not think you will find any trouble about it not being uniform'.[74]

American imports of high-grade steel continued to grow, reaching a peak of nearly 10,000 tons in 1873 (Table 1: 3). Imports declined during the depressed years of the early 1870s, but there was some restoration to their former levels in the early 1880s. However, by then American crucible steel production was about 80,000 tons, and so the percentage of the trade in the hands of foreign steel producers had fallen drastically. Concluded the *Sheffield Independent*: '[US] dependence on Sheffield for steel of any kind is over and gone'.[75] Vickers, which had enjoyed a trade in bar and sheet steel with America in 1864 of £83,000, found that its business had evaporated to £4,000 by 1885.[76]

Sheffield, however, still enjoyed a good trade in the finer grades of

Table 1.3 *American imports of fine steel (net tons)*

Year ended June 30	Valued above 7 but not above 11 cents	Valued above 11 cents (10 in 1884)	Total	Annual US crucible steel production
1867	6,328	1,018	7,346	16,964
1868	4,764	536	5,300	19,197
1869	6,454	432	6,886	19,643
1870	4,145	976	5,121	29,911
1871	7,372	818	8,190	31,250
1872	7,427	993	8,420	26,125
1873	7,717	2,206	9,923	31,059
1874	4,500	4,189	8,689	32,436
1875	3,818	2,954	6,772	35,180
1876	3,786	532	4,318	35,163
1877	2,540	406	2,946	36,098
1878	2,350	285	2,635	38,309
1879	2,405	237	2,642	50,696
1880	3,960	339	4,299	64,664
1881	5,362	521	5,883	80,145
1882	4,924	534	5,458	75,973
1883	4,419	382	4,801	71,835
1884	3,472	398	3,870	53,270

Source: *BAISA* 19 (12 August 1885), p. 212; American Iron and Steel Institute, *Annual Statistical Reports* (New York, 1918), p. 23.

steel.[77] Although Henry Disston, the Philadelphia sawmaker, began experimenting with crucible steel melting in the 1850s, until after the Civil War virtually all the steel plates for the US saw industry were imported from Sheffield.[78] In the 1860s the Pennsylvania steelmakers made inroads into this trade. Richard M. Hoe & Co, of New York, began buying its steel from such firms as Hussey, Wells in this period and deserted its Sheffield supplier, Sanderson Bros.[79] The quality of US steel was evidently satisfactory, but Sheffield steel was not entirely ousted. A Marsh Bros' agent noted, in 1867: 'Distin [sic] has long made steel for large saws. Circulars he buys Jessop's.'[80] Disston was still using Sheffield steel in the 1870s;[81] and as late as 1900 the firm bought Sheffield Mushet tool steel for inserted tooth saws. Hoe's continued to buy quantities of Sheffield steel throughout the century and remained committed to low tariffs on imported steel.[82] Welch & Griffiths, a Massachusetts sawmaker, used only Jessop's saw steel.[83] The Eclipse Keystone Saw Works, Cincinnati, made saws from Jessop's and Singer, Nimick steels – each brand being preferred for a different type of saw.[84] The San Francisco firm, the Pacific Saw Co, also imported Jessop's plate.[85] Sheffield steel was used by Simonds, another prominent American sawmaker, even after the firm built its own crucible steel plant in 1900.[86] E. C. Atkins & Co, the famous Indianapolis works, also obtained its steel from Sheffield in the late nineteenth century.[87]

New England manufacturers were particularly loyal to the Sheffield product – a loyalty expressed in the formation of the Consumers of British Iron & Steel Society in Boston in 1873. The Society, composed of various New England concerns allied with Sheffield's agents in America, came into existence to combat higher tariffs on imported steel.[88] Opposition to higher duties reflected the fact that axemakers such as Collins, Weed & Becker, and Douglas, and planemakers such as the Stanley Co, used substantial quantities of English steel in the 1870s.[89] Like the cutlery manufacturers, they had tried American steels, but had not found them entirely satisfactory.[90] US arms manufacturers also showed no disposition to use domestic steel, believing that English methods resulted 'in a more homogeneous staple' and accusing American steelmakers of making 'more haste than good speed'.[91] In the 1870s England remained the sole source of supply for the American arms industry.

Sheffield's technical ability in handling large masses of crucible steel was greatly superior to the Americans'.[92] Thus, Sheffielders who visited the Pittsburgh crucible steel industry were by no means overawed. Robert A. Hadfield was a guest at Hussey, Howe's Works on 17 July 1882, when the crucible steel industry there was clearly in full swing. Describing the visit and his meeting with two Sheffielders (the Cappers), he wrote:

Met M. Hussey Jnr., M. Wheeler foreman supt., M. Charles Capper, works manager in one dept. Employ 900 men, 12,000 tons per annum, 2 Siemens open hearth furnaces, also gas pot holes. Pots (plumbago) carry 90 lbs & more, last 6 rounds, saw some daubed where worn and used again. Taken a contract against Jessop's and Firth's for 1,200 tons steel for cultivator teeth. Price 9.4 cents per lb … [I] got George Capper (now working as hammer foreman) on one side, and wanted anxiously to know what American steel was like. 'Well' says he 'it lacks body and had not the quality of good English steel, it stands too much heat'. Also said they put such common stuff in the pots that no wonder quality was poor … Very hot day, men nearly naked and sweating away. Pulling 90 lb pots out of the hole like fun. Head melter earning $12 per day (£2!!). Puller out $5. No wonder men are tempted to go out to the States. These works are the oldest steel works in Pittsburgh. Cannot say that their warehouse and stock was imposing. Did not look as big as Jonas and Colver's [Sheffield]. Heard they could get slack for about $1 per ton at their works. Cheaper than in Sheffield. Noticed gas producer very near to Siemens furnace. Both Cappers anxious to know if M. Hadfield was coming out to the States before long, fancy from what they let drop, they intended starting a forge of their own, said there was plenty of room for such an establishment here. Noticed several of Davy's steam hammers, so with English hammers, and English hammermen, why should not American works be much behind English Steelworks. Noticed they were very strict about letting people pass the gates, etc.[93]

Table 1.4 *Steel production in Allegheny County*

Year	Number of steel works	Net tons crucible steel ingots
1874	11	17,915
1875	14	22,942
1876	14	25,009
1877	14	24,747
1878	14	27,866
1879	18	40,142
1880	17	52,136
1881	17	61,256
1882	18	59,596
1883	20	59,128

Source: Pittsburgh Chamber of Commerce, *The Mercantile, Manufacturing and Mining Interests of Pittsburgh* (Pittsburgh, 1884), p. 123.

At this date, the Pittsburgh crucible steel industry still lagged behind Sheffield in output (Table 1: 4). Annual figures on the Sheffield output are lacking, but an exhaustive examination of the available evidence suggests that the figure was over 100,000 tons per annum by the early 1870s.[94] This was probably a peak period for crucible steel production in Sheffield and America. After that there was a decline, though further peak years occurred during the First World War, reflecting the increased use of crucible steel in the engineering industries.

For critical applications in tools and machinery, crucible steel was never supplanted, despite Bessemer's boast that his converter could produce cheap, high-quality tool steel.[95] However, the bulk steelmaking processes supplying puddled, Bessemer, and open-hearth steel offered serious competition in the final quarter of the nineteenth century.[96] In America the most expensive grades were bought only after a thorough search for cheaper alternatives, a fact noted by the manager of the Chicago branch of Sanderson Bros of Sheffield, who emphasised that 'there are very few people ... who wish to buy the very high quality and correspondingly high priced grades of tool steel'.[97] Already in 1867 Abram S. Hewitt was keenly interested during his visit to Europe and the Paris Exposition as to whether Bessemer steel equalled the product of the crucible.[98] He concluded rightly that the day when the crucible became obsolete had not yet dawned. But that day did come nearer with the adoption of the open-hearth process, which was quite capable of producing very good qualities at a cost considerably less than its competitor. Satisfying the desire for economy, its adoption was rapid, resulting in lost American orders for the Sheffield manufacturers.[99] Production of open-hearth steel was rising eight times as fast as crucible after the mid-1890s, and almost four times as fast as Bessemer, surpassing it in 1908 (see Appendix). Unlike Bessemer, open-hearth steel had sufficient quality to compete with the crucible product.[100] Some firms even took the opportunity to sell open-hearth and Bessemer steel as the higher-grade article. According to a historian of the Burgess Steel & Iron Works, Ohio, it was this firm's practice of selling open-hearth steel as crucible that caused the Crucible Steel Co to buy it out.[101]

Despite these trends, Sheffield continued to sell steel in America. In 1893 a New York pocket-knife manufacturer stated that: 'The steel made in the American mills is just as good as Sheffield steel ... but to some extent we use the Sheffield steel on account of a conviction on the part of some of the American dealers that Sheffield steel is better than the American.'[102] However, the use of Sheffield steel may not have been due to simple prejudice. Remarked the Sheffield delegate of the Mosely Industrial Commission to America: 'Sheffield steel is used in the manufacture of the best cutlery, the reason given to me why American steel is not used being that its temper varies so much, while the temper of English steel is more even.'[103] In the 1890s and 1900s the American Axe & Tool Co, composed of the fourteen leading axe companies, still advertised axes of best English cast steel.[104] One American cast steel and toolmaker, who criticised domestic steel, observed: 'There are several firms in this country that make good steel at times, but the all important question with the consumer is to know who makes good steel all the time and this I will answer by saying not one of them.'[105] The experience of the Whitin Machine Works appears to verify this: in 1873 the firm had declared that American steel was acceptable, but in 1895, after some trouble with the domestic product, had reverted to the English.[106] Even at the end of the century, then, the debate over the respective merits of American and English steels continued and so there remained 'in some quarters an idea that only England can produce tool steel of the highest class'.[107]

In Sheffield at the end of the nineteenth century single 'orders from the USA for 500 and 600 tons of crucible steel for making tools were not uncommon. In busy years every single melting hole in Sheffield was occupied and working to full capacity, and even then it was not unusual to be six or seven months behind in one's orders in the melting department. In those days not less than £100,000 worth of crucible steel was dispatched each month from [England] to the United States.'[108] Sheffield's specialised product knowledge allowed it to adapt rapidly to changing fashions and demand. In the 1880s and 1890s several firms, notably J. H. Andrew, Cocker Bros, Samuel Fox, and Arthur Lee & Sons, enjoyed a flourishing American trade in high-grade crucible steel wire. Samuel Fox of Stocksbridge, near Sheffield, made a great success with the introduction of his crucible-steel-ribbed umbrella.[109] Arthur Lee (1842–1918), whose numerous visits to America before 1870 had 'left a lasting influence on him and upon the firm',[110] after 1877 began producing crinoline steel strip for the US, where cold strip steel for skirts was not produced at that time. The trade was extended by the founder's sons, especially Percy W. Lee, who visited the US in 1896 and 1898, bringing home orders for wire-drawing plates and the latest American wiremaking machinery for installation at the Crown Works. Other Sheffield exports to America at this time included crucible steel engraving plates, engravers' tools and magnets.[111]

By then David E. Park of the Park Steel Co and a number of his competitors saw advantages for themselves and the American industry if the leading crucible steel producers combined.[112] Like other combinations at that time, the desire for an assured supply of raw materials seems to have been more significant in encouraging integration than the desire to fix price and production schedules. The thrust of company policy in the early years, seen in the organisation of the St Clair Furnace and Steel companies, was towards making the combine 'absolutely independent as regards raw materials of all kinds', besides reducing the cost of manufacture to a minimum.[113] According to one report: 'substantially, all its coal, coke and basic pig iron requirements are produced by the company and its subsidiaries. Nearly all the iron ore requirements are purchased under contract from Synder Mining Company, 50 percent of the capital stock of which is owned by Crucible'.[114]

Since Crucible Steel absorbed Sanderson Bros' Syracuse Works in the merger, it is tempting to view 1900 as the end of an epoch as regards Sheffield's trade with America. Such a view would be mistaken. Sheffield subsidiaries such as Firth Sterling were still in business in the US, and Jessop's and Edgar Allen were yet to begin production in America. There was still room for the independent manufacturer, even though Crucible Steel accounted for 95 percent of domestic crucible steel production through its thirteen plants.

Nevertheless, the formation of Crucible Steel is a symbol of the profound contrast which existed between the Sheffield and American industries. Within only a few decades an industry based upon a large number of small producers had been transferred across the Atlantic and transformed into something entirely different: a consolidation of large

firms concentrating on their own specialities and with an adequate supply
of raw materials. Such a consolidation would have been unthinkable in
Sheffield at that time, with its 150 or so producers, only twenty of whom
could be classed as fairly large, and demonstrates how far the American
crucible steel industry had moved away from its Sheffield origins.

2

SCIENCE AND ART: SHEFFIELD AND
AMERICAN CRUCIBLE STEEL
TECHNOLOGIES CONTRASTED

Let me restate the belief that the reputation of Sheffield tool
steel depends more on the acute observation of workmen, or
managers who have been workmen, than on anything else.

Harry Brearley, *Steel-Makers* (1933), p. 25.

When J. Stephen Jeans toured American crucible steel works at the end of
the nineteenth century, on behalf of the British Iron Trade Association, he
would have seen the melter and 'puller-out' producing steel in much the
same way as in English furnaces. He concluded: 'There is little to dis-
tinguish American from British crucible steelmaking if we except the fact
that in the United States anthracite coal or natural gas are largely used as
fuels in the place of coke, the usual fuel employed in English works.'[1] This
seems self-evident, since with Sheffield's reputation as the pre-eminent
exponent of the method of making high-quality steel by melting bar iron
in clay crucibles it was natural that America embraced its innovations.
However, due perhaps to his unfamiliarity with crucible steel manufacture, Jeans missed many of the subtleties involved, and his view does little
to explain why there was still a market for Sheffield steel in America even
in the twentieth century. This chapter, therefore, contrasts English and
American crucible steel technologies.

In Sheffield the cementation of Swedish iron bars was the initial stage in
the production of crucible steel.[2] These bars, which contained only about
0.05 to 0.15 percent carbon and were therefore too low in carbon content
for tool steel, were packed in alternating layers of charcoal in a converting
furnace. These furnaces, which became a familiar feature of the industrial
landscape in Sheffield in the nineteenth century, consisted of two rec-
tangular chests, with fire-bars underneath, surmounted by a bottle-
shaped chimney. The size of the chests varied from 8 to 15 feet in length,
and from 2½ to 4 feet in width, and they were generally about 3 feet deep,
with a capacity of from 8 to 13 tons of bars. The furnace was sealed with a

layer of 'wheel-swarf' from the bottom of Sheffield grinders' troughs and the bars were then heated until the carbon from the charcoal was absorbed.

The average cementation furnace would take a couple of days to reach the required temperature of about 1,000–1,100°C, constant care being taken to keep the chests airtight and to maintain the temperature at the correct level. Firing would take about a week, the furnace then being allowed to cool gradually for several days, after which the bars were unpacked and sorted by fracture (they were now brittle) into various tempers. During cementation, the bars – which had been transformed into a crude type of steel – became covered with surface blisters, hence the name 'blister bars' or 'blister steel'.

An important consideration was that the bars were not uniform in carbon content, since the outside of the bars absorbed more carbon than the centre. To increase the homogeneity of this blister steel the bars were bundled (or 'faggoted') and heated and forged together, so producing 'shear steel'. If the process was repeated, by further shearing and welding of the bar, 'double shear steel' resulted.[3] The single or double shear bar was afterwards, by forging and rolling, drawn into thick strips suitable for cutlery. For the manufacture of high-class table cutlery, butchers' knives and any class of knife which had an iron back with a cutting edge welded on, shear steel was superior to the finest cast steel, and was reputed to hold its own against all comers.

The diffusion of carbon by forging did mechanically what the Huntsman crucible was to do chemically. Huntsman's secret, unsuccessfully guarded, and the development of his process have been well described by several authorities.[4] In principle it was a logical step from the production of shear steel. As devised by Huntsman in 1741, the process entailed the fragmenting of cemented bars and melting the pieces in a clay crucible. Also packed into the crucible was other material that might serve as a flux or contribute desired qualities to the steel. The molten steel could be cast into ingots direct from the crucible, or the contents of several crucibles might be poured together and 'teemed'. Either way, Huntsman's method resulted in a product which was highly uniform.

Such is a simple description of the process.[5] In actual practice crucible steelmaking was anything but simple. By 1850 the practical production of steel had more than out-run its theoretical basis. The mechanical and structural theory of metallurgy had made little progress after Réaumur had opened up these fields at the beginning of the eighteenth century, and though there were soon plenty of descriptions of the Sheffield methods the great metallurgy books of the nineteenth century largely confined themselves to giving details of cementation procedures and practical melting operations.[6] What was lacking was an understanding of the science of metallurgy. As Dr John Percy admitted in his treatise published in 1864, one of the first really detailed accounts of steelmaking: 'the science of the art was still in a very imperfect state'.[7] Thus the most commonplace features of crucible steel manufacture, such as the formation of blisters on the steel and the peculiar superiority of Swedish irons, were still a subject of debate at the end of the nineteenth century.[8]

The chemist was an unfamiliar figure at steelworks. The idea of analysing steel in a laboratory with a view to improving its commercial application was virtually unknown. One of the most critical tests – the calculation of the carbon content of the steel – was accomplished by simply fracturing the bar and gazing at the crystalline structure, a method which in experienced hands gave a reading accurate to within a fraction of a tenth of one per cent.[9] It was some time before the wider significance of this was recognised.[10] Henry Clifton Sorby (1826–1908) had begun his work on the metallography of steel in the 1860s, but it was to be some twenty years before his results were followed up.[11] Not until 1891, when Albert Sauveur (1863–1939) set out to continue Sorby's research in a modest laboratory at the Illinois Steel Co, was the importance of the microscopic examination of steel realised by firms.[12]

Meanwhile 'rule of thumb' methods predominated. The detailed recipes of the Sheffield steelmakers were cloaked in secrecy. Remarked the Sheffield steel manufacturer Henry Seebohm, after his townsmen had refused to entertain a visit from the Iron and Steel Institute in 1884: 'Sheffield inventors have learnt by bitter experience that secrecy is the only protection for improvements; and if they think they have found a goose that is going to lay golden eggs, they lock and double-lock the fowl-house door'.[13] Although foreign rivals were occasionally allowed access to Sheffield steel furnaces, the general attitude was one of concealment – an attitude which hardened as the nineteenth century wore on.[14] Americans who visited Sheffield were often, to their surprise, politely (or not so politely), turned away. In 1882, Samuel Osborn, the famous Sheffield tool steel manufacturer, replied to an American request for information: 'It is a very great trouble for any kind of foreigner to get into any kind of special works now. We refuse all that are strangers to us. I think perhaps John Bull is more sore than anything else, because other countries can send us their products and ours are virtually prohibited from theirs.'[15] Even some of the more progressive Sheffield makers ran into difficulties with the entrenched attitudes of their fellows, as when Seebohm encountered opposition to his plan to introduce coloured labels to denote carbon content, because it was said to destroy some of the mystery of crucible steel.[16] Sheffield steel had to have that indefinable something called 'body', exotic recipes were compounded, and everything from the clay to the water was held responsible for Sheffield's legendary quality.[17]

In these circumstances science was considered an occupation of the leisured classes, rather than as an adjunct to trade, and in the steel industry the major discoveries were made by men with little formal training.[18] Though the need was identified by 1862, not until about 1884, when courses were begun at the Sheffield Technical School, was metallurgy taught as a subject in Sheffield.[19] Links between the world of science and the Sheffield steel industry were not entirely lacking, as two historians have recently emphasised, but it would be stretching the evidence to suggest that the Sheffield methods were scientific in the modern sense.[20] The channels for systematising and formulating knowledge and for replicating results were lacking and this posed formidable difficulties for entrepreneurs. At mid-century steelmaking institutes and journals were non-existent, and even when periodical literature began to appear in the 1870s, there was little consideration of chemistry and physics.[21]

American technical literature began to appear as early as 1814, when Professor Thomas Cooper of Dickinson College, Carlisle, Pennsylvania, used various English and French authorities to compile a 180-page treatise on steelmaking.[22] Until the publications of G. H. Makins, Henry Osborn, Frederick Overman, and Percy in the 1850s and 1860s, however, there was little else apart from a few scattered references in the *Journal of the Franklin Institute* and the publication of selected English patents.[23] An American may have had access to some of the European accounts of the Sheffield methods, such as those by Le Play and by Swedish engineers, but, again, these were largely concerned with practical details, and even foreign visitors were loathe to give away too many secrets, especially if they hoped to begin manufacturing themselves.[24] A modest collection of contemporary textbooks by Lardner, Nicholson, and Rees, would have completed the selection of available metallurgical literature in the 1860s.[25]

Americans were quickly off the mark in providing a formal metallurgical education. In the 1850s and 1860s George J. Bush introduced courses in metallurgy at Yale and was instrumental in establishing the Sheffield Scientific School there. However, when the School offered scientific advice and consultation to the American Silver Steel Co at Roxbury Station, Connecticut, the results were disastrous, proving that in the absence of a scientific basis for the industry, which persisted to a greater or lesser extent throughout the nineteenth century, the skill and experience of the individual workman were the only reliable yardstick for the production of steel.[26] A French visitor, Frédéric Le Play recognised this: 'the humble workmen ... are the true metallurgists of Yorkshire'.[27] The ability of Sheffield to produce its own body of skilled workmen was not the least reason for its continued success and helps explain why the trade remained localised there.[28] It also accounts for the slow progress of other countries in acquiring the necessary metallurgical know-how.[29]

Even the making of the crucibles was an art. The most important constituent was Stourbridge or Derby clay which was mixed with a small amount of coke dust to provide the necessary strength at high temperatures. The mix of ingredients, or 'grog', was another source of individual prejudice. Admitted Harry Brearley: 'It would be a difficult matter to induce a Sheffield pot-maker to leave out any one constituent of his mix, and equally difficult to persuade him to substitute any other clay for the one he has long been accustomed to.'[30] Potmaking began by adding water to the clay and then treading it with bare feet for a period of up to two hours.[31] The clay was then moulded into crucibles by hand and set aside to dry, the drying process taking about three weeks. The pots were extremely fragile and often made on site, so it was not unusual to find a pot-maker working for different firms during each week. There was no place for machinery. Even in the 1920s, potmakers still trod the clay with their feet, since it was claimed that any impurities or coarse fragments (which could cause a costly or dangerous 'run' during the melt) could be more positively detected. Only one or two firms employed mechanical devices for pot-moulding by the 1920s, even though such machines had been available for decades.[32] Nevertheless, one man and boy were capable of making 65 to 75 pots daily with each pot capable of melting three rounds of steel per day.[33]

After inspection the crucibles were ready for the furnace, where they were annealed with extreme care, the pots being placed upon an annealing grate and heated very slowly for several hours. They were then lowered to the firing grate, where each crucible was placed upon a small brick to prevent its coming into contact with the bars. It was then packed in coke or coal and heated for an hour or so before receiving its 'charge' of metal.

The furnace was usually a separate building and in Sheffield typically coke-fired, although some used coal, and gas-firing was growing in importance in the twentieth century. In gas firing, however, there was a greater risk of the crucibles breaking and its appeal was limited. The life of the English furnace was about four weeks. Occasionally for high carbon steels five weeks might be the norm, but usually the melting holes were knocked and relined every fourth Monday (the 'building day') and this was frequently paid for as a full melting day's work.

Careful heat-control was essential in the furnace – a difficult job, since the coke furnaces were governed entirely by the 'flues' or the height of the stack. A fire-brick or a piece of paper was usually employed to vary the temperature and air-flow within the melting holes and this crude method proved remarkably effective in the hands of a skilled melter.

The experience of the melter was essential, too, in the final melting stages. Only he could decide, in the absence of pyrometers and similar gauges, when the steel was sufficiently 'killed', or rid of occluded gases. The old method adopted for killing was to keep the metal molten for varying periods; but later an aluminium pill was sometimes added to remove the most obstinate gases before the metal was teemed. Whatever technique was used, the trained eye decided when it was time to terminate the melt. A mistake at this stage, such as withdrawing the pots too soon, or allowing them to stand too much heat, and the whole charge would be scrap.

Once the melter had decided to his satisfaction that the steel was sufficiently dead-melted, the 'puller-out', protected by wet sacking, began retrieving the pots. This demanded great physical strength and careful timing, since at high temperatures the pots were fragile and could be easily broken by clumsy use of the tongs. Once the crucible was withdrawn and stood ready for teeming, the autocrat in the furnace – the melter – stepped forward. His difficulties were well summarised by a Sheffield steelmaker, David Flather:

> When you remember that the man who has such work to do, has within two feet of his hands, a white-hot crucible, which, with its contents, will generally weigh about 70 lbs, that he has to pour the steel down such a small opening, without splashing and without hesitation, that he must not touch the sides of the mould, but must pour in a gentle stream till the mould is full, and must keep on filling mould after mould until his crucible is empty, and that he will, in the space of about twenty minutes, lift and pour from 10 to 15 cwt of steel in this manner, I think you will agree that a steel melter's work is not by any means easy.[34]

Finally, as the ingot was poured, a 'dozzle', or fire-clay sleeve, was inserted which allowed a reservoir of molten steel to feed down into the shrinkage cavity or pipe which formed on cooling.

For larger ingots the contents of innumerable crucibles were teemed together. This Sheffield speciality, which was surpassed only perhaps by Krupps, was described by the American engineer, William Sellers, who noted that: 'From the great number of pots used, and the necessity of bringing them to the proper heat, and pouring into one reservoir at the same time it was necessary to have all the men as thoroughly drilled as a regiment.'[35] The military analogy was also employed by the journal *Engineering* when it described single castings of 25 tons poured from 576 pots, holding 100 pounds each, which were teemed at the rate of one pot every half-second within five minutes.[36]

In Sheffield the ingot was usually passed to the forge for hammering, which was also done with great care and attention, overheating being strictly guarded against to avoid decarbonisation. Hammering or rolling was not always done by the same firm. The large number of small manufacturers, and the fact that tool steel was a relatively costly material with a limited demand meant that it was found desirable to provide public mills and forges where the ingots could be expertly rolled or forged at a trade list price, and even the largest firms sent their ingots to these when making the more unusual sizes. After the ingot was broken down into billets and converted into oversize bars, the final size and shape were produced by 'tilting'. Sat on a swing-chair, and passing the heated bar beneath a broad hammer, the skilful hand and eye of the tilter gave the steel its final fine grain and uniform structure.[37] The bar of tool steel was then ready for the customer.

In what ways did American practice differ? The lack of certain natural resources and the need for a more scientific method to overcome these handicaps resulted in a process which differed in several important respects.[38]

American crucible steelmakers soon abandoned the traditional practice of spending several days in cementing their iron and preferred to carburise and melt in one operation. The pioneer in this field was Curtis G. Hussey, who, in the 1860s, succeeded in making cast steel direct from iron bars, a method which was bitterly attacked by Sheffield importing agents in America.[39] Hussey's methods are not known in detail; doubtless they involved the melting of wrought iron with an appropriate amount of cast iron or charcoal, which provided the correct amount of carbon in the crucible. By the 1880s this had become the standard practice in America, and converting furnaces fell into disuse.[40] To a certain extent, similar developments occurred in Sheffield, where a direct method of melting had been patented by William Vickers as early as 1839.[41] By the 1880s Sheffield steelmakers were making the last additions to their ranks of cementation furnaces, since it was found perfectly acceptable to melt Swedish bar iron, with a suitable proportion of Swedish cast iron, directly in the crucible.[42] In the 1860s Vickers' extensive River Don works could be built without any converting furnaces. However, although cementation furnace-building appears to have reached a peak in Sheffield by about the

1870s, the time-consuming technique of producing blister steel was not discarded and was still reserved for the highest class of tool steel even in the twentieth century.

In America the gas-fired furnace was in general use, though oil burners were also common. The gas was mixed with air and directed into the melting hole to provide a very intense heat. The melting hole itself, with the brickwork inclined towards the crucibles, also concentrated the heat. At the Crescent Steel Works in Pittsburgh various improvements were quickly incorporated into the original furnace design to prevent it cracking at high temperatures. The melting furnaces were also raised above the level of the moulding floors, so forming a continuous bench along the furnace against which the ingot moulds could be rested, thus doing away with teeming holes which required the services of an extra man in the melting crew. This was said to require only a third of the labour needed in an old-style melting house.[43] At first the life of a Siemens gas furnace in the US was from four to six weeks, not very different from the Sheffield coke-hole, but American furnacemen became skilled at retopping (by rebuilding only the top of the furnace so that work was not interrupted), and soon six to twelve months was usual.[44] As a rule, two shifts were employed in working the furnace, each gang obtaining three heats during the shifts; the second gang relieving the first after the third heat was completed, at whatever hour that might be. The furnace was worked continuously from Monday until Saturday morning, when any necessary repairs were conducted. Inside the furnace the crucibles rested upon a coke bed with a hole through to a vault below, so that if an accident happened and a charge was lost the steel could fall through, thus ensuring that there was little interruption. Each melting chamber had six crucibles beneath three covers lined with fire-brick; and as each cover served two crucibles, it was unnecessary to move more than one at a time when placing or removing the pots. Regulation of the heat on the crucibles was accomplished by means of valves, another stark contrast to the Sheffield practice.

In America, too, the pots were charged differently. In some cases the pot was charged cold; in others it was filled hot and set back, since it was claimed more heats were obtained in this way. The weight of the American charge – from 90 to 110 pounds – was a good deal heavier than Sheffield's average of 70 pounds, but the gas-fired furnace was much shallower than the coke one, enabling the American 'puller-out' to bring even his heavier pot onto the floor with a single lift; whereas in Sheffield a double lift and extra care were necessary.

The American crucible pot, in fact, bore little resemblance to its Sheffield counterpart. The early development of the American crucible steel industry had been hindered by the unsuccessful search for an equivalent to Stourbridge clay. Instead, largely due to the efforts of Joseph Dixon, who set up a company for their manufacture, plumbago or graphite pots were adopted. The pots were tough and durable, could be produced in bulk, and could be transported easily. In Sheffield the pots were far too fragile to be moved far and only enough crucibles were made for the next day's run. The robustness of graphite meant that it was possible to obtain any-thing from five to ten heats with a plumbago crucible as compared with three heats maximum from the Sheffield pot.

So far, all the advantages lay with the plumbago pot. However, the graphite, containing as it did a high percentage of pure carbon, gave rise to a great deal of irregularity in the finished ingot. The molten steel absorbed carbon from the pot and, though it was possible to allow for this, it was impossible to predict its extent. An analysis of one such heat of 18 percent tungsten high-speed steel found the following:[45]

Ingot Number	Carbon %
1	0.88
2	0.74
3	0.57
4	0.77
5	0.74
6	0.85
7	0.78
8	0.88
9	0.92
Average	0.79

The results show the degree of variation in successive heats, which was probably due to local temperature conditions in the furnace. This can be compared to Sheffield methods which allowed a staggering uniformity in heats and a low carbon content. One metallurgist examined 24 ingots and found no greater variation in carbon than 0.06 percent.[46]

In America, in an attempt to correct this deficiency, ladle teeming was introduced. Sometimes as many as 30 pots were put into a ladle at once; in other cases the melt was split into two smaller receptacles. Thus a degree of uniformity was established, which was closer to the Sheffield figure. Mechanical devices, such as ladles on rails or pulleys, assisted the process, and these were also essentially alien to the English furnace. When it came to the single pot, however, the Sheffield steelmakers could undoubtedly work to a much closer specification. In America it was often difficult to control the flow of metal and the likelihood of splashes and imperfections on the surface of the ingot was increased. It was probably for these reasons that Brearley referred, contemptuously, to the 'American slop method'.[47]

Though uneconomic in some respects, the Sheffield system was sometimes less wasteful than the American. In the production of tungsten steels the losses of tungsten in Sheffield plants were considerably less than those in the US, something that one observer attributed to the extreme care and attention to detail.[48] Something like 20 per cent of tungsten was added to the crucible charge with the expectation of obtaining better than 18 per cent tungsten in the finished steel; all croppings and trimmings being re-melted.

Both in Sheffield and America much depended on the most critical element – the class of material from which the steel was made. The view of Sheffield workers was expressed in a well-known local phrase: 'If you put the devil in a crucible pot you will get the devil out.' Huntsman had begun by breaking up Swedish iron bars and that practice had been followed religiously throughout Sheffield's history.[49] Swedish irons made from Dannemora or Oregrund ore were probably those with the highest reputation for producing the finer qualities of steel, but there were several varieties and each firm jealously guarded the particular brand it used.

During the First World War, a Section of the Ministry of Munitions arranged for a trial between English and Swedish bar irons, which was said to show that the domestic product was at least as good as its competitor.[50] However, this did little to dent the popularity of Swedish iron, especially since imports of American iron during the war did not prove equal to the Swedish. The opinion of most of the experienced metallurgists in Sheffield in the 1920s was that Swedish iron was unequalled. Local prejudice and conservatism may have had something to do with this, but that would hardly have been strong enough to persuade the nineteenth-century Sheffield steelmaker to pay up to £34 a ton for 'Hoop L' Swedish iron when he could get English bar iron (for example, 'Best Yorkshire') at £18 per ton or less. Trial and bitter experience were probably more important in convincing manufacturers of the virtues of Swedish iron, which, with its freedom from impurities such as sulphur and phosphorus, provided a secure foundation for consistent results at a time when the chemistry of steelmaking was only poorly understood.

American makers, apparently, did not share this view of the merits of Swedish iron. As we have seen, the early development of the Pittsburgh

Table 2.1 *Summary of costs for crucible furnaces*

	Coke-fired (cost £900)			Gas-fired (cost £7,000)		
	£	s	d	£	s	d
Depreciation and interest		2	3		6	0
Repairs		4	6		2	4
Fuel	2	1	1		5	6
Crucibles		19	0	2	4	10
Labour	1	16	9	2	0	0
Total cost per ton of liquid steel (less raw materials cost)	5	3	7	4	18	8

crucible steel industry was characterised by the utilisation of domestic ores. This practice set a trend, and American usage of Swedish bar iron seems to have been a good deal less than in Sheffield.[51] In America, when quality was the prime consideration, melters often settled for Swedish iron or a combination of Swedish and American iron. However, other steelmakers were more self-sufficient. Replying to the suggestion of an English authority that the most satisfactory results in the production of high-speed steel could only be obtained by using solely the purest qualities of Swedish irons, Dr John A. Mathews, of the Halcomb Steel Co, argued that: 'Swedish iron is not necessary. We get equally good results using Swedish or a great many of our domestic irons which in analysis are as good or better than Swedish iron.'[52] Clearly, not all American steelmakers accepted the traditions of the past as conclusive.

This leads to a consideration of the comparative merits of the two systems. Who made the better steel, and at what cost?

The Sheffield methods resulted, through the use of natural resources, in a highly uniform and satisfactory material. It is difficult at this stage to assess the quality of old Sheffield steel, but a recent analysis of some surviving samples has shown them to be remarkably 'clean' even by modern standards.[53] Tonnage production, though, was considerably less than the American. The greater capacity of graphite pots, and the fact that American furnaces were worked for six heats instead of two or three, meant that US makers could beat the English tonnage by four or five times. However, crucible and labour costs were also higher in America. David Carnegie, writing in 1913, provides an interesting comparison of English and American costs for a coke-fired Huntsman crucible and a gas-fired American furnace (Table 2: 1).[54]

It was in the price of labour, crucibles and fuel that the greatest differences occurred in the costs of production. In the early days of compe-

Table 2.2 *Crucible steel wages in Sheffield and
America 1872*

	Sheffield wages per week	Pittsburgh wages per week
Melter	$12.10	$47.83 ($63 in 1874)
Puller-out	7.02	17.55
Cokers	4.86	19.00 (Gasmaker)
Pot-maker	9.68	—
Converter	4.88	24.00

Source: E. Young, *Labor in Europe and America* (Washington, DC, 1875), pp. 325, 765.

tition between the two processes some of the differentials were even more pronounced. This was particularly true of labour costs. Data for the 1870s (Table 2: 2) show the premium placed in America upon the vital services of the melter, and the great advantage this gave to Sheffield manufacturers in terms of relative costs.

Unfortunately for Sheffield, American wages did not remain at this high level. By the 1880s the wages paid to American melters had fallen to about $34 as compared with about $15 in Sheffield.[55] In the 1890s there was another reduction, and the highest class of skilled men in Pittsburgh were receiving no more than $20 per week.[56] By the 1920s, though British wages for crucible steel furnacemen were still lower than those paid in American plants, the difference was marginal.[57]

Nevertheless, Sheffield could still ship steel at prices below those of the American maker even after the First World War. On the basis of Carnegie's figures this would appear to be impossible. However, it must be remembered that they refer to the more common varieties of crucible steel. When it came to producing the higher grades of tool steel and high-speed steel costs could be vastly different, varying in Sheffield from £20 to £158 per ton of liquid steel. Production of these steels was much more labour intensive, so increasing Sheffield's competitive edge over the US. This advantage was pressed home in the lengthy finishing stages in the forging mill. An American noted the special significance in the manufacture of high-speed steel of the relatively low wages paid in Sheffield to rollers and hammer finishers: in 1921 these skilled workers were still paid less than the average common labour in US mills.[58]

It was labour costs and the cheaper price for crucibles which offset Sheffield's disadvantages as regards fuel. American makers had access to abundant supplies of natural gas and the thermal efficiency of plumbago pots was twice that of clay ones. Sheffield's use of fuel was far from efficient. The coke-fired furnaces were shut down every night and 'were lighted afresh every morning with the same sleepy interest that goes to lighting the kitchen fire; and, likewise, the team were not fully awake until after breakfast time'.[59] Americans found it difficult to comprehend how this tremendous heat wastage was tolerated.

The introduction of ladle teeming had allowed Americans to make up some ground in the control of uniformity and quality. As regards the finished product one steelmaker, T. Holland Nelson, had no doubt 'that if the American manufacturer puts as good material into his crucible as his English or continental competitor, despite the difference in the methods of production, he can obtain quite as good a steel in the ingot with a considerably increased tonnage'.[60] However, it was not always the case that American melters used the best raw material. The variable quality of American steel in the nineteenth century was at least partly due to a lack of uniformity in domestic ores and the practice of charging the crucibles with wrought-iron and scrap.[61] Moreover, as T. Holland Nelson himself admitted the quest for tonnage damaged the reputation of American steel. Sheffield's concern with quality extended far beyond the melting process. In America higher output led to the substitution of rolling for hammering with its consequent increased risk of overheating and decarbonisation. Great care usually avoided this problem in Sheffield. Some hammerers even preferred water-powered hammers, because they gave a more even blow and a better 'feel' for the steel. These were some of the reasons why Sheffield steel continued to be imported into America well into the twentieth century.

One puzzling feature which remains to be explored is why Sheffield makers did not improve their competitive advantage by adopting the cheaper regenerative gas furnace, which had been almost universally adopted in the US by the 1880s. Despite the huge savings involved few of these furnaces, as some Americans were surprised to discover, had been laid down in Sheffield. Vickers had built a Siemens gas furnace in 1871–2, which cut fuel and furnace-repair costs by nearly two-thirds.[62] Sanderson's had added Siemens gas furnaces at its Darnall Works in 1871.[63] In 1885, when Samuel Osborn took over William Butcher's Works, the new installation included a 24-hole gas crucible furnace.[64] Firth's changed to gas in 1907–8, when it constructed new works at Tinsley.[65] Jessop's had joined the field at the turn of the century with a 72-pot furnace worked by producer gas.[66] Traditional coke-holes, however, still accounted for something like 80 percent of the output, and they were still reserved for the highest class of tool steel.

The capital cost of a gas furnace was certainly beyond the means of many of Sheffield's small producers, in an industry which, in the past, had been typified by its relative ease of entry. Conservatism may also have been involved. Brearley, noting the failure to adopt the gas furnace, criticised his fellow steelmakers for their state of 'blissful satisfaction' with well-tried methods which meant that: 'Over a period of one hundred years one looks in vain for an improvement of first-rate or even second-rate importance.'[67] However, it would appear to be a mistake to stress this too much. 'There is unquestionable evidence', wrote David Carnegie, 'from Patent Office records that much time and talent have been expended to perfect this [crucible] process'.[68] He listed an impressive series of improvements, many of which originated in Sheffield, including everything from gas regenerators to movable furnace bottoms.[69] When it came to devising innovations in crucible steelmaking there was certainly no shortage of ideas. When these failed to be adopted it was more often for practical reasons than because of ignorance or conservatism.

The chief objections to gas melting were technical ones. Plumbago pots, largely because of their unfortunate effects on the uniformity of the steel, were never popular in Sheffield for melting the higher grades, despite the fact that they could be easily obtained from such firms as the Patent Plumbago Crucible Co of Battersea.[70] When clay pots were tried instead, they cracked. Another problem, discovered by Osborn's, was that it was found difficult to maintain a uniform temperature throughout the gas melting furnace with a consequent adverse effect on the steel.[71] A furnace designed by Dawson, Robinson and Pope to meet this difficulty was patented in 1898 and went into successful production at Jessop's Works. The saving in fuel was said to have been at least £2 10s on every ton of steel made, only 1¾ tons of slack being used as against three tons of high-class coke in ordinary coke-hole practice.[72] Some firms spent heavily on trying the new methods. Edgar Allen's incurred heavy losses in experimenting with the crucible gas furnace in the early 1890s. Only after extended trials did the directors decide to abandon the idea, opting instead for the Tropenas Process (a modified Bessemer converter), which they found superior to any other furnace.[73]

The logic for the adoption of the gas furnace was strengthened during the First World War and the 1920s, when the supply of good coking coal diminished and increased tonnages meant that carbon steel could no longer be treated with such care. Indeed, one Sheffield steelmaker, in 1921, argued that there was not 'the slightest reason why Gas melted steel should be in any way inferior to Coke melted material, providing ordinary care and reasonable intelligence are used'.[74] But by then, postwar difficulties had rendered the utilisation of new techniques more problematical. Huntsman's coke-hole and crucible technology, therefore, based upon tradition and conducted mostly in small-scale works, remained much as it had been in the early nineteenth century.

Apart from minor improvements and an increase in tonnage (which really depended as much on demand and social attitudes as technical innovations), it is difficult to see how the Sheffield methods, which were so ideally suited to local conditions, could have been improved. The techniques, it is true, were expensive in fuel and labour, but the individual attention and craftsmanship may have been critical in preserving part of Sheffield's American trade. Whilst in some sectors of the steel industry the only manual labour needed to turn limestone, coal, and iron ore into steel was pulling a lever or turning a wheel, the crucible steel industry, with its reliance on human skill and muscle, preserved its own unique flavour. Improvements which would take high-grade steel production into the twentieth century had to wait for an entirely new process – the electric furnace.

3

THE RESPONSE TO A NEW TECHNOLOGY: ELECTRIC STEELMAKING

> Up-To-Date contrivances notwithstanding, no method of steelmaking has been found, which, for all-round excellence, can compare with the original practice ... of melting in sealed clay crucibles in the coke-fired furnace.
>
> Introductory quotation from *A Brief History of the Firm of B. Huntsman Ltd 1742–1930* (Sheffield, 1930).

For high-grade alloy steel, cutting tools, die steels, and stainless steel, metal must be refined and melted under strictly controlled conditions, often at a higher temperature than in the crucible, and in such a way that impurities are reduced to a minimum. Where a fuel such as coke is burned in the furnace some contamination is unavoidable; therefore, the way was open for the introduction of a process that would eliminate this problem.

Electric steelmaking, which was to completely supersede the clay crucible and coke-hole, had a comparatively recent origin.[1] Its beginnings may be traced to the discovery of the electric battery and the experiments of Sir Humphry Davy, but the first electric furnace of any practical importance was constructed in England by Sir Charles William Siemens in 1878, which he used mainly for melting metal. The smelting of iron ore was a later development; in 1898, Captain Stassano, in Italy, patented his electric furnace for this purpose, and in the following year demonstrated the working of his process.

Siemens' original design consisted of a crucible and two rods for conducting the current. The metal to be melted was placed in the crucible, making electrical contact with the lower pole; then the other rod was lowered until an arc was struck between this rod and the metal in the crucible. Nearly all of the early electric furnaces were of this type. In France, Héroult, and in Sweden, Kjellin, succeeded in adapting the design to the production of good-quality steels. The original patents of these pioneers of electric steelmaking were taken out in about 1900.[2]

46

Table 3.1 *Summary of costs per ton of liquid steel – Héroult furnace*

Cost of plant, £2,000 approx.	£	s	d
Depreciation and interest	0	2	4
Repairs to walls, roof and mechanical plant (roof lasts about 80 heats)	0	2	6
Power, 750 kw hours at 0.3 d. per unit	0	18	9
Power, heating up at weekends	0	1	0
Electrodes, 30–40 lbs (average 35 lbs) @ 2d per lb	0	5	10
Labour – 1 melter, 1 helper and 4 labourers	0	6	0
Management expenses (50 per cent of labour)	0	3	0
Cost per ton of liquid steel (less raw materials cost)	1	19	5

After this, development was rapid. The commercial possibilities of the new processes invited official scrutiny. In view of the great importance to Canada of developing the electric smelting of iron ores, the Canadian Government, in 1903, appointed a Commission to report on the electro-thermic processes operating in Europe for smelting iron ores and making steel. The Commission visited Europe in 1904 and saw (amongst others) the Héroult and Kjellin furnaces in commercial operation making steel and ferro-alloys. It also engaged an English metallurgist, F. W. Harbord, to conduct experiments with the new furnaces. A report was published after the Commission's return, which concluded, encouragingly, that 'steel equal in all respects to the best Sheffield crucible steel can be produced . . . at a cost considerably less than the cost of producing a high-class crucible steel'.[3]

The electric furnace had very definite advantages in its operation. There was no contact with deleterious gases from fuels such as coke, ensuring a lower phosphorus and sulphur content in the steel; greater homogeneity could be achieved when making large ingots; the temperature was easy to control; and production could be conducted intermittently with very little loss of efficiency. In economic terms the electric furnace had a marked edge over the older crucible process.[4] David Carnegie gives an interesting breakdown of costs which can be compared with the earlier figures for the Huntsman crucible (Table 3: 1).[5]

The electric furnace, in most cases, was still too costly to compete where tonnage was the chief requirement in the finished product. Never-theless, its numerous advantages for high-grade steel production meant that its eventual success was assured.

Statistics for US steel production show that by 1930 the electric furnace had almost completely replaced the crucible for producing ingots and castings (Table 3: 2). Though the comparative statistics are unavailable,[6]

Table 3.2 *Production of US and UK crucible and electric steel (tons)*

Year	US crucible*	US electric*	UK electric**
1908	63,631	–	–
1909	107,355	13,762	–
1910	122,303	52,141	–
1911	97,653	29,105	–
1912	121,517	18,309	–
1913	121,226	30,180	–
1914	89,869	24,009	–
1915	113,782	69,412	22,000
1916	129,692	168,918	46,709
1917	126,716	304,543	98,592
1918	115,112	511,364	125,448
1919	63,572	384,452	77,000
1920	72,265	502,152	89,100
1921	7,613	169,499	26,500
1922	28,606	346,039	39,400
1923	44,079	515,872	64,200
1924	22,473	432,526	64,500
1925	19,562	615,512	64,100
1926	15,493	651,723	60,800
1927	9,036	666,087	74,400
1928	7,769	802,260	78,400
1929	6,645	951,431	86,800
1930	2,253	612,599	76,000

Source: *Annual Statistical Report of the American Iron and Steel Institute* (1918), p. 24; (1930), p. 26. **NFISM, *Statistics of the Iron and Steel Industries* (1931), p. 9.

certainly no such thing had happened in Sheffield by that date. 'In England', remarked a Sheffielder in 1929, 'the higher grades of these [carbon tool steels] are still manufactured by the crucible process.'[7] Amongst the reasons for this fact, observed G. I. H. Finch, was 'the still persistent belief, long since proved to be without foundation, that electric steel is inferior to crucible steel'.[8] As if to verify that statement, the views of Jessop's American sales director, Frederick C. A. H. Lantsberry, may be added (alongside those of Huntsman's quoted at the opening of the chapter): 'The modern tendency is to produce high-speed steel in electric furnaces, but in the author's works ... the practice is to adhere to the old crucible process ... [which] demands the use of raw materials of the highest degree of purity so that the resulting product has of necessity certain inherent qualities which are not to be found in the electric furnace product.'[9] One authority still thought the crucible process important enough to devote a paper to it before the Sheffield Metallurgical Association in 1927, which extolled its virtues and pointed to the fact that the value of its product in Sheffield was greater than ever.[10]

Table 3.3 *Electric steel furnaces installed 1910–23*

	1910	1913	1915	1916	1917	1918	1919	1920	1921	1922	1923
United States	10	19	41	73	136	233	287	323	356 ⎫	438	456
Canada	3	3	2	8	19	36	43	40	43 ⎬		
Others	101	118	170	222	316	464	485	–	562		

Source: A. Stansfield, *The Electric Furnace for Iron and Steel* (New York, 1923), p. 12. NFISM, *Statistical Report* (1918), p. 7, shows total electric furnaces built or building in UK in 1916, 91; 1917, 127; 1918, 147.

Here, it seems, in comparison with the US, are the ingredients of that familiar story of the British industrialist's failure to adapt to changing technologies. However, the evidence is not as clear-cut as that. In both England and America adoption of the electric furnace took time and in the beginning it was the Americans who lagged behind European developments. Statistics for the installation of electric steel furnaces (Table 3: 3) show that not until after the First World War did the US establish a significant lead over other countries.[11]

In the nineteenth century Americans had made important contributions to electric steel metallurgy.[12] Robert Hare, a Philadelphia chemist, born in 1781, is credited with constructing the first electric furnace, which with only battery current converted charcoal into graphite. In 1886, another American, Charles Hall, invented a process for making aluminium, using an electric current. Two brothers, Alfred and Eugene Cowles, who had worked with Hall, applied the principles of electric melting to the production of aluminium bronze. In 1891, Edward G. Acheson, an American who had been associated with Edison, used the electric furnace to convert coke, sawdust, sand, and salt into a new substance, carborundum, which found applications in grinding. Acheson also made by far the purest graphite obtainable, again with electricity.[13] Edward A. Colby had also taken out basic patents on the electric furnace in the 1890s.[14] Despite these promising beginnings, however, commercial application of the electric process was slow.[15]

In 1906, Henry Disston & Sons, the Philadelphia sawmakers, laid down the first low-frequency induction furnace, and began experimental heats with the new process.[16] In the same year the Halcomb Steel Co, at Syracuse, New York, commenced the commercial production of electric steel.[17] The Firth Sterling Steel Co, Pittsburgh, followed shortly afterwards in 1908, and there were further installations at the Illinois Steel Co and the American Steel and Wire Co. The furnaces were, typically, of European design.

In many quarters, however, it was felt that the electric furnace was a complement to, rather than a substitute for, the clay or graphite crucible. As late as 1916, in a paper presented to the American Iron and Steel Institute, the president of the Halcomb Steel Co, Dr John A. Mathews, stated: 'With the advent of electric furnaces we have a rival which claims to make steel equal to the best crucible steel ... nevertheless, we are building four new crucible furnaces at the present moment.'[18] At Disston's, despite an early start, in 1920 the old crucible method was still supplying the firm with nearly twice as many steel ingots as the electric furnace: 5,176 tons to 2,852 tons.[19] In 1925 a Sheffield visitor to Disston's noted: 'They have 2 Elec. Furs. 16 ton and 4 ton & a lot of Gas Crucible Holes, but ... before long [they expect] to reduce the number of crucibles and switch over to Elec. more.'[20] Firth Sterling also retained crucible steel melting in the 1920s; the traditional methods accounting for one-third of annual capacity in 1930.[21] The crucible was still retained, it appears, where uniformity and quality were the prime consideration and though the electric furnace had moved to the forefront of high-speed steel production in the US by 1930, only during the 1920s did it displace its forerunner.[22]

There were practical reasons why some metallurgists refused to consider electric steel as an equal to its predecessor. Electric melting was not simply a convenient short-cut; it demanded skilled labour fully conversant with its own peculiar problems. For some metallurgists it was a question of 'wait-and-see', especially since early experiences with the new method did not always fulfil expectations.[23] Halcomb's steel furnace did not operate successfully, and was considered a failure until Dr John A. Mathews organised it on a regular commercial basis after 1908.[24] Some of the more extravagant claims made on behalf of the electric furnace by its inventors, such as the belief that it could produce the finest quality tool steel from either scrap or materials of only moderate purity, appear to have hindered its development, especially in England.[25] 'Inferior scrap can be converted to a tool steel or alloy steel of any desired composition', declared one journal in 1913 in a review of an electric furnace at Darwin & Milner's, Sheffield.[26] But crucible steelmakers, whose whole training and experience were based upon the manufacture of the highest grade of steel, were sceptical. Electric steelmaking, therefore, in both Sheffield and America only found ready acceptance for melting the less special of the special steels or for cheaply reducing scrap. In Sheffield, the pioneers in the field, Edgar Allen's and Firth's, used their furnaces either to prepare steel for casting or to further refine material from a Siemens furnace.[27] Hadfields, in the First World War, used its impressive array of electric furnaces exclusively to melt down scrap metal.[28]

There was also the question of costs. The capital investment required for the installation of an electric furnace (Héroult) was more than double that for the old clay crucible. Also, although the electric furnace was significantly cheaper than the crucible, the difference depended very much upon the cost of electric power. The electric furnace was, therefore, rapidly taken up in Scandinavia, where economic developments had resulted in the availability of cheap hydro-electric power. America was also well to the forefront in the utilisation of hydro-electricity and, although the price of electricity from regions such as the Great Lakes was much higher than in Scandinavia, it could be as little as a quarter of its cost in Sheffield.[29]

Nevertheless, developments in Sheffield before 1914 were as impressive as those in America. Since the first electric furnaces in the US were installed by one Sheffield subsidiary (Firth Sterling) and one with very strong Sheffield links (Halcomb Steel Co), it is not surprising to find that in Sheffield itself there was early interest in the new process. In 1893 the director of the engineering firm of Thwaite, Tozer & Co wrote, at the suggestion of Professor Arnold of Sheffield University, to Robert A. Hadfield to inform him of his 'Electro-fusion System of Crucible-Steel-Melting'.[30] Hadfield was inclined to defer consideration of the subject on economic grounds, since he had 'heard only recently from two reliable sources in America, where they are certainly ahead of us in this line, that the application of electrical energy to heating or similar operations is still much too costly to be practicable except for very special purposes'.[31] Nevertheless, he was later to join and help finance experiments on electric melting. In 1903 it was also reported that W. Edgar Allen was in France gathering information on electric furnace improvements.[32] In October 1906, Robert S. Hutton, the son of the Sheffield silversmith, James E. Hutton, who had become interested in electro-metallurgy in Manchester and had continued his studies in America, presented a lecture on 'The Electric Furnace and its Application to the Metallurgy of Iron and Steel' to the Sheffield Society of Engineers and Metallurgists.[33] His talk succeeded in arousing the interest of Sheffield's steelmakers.

By 1906 Arnold had organised a Steel Research Committee at Sheffield University composed of the city's leading steelmakers to conduct experiments into electric melting. The subsequent research reports recognised the potential of the electric furnace.[34] Vickers had designed an electric furnace based on the Grondall-Kjellin design and one of them had been installed by the American Electric Furnace Co at Niagara Falls.[35] High-speed steel manufacturers were also showing an interest in electric melting at this time.[36] In 1910 Edgar Allen's made the first melts of electric steel in Sheffield in a 3½-ton Héroult furnace.[37] A year later, Firth's and Jessop's began production;[38] there was also an experimental model at Sheffield University; and another electric furnace installation planned by Kayser Ellison. Output for 1911 in England was projected at about 13,000 tons.[39]

The demand for special castings and shell steel during the War gave a tremendous impetus to the electric steel industry. Even the more conservative Sheffield metallurgists had to try the latest methods as the supply of coke and pure base metals for the crucible diminished. Vickers, in 1916, added a 2½- and 3-ton Héroult furnace, making its total four; Firth's, two 7-ton, two 6-ton, a 2½- and a 1-ton furnace, making its total eight; while Hadfields made its total ten by adding four 8-ton, one 3½-ton and one 1½-ton furnace.[40] Osborn's installed its first electric furnace, a Héroult, in 1915, and had added two more within a year.[41] Brown Bayley's also installed an electric furnace in 1915 to produce stainless steel.[42] Kayser Ellison was operating four electric furnaces by 1917, including two of the Greaves-Etchells type.[43]

The Greaves-Etchells furnace was designed in Britain to meet the special requirements of the Sheffield steel industry. By 1923 over 20 of these furnaces, ranging from 500 lb to 20 tons, had been erected in the Sheffield area for the production of high-grade alloy steels. In the US two furnaces were supplied to the Halcomb Steel Co, and five to the US Navy Yard. Greaves-Etchells furnaces were also installed by the Ford Motor Co, and by the Holmes Foundry Co, in Michigan, and were used for melting cast-iron borings and refining cupola iron for casting motor cylinders and piston rings. By 1923 over 60 furnaces of this type had been installed, and its makers considered it second in the world as regards electric tonnage output (the first was the Héroult).[44]

In the 1920s in America development of the electric furnace continued apace; production rising from about 500,000 tons in 1920 to nearly double that figure in 1929. The growth of production in Sheffield was comparatively slower and by the end of the decade the crucible had still not been entirely dislodged. In some firms the older method languished alongside the electric furnace and the two processes could occasionally be seen together in the same advertisement.

Demand seems to be the important factor here rather than conservatism. The automobile industry exerted a tremendous pull on electric steel production in the US. This was less true in Sheffield, especially since the city's embryonic motor-car industry declined in the interwar years, and so the steel industry lost the chance of supplementing its idle armaments capacity. When demand was sluggish and only small quantities of high-grade steel were required, the clay pot still served the purpose well enough for many manufacturers. At Balfour's the last crucible furnace was not extinguished until 1947, not because it was uneconomic, but because the average age of the team was fifty-nine and no replacements were forthcoming. Arthur Balfour's son, Francis, is said to have defended the crucible literally to its death, an enthusiasm which ended with a spectacular and disastrous attempt to run the furnaces continuously at the Broughton Lane Works.[45] Several Sheffield firms re-opened their crucible melting holes when the Second World War increased the demand for high-speed steel. Wardlow's produced 400–500 tons of tool steel by the traditional methods at Abbeydale in 1941–4.[46] Even after that crucible steelmaking lingered on in some factories and the last furnace did not close down until 1968.[47]

Considering the problems of adjustment that Sheffield faced in the interwar period, its record is still a creditable one. There is certainly little evidence to support the erroneous view that in Britain there was 'insufficient attention to electric metallurgy'.[48] Sheffield remained in the forefront of many developments in electric steel technology. Improved motor-generators set for high frequencies resulted in the first commercially viable coreless induction furnace designed in 1922 by Edwin F. Northrup of Princeton, New Jersey. In 1927 Edgar Allen's installed the world's first high-frequency electric furnace of this type.[49] It was to be the eventual replacement for the crucible in Sheffield for the production of tool steels and early stainless steel, since the arc furnace had never been wholeheartedly embraced for high-speed steel production.[50] Introduced in increasing numbers in the 1930s, high-frequency induction furnaces contributed to Sheffield's reputation as the most concentrated centre for electric steel production in the world.

Even had the electric furnace been adopted on a more widespread basis in Sheffield, it is doubtful whether it would have helped the city retain its high-speed steel trade with America in the 1920s. This trade suffered an irreparable blow when the electric furnace removed two of the traditional advantages that the crucible steel industry had enjoyed in Sheffield: the lower cost of labour and the cheapness of crucibles. Henceforth, trade with America would be conducted on a far more equal basis, with America perhaps now possessing the greater advantage with its cheaper electricity. Nor could Sheffield rely on its traditional skills in mixing metals; another result of the electric process was a much greater uniformity in steels.[51]

Part two

THE DEVELOPMENT OF SPECIAL STEELS

4

THE RISE OF ALLOY STEELS

[I] cannot but think that the special question of steel alloys or combinations will be eventually found to possess considerable practical importance to the world at large, and perhaps be the means of eventually enabling our civil and mechanical engineers to design and carry out works of a magnitude which, notwithstanding the great strides made during the last few years, even at present are not possible.

Robert A. Hadfield, 'Alloys of Iron and Chromium', *JISI*, 1892, ii, pp. 49–50.

Strictly speaking, all steels are alloys, since even 'ordinary' steel contains up to 1.5 percent carbon, an element which has a greater effect than any other on the properties of iron. Many other steels in the nineteenth century included various elements such as manganese, aluminium, and titanium, which were added to the crucible to remove unwanted ingredients or eliminate mechanical defects. Josiah Heath's patent in 1839 for the addition of 'carburet of manganese' to crucible steel greatly improved its welding quality and lessened the cost. However, the term 'alloy steel' or 'special steel' is usually reserved for steel which 'contains one or more elements other than carbon, in sufficient proportion to modify and improve substantially some of its useful properties'.[1] Sheffield occupies a particularly important place in the development of such steels.

To repeat an earlier observation, in the 1850s there was little metallurgical literature of any value. Manuals of steelmaking tended to codify available technical data on melting and casting, whilst ignoring chemistry or physics. The inadequacy of metallurgical theory, which ensured that a satisfactory definition of steel based on carbon content was only reached in the 1860s, meant that the development of alloy steels was very much a post-1850 phenomenon.

Nevertheless, important work had been done in the early part of the nineteenth century.[2] Michael Faraday and James Stodart, a London instrument maker and cutler, devoted much time and energy to the question of 'artificially' improving cutting edges and decreasing corrosion by adding elements to steel.[3] The practical side of their experiments was carried out with the help of the Sandersons and Charles Pickslay in Sheffield. Faraday's work, however, did not find any commercial application, though it provided inspiration for others. In France, Berthier, in a report published in 1821, documented the results of the introduction of chromium into cast steel and his treatise on assaying presented the first comprehensive statement of the alloying performances of the various elements.

The age of alloy steels, however, is generally regarded as having been inaugurated by Sir Robert A. Hadfield (1858–1940) with his research on manganese steel. Hadfield was the son of Robert Hadfield (1831–88), the owner of Hadfield's Steel Foundry, in Attercliffe, Sheffield, and one of the pioneers of the manufacture of steel castings.[4] The younger Hadfield took over the company after his father's death and during his lifetime he built up the firm he had inherited into one of the largest steel foundries in the world. Alongside his business career, he established an international reputation as a metallurgist for his work on alloy steels. His published output included over two hundred technical papers and addresses, bringing him numerous honours from scientific and public bodies.

However, although Hadfield was to achieve fame in both his scientific and business careers, it was as a metallurgist that he achieved his most striking success. He refused the chance to go up to Oxford or Cambridge, preferring instead to serve a brief apprenticeship with the local tool steelmakers, Jonas & Colver. After one of his first days there, he noted in his diary on 25 January 1875: 'I like it pretty well ... and I think I shall do very well'.[5] He received tuition in chemistry from Mr A. H. Allen, a leading analyst, and began his own experiments in steelmaking at the Hecla Works, even persuading his father to allow him to install his own furnace in the basement of the family home, Ashdell Mount. Once again, Hadfield recorded these events in his diary: 18 May 1876, 'Had my furnace going, melted steel'; 24 May 1876, 'Melted steel in 25 minutes'; 5 April 1877, 'Having a furnace built at home'.

In 1878 Hadfield visited the Paris Exhibition, which introduced him to the research of the metallurgists of the Terre Noire Co, who had succeeded in producing ferro-manganese with as much as 80 percent of manganese and only a small amount of carbon. (Previously, manganese had been added to steel in the form of spiegeleisen, a white pig iron with about 20 percent of manganese, but since it contained about 5 percent of carbon it was unsuitable as an addition to low-carbon steel.) The Company's descriptive pamphlet, which was translated by the young Hadfield,[6] showed the beneficial effects of additions of manganese to steel of up to 3 percent; further quantities, however, made the steel very brittle. On his return Hadfield resumed his own experiments, which were to be briefly interrupted by a visit to America in 1882, by focussing his attention on additions of both manganese and silicon to steel.

In his laboratory notebook Hadfield recorded the following observation on 7 September 1882: 'Was led to make the following expts. with a view to making a v. hard steel for trams' wheels. They have led to some very curious results, perhaps most momentous results, that may to some extent quite alter metallurgical opinions as to alloys of iron & steel.'[7] Hadfield began by making an experimental melt with silicious pig iron, soft iron, and rich ferro-manganese, the material introduced by the Terre Noire Co. This was found to contain 7.45 percent of manganese, and on casting it into a wheel it proved to be very difficult to cut with steel tools, but to be useless as a grinding material, as the surface glazed instead of cutting. A second melt followed, dispensing with silicon, and containing 1.35 percent of carbon and 13.76 percent of manganese. Hadfield found the ingot 'very tough, most peculiar fracture... To all appearances it looked v. soft & I thought this is no use ... I said fetch a file when lo & behold it took serations off file like an emery wheel... *Notwithstanding this it was exceedingly tough & very difficult to top ingot.*' As a turning tool it quickly lost its edge, and as this was attributed to the heat of the process having destroyed its temper, the tool was reheated to 900–1,000°C and quenched in water (the normal hardening procedure). But surprisingly the metal became slightly softer and much tougher than before. Moreover, although containing over 80 percent iron, it was non-magnetic. These astonishing findings, which were a reversal of the ordinary behaviour of steel, fully justified Hadfield's confident prediction of the epoch-making nature of his discovery. When he came to cast a wheel with manganese steel, Hadfield could hardly conceal his delight at the results: '*Wonderfully tough*, even with a 16 lb hammer c[oul]d hardly break it... Not a *blow-hole in the wheel, sound as metal*. Really grand. Hurrah!!!'.[8]

Hadfield immediately patented his findings in 1883–4, and then embarked on five years of confirmatory experiments.[9] It was eventually shown that the best results were obtained with 12–14 percent manganese, with carbon about 1 percent: this gave a material that was relatively soft, but capable of becoming intensely hard when it was deformed. Thus, it could be marked with a chisel, but it was impossible to cut it with the same tool. This complicated the manufacturing problem, since, as Hadfield himself pointed out: 'it is simply impractical to machine it, which is one of its drawbacks, it being so hard, or rather although the tougher percentage is not so extraordinarily hard to file, still no turning or other tool steel will practically touch it'.[10] Before the advent of high-speed steels, it was commercially impossible to machine manganese steel, and usually parts could only be surfaced by grinding. It was, however, a good material for steel castings (a speciality of Hadfield's company) because of its low melting point; though, on the other hand, its high contraction rate and the fact that a high manganese material has a highly erosive effect on silicious lining materials and clay crucibles presented difficulties that were only overcome after lengthy trials. Nevertheless, Hadfield's experience in the manipulation and control of the material and its heat treatment made it possible to successfully produce rails, sheets, plates, and even complicated assemblies such as track layouts. Much of the equipment laid down at Hadfields in Sheffield, such as the blooming and finishing mill for manganese steel rails, was the first of its kind in the world.[11]

There were also problems of application. The high electrical resistance of manganese steel, which produced difficulties for electric traction systems, and its non-magnetic nature, which interfered with the working of the magnetic brake, presented problems which were only solved after time-consuming experiments and discussions with tramway and railway engineers.

This explains the delay before Hadfield announced his discovery to the world, by an exhibit at the Institution of Mechanical Engineers in 1887. He later gave a full account of the new steel to the Institution of Civil Engineers and the Iron and Steel Institute in 1888.[12]

Hadfield and his father believed that the material would be ideal for railway wheels. In 1885 Hadfield himself reported that he had made a wheel with 18 percent manganese and 'had about 50 blows at it with a heavy sledge hammer without in the least way damaging it'.[13] But other possibilities also suggested themselves. Continued Hadfield:

We are going to have it tried in a short time for rails & tyres here, as we believe it will last much longer than anything yet introduced... We also think it may be applied for saw plates & thus do away with all the hardening & tempering which cause so much annoyance and trouble owing to the plates warping, etc. Also for springs to do away with hardening in the same way. Please also do not overlook the matter of casting safes as this will be very valuable, indeed we have just made a sample safe for Chubb's the great safe builder here & they wrote us a few days ago saying the only drawback was that owing to its extreme hardness the difficulty was to work it up into form.

We have had several picks cast lately & the person who has tried them reports to us they stand very well indeed & possess the great advantage that when requiring re-sharpening & re-hardening the workmen in charge cannot possibly spoil the material by cracking it in the hardening, as of course this material when put into water is not in any way hardened.

[And] we believe this material is specially adapted for all classes of agricultural work such as reaping machine fingers, shares, skifes, etc., etc., which could be much stronger than chilled iron & yet very hard.[14]

Further experimentation led to the disappointment of some of these hopes for the curious new alloy. Manganese steel did prove to be ideal for safes; not only was it undrillable and hence more burglar-proof than conventional steel, but cast safes saved labour by making obsolescent the older process of welding together plates. On the other hand, manganese steel proved unsuitable for edge tools, since by the time the material became work-hard it had lost its edge. Other novel ideas also fell by the wayside. Horseshoes made of the product glazed over so that the animals were unable to stand; whilst manganese steel pokers, which were intended to exploit the material's extraordinarily low conductivity, were made fragile by the heat. During the early trials with his new steel Hadfield devoted most of his energies to constructing tram or railway wheels and by late 1883 he had patented one with an inside boss of soft steel, so that it could be easily bored, and with the arms made from tough, rolled steel. When tested in actual use, however, the manganese alloy was satisfactory for the wheel treads, but was unsuited to absorb the attritional wear on the flange, where there was no shock.

While Hadfield pondered these problems, the novelty and high cost of manganese steel did not prove popular with engineers. Complained Hadfield to his American agent in 1884: 'The material is being tried for a considerable variety of purposes but people are so slow on this side & inventors here have so many prejudices'.[15] Not until 1892 was the real breakthrough made when Hadfield and his assistants supervised the first melts of manganese steel in the US at the Taylor Works, New Jersey.[16] It was thus in America where the product was to win its first widespread acceptance and so US industry was the first to enjoy the full benefits of manganese steel; not only did the alloy establish a completely new branch of the steel industry, but it was to have an enormous impact on efficiency and productivity in a variety of manufacturing and extractive activities. Though Hadfield and the Taylor Co found the product of little use for car wheels, it was quickly realised that it had great potential for tram and railway trackwork. On 28 August 1894 the Taylor Co, allied with William Wharton Jnr & Co, of Philadelphia, cast the first manganese steel frog, which was installed in Brooklyn, New York, at Fulton Street and Boerum Place. Its astounding performance under traffic averaging one car every 27 seconds throughout the day prefigured an application that was to be world-wide. Manganese steel also proved pre-eminently suitable for the jaws of stone- and ore-crushing machinery, dredger-pins, mining wheels, and paper-pulp-beaters. To market and produce such products, the Sheffield firm of Edgar Allen's acquired a plant at Chicago Heights, Illinois, in 1910.

By that date, substantial orders had at last begun to arrive at Hadfields. In 1897 Hadfields pointed out 'that less than four years ago its application was confined to about half a dozen purposes, [though now] its various applications have reached nearly 40 classes of articles, each bringing in a steady stream of orders'.[17] Early trackwork trials had been made in Sheffield in 1901, which began a short four-year period of intense competition with the traditional crucible product. Manganese steel's superior toughness, though, meant that its success was assured. As an example of its remarkable wearing properties in such situations Hadfield could point to the experience of the Sheffield Corporation Tramways in Fitzalan Square; one manganese steel layout installed in 1907 lasted for twelve years, forty-eight times the life of a carbon steel layout. On European railways the decisive event occurred in 1907 when Schneider, the French steelmakers, rolled manganese steel under Hadfield's licence for the new Paris Metropolitan Electric Railway. A year or so later the Metropolitan Line, London, followed the lead when similar track was installed between Farringdon and Aldgate.[18] By then Hadfields was enjoying a brisk business with British local transport authorities, as the alloy became the standard material for heavy duty rails.

While he was researching manganese steel, Hadfield was also experimenting with a silicon alloy. According to his own account the work had stemmed from his desire to produce a steel suitable for a cast grinding wheel in place of the old emery wheel by melting together steel scrap and silicon spiegel.[19] The experiments continued during 1883, and it was finally in 1884 when Hadfield discovered an iron-silicon alloy, low in carbon and containing from about 1.5–5 percent of silicon; and in 1885 silicon steel with higher carbon. Patented in 1884 and 1886, the low-carbon silicon-iron alloy, known afterwards simply as 'Silicon Steel', was the subject of numerous chemical and mechanical tests which were finally embodied in a paper read by Hadfield before the Iron and Steel Institute in 1889.[20]

Hadfield's results ran counter to accepted theory which generally regarded silicon as a harmful addition to steel. It was found, after many years of costly research, in which Hadfield was aided by (Sir) William Barrett and Mr W. Brown, that the steel possessed remarkable electrical and magnetic properties, which rendered it particularly suitable for use in the manufacture of electrical transformers. The results of the investigations were embodied in joint papers by Barrett, Brown and Hadfield, read before the Royal Dublin Society in 1900, and before the Institution of Electrical Engineers in 1902.[21]

Again, as with manganese steel, it was some time before there was any practical application of the new alloy, a delay which was not so apparent in the US. Hadfields, being mainly steel founders, had not the necessary mills and forges to finish the steel, and could only supply it in ingots. The finishing of these into sheets, therefore, had to be entrusted to Joseph Sankey & Sons, of Bilston, Staffordshire, which finally undertook the complete manufacture of the material, using the brand-name 'Stalloy'. At a later stage, Messrs. Lysaght also undertook its manufacture. Consumers, though, still complained about the high cost, especially in the early stages of production when there was much wastage. These were amongst the reasons why, despite its invention in 1883–4, silicon steel was not produced in commercial quantities until about 1906.

In America, though, with its rapid development of electric power, Hadfield's silicon steel was swiftly taken up under licence. The use of the alloy removed a stumbling block in the design of alternating current transformers. These transformers, distributing electricity to local neighbourhoods, had been found to develop disconcertingly high electrical losses, which prevented the construction of large-scale devices. Hysteresis and eddy current losses in the transformers meant that in 1896 the distribution system in Sheffield lost 30 percent of the power generated. In contrast, the efficiency of modern transformers, made from alloys based on Hadfield's work, is over 99 percent.[22] The first transformers using silicon steel had been constructed in Sheffield by 1903 with Hadfield's help.[23] In June 1903 Walter S. Moody, the chief transformer engineer of the General Electric Co in America, wrote to Hadfield expressing an interest in these developments, having heard about them from a subsidiary, the British Thomson Houston Co. Hadfield supplied the relevant information and his patent allowed Moody to experiment successfully in rolling the steel in large tonnages, so revolutionising transformer design and dramatically reducing running costs.[24] The American Sheet and Tin Plate Co, one of the associated companies of the United States Steel Corporation, and the Westinghouse Co, also became licencees;[25] and by 1908 Hadfield estimated that a quarter of a million silicon steel transformers had been constructed in America.

Hadfield's endeavours did not occur in isolation. In the late 1880s, F. Hall of Jessop's researched the effects of nickel in steel almost simultaneously with James Riley of the Steel Co of Scotland. The resulting nickel steel alloys rapidly established their value, particularly for armour plate.[26] From the 1890s Professor John Oliver Arnold (1858–1930) at Sheffield University led the search for new alloys with his development of phospho-magnetic steels, his Admiralty work on fractures, and his investigations on stress testing.[27] In 1899 Augustus F. Wiener, an Austrian, brought the element vanadium to his notice and Arnold soon showed that it greatly improved the tensile strength of steel.[28] Arnold's secret researches were subsequently leaked, forcing Wiener to copyright the results in the *Engineer* in 1904.[29] By then the remarkable tensile properties of chrome-vanadium steel had been extensively investigated by J. Kent Smith at Willans & Robinson's Ferry Works, Flintshire, with Arnold himself carrying out the alternating-stress tests. The publicised results were noticed by executives of the Ford Motor Co who, believing, as Arnold had suggested, that the lightness and strength of chrome-vanadium steel would be ideal for automobile parts, later hired J. Kent Smith to produce the alloy commercially.[30] In Sheffield Vickers likewise began manufacturing vanadium steel for the motor industry at this time. Arnold in the 1900s and after also investigated molybdenum as an alloying element,[31] alongside his other work on nickel, chromium, tungsten, tantalum, and uranium additions to steel. These pioneering researches provided alloys for the advancing machine-tool and engineering industries and his published results embodied a path-breaking survey of the constitution of complex steels.

At Sheffield University Arnold presided over one of the most advanced – perhaps the most advanced – steel research facilities in the world.[32] Arnold provided a direct link with the scientific tradition founded by Henry Clifton Sorby (indeed the two men had been close friends!) by bringing a greater awareness to firms of the benefits of applying accurate methods to the testing and measurement of steel. Arnold's services were available to dozens of the city's steel firms by means of the Sheffield Steelmakers Ltd and the Sheffield High Speed Steel Association – more or less secret organisations which retained Arnold as consultant for an extremely modest fee.[33] Besides providing this important bargain-price facility for metallurgical trouble-shooting, Arnold's formidable and fiery personality proved a great asset in law suits, notably in the patent wrangles over high-speed steel, where he could always be found vigorously upholding Sheffield's reputation as the world's premier steelmaking centre.[34] More importantly, Arnold exerted a powerful influence as a teacher, not only providing trained metallurgists for the city's industry, but also bringing together manufacturers, scientists, and students by means of the Metallurgical Society which he founded in 1890.[35] By the 1900s many of his past students had begun careers in Sheffield steelworks, where they helped establish research laboratories. By 1915 Arnold was able to inform Hadfield that 'researches are always proceeding in the Sheffield works ... [and] most of the big Sheffield works have their own research laboratory'.[36] Most famous of all was the Brown–Firth Research Laboratory, founded in 1908.[37] These institutions provided a seedbed for the development of pyrometry, metallography, and dynamic mechanical testing, and epitomised an increasingly science- and research-based approach that was to place Sheffield in the forefront of alloy steel technology by the 1900s[38] – a pre-eminence that was also reflected in the development of high-speed steel.

5

THE EVOLUTION OF HIGH-SPEED STEEL

It seems curious that after Messrs. Taylor and White, in 1900, indicated the lines on which a decided advance in tool-steel manufacture could proceed, it was left to English steelmakers to place regular commercial brands of high-speed steel on the market ... [which] give results so approximately uniformly excellent that to attempt to minutely tabulate their merits and decide which is the 'best' is almost a waste of energy.

J. Vose, 'Notes on High-Speed Steel',
American Machinist 27, Pt. 1 (5 May 1904), p. 586.

Tool steel is the oldest kind of steel, yet its manufacture as a speciality dates back little more than a century. Until then, the usual machining process entailed softening or annealing the metal to be cut, and hardening the tool which was to do the cutting. Before the discovery of self-hardening steel the invariable custom was to plunge the ends of the crucible high-carbon steel cutting tool into water, a procedure which often resulted in cracking.

This problem was solved not in Sheffield, but in the Forest of Dean in Gloucestershire, where, in 1868, Robert F. Mushet (1811–91), the son of the famous Scottish ironmaster, David Mushet, found that the addition of finely powdered wolfram ore (tungsten) produced a steel which did not require anything but cooling in the open air to give it a cutting edge hard enough for lathe and other similar tools.[1] To some extent, Mushet's work had been anticipated by the Austrian chemist, Franz Köller, but it was largely due to Mushet that the self-hardening steel was produced commercially. 'R. Mushet's Special Steel' ('RMS'), as it came to be known, the forerunner of modern high-speed steels, contained about 7 percent tungsten (hence the term 'tungsten steel'), and made possible a 50 percent faster cutting speed.

Mushet decided against taking out a patent, perhaps wary after the

66

experiences of Cort and Heath, and kept the recipe and complicated preparatory processes secret. Instead, a vigorous sales campaign was launched and the Titanic Steel & Iron Co Ltd of Coleford, Gloucestershire, was established to supply the demand. There was immediate interest from the trade press,[2] but the Titanic soon ran into difficulties, largely, it has been suggested by the Mushet's historian, because the company was under-subscribed and disagreements occurred amongst the directors.[3] Fortunately for Mushet, production was immediately taken up by Samuel Osborn (1826–91) of the Clyde Steel & Iron Works, Sheffield, who, after a modest beginning in 1852, had expanded his business in 1868 with the acquisition of Shortridge, Howell & Co Ltd, in the Wicker, Sheffield. This works consisted of converting furnaces, crucible melting holes, steam hammers, rolling mills for both sheets and bars, so ideally equipping Osborn to produce Mushet steel.[4]

The arrangement was simple: Samuel Osborn acquired the sole right to manufacture 'R. Mushet's Special Steel', with Mushet to receive a royalty on every ton sold. The whole manufacturing process, though, was shrouded in secrecy. The mixtures for the steel were compounded at Mushet's Works deep in the Forest of Dean and the treatment and further preparation of the ores were also done outside Sheffield. Elaborate methods were devised to conceal the destination of the mixture after its departure from the Forest of Dean, workmen were sworn to secrecy, and not even all the partners knew the secrets of manufacture. Robert Mushet himself never visited Sheffield.[5]

The fame of Mushet's special self-hardening tool steel spread quickly under Samuel Osborn's enthusiastic salesmanship. As early as 1872 excellent reports were received from America,[6] where it was advertised in the *Iron Age* as turning out 'at least double work', with the ability to cut 'harder metals than any other steel'. Osborn soon found, though, as did other Sheffield makers, that the American market had its dangers, and financial fluctuations there were amongst the factors which pushed the company to the edge of liquidation in 1874.[7]

It proved to be a temporary setback. Renewed credit and orders from across the Atlantic soon ensured that the Americans became the most important of Osborn's customers after the mid-1870s. 'Samuel Osborn & Co, is coming out as a very strong firm', its director was able to write to a New York agent in 1875, adding for good measure: 'Begin to use English steel at once if you intend to stand high with your heads'.[8]

Osborn was in touch with America by 1872.[9] On 10 November 1875, he personally visited the country, touring Canada, Chicago, St Louis, and New York, and meeting Sheffield steelmakers such as Charles Halcomb of Sanderson Bros.[10] Upon his return to Sheffield in December, Osborn found that 'all had gone well at the works ... [and] some very nice orders have come up [from Canada and the US]. This includes lots of Mushet's Special Steel'.[11] Continuing orders from America ensured a return visit in 1876, which gave Osborn the opportunity to view the Centennial Exhibition in Philadelphia.[12] Shortly afterwards, B. M. Jones & Co, in Boston, became Osborn's main American agent, beginning a long and rewarding association for both parties.[13] After another American business trip in April–June 1883, a delighted Osborn wrote to Jones: 'The demand goes on growing and we are making [Mushet steel] more uniform and better than ever we did.'[14] Business remained good in 1888, the date of the Sheffielder's final excursion to the US, when he informed one of his American friends: 'We are very full of work in all departments and B. M. Jones & Co send us some good orders.'[15]

Osborn's salesmanship and the efforts of the Boston agency soon made Mushet's steel and Samuel Osborn & Co virtually synonymous. Towards the close of the century, it was slowly discovered that the substitution of chromium and manganese improved the performance of tool steel; during the 1890s low-manganese tungsten-chromium steels were being produced.[16] One of Osborn's associates, Henry Gladwyn, showed that even better results were obtainable if the cutting portion of the steel tool was re-heated after forging and cooled in an air-blast: air-hardening thus became the slogan instead of self-hardening.

Despite the aura of secrecy, Mushet tool steels were copied and rival Sheffield firms such as Edgar Allen were advertising their own versions of self-hardening steel by the early 1880s. Sanderson Bros, too, both in Sheffield and America was marketing highly advanced tool steels by the 1890s. Competition thus became very keen, but as Frederick W. Taylor (1856–1915), the famous American industrial efficiency expert, observed: 'It is a remarkable fact that the successors to Mushet in the tool steel business, even up to the time of the Taylor–White invention, probably retained one-half of the business in self-hardening tool steel throughout the world. This is an unusual record for any one firm in the manufacture of any standard article.'[17]

Taylor himself began research on the properties of these steels towards the end of the century at the Midvale Steel Co in Philadelphia. In the machining of the tyres, axles and shafts, in which Midvale specialised, Mushet tool steel was in regular use. In 1880, Taylor was appointed foreman of the machine shop and quickly embarked, with the sympathetic encouragement of the company president, William Sellers, and the help of five technical assistants from the Stevens Institute of Technology, upon a study to determine which tool steels were best suited to special kinds of work.[18]

Taylor soon established that Mushet tools could be driven at a much higher speed, aided, in contradiction of Mushet, who said that tools must be run dry, by liberal quantities of suds. Not only that, but the idea of re-serving Mushet tools only for special use was found to be a fallacy, since they showed their greatest gain in cutting time on soft metals – a 90 per-cent improvement on soft cast iron, compared with 45 percent on hard steel or chilled cast iron. In 1883, it was also discovered that the machines in use at Midvale and elsewhere had quite inadequate feed power.

Perhaps Taylor's greatest contribution stemmed from his assiduity in tracing all the various factors involved in cutting metals. Similar experi-ments were carried out at the same time by the Manchester Association of Engineers, the Manchester School of Technology, and Armstrong-Whitworth Ltd, but they were not as wide-ranging or systematic as Taylor's.[19] In his detailed analysis of Mushet steel Taylor found 2.2 per-cent carbon, 1.8 percent manganese, 0.3 percent chromium, and 7 percent tungsten, and succeeded in proving, with the help of the metallurgist Maunsel White (1856–1912) at the Bethlehem Steel Works, that it was the manganese content which gave the steel its self-hardening character-istic. Further examination showed that, as regards the self-hardening property, chromium was an effective substitute for manganese and also gave better performance. Both the chromium, up to 3 percent, and the tungsten content, to as high as 12 percent, were increased, and silicon added to improve shock resistance. When these experimental tools were heated to different temperatures quite astonishing results were achieved.

Taylor and White discovered that self-hardening steels of the tungsten–chromium type developed their best cutting properties when quenched just below their melting point, a treatment which many authorities be-lieved would irrevocably ruin any tool steel. Astoundingly, however, such tools removed metal even when their cutting edge was heated to a visible red. At the Paris Exhibition in 1900, the new tool steel was placed in an American lathe, and its performance at 'red hardness' caused a sen-sation.[20]

Later, Taylor summarised his endeavours, which had lasted over twenty-six years, and cost an estimated $200,000, in his classic address, 'On the Art of Cutting Metals', to the American Society of Mechanical Engineers in New York in 1906.

Contemporaries recognised the profound implications that Taylor-White treated steel, which could perform two to four times as much work as other tools, had for the development of machine-tool technology.

Wrote one authority: 'it is plainly apparent that we are on the eve of a complete revolution in shop practice which will necessitate the use of more powerful machinery and a complete change in the time-honoured method'.[21] Yet, in metallurgical terms, the Taylor–White process did not represent such a sharp break with the past. The Americans invented a heat treatment, not a new alloy, Taylor himself pointing out that 'tool steel of excellent quality for making high-speed tools existed and was in common use several years before our discovery was made'.[22] The change from air-hardening to high-speed steels was rather a matter of evolution than a distinct invention.

As early as 1819, Faraday had made experiments with alloy steels at the Royal Institution and with Sheffield assistance succeeded in producing chrome steel, though not on any commercial scale.[23] Julius Baur of New York was granted an American patent on chromium steel in 1865, but it never seems to have been applied in the field of tool steels. Henri Brustlein of the French Holtzer works began to experiment in the addition of chromium to steels in 1876 and published a number of his results in 1886 in a paper before the Iron and Steel Institute.[24] Sir Robert A. Hadfield summarised much of the work on chromium steels in another paper before that body in 1892.[25] Dr John W. Langley informed the American Society of Civil Engineers in the same year that self-hardening steel required not only tungsten, but also high additions of chromium and manganese.[26] By the 1890s the high manganese of the self-hardening steels, including the original Mushet, was replaced by some manufacturers with chromium. One of the pioneering firms appears to have been the Holtzer Steel Works and resulted from Brustlein's investigations. In 1894 steels of the true chromium–tungsten type were being manufactured by both the Midvale Steel Co, which acquired technology from France, and Sanderson Bros, a Sheffield subsidiary at Syracuse, New York, which appears to have arrived at its results independently.[27] At Syracuse, Dr Edmund L. French was instrumental in introducing both chromium–tungsten and, later, chromium–molybdenum steels.[28]

Why, then, was Mushet steel not driven at red heat? Here it seems is a clear instance of tool steel technology out-pacing machine-shop practice on both sides of the Atlantic. As Fred M. Osborn wrote, when discussing the Taylor–White process: 'it had been practiced long before, among smiths, but it was not appreciated by those in greater authority in engineering works'.[29] According to Taylor, Mushet steel was for many years looked upon as a curiosity. Once its suitability for cutting very hard forgings was recognised it was usual to have one or two prized bars of Mushet steel available in machine-shops for use on particularly difficult work.[30]

But almost no effort was made, either in Europe or America, to build machines with higher driving speeds, which could maximise the cutting potential of Mushet or other self-hardening tools.

That the development of high-speed steel was, to a certain extent, evolutionary rather than revolutionary goes some way towards explaining the following paradox: Sheffield and not America reaped the commercial benefits of the process in its early days.

Sheffield was ideally placed to take full advantage of the Taylor–White treatment and as Professor J. O. Arnold remarked: 'The steel makers of Sheffield were not slow to take this hint'.[31] Among their advantages were: when Taylor recommended high-speed steels in the lower carbon range, they may have been made in England for at least from three to five years previously; the Sheffield crucible process, with its exacting standards and high uniformity, was especially suited to the production of the new and increasingly exotic mixes; Sheffield, with its wide range of European and American contacts and advanced research laboratories, was able to absorb rapidly the latest findings; the patent specifications of Taylor and White were fairly limited.

The latter consideration became important in 1907 when the Bethlehem Steel Co sued the Niles-Bement-Pond Co, of Philadelphia, in a test case involving the Taylor–White patent. Bethlehem, hoping to put an end to the widespread infringement of the new process, soon found itself involved in a two-year struggle involving both British and American manufacturers. At the trial, managers and smiths from Firth Sterling, a Sheffield subsidiary in Pittsburgh, and the Crescent Steel Co testified that 'they had as a matter of everyday business used with regard to Mushet, Titusville and Sanderson Steel, heats which were those of the Patentees long before the Patentees disclosed their so-called invention'.[32] Bethlehem found a useful ally in Charles H. Halcomb, the Sheffield-born former manager of Sanderson Bros, Syracuse, who argued that Taylor and White were 'responsible entirely for High-Speed Steels'.[33] But other Sheffield makers were less helpful. Faced with a significant threat to their livelihood, Sheffield manufacturers quickly marshalled their resources and evidence to form an association to oppose the patentees. When representatives from Bethlehem travelled to Sheffield to collect evidence, they were dismayed to find that 'the combination is a stronger and tighter one than we imagine, and if a man testified for us as to Sheffield matters he would have to get out of Sheffield hereafter'.[34] Henry Mushet, Fred M. Osborn and Professor Arnold attended the hearings to give evidence on behalf of the defendants, basing English claims on prior knowledge and use, expert construing of publications, the supply of heat-treated tool steel to the US before 1900, and tool steel labels and directions.[35] These efforts met with success when the decision was given against Bethlehem in 1909, allowing both English and American makers unrestricted access to the fruits of Taylor and White's work.[36]

Diffusion and application of the Taylor–White process were, therefore, very rapid. Even before the Paris Exhibition news of Taylor and White's success had spread beyond the Bethlehem workshops.[37] Arthur Balfour, of Seebohm and Dieckstahl Ltd, learned of the process in Chicago and rapidly discovered both composition and treatment. With the benefit of the firm's experiments along similar lines, it was but a short step to producing and marketing the new steel in 1901 under the brand-name 'Capital'. According to Balfour it did not take 'long to discover that by varying the mixture and keeping the carbon out from the beginning [instead of burning it out] they could produce a steel which by ordinary treatment would give a better and far regular result than the Taylor–White method'.[38] Thomas Andrews & Co introduced its 'Wortley' special self-hardening tool steel which performed close to red heat and was designed to 'meet the demand for a material that will stand the very high speeds and heavy cuts now employed in modern machine work'.[39] Jonas & Colver Ltd, entered the market with its 'Novo' steel in 1902, and by 1909 the firm's output was said to be larger than any other concern.[40] Firth's had also observed the latest advances at the Chicago and Paris Exhibitions and manufacture was begun almost immediately in August 1900. Production of Firth's 'Speedicut' steel was at first small – only 100 tons in 1902 – but by 1916 the figure was nearer 1,000 tons a year.[41]

Samuel Osborn & Co, not surprisingly, quickly up-dated its old Mushet steel. One of the firm's directors, Arnold Pye-Smith, had watched events at the Paris Exhibition and reported: 'My opinion is that if [Taylor–White steel] enters seriously into competition with RMS it will not replace it in very many cases & it seems also that probably RMS may be made suitable for the treatment'.[42] Osborn's was therefore soon analysing various Sheffield and American steels.[43] By 1905 the firm had laid down a completely new plant for the production of high-speed twist drills and milling cutters, which was said to embody the latest and best features of American and Continental practice.[44]

In 1903, when Manchester engineers organised their trials on the new high-speed steels, John Brown's, Charles Cammell's and Vickers, were ready to participate with their own versions of the metal.[45] When the Iron and Steel Institute visited Sheffield in 1905, nearly all the carbon tool steelmakers, including Jessop's, Saville's and Beardshaw's, were involved in production and numerous public demonstrations of the cutting properties of high-speed steel were staged.[46] At this date, Sheffield makers were producing a full range of high-speed steels, even providing lower performance tools (in Jessop's case, ordinary 'High-Speed' as well as 'Extra High-Speed') for engineering firms which did not have lathes powerful enough to cope with the latest steels.

In Professor Arnold's words:

> The net result of these collective Sheffield experiments between, say, 1900 and 1910, was to produce a turning alloy with a thermal stability up to 650 deg. C, a distinct red heat, or in other words, an advance of 400 deg. C over the plain carbon steel of 1740. The result, of course, is that cuts, traverses, and speeds which even in 1890 would have been dismissed as a madman's dream are now calmly accepted as facts. To put this advance in another way, the 1740 turning tool would before breaking down remove 15 cubic inches of material, whilst ... a second quality modern high-speed steel will remove, say, 215 cubic inches.[47]

In the first decade of the twentieth century the export of high-speed steel to America became a regular feature of the Sheffield trade.[48] A perusal of the leading US journal, the *American Machinist*, shows that the Sheffielders quickly made an impression on the US market.[49] So great was the saturation of English high-speed steels that one American correspondent complained: 'When it comes down to actual performance ... it will be found that a number of American high-speed steels on the market will do fully as much work as these much flaunted English tool steels'.[50] Nevertheless, it was generally admitted that the Sheffield varieties had lived up to their advertised claims.[51] By 1906 an English engineer noted that high-speed steel had made considerable headway in American machine-shops and that the special steels all came from England.[52]

There was still plenty of room for debate, since high-speed steel was far from being a standardised item. Before long 'new', 'improved', and 'superior' brands of high-speed steel were being marketed with expensive ingredients such as vanadium, cobalt and molybdenum.[53] Here the literature becomes very murky. Vanadium found its way into the composition of tool steel by 1906, and it seems that Sheffield led the way with research carried out at Sheffield University at the turn of the century.[54] John Brown's and Osborn's can be identified as pioneer users.[55] Dr John A. Mathews, a metallurgist at the Halcomb Steel Co, Syracuse, was awarded a patent for vanadium in high-speed steel in 1905, though he credited English steelmakers as being first in the field.[56] Paul R. Kuehnrich, a German-born Sheffield metallurgist at Darwins Ltd, was amongst the first to explore the possibilities of cobalt as an alloying element in tool steel.[57] But, henceforth, English and American developments ran so closely together that it is frequently impossible to separate them. Before the First

World War, the so-called '18–4–1' steel (18 percent tungsten, 4 percent chromium, and 1 percent vanadium, with 0.7 to 0.8 percent carbon) was almost universally made. There was still intense rivalry between individual makers and Sheffield still preserved a corner of the American market, but, by the second decade of the twentieth century, the technological lead created by Mushet in his Forest of Dean hideaway had been closed.[58]

6

CONTRARY TO NATURE:
THE DISCOVERY OF STAINLESS STEEL

When I am asked if I discovered stainless steel I say 'Yes'.
Harry Brearley, *Stainless Steel.*
The Story of its Discovery (1924), p. 22.

It is difficult to imagine a world without stainless steel – a world in which, without the use of liberal quantities of paint, grease, and oil, even the most expensive steels inevitably stained and became corroded. Most textbooks on the history of metallurgy credit Harry Brearley, the Sheffield metallurgist, with the discovery of stainless steel in 1914. It is unusual, however, for a discovery not to have had its precursors and stainless steel is no exception. Its development led to some interesting exchanges in Anglo-American technology.

In 1948, an American metallurgist, Carl A. Zapffe, surveyed the available evidence and, after dividing the contribution of discoverers of stainless steel into constitution of alloys, corrosion resistance and industrial usefulness, he credited six pioneers with priority in each classification.[1]

Investigator	Discovery
L. Guillet	Compositions and primary metallurgical
A. M. Portevin	characteristics of the stainless steels – mart-
W. Giesen	ensitic, ferritic, and austenitic.
P. Monnartz	Stainlessness and the passivation phenomenon (also commercial utility of the chromium grades).
H. Brearley	Commercial utility of the chromium grades.
E. Maurer	Commercial utility of the chromium-nickel grades.

As with high-speed steels, the development of stainless steel was evolutionary rather than revolutionary. Chromium, ever since its discovery by Louis-Nicholas Vauquelin in 1797, was a common constituent in steels. Robert A. Hadfield's paper on 'Alloys of Iron and Chromium', presented to the Iron and Steel Institute in 1892, contained what he claimed to be the first correlated study of chromium steel.[2] Unfortunately, the high levels of carbon in the ferro-chromium available at that time and the unfortunate choice of sulphuric acid as a test reagent meant that Hadfield's high-chromium steels actually corroded faster than the low-chromium ones; thus the potential of chromium alloys was not recognised. Despite Hadfield's findings, however, the analysis of steels containing chromium was resumed towards the end of the century by Guillet and Portevin in France, Monnartz in Germany, and Giesen in England.

Chrome steel had found its way into commercial use in the 1860s at Julius Baur's Chrome Steel Works in Brooklyn, New York.[3] Nickel steels and the chromium-nickel steels, which contained a few percent of the alloy, had been well known in the late nineteenth century to naval ordnance manufacturers, and before the First World War the information was gradually extending to the emerging automobile industry. In America, there is evidence that C. Dantsizen, a metallurgist at the General Electric Research Laboratory in New York, had experimented with low-carbon chromium alloys in the rustless range for use in turbine blades before 1914. Similarly, Eduard Maurer and Benno Strauss, at the Krupp Works, had produced chromium–nickel steels with a view to their commercial application.[4]

As Zapffe observed, what was surprising was not that the breakthrough in research on stainless steel occurred in the twentieth century but that it had not happened sooner. In 1914, a Sheffielder, Harry Brearley, entered the picture to explore the commercial possibilities of stainless steel and to lay claim to its discovery.

Harry Brearley (1871–1948) was, at the time of his discovery, a metallurgist at Thomas Firth & Sons.[5] He had begun work for the company about 1882 as a cellar-lad ('nipper') in the crucible furnace, where his father had been a melter for about forty years. In 1901, having acquired skill as an analyst, he left Firth's to establish a chemical laboratory at Kayser Ellison's. Two or three years later he returned to Firth's to take up a post at the firm's Russian Riga subsidiary as a chemist. Eventually, when his tenure at Riga ended, Brearley was invited by Firth's to assume responsibility for the Brown–Firth Research Laboratory. Alongside these activities he also had an interest in a private metallurgical consulting practice; by the inclusion of a special clause in the Firth contract he was able to continue this business which operated as the Amalgams Co.

In May 1912 Brearley visited the Royal Small Arms Factory at Enfield for a routine study of erosion and fouling in rifle barrels. In his report dated 4 June 1912, he remarked: 'it appears desirable to make observations with steel containing much higher percentages of chromium'. As Brearley pointed out later, this interest in a higher chromium content was entirely fortuitous, and stemmed simply from studying certain problems of ordnance rather than any intention of discovering stainless steel.[6] The first bulk cast of this chromium steel was made at Firth's in July 1913 and a second electric furnace cast, containing 0.25 percent carbon and 12.86 percent chromium, followed on 20 August 1913. Brearley was intrigued by the fact that pieces of experimental billet material, which had been left outside, had not rusted. When microscopic observations of these steels were made, one of the first things that Brearley noticed was that the usual re-agents for etching the polished surface of a micro-section had no effect. The chromium had made the steel stainless!

Brearley suggested that the steel might be useful for cutlery. By the end of 1914 steel had been dispatched to two firms, but had been rejected because of problems with forging, grinding, and hardening – almost certainly because the forging temperatures used were the traditional ones for carbon steel, whereas martensitic chromium steels require greater values. On 20 May 1914, for example, Joseph W. Ibberson, the head of an old-established cutlery firm, replied to Firth's:

From the Special Steel – Self Hardening Rustless – we have worked up several table blades which we send herein. The blade marked with a 'V' by glazing, has been exposed outside for ten days, and each day water has been poured over the blade, so that you will see your claim 'Rustless' has some merit. In our opinion this steel is unsuited for Cutlery steel: it is too hard to work and is almost impossible to grind, and the polished surface is dirty and bad colour.[7]

Much to Brearley's annoyance Firth's showed little interest in the new steel. It should be remembered that the rusting of iron and steel was accepted without question at this time. According to Brearley the cutler who made the first stainless knives said: 'Bloody likely, it would be contrary to nature'; whilst Firth's directors, though they agreed that 'there is no doubt as to [the steel's] rustlessness', believed that this was 'not so great a virtue in cutlery, which of necessity must be cleaned after each using'.[8] In the summer of 1914, however, Brearley met the manager of R. F. Mosley's, Mr Ernest Stuart, and another attempt was made to manufacture knives. After initial failures, due to the hardness of the steel, the production problems were eventually solved and success was achieved.

Through the Amalgams Co Brearley bought a hundredweight of the steel from Firth's and made it all into stainless steel knives. Brearley credited Mosley's with pioneering the use of stainless steel for cutlery, and, though he also paid tribute to the help of his brother and others, he gave himself the honour of stainless steel's discovery.

Brearley's enjoyment, however, was marred by a dispute with Firth's concerning the rights to the product and its marketing. The exact nature of the argument – which was to spill over into the local press – is difficult to discover. Only Brearley's account has come down to us, since Firth's made few public statements on the matter. Part of the trouble stemmed from Brearley's character. He once described himself as by nature 'a rebel',[9] and it seems clear that he liked the role of gadfly, a stance which he publicised with numerous self-promoting statements. Generally, the dispute was over the question as to whether an inventor, employed by a company, had any rights in the outcome of his endeavours. Brearley, believing that his interest gave him at least a half-share in decisions on the new product, became convinced that Firth's directors were intent on denying him 'any credit or voice in the matter'. So Brearley resigned.[10]

By 1915 he had accepted a post as works manager of Brown Bayley's Steel Works, where, with the help of an electric furnace, the manufacture of stainless steel was begun.[11] News of the remarkable new steel spread quickly in Sheffield's manufacturing community and favourable reports appeared in the local newspapers.[12] Between the beginning of 1915 and the summer of 1917 Firth's produced 1,000 tons of stainless steel, Brown Bayley's about 600 tons, and John Brown's, Sanderson Bros & Newbould, Howell's and Hadfields had started production. In February 1915 Firth's disclosed details to the manager of their Pittsburgh plant, L. Gerald Firth, and the first American ingot was cast on 3 March 1915 and immediately shipped to a knife factory.[13]

No attempt appears to have been made to apply for a British patent. But at this point Brearley was approached by a seventy-five-year-old stranger, Mr John Maddocks, who had been associated with the textile trade. He told Brearley that he knew America well and had had considerable experience with patents. The result of their meetings was an application on 29 March 1915, at the US Patent Office, for rights on the new chromium–iron alloy. This attempt failed. Not to be thwarted, Brearley enlisted the help of Sir Robert A. Hadfield, Dr J. E. Stead, and F. W. Harbord, who provided technical letters in support of Brearley's next application. The result was that American Patent No. 1,197,256 for 'Improvement in Cutlery' was ultimately granted for articles with 'stainless properties' in the chromium range of 9–16 percent, with carbon below 0.70 percent.

Brearley, with his hands full with developments at Brown Bayley's and the war effort, was not very involved with the US at this time and could not take up Maddock's suggestion that they visit America to dispose of the patent rights obtained in September 1916. Despite their earlier differences, Firth's became interested again and, no doubt with the intention of utilising their Pittsburgh Works, decided to buy a half-share in the patents. In 1917, therefore, the interested parties formed the Firth–Brearley Stainless Steel Syndicate to licence the manufacture of the product world-wide. Share capital was £30,000, split equally between the Brearley and Firth interests.[14] In Brearley's tart description, it was 'a business organisation; it made nothing and it sold nothing, but it issued licences relating to stainless steel with authority deriving from patents; it also interfered with trade, as far as its powers reached, and sometimes a bit beyond, for the benefit of its supporters'.[15]

To exploit the American patent, the Sheffielders immediately planned the formation of a sub-syndicate, the American Stainless Steel Co. Lewis J. Firth, the president of Firth Sterling in Pittsburgh, began recruiting likely candidates and G. Ethelbert Wolstenholme (1875–1940) of Firth's left for America in 1917 'to create enthusiasm in the manufacture and use of Stainless Steel' and to impart the necessary production information to the American Stainless Steel Co and the other privileged firms.[16]

In America, though, Brearley did not have the field entirely to himself. It was at this point that a gifted and dedicated American metallurgist, Elwood Haynes (1857–1925), put forward his own claims for the discovery of stainless steel. Though often credited as a joint-sharer in the technical development of stainless steel, Haynes has remained a rather shadowy figure. However, a recent study, based on the newly-opened Haynes Papers, at Kokomo, Indiana, has illuminated his contribution.[17]

In 1881, while writing a senior thesis, 'The Effect of Tungsten upon Iron and Steel', Haynes had experimented with tungsten–chromium steel, a forerunner of the Taylor–White tool steel alloy. Continuing his work, Haynes developed a high-speed alloy, 'Stellite', which contained high percentages of cobalt, molybdenum, and chromium. Eventually, he established a company for its manufacture.[18] As early as 1887 Haynes had begun experiments to find a non-rusting alloy suitable for cutlery manufacture. In an important series of trials in 1911 and 1912 he made various items from chromium–iron alloys, including cold chisels, wood chisels, and auger bits. He learned that, when properly heated and annealed, the tools showed good cutting qualities and held their lustre in the air under all conditions. Initially, Haynes had put his findings to one side while he devoted his energies to 'Stellite', but, learning of developments in England, he resumed his investigations and renewed his patent application.

Haynes' stainless steel application antedated by several days the one by Brearley on 29 March 1915. Both the Haynes and Brearley applications were initially rejected. Brearley's formidable list of references, however, and the fact that he stressed the need for hardening and tempering to max-imise the steel's rustless properties, appeared to do the trick and in June his request was accepted, whilst the Patent Office continued to reject Haynes's claim. The American's response was to appeal and apply for an interference order. He did not deny that Brearley had 'discovered practi-cally the same properties in chrome-steel', and added: 'I am practically certain that his discovery was made independently of any discoveries made by me'.[19]

Though Brearley argued that Haynes' broader range of composition (from 4–60 percent chromium) included materials that could not be hardened by the usual processes into commercial blades, the American had a strong case and on 31 July 1917 an interference order was granted. Ethelbert Wolstenholme met Haynes on 18 February 1918, and cabled to Sheffield: 'Regret that under American law conditions Brearley patent is greatly diminished in value by claims secured by Haynes. Haynes there-fore insists sharing equally with you stock allotted.'[20] Rather than risk the expense and delay of litigation, an amicable solution was soon found in the merging of the Haynes–Brearley interests into the American Stainless Steel Co, which was registered in Pittsburgh in 1918 with a share capital of $150,000. Of the issued capital, the Firth–Brearley Stainless Steel Syn-dicate held $50,000, Haynes $40,000, and American steel firms (Bethle-hem, Carpenter, Crucible, and Firth Sterling) $40,000.[21] On behalf of the English interests, Lewis Firth and James Kinnear (d. 1922) of Firth Ster-ling, took their seats on the seven-man board, to which Haynes could also nominate two members.

With matters in America settled and with war-time Government restric-tions on the use of stainless steel lifted (it had been commandeered for aero-engine valves), the Firth–Brearley Stainless Steel Syndicate set to work issuing licences and collecting royalties. This involved a good deal of ground-work; the patent had to be defended, firms manufacturing or exporting stainless steel without a licence had to be brought to book, and cutlery firms and the public needed fully alerting to stainless steel's useful-ness and reassuring that the new knives would cut satisfactorily and that they were non-poisonous. As far as it was able, the Syndicate also tried to maintain quality standards amongst the licencees. An organisation in which Harry Brearley and Firth directors rubbed shoulders was perhaps not entirely conducive to harmony and it was not long before they were at loggerheads.[22] Nevertheless, after a few difficult years in the early 1920s when no dividend was paid, the Syndicate, under the efficient secretary-ship of Edward Gadsby, produced a handsome return. The Syndicate minute books show total income of £197,241 in the period 1923-33, which enabled the payment of an average yearly dividend of 28 percent (in 1931 a dividend of 50 percent was paid!).

Though Brearley occasionally chafed at the arrangement, the Syndicate proved a success and Firth's did a good deal to advertise the product. Publicity booklets were issued and in 1928 Firth's acquired the firm of Padley & Price in Blackheath, Birmingham, to mass-produce stainless steel sheets.[23]

The Syndicate's arm also stretched across the Atlantic through Lewis and Gerald Firth in Pittsburgh, where it was able to play an important role in the American development of stainless steel. Regular visits by Firth's Sheffield directors emphasised to the Americans the usefulness of the new alloy. Frederick Best, a director in the Syndicate, wrote from New York in 1919:

I have been urging upon the Firth Sterling Steel Company and the Washington Steel & Ordnance Company, as well as the other privileged firms ... the advisability of taking up the manufacture enthusiastically and to do everything they possibly can to create a demand, and I believe they are just beginning to realise the possibilities of the enormous output for the many thousand purposes for which this material will undoubtedly be adopted.[24]

Sheffield's advanced technical help and scientific expertise in stainless steel manufacture were also made available to the Americans. In 1922, for example, it was decided that Best and Brearley should advise them to appoint a technical manager, who should spend some time in Sheffield 'in order to get thoroughly informed as to the extended uses for which Stainless Steel is being utilised on this side; how such uses can best be developed; and also to obtain any further information on the many points which arise in connection with the manufacture and treatment of Stainless Steel Articles'.[25] More importantly, Sheffield know-how stiffened the resolve of the American Stainless Steel Co, when it defended its patent rights against the Ludlum Co of New York in a famous test case in 1920. Brearley attended the trial in New York in 1921-2, where he gloried in his three-hour spell in the witness box. He reported to Sheffield: 'I am quite satisfied with our position ... Our barrister – [Charles] Neave – was a splendid chap. I am glad he didn't cross-examine me. The defendant's barrister was poor stuff and I enjoyed his cross-examination; getting a good deal more out of it than he did.'[26]

Brearley was over-confident, though, and to the great dismay of the

American Stainless Steel Co the case was initially awarded to Ludlum, causing the Sheffield Syndicate to galvanise itself into action. A 'strong letter' was dispatched from Sheffield with regard to the suggestion of one American board-member that it would mean dissolving the arrangement; an appeal was lodged; and Harry Brearley drew up a detailed report to assist the American company in contesting Judge Learned Hand's 'erroneous conclusions'.

The appeal was won in 1923 and the American Stainless Steel Co was able to enjoy the fruits of its endeavours. The wide chromium ranges embodied in the Haynes–Brearley patents were now a formidable barrier to infringement; coupled with Sheffield's steelmaking expertise and Haynes' own hard-line on royalty matters, they ensured highly profitable returns. The complete financial statements of the American company are not available in the files of the Sheffield Syndicate, but evidence elsewhere shows that the Americans paid a 24 percent dividend each year during the period 1925–9; and even in the 1930s there were high earnings, with a 36½ percent dividend in 1932 on profits of $300,000.[27]

After the First World War research on stainless steels proceeded rapidly in Sheffield. In June 1920 the firm with which Brearley had become associated – Brown Bayley's – pioneered the production of an important class of the low-carbon, high chromium–iron alloys, a variety later commonly known as stainless or rustless iron.[28] At the Brown–Firth Research Laboratories Dr William H. Hatfield (1882–1943), Brearley's successor, also made important progress in the field of austenitic chromium–nickel alloys.[29] After Strauss and Maurer had initiated the development of the modern high chromium–nickel steels in the Krupp laboratories from 1909 to 1912, about ten years later the Firth–Brearley Stainless Steel Syndicate acquired British rights on the German patents in exchange for Firth's martensitic expertise and under an agreement which prevented German and British makers exporting stainless steel to their respective countries. Thus under Hatfield's guidance began the production of the famous '18-8' (18 percent chromium, 8 percent nickel) variety, which was brilliantly produced and marketed by Firth's as 'Staybrite'. The 18–8 alloy, which in its use in articles that do not require a cutting edge has become the most widely used type of stainless steel, was described by an American as 'really a very wonderful alloy, and has given the utmost satisfaction when made into all manner of tools, utensils and equipment which must be kept scrupulously clean, which must not contaminate the materials handled, or which must resist severe corrodents'.[30] In 1923, Firth–Brown began, at the instigation of leading British chemical engineers, to produce large masses of such steel for chemical plant. American manufacture began shortly afterwards so that by 1928, when Hatfield visited the US, he found that '18/8 steel was being produced on a very extensive scale, and was regarded as an indigenous product'; he quickly pointed out, however, that the 'composition originated in this country in [my] laboratories: it is a British development which subsequently spread to other countries'.[31] Hatfield also emphasised the importance of Sheffield's role when Henry Ford in about 1930 began fitting his cars with 'rustless iron fittings' of 'Allegheny Metal', recalling that he had made Allegheny Steel Co personnel aware of the 18–8 composition when they visited Firth's in 1926 and when he had visited the Allegheny plant in 1928, at which time he had also visited Henry Ford in Detroit.[32]

The relatively high cost of the low-carbon ferro-chrome used in these developments spurred the search for methods of producing low-carbon, high-chromium steels from other materials. Again Sheffield played an important part, since the first effort along this line in the US was made in 1926 by two Sheffield brothers, Alwyn and Ronald Wild, who presided over the Rustless Iron Corporation in Baltimore. During the period 1926–31, they placed the direct production of stainless steel and iron ingots from chrome ore, using ferro-silicon as a reducing agent, on a practical working basis.[33]

Thus, whatever Elwood Haynes' rights concerning the initial discovery, in many key stainless steel developments America lagged some way behind Sheffield. 'We pride ourselves on being a progressive people', admitted Dr J. A. Mathews of the Crucible Steel Co of America, 'yet in the matter of adopting stainless steel for general use we are far behind our conservative British cousins. The use of stainless steel in Great Britain in its various applications has gone ahead very much more rapidly than it has in America.'[34] Brearley's research occurred in the perfect setting, in a city with the technical ability in working steel and with cutlers and steel manufacturers eager to try the new material. Moreover, Brearley's original composition (0.3 percent carbon, 0.3 percent manganese, 13 percent chromium) was not improved upon for ten years, and his statements that such steels should be made in the electric furnace, that they should be hardened and polished to give maximum results, and that they were particularly useful for cutlery, became the basis for the industry in its early years and the cornerstone of its later successes. By 1930 yearly US production of stainless steel was about 60,000 tons – probably about half the total world output (unfortunately the Sheffield figures are lacking) – and it was percolating into almost all facets of the manufacturing arts, providing inspiration for technologists, engineers, toolmakers, architects, and designers.[35]

Part three

SHEFFIELD STEELMAKERS AND TOOLMAKERS IN AMERICA

7

TRANSATLANTIC SPECIAL STEELS I:
THE CRUCIBLE STEELMAKERS

There are numerous reasons for the great advantage which the
United States holds over [England] in the manufacture of steel,
two of the greatest being that [American] manufacturers are
always on the alert for improving the methods and lessening
the cost of manufacture ... [and] I think the laboring men in
America are far more sober and industrious than in England.

A Sheffield director (Firth's) in Pittsburgh,
quoted in *American Manufacturer* 68 (2 May 1901), p. 571.

The rise of the American crucible steel industry had important reper-
cussions for Sheffield. More so, since the town's largest crucible steelmakers – Sanderson's, Firth's, and Jessop's – had all made substantial
additions to their melting capacity in the 1860s and early 1870s. These
firms, together with other large producers such as Vickers and J. H.
Andrew, although they represented only a very small percentage of the
total number of manufacturers, were probably responsible for about half
of Sheffield's crucible steel output.[1] Faced with the loss of a major market,
these makers, paradoxically, became even more closely involved with
America, as they responded by transferring some of their manufacturing
activities across the Atlantic.

Sanderson Bros had been founded by Thomas Sanderson and began
producing steel in the early nineteenth century, the enterprise first trading
under the name of Naylor & Sanderson. On the retirement of Naylor, the
firm of Sanderson Bros & Co was formed by the founder taking his
brothers, John and James, into partnership. After Thomas Sanderson's
death in 1836 the firm was led by these two men. When they died in the
1850s, the family connection was maintained by Henry Furniss and
Edward Hudson, nephews of Thomas Sanderson, and Edward Fisher Sanderson, the son of John Sanderson.[2]

Sanderson's quickly established itself as one of the leading Sheffield

steel firms. Edward Sanderson contributed to Dr John Percy's pathbreak-
ing book on metallurgy and the company supplied technical help to Faraday in his pioneering work on alloy steels.[3] The Sanderson Works
attracted numerous foreign visitors, including the famous Swiss steelmaker Johann C. Fischer, who, in the 1820s, observed that their steel 'was
a really first-class product and its uniformity leaves nothing to be desired'.
He added: 'They trade with North and South America'.[4]

Sanderson's was said to have been amongst the first firms to realise the
value and extent of the American market.[5] Edward F. Sanderson (1800–
66), who was to become the leading spirit at the company, resided principally in New York from the 1820s, eventually becoming a naturalised
American and only returning to Sheffield as the senior partner in later
life.[6] Largely due to his efforts, Sanderson's brands soon became 'well-
known to the machinists of the United States, as indicating the best qualities of cast steel sent from England'.[7] By 1832 the company's American
trade and reputation were sufficiently important for it to issue a warning
statement to its American customers 'with whom, for nearly 30 years, [it
had] had intercourse in business' when a rival Sheffield concern attempted
to pass itself off in the US as the successors to Naylor & Sanderson.[8]

In New York Edward F. Sanderson not only kept his eye on trade. In
1840 the owners of the Adirondack Iron & Steel Co, who were responsible for one of the most ambitious ante-bellum efforts to manufacture
steel from American ores, appear to have interested him in their venture.
Sanderson was particularly intrigued by American ore and wanted to give
it a true test using 'his patented method of smelting'. In April 1841 he
visited the Adirondack Works, ostensibly on a fishing trip. However, one
of the proprietors remarked:

[the] brother of the famous steel manufacturer of England, goes more to see,
examine and report to his brothers, on our mining and other property than to fish.
The Sandersons have read about our ores, and are wishing, I understand, to
undertake at our place in working the ore upon a new plan lately invented by one
of them by which the rich magnetic ores can be worked at a vastly less expense
than by the old processes.[9]

These plans did not proceed very far, though steps were taken to provide the necessary bricks for the furnace, and probably Sanderson's direct
process was not a success.[10] Nevertheless, the episode shows that Sheffield
was aware of American developments and that there was some interest in
investing capital.

More continuous are the records of Richard M. Hoe & Co, the New
York sawmakers and printing press manufacturers.[11] In 1828 Hoe had
decided to fabricate his own circular saws from cast steel, but he was hin-

dered by the lack of skilled grinders and the quality of domestic steel from Philadelphia. The problem was brought to the attention of Edward Sanderson, so beginning an important relationship for the New York company.

Sanderson's offered Hoe's the services of John Wheatman (ca. 1812–73), one of the firm's most accomplished sawmakers, who was to remain with Hoe for many years. Three sawmakers and one handlemaker, a large number of saw blanks, and quantities of finished saws and files, were also needed. Soon Sanderson's was sending regular shipments of saw steel to Hoe alongside large consignments of files and rasps.[12] 'The firm would for many years boast it was using the very finest English steel', writes Frank E. Comparato, 'obtaining it by frank complaints and unsolicited advice despite the humbling financial arrangements then in existence'.[13]

The following extracts give a flavour of the exchanges:

Hoe to Sanderson, 29 August 1843.
I am sorry to be compelled to say that the last lot of our cir[cular] saw steel was of a quality so poor, that it would destroy our sales entirely if continued ... If we attempt to heat it hot enough to harden sufficiently high it will fly and twist into all manner of shapes, rendering it impossible to hammer a plate straight.

Hoe to Sanderson, 18 October 1843.
You will please remember by your own workmen using care in rolling, to have the scales well beaten off & the plates rolled even in thickness ... We hope to wait on you with a large order, but are very sorry to see that you have charged 30/- for this lot, as we expected it at 28/- & we are making great calculations on the business.

Hoe to Sanderson, 13 November 1843.
The cheap Mill Saws sell rapidly and we wish you to be very careful to *sustain the quality* of the steel & make them a *trifle harder* ... I sincerely hope that you will be able to improve the quality of the mill saws to render them equal to those made by Jessops 12 cent steel. If you can do so at the low price we sell them we shall sell immense quantities [?] at least to call for steel to the value of 30,000 dollars per annum.[14]

These extracts should not give the impression that there was any strain in the relationship. Amongst all the grumbles and requests for faster deliveries in the letter of 18 October 1843, Hoe wrote to Sanderson: 'I am happy to feel assured that you will look after the quality of the steel made for us.' Even after the success of the American makers, Hoe remained, to some extent, committed to English steel and firmly opposed higher tariff rates.

This linkage facilitated exchanges of technology. The Sheffielders were asked to keep their eyes open for any improvements in printing press manufacture.[15] Richard Hoe was soon in Sheffield, in 1838, visiting the

Sanderson Works, demonstrating his recently invented saw-grinding machine to interested parties, and buying patent rights. The British and Scottish saw machinery patents taken out by Hoe had cost about $4,000 – advanced by Sanderson's. By 1857 Hoe's indebtedness to the Sheffield firm had reached $23,000, giving Sanderson's a considerable interest as Hoe's printing press agents in Europe.[16] Hoe also required, besides saw steel, best quality screws and nuts, printing press materials, grindstones and back saws.[17] In 1858, when a new saw supervisor was needed, Wheatman was asked once more for help; he replied by sending out from his own firm in Sheffield a sawmaker and his family and an order for steel.[18]

In the 1860s, however, Hoe's began buying steel from American crucible steelmakers in Pittsburgh, New York, and Philadelphia, and though the New Yorkers continued to order steel and files from Sanderson's in the 1870s, Sheffield was no longer the sole source of supply.[19] By that date Sanderson Bros had entered the American market more directly.

In 1869 Sanderson's was registered as a limited liability company with a capital of £150,000 and under the guidance of its newly appointed managing director, Charles Henry Halcomb, it was decided to begin manufacturing in the US. The decision not only reflected increasing American competition which had taken away customers such as Hoe, but also the effects of the tariff. In 1872 the company noted an 'uncomfortable restlessness at the American Customs House ... where the authorities persistently made efforts to raise the duty'.[20] Besides avoiding heavy duties, the main intention seems to have been to replicate Sheffield methods of crucible steel manufacture in America, though the firm was, perhaps, not unaware of New York State's other advantages. Two Sanderson directors, who visited the Adirondacks before the foundation of the American works, 'were amazed at what they saw. They found mountains of ironstone as fine as the Dannemora and Swedish brands [and] under the primeval forests [were] stored inexhaustible supplies of rich, black ore, and which extend[ed] over a district as large as all Yorkshire.'[21]

The venture involved the purchase of the Geddes Steel Works at Syracuse, New York, in 1876, from Sweet's Manufacturing Co. Sweet's had been established in 1871, with a capital of $250,000, by William A. Sweet (1830–1904), whose manufacturing activities dated from about 1858 when he became involved with his brothers in the production of cutter knives for mowers and reapers. In 1863 Sweet successfully began the manufacture of steel, under the style of the Onondaga Steel Works, using converting furnaces and gas-fired melting holes, apparently of his own design.[22]

Sweet's activities were well known in Sheffield. Jessop's had supplied steel for his reaper cutters.[23] The Marsh Bros' correspondence with its New York agents (1863–7) also documents a number of dealings with the American. After a protracted wrangle over a consignment of steel which, according to Sweet himself, was lacking in hardness, Theophilius Monk of Marsh Bros visited Syracuse. He was less than impressed. 'Mr Sweet may have got some fresh workmen, changed his process a little, or changed his test but the steel is exactly as before', he reported.[24] The Sheffield firm eventually came to the conclusion that Sweet's metallurgical tests were 'absurd'[25] and added, contemptuously: 'Sweet's employ entirely inexperienced workmen to grind and believe any laborer suitable for that branch.'[26] Sweet was also known to Samuel Osborn who, after their meeting in Sheffield in 1878, declared that they were of a 'kindred nature', though this feeling did not prevent Osborn from later refusing Sweet's request for details of the company's polishing machines.[27]

Sweet prospered, however, moving into the manufacture of steel goods, such as springs, tyres and crowbars. In 1872 Sweet's Manufacturing Co purchased the old distillery property in Geddes and converted it into a steel works. It was this concern which, in 1876, was sold to a stock company organised under the title of Sanderson Brothers Steel Co, with a capital of $450,000.[28] William A. Sweet became general manager until 1883 when he sold out to the English stockholders. A company circular described the arrangements and the firm's intentions:

Sanderson Bros Steel Co, Syracuse, NY
16 Cliff St, NY. August 24, 1876.
The new company has purchased from Sanderson Bros and Co, all their stocks of steel in America, their good-will, and the exclusive right to use their name, trade marks, patents, peculiar modes of preparing crucibles, mixtures for melting, methods of manipulating, and all confidential information of whatever kind employed in the Sheffield process of steel manufacture; and will continue to use the finest brands of Swedish Dannemora iron for the foundation of Sanderson Brothers' American best cast steel.

With the advantages of abundant capital, a competent manager, and skilled workmen practically trained at the works in Sheffield, together with the most approved machinery, the new company combines ample facilities for promptly furnishing the identical uniform qualities and tempers of steel hitherto supplied from Sheffield.[29]

Edward Frith, Treasurer.

Production was soon underway with the traditional Sheffield methods. The company made its own clay pots, possibly from imported clay, and used best-quality Swedish iron. The location on the line of the New York Central and Hudson River Railroad and on the Erie Canal favoured the handling of large quantities of raw materials, and gave access to the tool steel demand from New England, the Midwest, and Canada. Converting furnaces and coke-holes, capable of producing 2,500 tons a year, enabled the firm to pursue its policy of manufacturing only the highest grades of tool steel.[30]

The partnership was greeted with some enthusiasm in America, where it was viewed as a logical step towards reaching the English standard of uniform qualities and tempers. In Sheffield, however, the endowment of Americans with local expertise met with disapproval from the editors of the *Sheffield Independent* who regarded it as 'simply a queer way of getting out of a business, to be watched as a curiosity'.[31]

In 1881 the directors of the Sheffield firm reported that they 'were quite satisfied with the success of their scheme' and the Syracuse manager visited Sheffield to procure more workmen.[32] At this time the Syracuse works employed about 250 men, had an annual product approaching $800,000, and sold its steel through agencies in Boston, Chicago, and St Louis. Despite a disastrous fire in 1887, the firm believed it 'had acquired an exceedingly valuable position' in the US.[33]

Technically, the Syracuse company occupied an important position in the tool steel industry in the later nineteenth century. In the late 1890s, steels of the chromium–tungsten type were being manufactured, laying the groundwork for the Taylor–White process.[34] Edmund L. French, who became Sanderson's chemist in 1897 and was later a head of Crucible Steel of America, played an important part in this development. So, too, did Samuel S. Buckley, who had joined Sanderson's sales and development department in 1899 and was later to found the Onondaga Steel Co. Buckley not only pioneered molybdenum additions to tool steel, but also, in collaboration with E. L. French and W. B. Brookfield, placed on the market a number of years later the first high-speed steel produced in America.[35]

Commercially, though, the Syracuse operations may not have been as successful as the directors had hoped. The Sheffield methods were gradually abandoned: the coke-holes being replaced by gas furnaces in 1884, and the cementation furnaces discarded in 1898. Output rose only gradually from 3,000 tons in 1882, to 5,000 in 1892, and 7,000 in 1901.[36] Faced with crucible steel's declining share of the market, sluggish demand for such steel in this period (see Appendix), and a proposed merger of America's leading crucible steelmakers, the Sheffield firm relinquished its Syracuse branch to the Crucible Steel combine in 1900.[37]

Charles Herbert Halcomb, son of the Sheffield managing director, who had come to Syracuse in 1881 at the age of twenty-two, became the president of the Crucible Steel Co of America, ensuring that a Sheffielder became the first head of the world's largest crucible steel producer. Halcomb and metallurgists trained at Sanderson's continued to have an important influence on tool steel manufacture in the US. In 1905 Halcomb erected the Halcomb Steel Co in Syracuse with 400 workmen and a capital of $900,000 to make tool steel. Shortly afterwards, Dr John A. Mathews began his pioneering work on vanadium tool steel alloys at the company, which was also in the forefront of electric steelmaking. In 1911 the Halcomb Co became part of the Crucible Steel Co, once more linking it with the old Sanderson plant at Syracuse, which had continued with the old crucible process. Greatly expanded during the War, both plants were reported to be producing at full capacity in 1924.[38]

A partnership with an already established American enterprise was also the means adopted by Thomas Firth & Sons Ltd to penetrate the US market in the 1890s. The firm had been founded in 1842 by Thomas Firth and his two sons, Mark and Thomas, and specialised in the production of crucible steel, files and saws, and, later, gun forgings.[39] In the early days the Birmingham market was the most important, but Mark Firth (1819–80), who became the leading member of the firm, quickly built up 'an immense American connection',[40] which, despite the tariff, was looked after 'very vigorously' through the 1880s.[41]

In 1895, largely at the suggestion of their American agents, Abbott & Wheelock, Firth's seriously considered manufacturing in the US. The board initially rejected the idea, but the deteriorating trading situation forced it to think again. On 14 September 1896, the Firths convened an extraordinary general meeting at the Norfolk Works to debate once more such an unprecedented step.[42]

The board reviewed its increasingly unfavourable American prospects. Sanderson Bros of Syracuse had recently obtained the drill steel orders of one of Firth's most important customers and the company had 'no doubt that if the Morse Co – the leading manufacturers in the Drill trade – were to transfer their business to an American company, the other Drill makers would soon follow and it would have a very serious effect upon the Company's general Tool Steel business in the States'. Moreover, the duty on best cast steel sent to the US (which was likely to rise) was £12 per ton, whereas Swedish iron could be bought in America at Sheffield prices subject to only £2 8s duty per ton. Edward Firth, the chairman, however, argued that his firm had no one of sufficient calibre available to run such a business and he strongly opposed the idea because it would lead the company into 'endless difficulties'. But Lewis J. Firth vigorously defended the plan and, highlighting Firth's trading difficulties, argued that there was an opportunity for the company in the US since the 'Americans as a rule used inferior Iron and for this and other reasons the steel had not the uniformity of temper which was so important'. He recommended sending George Henry Firth to the US, a man 'very expert in the selection of ingots according to temper', and stated that he himself would be willing to devote three to four months each year to the American business. Bernard Firth agreed and also believed that in America George Firth would 'not have the disadvantage he has at these Works of being amongst men with whom he has been in intimate relationship from his youth and yet whom he was expected to manage'. The meeting, therefore, finally resolved to begin manufacturing in the US in association with a Pittsburgh concern. The directors 'candidly admit the difficulties in the way of superintending a business carried on at such a distance, but they believe they are not insurmountable'.

The subject of Firth's attentions was the Sterling Steel Co of Demmler, Pennsylvania, managed by Charles Yandes Wheeler (1843–99).[43] The latter, who had been trained at Hussey, Howe's Pittsburgh crucible steel works, had pioneered the manufacture of shells in America. Like the Carpenter Steel Co, of Reading, Pennsylvania, Wheeler was in close contact with Europe's more advanced projectile makers, and had acquired technology from W. G. Armstrong & Co and the Firminy Works in France.[44] The concentration on shell manufacture, however, had led to the neglect of Wheeler's tool steel business, offering Firth's an attractive opening.

In 1896, therefore, the Demmler projectile and tool steel departments were brought together as the Firth Sterling Steel Co. Firth's was to subscribe £50,000 to raise the ordinary share capital of the firm to £120,000; £1,000 was to be spent on expanding the output of the crucible steel department from 200 to 2,000 tons a year, and George Firth (1857–1904) was sent over as supervisor. By 1898 Firth's American crucible steel was 'giving satisfaction' and the following year the first 'good dividends' were reported. At this point Firth's increased the value of its investment to £250,000, equal to two-thirds of the capital, and there were large undivided profits. After Wheeler's death, Lewis J. Firth became president of Firth Sterling, a £45,000 mortgage on the property was paid off, the Wheeler shell patents were purchased at bargain-price, and in 1901 extensions to the crucible steel department costing £60,000 were initiated.

In that year, one of the Firth directors (probably Lewis Firth) told a Pittsburgh reporter:

Our business from the Pittsburgh plant for the last year was simply enormous. The plant is being worked full turn and to its greatest capacity, but it is impossible to supply orders. Primarily, the tariff on iron and steel drove us to establish a plant at Pittsburgh, and the advantages of this territory have so impressed themselves upon us that the mere tariff question is a bagatelle compared to other reasons. All English steel manufacturers recognise how far ahead the United States is and I can mention several Sheffield firms who have either secured a site for a plant, or are negotiating for one, in Western Pennsylvania.[45]

From that date, until about 1912, the substantial dividends from the Pittsburgh Works became a recurrent theme in the Sheffield company minutes. In 1908, for example, reference was made to the 'handsome return' on the US investment, which the board attributed 'principally to the successful efforts of Mr. Lewis Firth', who was voted £500. Scattered data in the directors' files show the reason for the firm's delight. In 1908, after several years of steadily increasing orders for projectiles and tool steel, Firth's collected in cash and stock dividends a profit of £31,038 from Pittsburgh; about forty percent of the Sheffield company's total £78,804 profit for that year! At the end of 1909 Firth Sterling's profits for seven months were £106,000 ($530,000), enabling the payment of a 10 percent dividend, with £70,000 cash in hand. Firth's had happily timed its American involvement to coincide with peak years in crucible steel demand (see Appendix). Moreover, a steady stream of US Government shell orders ensured that the ordnance side of the business made average yearly profits of £28,940 in the period 1897–1909; and Firth's was also paid royalties for its projectile expertise.

By then Firth's had moved the shell business to Washington, DC, a plan dictated not only by the expansion of tool steel capacity, but also by the armaments' outlook. Despite steady profits, the Firths were only too aware of the precariousness of the projectile trade in America; competition for the limited American market from domestic manufacturers such as Bethlehem Steel was increasing and there were rumours that Sir Robert Hadfield, who had 'spoilt' American prices by introducing European competition, was about to become allied with a US concern. Government requirements were also becoming more stringent and Firth's, as Hadfields was to experience, had difficulty in maintaining quality in America and in meeting deliveries. In 1907, therefore, the Washington Steel & Ordnance Co was formed by splitting the Pittsburgh business in half, with $750,000 as the paid up capital of both companies, which were under the presidency of Lewis J. Firth. The ultimate intention was to sell the Washington Works as soon as possible for about $2 million, leaving the McKeesport plant free to concentrate on tool steel. Bernard Firth visited the Pittsburgh site in 1909 and reported: 'Trade in America is undoubtedly good and the next two years ... are likely to be very big ones indeed, and I think there is little doubt that these Works will be fully occupied.'

Before the First World War Firth Sterling established a reputation as the

leading American high-speed steel producer (see Table 8: 1) and continued to contribute good dividends to the Sheffield parent. Its profits in
1912 of $225,000 (£45,000) yielded dividends of about 12 percent and
returns remained satisfactory until 1918. By then production of stainless
steel had begun at Firth Sterling under the direction of L. Gerald Firth, the
son of the president. It proved impossible to dispose of the Washington
Works, despite an attempt to interest Hadfields, though it was fully utilised during the War when it made naval shells for the Allies, allowing
Firth's Sheffield Works to concentrate on the production of army projectiles.

In the interwar period rapidly changing economic conditions caused the
fortunes of Firth Sterling to fluctuate (see Table 7: 1). In 1920 and 1922
the American company again provided a 'substantial' part of the Sheffield
company's credit balance: it had organised the formation of the American
Stainless Steel Co, another lucrative source of income;[46] it was one of the
American pioneers of electric steelmaking; and under the direction of
Lewis and Gerald Firth its reputation for fine steel was maintained with
the introduction of stainless steels and Krupp-licenced tungsten carbide
cutting alloys.[47] On the other hand, the Washington business had been
liquidated in 1921 because of dwindling orders and it was to be another
nine years before the firm was able to sell the site to the US Government
for $525,000. Tool steel demand was also poor and after a series of losses
Firth's considered selling its Pittsburgh investment in 1928. Healthy
profits and a 7 percent dividend for that year, however, caused Firth's to
defer any such sale, but its declining presence in the US was marked by the
closure of its main American sales office at Hartford, Connecticut, in
1930.

In 1930, Lewis Firth proposed an ambitious $1 million programme of
expansion at McKeesport, which, after an extensive review, was accepted
in principle by the Sheffield board. The depression, however, effectively
scotched the plan and ushered in a decade of poor trading. Lewis Firth,
who was to celebrate his eightieth birthday in 1937, having successfully
resisted an attempt from Sheffield to retire him three years before,
remained on the board, with his son Gerald as president. But by the
Second World War Sheffield no longer had an active interest in the management of the Pittsburgh plant and relations with it had become, in the
words of the Firth Brown director who travelled to America in 1944 to
sell the investment, 'entirely passive'.[48] Firth's American involvement
ceased and the proceeds of the sale were invested in Firth Brown Steels in
Canada.

Like Firth's, other Sheffield steel enterprises were attracted to Pitts-

Table 7.1 *Firth Sterling Steel Company's performance*

Year	Profit ($)	Year	Profit ($)
1924	60,011	1935	318,459
1925	171,486	1936	378,991 (8 months)
1926	108,884 (loss)	1937	No data
1927	113,663 (£22,730 loss)	1938	No data
1928	427,276	1939	357,646
1929	No data	1940	819,260
1930	109,428 (loss)	1941	2,583,410
1931	335,273 (loss)	1942	5,392,439
1932	283,598 (loss)	1943	3,457,595
1933	73,699 (loss)	1944	1,091,636 (7 months)
1934	44,113 (£5,229)		

Source: Firth Brown Directors' Minute Books, Nos. 6–9.

burgh at the turn of the century. Seebohm & Dieckstahl Ltd planned the erection of an American plant in the area. Representatives were despatched and negotiations were opened with a view to forming some kind of amalgamation with Firth Sterling.[49] This plan, however, was later discarded. William Jessop & Sons, however, another crucible steelmaking concern with strong American links, did move to the Pittsburgh area after 1900.

Jessop's had been founded in 1793. It was Thomas Jessop (1804–87), the second generation head of the enterprise – a man known in America as the 'Steel King' – who was chiefly responsible for developing the firm into one of Sheffield's leading manufacturers of crucible steel. Under his guidance and travels abroad the company's most lucrative trading links, especially with the US, were established.[50] The firm had been doing business there since about 1828, when Thomas Jessop made his first visit to New York, supplying saw plates and tool steel to both the West and East coasts of America.[51] Thomas's brother, Henry (d. 1849), was sent to New York to reside there permanently. The company was a pioneer in sending crucible steel cutlery blanks to the US, a policy which brought rich dividends, but encountered opposition from Sheffielders who declared that Jessop was ruining the home cutlery trade. In the words of one report: 'at one time no local house did a better or more lucrative trade with the United States. Their profits on their American business were in some years enormous, and such as probably will never be made by any English house in the future.'[52] Before the advent of American competition Jessop's developed an extensive US connection with branches in six of the major American cities by the 1860s.[53]

The success of the American makers and the tariff, however, severely damaged this trade. By 1901, Jessop's had begun the construction of a crucible steel works on a 400-acre site at Washington, Pennsylvania, at a cost of £100,000. At this late date no attempt was made to follow the old Sheffield methods. Fuelled by natural gas, the furnaces were designed to manufacture not tool steel, but sheet and bandsaw steel.[54] The latest American labour-saving devices were installed and, though some initial difficulties were encountered in finding sufficient numbers of skilled workmen, one director was so pleased at the result that he intimated that he would like to 'scrap' the Brightside Works in Sheffield.[55]

Though little is known of Jessop's American business, the factors leading to the building of the Pittsburgh plant are clear. According to one of the firm's directors, 'the predisposing cause leading to the decision to lay down plant in the United States was the recent combine among American crucible steel manufacturers. As the recent American duty on crucible steel amounted to $50 per ton and as fuel was cheaper in America than in England ... they had decided to open up in the United States.'[56] Jessop's feared that the Crucible Steel Co of America would shut out the foreign maker, largely through restrictive trading practices.[57] The directors were also impressed by the energy of American workers and the widespread use of labour-saving machinery, believing that: 'The men in America do as much as they possibly can; over here they turn out as little as possible.'[58]

The American subsidiary succeeded in preserving its niche in the US market for the production of saw steel, supplying, amongst others, Atkins and Hoe's. Production had more than doubled by 1920, an electric furnace had been installed, and new lines in alloy and stainless steels for automobiles and aeroplanes had been developed.[59] However, Jessop's Pittsburgh ties were severed in the early 1920s when the American branch was sold. The reasons for this are obscure, though Jessop's postwar difficulties in Sheffield, which resulted in the firm temporarily suspending its operations, probably influenced the decision. When a director of the Sheffield sawmakers Spear & Jackson visited Jessop's in 1925 he commented: 'Sheffield have no connection directly or indirectly with Washington now', though he observed that machines made in Sheffield were still in use.[60]

Jessop's maintained its selling organisation in America, even after its take-over by Birmingham Small Arms in July 1919.[61] Jessop's was brought into close contact with Burton Griffiths, which not only acted as BSA agents in America, but also handled American machinery imports into England. Jessop's, with its expert knowledge of steels and tools, provided intelligence for Burton Griffiths, and so helped maintain and extend the sale in England of American machinery.[62] The US trade was still the most important, at least in the early 1920s, of Jessop's overseas markets. Frederick C.A.H. Lantsberry, president of Jessop's New York office, travelled extensively at this time pushing the company's tool steels.[63] But, as with other Sheffield high-speed steelmakers, decline set in during this decade, reflecting the falling American demand for English high-grade steel.

8

THE RISE AND DECLINE
OF SHEFFIELD'S HIGH-SPEED STEEL
TRADE WITH AMERICA, 1900–30

The reputation for superiority once enjoyed by Sheffield steels is not much of a selling argument now, as the standard qualities of [American] mills are right in the front rank with very few exceptions.

SCL BDR 134. Report of A. Balfour & Co's Boston agency, 2 May 1922.

The introduction of high-speed steel revitalised Sheffield's tool steel trade with America. Shortly after the turn of the century the new high-speed steels began finding their way across the Atlantic. Samuel Osborn & Co, the most famous of Sheffield's tool steelmakers in the US, was shipping small quantities of the new steel to its Boston agents as early as 1902, as the company records show:[1]

Shipments to B. M. Jones & Co of RMS

		Tons
March	1902	38½
June	1902	38½
September	1902	25
October	1902	12
(Mushet High-Speed)		2
Total for 43 weeks		116

The shipments are a reminder that only small tonnages were made (in 1914 Sheffield production was only 6,000–7,000 tons),[2] but since the value per liquid ton could be as high as £160, the Boston orders represented a valuable trade item.

Osborn's was keen to know from Jones of any complaints from customers after comparing RMS with the newer high-speed steels. The company was aware that its earlier technological lead with RMS had been cut. 'We have found that in England many of our customers have for a time stuck loyally to RMS', wrote Osborn's to Jones, 'and been in favour of it, then suddenly a change. A rival gets trials and heats RMS with a high-speed steel and so off go the orders and we have to attack the position being on a level with all other H[igh] S[peed] makers.'[3] Attacking the position meant up-dating RMS with the newer high-speed steels and the company's records show the activity this entailed.[4] By 1905 Osborn's was personally placing Mushet High-Speed Steel in the hands of its best American customers and was receiving from Jones a testimony to the quality and toughness of the product.[5] By 1906 the company was thanking Jones for the 'splendid orders which you have been sending in recently'.[6]

At this time Sheffield's high-speed steel trade with America appears to have reached a peak, one newspaper, in 1906, referring to a 'phenomenal' trade of 100 tons per week.[7] A year later Sheffield was supplying America with almost a half of its annual consumption of 4,000 tons of high-speed steel (Table 8:1).

However, in 1907 Osborn's expressed concern at various factors which were beginning to erode Sheffield's position in the high-speed steel trade – factors which were eventually to force the city's manufacturers to form the High-Speed Steel Association to set prices and protect their interests.[8] Osborn's became worried about 'not only the abnormal advances that have recently taken place in the cost of special alloys, but also the gradual all-round increase in the cost of the production of high-class steels – partly due to the more exacting demands of steel users, but of course chiefly due to the advances in wages, fuel and material, [which] render it absolutely necessary that we must realise better prices if we are to carry on a profitable business'.[9]

Osborn's, therefore, forwarded to Boston a revised price list:[10]

R. Mushet's Special Steel	1/- per lb net without any discount
Mushet High-Speed Steel	1/6 per lb „ „ „ „
Mushet High-Speed Steel (434)	1/9 per lb „ „ „ „
Titanic Cast Steel	46/8 per cwt „ „ „ „
Spindle Steel	31/6 per cwt „ „ „ „
Twist Drills	Our list less 10% discount

Osborn's added: 'We are afraid these prices will not leave margin for the usual Agency profits, but we hope the extras on *R. Mushet's Special Steel* and *Mushet High-Speed Steel* and the advances you may in some

Table 8.1 *Annual consumption of high-speed tool steel in the United States, 1907*

Manufacturer	Brand	Estimated production
Jonas & Colver, Sheffield	Novo	560
Firth Sterling, Pittsburgh	Blue Chip	480
Crucible Steel, Pittsburgh	Rex A	455
Bethlehem, South Bethlehem	BHS	330
[?]	Excelsior*	255
Midvale, Philadelphia	Midvale	255
Burgess, Pittsburgh	Burgess	195
Jessop, Sheffield	Jessop	180
Osborn, Sheffield	Mushet	180
Spencer, Sheffield	Velos	176
Bohler, Sheffield and Austria	Bohler Rapid	150
Allen, Sheffield	Allen	140
Colonial, Pittsburgh	Colonial	126
Halcomb, Syracuse	Halcomb	125
Baldwin, Wheeling	Hudson	110
Carpenter, Reading	Zenith	85
Bourne-Fuller, Cleveland	Scott IXL	70
Heller, Newark	Heller Bros	25
International High Speed, NY	International	25
[?]	Victoria	10
[?]	Semanola*	5
	Total	3937

Source: EMHL Acc 1770. Series II, Box 17, Folder 2. Memo re Taylor–White Tool Steel, 6 August 1907. The figures are approximations made by the Bethlehem Steel Co for the patent case against Niles-Bement-Pond. *denotes unidentified imported brand, possibly from Sheffield.

cases be able to obtain, will realise enough to pay interest on Stock and such Agency expenses as are chargeable to us.'[11]

By 1907 Osborn's found to its dismay that it was no longer profitable to sell the less special of the special steels in the US, such brands as Titanic cast steel being sold at an agency loss. American buyers still had some regard for Sheffield's more uniform product, but domestic tool steel was now beginning to undercut English prices. In some brands Osborn's described the American trade as a 'bread and cheese' business, though the directors added quickly that they were glad to have it. In 1907, therefore, they approached B. M. Jones with the idea that new arrangements be made by which Jones became a purchasing agent – in other words, bought and sold its own stock.[12]

The correspondence is not extant after that date, but it seems clear that Osborn's trading difficulties increased. A Journal and Ledger relating to B. M. Jones & Co from the 1918–20 period show an absence of orders and the winding down of the trade.[13] By then the First World War had seriously disrupted the American trade for Sheffield makers and the post-war slump, when high-speed steel production fell from 20,000 tons in 1918 to about 10,000 tons in 1920, brought further problems. The *Iron-monger* predicted gloomily that 'there does not seem to be much likelihood in the near future of America becoming a buyer of English high-speed steel, as she can now produce more than she could consume'.[14]

In 1921 a correspondent for the *Iron Age* calculated the export charges on a large shipment of Sheffield tungsten tool steel landed in New York and found that the total delivered cost was £531 per gross ton.[15] This meant a net cost in New York of about 83 cents per pound, as compared with the prevailing American price of about $1.15, leaving only 30 cents or so to cover selling and warehouse costs and any eventual profit. Since the relative cheapness of English high-speed steel was entirely due to the depreciation of sterling against the dollar, the slightest advance in the exchange rates to $4 would mean that Sheffield makers would have to reduce their prices to compete, a difficult task since their export prices were the same as their home prices.

Nor was this the only problem for Sheffield traders in the 1920s. Steeply rising raw material costs inflated the price of high-speed steel from £150 per ton in the 1900s to £420 per ton in 1920.[16] Another complicating factor was the old spectre of increased import duties posed by the Fordney McCumber Tariff, which the Sheffield makers viewed as a serious threat to their US trade. Sheffield manufacturers drew up the most detailed criticisms of the proposed tariff in the form of a memorandum submitted to the Foreign Office, which attacked the valuation and administrative provisions of the bill and predicted the virtual extinction of Sheffield's steel trade with America.[17]

One of the city's most prominent steelmakers, Arthur Balfour (later Lord Riverdale), galvanised opposition to the measure and employed his administrative talents as chairman of the American Tungsten Steel Importers' Commission in New York. This had been organised primarily by Sheffield industrialists to watch the interests of British trade in the US, especially in the materials which were manufactured in Sheffield, namely high-speed steel and crucible carbon tool steel.[18] The Commission kept in constant touch with the British Embassy in Washington, and assisted the latter with information to combat the higher rates.

Government action was slow. In May 1921 Arthur Balfour was told that nothing could be done until information became available as to actual tariff proposals. 'This is cold comfort for the British industry; but is as much as we can do while the attitude of the USA continues to be as it is at present', remarked the Foreign Office.[19] Nevertheless, the Foreign Office did recognise the importance of the high-speed steel industry and thought it advisable for the British ambassador in Washington, Sir Auckland Geddes, to take any measures that might at any time prove useful.[20] By March 1922 Balfour was informed that all possible representations had been made to the US authorities and that nothing further was to be gained by sending experts to Washington, since no public hearings were being held. The only useful step, thought the Foreign Office, was to encourage American importers to spread their views in the press, with perhaps the help of Swedish representations.[21]

Foreign Office memoranda from the Commercial Counsellor and the Secretary of State show that there was pessimism over the future of Sheffield's steel trade with the US, especially with respect to carbon tool steel. They emphasise the extremely limited nature of the trade at that time. Remarked the Secretary of State:

At one time Sheffield manufacturers sold a fair quantity of carbon tool steels in this country, but the British steels have been replaced quite generally by American steels which have proved satisfactory in quality and very much cheaper. There are now only two importers that import any but negligible quantities of plain carbon steel from England and the carbon steel business of these firms is much less important than their business in tungsten steel ... [English steels] are sold to only a very few ultra-conservative consumers who willingly pay a considerably higher price merely because of their faith in the quality of the British steel. In view of these facts, it is evident that little English carbon steel would be imported over the Senate Tariff rates, but it is almost equally true that they do not and cannot come in under present conditions, except in almost negligible amounts.[22]

Nor was the picture very different with respect to high-speed steels:

total American consumption of those [fine] steels and the percentage relation of imports of high-speed steel to the total American consumption of that product is only slightly in excess of 1%. For a period of 10 years, imports of high-speed steels into the United States from Great Britain have shown no increase whatever. On the contrary they have declined.[23]

Arthur Balfour and his colleagues did not take such a resigned view of events and took the unprecedented step of forming a deputation and going to Washington to plead their case directly. The group comprised of its spokesman, Arthur Balfour, representing the company of the same name, Sydney Robinson, of Jessop's, and Peter McGregor, of Sanderson Bros & Newbould. The delegation, through the offices of Sir Auckland Geddes, stated its case before the Senate Finance Committee on 30 August 1921.[24]

After highlighting the extremely close connections between America and Sheffield steelmakers, and the parlous state of the Sheffield industry in the postwar slump, Balfour pleaded for a significant reduction in the proposed Fordney McCumber duties, arguing that it would be 'absolutely prohibitive' as regards Sheffield's high-speed steel trade with the US. Demonstrating his awareness of the implications of the tariff for world trade, Balfour asked the Committee 'to let us live and work and pay you back what we owe you. We owe you a vast amount of money, which is a great anxiety to us, and we feel that unless we can trade with you our difficulties are going to be enormous ... All we ask of you is to give us the best and squarest deal you can under the circumstances.'[25]

As it transpired, the best and squarest deal was not very dissimilar from the original proposals. There were amendments – a reduction to 45 cents per pound on high-speed steel, and 15 percent ad valorem – but as Balfour subsequently stated the reductions did not go far enough, and the cheaper grades of steel, from the Sheffield standpoint, were left in a most unsatisfactory position.[26]

The Tariff may have seemed the most significant trading threat to Balfour and his colleagues, but a close look at the extant business correspondence, some of it relating to Balfour's own firm, paints a slightly different and rather more complex picture.

Arthur Balfour & Co had grown out of the crucible steelmaking enterprise of Seebohm & Dieckstahl Ltd, a company with strong American links. Henry Seebohm (1832–95) had visited the US in 1879 and had been greatly impressed, whilst George Dieckstahl's son had emigrated there.[27] The firm's American trade, which had begun in the 1870s, was sufficiently important for the directors to consider the erection of a Pittsburgh plant in 1900 (see Chapter 7). The intention was not implemented, but in the 1900s the US was still the company's biggest customer, largely due to the trade in high-speed steel. Arthur Balfour (1873–1957), who was eventually to become chairman, had visited the US in 1887, which was said to have left him with a lifelong enthusiasm for American drive and efficiency that became an influential factor in the firm's progress.[28] Balfour returned in 1892 and found employment as a moulder in the Buffalo Works of the New York Car Wheel Co, and began his remarkable career by rising from the shop floor to general manager within four years. Meanwhile, his brother, Bertram, resided permanently in America until his recall in 1908 to help run the Sheffield business.

In the 1920s Arthur Balfour & Co still catered for the American high-speed steel trade through its 'Ultra Capital High-Speed Steel' agency in Boston, Massachusetts. The few American company records that have survived relate to this period.[29]

By 1923 the Ultra Capital High-Speed Steel Co was reporting a heavy increase in an already existing deficit. A reduced sales force; the inability to cover more than a very restricted area; the reluctance of steel users to buy, save in the very smallest possible quantities; and the apparent impossibility of securing the interest of the manufacturing trade – all these were mentioned as reasons for the low turnover: and business conditions were also bad. Despite advertising further afield by means of circulars, the results were not encouraging: 'almost every manufacturer, with the exception of those using tool steel as raw material, has stocks of steel left over from the 1917–1920 period, and orders are consequently few and far between'.[30]

Most of the company's business was centred around the Boston and Cleveland areas. Beyond these localities sales were hindered by a lack of working capital, something which the company had always lacked according to its reports. Consequently, the agency was reduced in 1921 to employing two 'travellers' to cover extensively the area within a 50-miles radius of Boston. Advertising, which had been inserted in the *Iron Age* during ten months of 1920 at a cost of $480, was dropped and so too was any further promotion in trade publications. The idea of sending trade representatives to the Midwest and Pacific was considered in 1921, despite the fact that the company had been unable to arouse interest in the Midwest by letters; but by 1925 the Accounts Report stated that it did not consider travelling in this direction worth the cost and no trips were planned unless a good reason presented itself. The agency even had to justify the purchase of a single Ford automobile by arguing that: 'Even if you cannot afford a car, you certainly cannot afford not to.'

As the firm admitted, a mobile sales force was a prime necessity in the US; its lack resulted in a loss of potential turnover. By 1923 the Reports listed a sad tale of lost chances – abortive attempts to supply double-bevelled cutlery steel, stainless steel sheets, and low-tungsten sheets for leather and rubber knives; the failure, after almost ten months, to place samples of lime-drawn high-speed steel into the hands of manufacturers who expressed a willingness to use it; the inability to supply the right kinds of shoe-die steel; and the difficulties with self-hardening steel, which had led to problems in half a dozen shops that had still not been solved.

Balfour's poor performance, no doubt, reflected the difficulties of post-war adjustment in Sheffield.[31] The problems resulted in a higher price for the English product. In 1922 the Boston agency admitted that the difference between laid down costs and American prices on high-speed steel sheets – 50 cents and 90 cents a pound, respectively – could not be bridged by salesmanship.[32] In the case of hacksaw sheets the Sheffield prices were higher than the prices quoted by at least two large domestic producers. In magnet steels, as regards price, aside from the fact that the English deliveries were not good enough for US firms, the company could not compete. This led to the agency endeavouring with some success to locate sources of supply in America and opportunities for selling US carbon tool steels, when Balfour steels proved too expensive, were not overlooked.

The Tariff played its part in the higher prices, but one of the Boston agents argued in 1927 that it was not the vital consideration:

No Tariff changes are going to help us much, if at all; in a majority of lines for which we find a call, high-speed steel, low-priced alloys, tempered strip steels, etc., etc., we are unable to compete even with other importing houses, Swedish and Austrian particularly. No Tariff or exchange fluctuations will alter that.

The impression gained from a close reading of the Balfour correspondence is simply that there was a lack of demand for English steel. The company felt unable to capitalise on the increased prosperity, arguing that this lay mainly with big business rather than with the small enterprises it relied upon for custom. By 1922 Balfour's could find no one anxious to buy British material in preference to the domestic, with the exception of one or two lines, which would never be worth handling, unless in conjunction with other larger and more profitable ones, and nowhere was business to be found which would give the firm a chance to import some of its specialities. Apart from the sale of drill rods and the trade in shoe-die steel in negligible quantities, the firm was not very optimistic about the possibility of selling high-speed steel to tool manufacturers in the US. By 1924 the company was preparing to turn its attention more to carbon and oil-hardening steels, and to specialities, gradually building up stocks of the former, and doing all it could to develop the latter, in which it was still dependent upon Sheffield. The comparison of Sheffield with domestic mills was no longer such a favourable one. In 1927 the Boston agency could point to twenty orders worth $5,000 on which the Sheffield manufacturers had disappointed their customers and so had lost the chance of future business. In shoe-die steel the once fairly steady business had been ruined by bad rolling and wrong composition of material.

The problems eventually proved to be insurmountable. As early as 1923, Balfour & Co was thinking of offering the agency stock on consignment terms. In 1931, when a favourable exchange rate prevailed, the company despatched a representative from Montreal to sell the high-speed steel stock. By 1932 the American agency, now under Adams & Osgood Steel Inc, had been liquidated.[33]

A similar fate befell Edgar Allen & Co, which, after relinquishing its manganese steel interests in America, had reverted after the First World War to the trade in high-speed steel through its New York and Chicago agencies. Incorporated in Illinois in September 1919, the firm supplied orders for special steels – Allen's Imperial Extra Special, Minerva Special Steel, Red Label Tool Steel, and Stag Steel – and, occasionally, for steels made specially for the American market, such as Allen's Chrome–Vanadium Steel. Most of the firm's business was in the East and Midwest with some orders for Oregon. From 1924, the earliest date from which evidence survives, Edgar Allen's order book for the US shows a modest and steadily declining trade through the Chicago and New York agencies.[34] In January 1925 orders from the Chicago agency were for only a few hundred bars, and though quantity is no indication of the value of the trade, since high-speed steel bars could cost £650 a ton, it was hardly enough to make the US trade worth the cost of the firm's own agency. The depression was particularly severe with the trade and in 1931 the orders taken were mostly cancelled.

Allen's had great difficulty in competing in the American market in the 1920s. In Sheffield attempts were made to keep up with the latest developments. In 1908 the firm had installed the first Héroult electric furnace in England. In 1920 a new 10-ton electric arc furnace went into production, to be followed in 1927 by the world's first high-frequency furnace. But results were mixed – the electric furnace was dismantled due to high running costs and, though the high-frequency process enabled Allen's to enter the market with its Stag Major super high-speed steel for the commercial drilling of manganese steel, the extra alloy content meant that the product was expensive even by British standards.[35]

In 1918 the British government lifted its ban on the export of tungsten steel to America, and Allen's quickly responded with a shipment of 50 tons with another 40 tons to follow. In the US in the immediate postwar period it was reported, reassuringly, that there was still a demand for Edgar Allen steel, and that some engineers in the US had been awaiting the opportunity of once more securing their favourite brands. More disconcertingly, it was also remarked that as a response to renewed Sheffield competition the American makers had severely cut their quotations for high-speed steel.[36] There is some evidence for this in the business correspondence. Concerning one firm which had been using Allen's steel for a number of years, the Chicago agency wrote: 'Our American competitors have gotten in there with a cheaper priced material which is evidently doing the work nearly as well as our Class E.' To compete, the firm had to consider the modification of its Stag Brand steel. Other experiments with special materials were conducted in an attempt to win business, but again price factors were a hindrance. For one order in 1929 the New York agency experimented with alternatives in manganese, but was not successful and had to cancel the order due to high production costs. High Sheffield prices were a source of concern to the New York agency, but the company felt that reductions could only be made on the larger orders.

More depressing was the fact that Edgar Allen products did not seem to meet the exacting demands of American industry. On more than one occasion there are complaints from American manufacturers that the Sheffield steel did not meet its specifications. In such a small number of orders this is, perhaps, significant, though it should be mentioned that complaints were nothing unusual to the high-speed steel manufacturer, who faced the problems of adapting a variegated product to the subtle demands of individual makers. Complaints range from a lack of hardness, to deficiencies in the uniformity of the shipment. On one occasion, a lack of straightness in the bars entailed a considerable amount of extra work in Chicago on the hand-press. On another, the agency informed Sheffield: 'We have had so much difficulty with supplying satisfactory steel to this customer that we request that you pay special attention to this order and do not ship it if you are not absolutely sure that it is free from seams.' Orders were also lost because of a 'lack of guts' in some of Allen's steel.

Allen's steel still performed well in trials.[37] The Sheffield product was advertised at Expositions in Cleveland and Philadelphia.[38] In New York attempts were made to open up new lines of business. Even though the company had not wished to enter the hollow-drill steel trade in the US, the large copper mines were canvassed for orders and Allen's drill steel was entered in tests with competing brands for this business, the only Sheffield steel so represented.

By 1928, however, it had ceased to be profitable for the firm to operate its own branch in the US (according to the company's historian this was due to the cumulative effects of the Tariff). The Edgar Allen Steel Co Inc was transferred to A. Milne & Co, the original name being retained, and the company continued to sell Edgar Allen tools through a warehouse in New York and a branch office in Detroit.[39] Later, the name was dropped, and Milne's, with whom friendly business relations still remained in the 1950s, continued to sell Sheffield tools until the Second World War, when difficulties made it no longer worthwhile, though orders still occasionally came in from the partners, H. Sears Hoyt and J. King Hoyt.[40] Visits were still made by the directors to the US, even though the former connection was effectively dead.

The 1920s also witnessed the demise of the American tool steel trade of J. H. Andrew & Co Ltd. Founded in about 1870, the firm had built up an important US business before 1914, specialising in tool steel, steel wire rods, and mining steel. It was said that most of the cables used in American suspension bridges were manufactured at Andrew's Toledo Works.[41] However, in 1921 the firm's New York agent, Charles Newman, reported that 'the War had brought about great changes in the position in America as regards the importation into [the] USA of Sheffield Steels in that owing to the English Steel Makers being debarred from carrying on their USA trade during the War a large number of competitive American firms had appeared and had temporarily, at any rate, captured the market'.[42] He added some gloomy remarks with reference to the proposed Fordney McCumber Tariff.

In view of the importance of the American market, however, the directors decided, after a careful review of the situation, that the 'Toledo' steel business should not be given up without a struggle. Newman recommended the setting up of a New York office instead of relying upon scattered distributors. After estimating the cost of such an organisation at $31,260 per annum, the company's overseas director, Capt. Kinloch, was sent to New York in 1923 to survey the situation on the spot. Meanwhile, the firm's American trade since 1911 was reviewed and its future prospects debated. The board decided that 'in view of the extreme narrowness of the margin between cost delivered USA Agent and sale price obtainable, it was felt to be impossible to adopt the suggested Sales organisation in America for sale of Tool Steels'. The Tariff had 'made it practically impossible to import [Andrew's] High-Speed Steel into the United States and sell it at a profit'. To make Andrew's steel more competitive, the New York agency pushed for reductions in the price of high-speed steel bars and bits, but the Sheffield firm was unable to comply.

In July 1925 Kinloch returned from the US and described in detail his impressions: he showed that it was no longer profitable for the firm to hold stock in America. In 1925 the US agency sold £4,486 of steel, but sales from Andrew's other and more lucrative markets in South Africa, Japan, Australasia, South America, Canada, and Russia, totalled £325,153. Having secured the board's agreement, Kinloch left immediately for the US to sell off as much of the high-speed steel stock as he could, before shipping the balance home before the end of 1925. Henceforth, new orders were to be executed from Sheffield stock as far as possible.

The prospects for the trade in wire rods were also poor. In 1925 the director reported to his shareholders:

There is no possibility of selling WIRE RODS in the States, until our costs of production are reduced by at least 25% which is quite impossible on the present prices of raw materials and a 47 hour week, whatever kind of plant we might have.

As you know, we had a very fine Wire Rod connection with America, up to the outbreak of War, at remunerative prices, but unless the costs of Domestic Rods in the States very greatly increases, or our costs are reduced very considerably, I hold no hope of regaining this business.

After the liquidation of the American stock a skeleton organisation was retained in the US for the selling of a few special lines which were less affected by the Fordney Tariff, and which did not necessitate the carrying of stock. The US staff was also retained to take advantage of a hoped-for alteration in the Tariff; but it was to be a fruitless wait.

9

TRANSATLANTIC SPECIAL STEELS II:
STEEL CASTING ENTERPRISES

> We pour some fluid iron or steel into a mould, and what have
> we? A metal liable to puzzle us with various kinds of often con-
> tradictory phenomena which may be of no consequence, or
> perhaps be annoying and sometimes hurtful. We congratulate
> ourselves on having taken all precautions to ensure a good
> casting, when lo! we hear a crack and find the subject of our
> pride a useless mass of metal.
>
> Paul Kreuzpointer, 'Riddles Wrought in Iron and Steel',
> *Cassier's Magazine* 19 (1900–1), p. 276.

Once the problems of pouring crucible steel into ingots had been
mastered, steelmakers began to explore the possibilities of moulding cast
steel to special shapes and sizes. In 1824 Frederick H. W. Needham of
London patented a process for making steel castings, but it was not used
commercially. In the 1840s, however, Johann C. Fischer, Jacob Mayer,
and Krupps discovered and patented the methods for the production of
steel castings as a regular business.[1] Continental improvements, which
had been derived from the Sheffield methods, were swiftly incorporated
into Sheffield practice. During the period 1850–80 a number of firms,
notably Butcher's, Cammell's, Firth's, Jessop's, Hadfields, Shortridge,
Howell & Jessop, and Vickers, successfully embarked upon the manufacture of steel castings.[2]

Produced by the teeming of innumerable crucibles into a specially
treated mould, such castings, some of which weighed several tons, represented the summit of metallurgical art at that time and resulted in some
of the most spectacular sights in nineteenth-century steelmaking. The
high shrinkage rates of such large masses of steel, the problem of finding a
sufficiently refractory moulding material, and the need for a highly
trained labour force, ensured that it was some time before steelmasters
had the processes fully at their command. Meanwhile, the details of

manufacture remained highly secret.[3] Since steel castings were relatively expensive, elaborate techniques and machinery had to be devised so that they could be produced with little additional finishing.[4] At Vickers a patented mill was used for 'breaking down' or roughing out railway tyres within minutes, and these were then passed hot to another mill, which rapidly rolled them truly to size.[5] When Abram S. Hewitt, the American ironmaster, came to Sheffield in 1867 he was presented, to his evident astonishment, with the spectacle of the mass-production of standardised cast steel castings on a very large scale indeed. At Firth's 'there seemed to be no greater difficulty in dealing with these large masses of steel than with the smallest ingot on the premises'.[6]

Crucible steel castings rapidly found favour in engineering and agriculture because of their tenacity, strength and lightness when compared with iron forgings. Cast steel proved ideal for the production of bells, a speciality of Naylor Vickers, which cast its first bell in 1855. Before the trade was rapidly satiated, due to the low replacement rate, a brisk trade was done with the US, where the capacity of steel bells to withstand low temperatures and their carrying power, which could bring together scattered Western rural congregations, made them very popular.[7] On the railroads, steel tyres, despite their high cost, superseded iron ones because they lasted five times longer.[8] American locomotive builders, who before 1860 had been rather conservative in their use of cast steel, were amongst the best customers for the new steel tyres.[9] In 1863 only 466 steel tyres were sold in the US; but by 1871, the figure was nearer 48,000.[10] Since the US had no steel castings industry, Americans either imported tyres or rolled them themselves from Sheffield ingots.[11] Krupp's was a major exporter of the finished article, but the records of the Baldwin Locomotive Co of Philadelphia show that several Sheffield firms were also important suppliers.[12] Baldwin's began using steel tyres in 1862, buying them through New York and the Philadelphia importing agency of Philip S. Justice, the first man to sell them in America.[13]

In 1865 Justice wrote to Baldwin's to inform the directors of a new venture:

It is proposed to start an Establishment in this city or neighborhood, immediately, for the manufacture of Cast Steel Tyres and heavy forgings of Cast Steel with the ultimate intention of making Cast Steel Rails as well. The superintendent for the present to be in the hands of Mr. Wm. Butcher of Sheffield who proposes to bring out a complete staff of men and machinery if necessary ... [and who] is the first manufacturer who made a solid Cast Steel Tyre in England and has had a very large experience in them, as well as all kinds of Steel. It is only reasonable to presume therefore that none of the ordinary contingent failures of a new concern will attend the present.[14]

William Butcher (ca. 1791–1870), alongside his brother Samuel, was the owner of the W. & S. Butcher Steel Works in Sheffield, and one of the town's most successful traders with America, where his mark on tools and cutlery was said to be a household word.[15] Besides chisels, gouges, and planes, 'no other house dealt so heavily in files';[16] by 1865 Butcher was reported to be making more files for America than had ever been prepared by a single maker.[17]

Butcher also seems to have been something of an engineer. He helped recruit workmen for the Pennsylvania Steel Co in Harrisburg, and was engaged by the firm to supervise the building of a Bessemer plant.[18] For some reason these plans were shelved, and Alexander Holley was appointed in Butcher's place to complete the project. Butcher himself removed to Philadelphia and with Justice's help built the William Butcher Steel Works in the city in 1867.

Norristown was selected as a site because of its proximity to several main railway lines which connected with the anthracite coal region. The easily available coal supply, apparently, had more weight with Justice and Butcher than the marshy character of the ground, which was later to prove a serious obstacle in both building and operation. During 1866–7 work was begun on the seven-acre site on the first buildings, which included the crucible melting shop, described as the longest wooden-trussed span in the country. On 10 May 1867, the stock of the company was subscribed and in June the charter officially launched the Butcher Works on its career.[19] Designed for the production of steel tyres, it also made ingots, railroad frogs and crossings, shovel steel, spring steel and a variety of other forgings and castings, together with steel for hoop skirts.[20]

Butcher's intention seems to have been to produce crucible steel on exactly the same lines as in Sheffield. A converting furnace, a shed for making crucible pots, a coke-hole melting shop, and imported Swedish bar iron were the main features. By the spring of 1867 the melting shop was completed and a tyre mill, built in England by Galloway Bros, was installed. This supplemented an English drill press and American machines, such as a boring mill erected by Bement & Dougherty in 1868.[21] The steel mixtures were dictated by Butcher and were entirely 'rule of thumb'; no record was kept of production and there was no laboratory to analyse heats. The first tyres were rolled from blooms imported from England, but almost immediately a gang of Sheffield melters teemed the first castings in the new melting shop and these were then punched and beaked under a hammer at the Bush Hill Iron Works of Matthews & Moore.

Butcher's steel castings were the first made commercially in the US, and they seem to have been well up to the usual Sheffield standards. The Works marketed cast steel car wheels, which, according to a test report by Messrs. A. Whitney & Sons, the Philadelphia car wheel makers, were of excellent quality.[22] The Philadelphia & Reading Railway Co also purchased a consignment of cast steel frogs, which were so satisfactory that some of them were still in use as late as 1894.[23]

However, the management was characterised as 'reckless and utterly wanting in system'.[24] Though Butcher's 'rule of thumb' methods were well-suited to the production of crucible steel, major problems were encountered when it became desirable to try other processes. The first departure from old lines occurred on 4 October 1870, when a contract was secured with the Keystone Bridge Co to furnish about 2,400 tons of steel for the Eads Bridge over the Mississippi at St Louis.[25] This was the first steel bridge erected in the US, but it brought Butcher little besides experience and scrap.

James B. Eads' rigid tests and demands for exceptional workmanship, which were to the limits of available metallurgical knowledge (and perhaps a little beyond), coupled with the Butcher Works' difficulties in working steel in such large masses, became a recipe for disaster.[26] Butcher's carbon steel bolts ruptured under test, and so Eads turned to the Chrome Steel Co headed by the New York metallurgist Julius Baur, who believed he had discovered a way to substitute chromium for the carbon in ordinary steel.[27] Convinced by Baur's materials and claims, Eads paid the Chrome Steel Co a $15,000 royalty to allow the Butcher company to manufacture chrome steel for the bridge. Eads' hopes, however, soon foundered as the Butcher Works delayed, tinkered with the mixtures, and delivered faulty material. Eventually, the use of steel in parts of the bridge had to be abandoned, the Philadelphia contracts were cancelled, and henceforth Eads relied upon Pittsburgh makers to complete his designs.

Sensing the need to keep abreast with the latest technologies, the Butcher Works in 1869–70 had also constructed one of America's first Siemens–Martin open-hearth furnaces. Its capacity was only 3½ tons, but, according to the firm's historian: 'this cupful of metal gave the bosses more agony than any combination of 50-ton furnaces can possibly cause our present day experts'.[28] The problems were exacerbated by the erection of another experimental open-hearth furnace, the 'Dolly' or 'Sellers'. In the first month of production in 1871 only three heats were run from the main open-hearth furnace. On 9 September 1871, after 92 heats had been completed with indifferent success, the furnace was closed down. The final heat solidified within the furnace and ensured its complete dismantlement, leaving the ingot as an unusual monument to the catastrophe in the shape of a convenient hitching post!

Apparently, William Butcher was 'quite dispirited by his lack of success'.[29] He reportedly set off with forty of his English work-force and leased another crucible site at the Freedom Iron Works at Burnham, near Lewistown, Pennsylvania.[30] Butcher's involvement in the Philadelphia venture ended, William R. Durfee became the superintendent, and the Sheffield interest was sold. Butcher himself died in November 1870,[31] and the presidency of the Works came under the control of William Sellers, the distinguished machine-tool builder and engineer of Philadelphia, who gradually effected a change in its organisation and the character of its products.[32] He renamed the company the Midvale Steel Works, installed a new foreman, acquired a skilful metallurgist from England, and ensured that henceforth a much more scientific approach was adopted to the problems of steel manufacture. In the words of C. A. Brinley, the chemist who was responsible for much of Midvale's later success:

The works had been brought into [its] low condition by the grossest carelessness, if not ignorance, in the direction of the details of manufacture. Good and willing men were not lacking, the bone and sinew had been there, practical skill in melting, heating and working steel had been there, and there had only been needed, to make the enterprise a success, a more accurate chemical knowledge of the difference between good and bad steel and a common sense and conscientious application of it in the direction of the work.[33]

Having carefully sorted and analysed the 3,000 tons of steel abandoned in the Works' yards, Brinley and his assistants successfully re-launched the firm's business in wheel and axle castings and re-started open-hearth production. Orders from the Pennsylvania Railroad in 1874, the US Army in 1875, and the builders of the Brooklyn Bridge in 1879, soon followed and their successful completion marked Midvale as one of the foremost American steel casting concerns. In contrast to Butcher's methods, Midvale's approach was part of a new era in steelmaking which demanded that steelmakers be led by books and a laboratory rather than by the older practiced techniques.[34] It was at Midvale that Frederick W. Taylor began his experiments on the nature of tool steel that were to have such a profound impact on machine-shop practice.[35] Midvale's prominence also brought it into contact again with Sheffield steelmakers such as Vickers and Hadfields.[36]

By the 1880s, Midvale's progress had become part of the general history of the American steel castings industry.[37] That industry can be said to have had its true beginning in Pittsburgh in 1870 when William Hainsworth, who had been born in England and had worked in steel foundries there, began casting steel from a small two-pot furnace.[38] Incorporated as the Pittsburgh Steel Casting Co, the first factory to manufacture steel castings exclusively, Hainsworth's enterprise grew rapidly, mainly due to the demand for agricultural machinery and implements.[39] A visit to Europe to acquire the necessary skill and technology enabled him to produce the first open-hearth steel castings in the US in 1875, and then, in 1881, the first castings manufactured by the Bessemer process.

However, although the field for steel castings was widening in the US, the product did not give universal satisfaction. Whilst English founders like Hadfields and Vickers were producing large marine castings for rudders and stern pieces, American firms, even the more advanced ones such as Midvale and the Pittsburgh Steel Casting Co, lagged far behind. In the period 1880–90, when the US Government turned to the steel industry to build the 'New Navy', it found that American founders lacked the necessary skills to produce heavy shapes for shafting, guns and armour. When the shafting of one of the Navy's most prestigious ships cracked, Albert Vickers communicated to the Secretary of the US Navy the insulting suggestion that instead of using 'palpably inferior and unsuitable American shafting he should look abroad where masters of the art were to be found'.[40] Five years later, in 1890, the Engineer-in-Chief of the Navy stated: 'I am obliged to report that we are having a most discouraging experience with steel castings.'[41] Great difficulty was experienced with moulding sands in the early days of the American industry and for many years firms such as Midvale lost money regularly on steel castings while trying one mixture after another. Not until James G. McRoberts, at the St Louis Steel Foundry Co, in 1891–3, began using a green sand mixture were the problems overcome.[42] Meanwhile the consequent lack of uniformity had damaging effects. Remarked one authority in the *Iron Age*: 'In going over the history of the business during this period – 1880, say to 1890 – one gets the impression that the castings were pushed on the [American] market before the art was fully developed, and with the result that steel castings fell into a certain disfavor which seemed to retard the progress of the industry for several years.'[43]

Whilst Americans struggled with the problems of moulding sands, Robert A. Hadfield and his team of foundry assistants led by the Mallabands were discovering and pioneering the manufacture of manganese steel castings.[44] Though it was several years before there were any significant sales of the new alloy, Sheffield's technological lead gave Hadfield the chance to introduce its manufacture into the US.

Hadfield had first visited America in June–August 1882, when he was twenty-three years old, in the company of Joseph Jonas, the director of the firm of Jonas, Meyer & Colver. The visit was intended to introduce the young Sheffielder to the metallurgical and business world in preparation for his role as director of his father's company. The visits to American steel casting and crucible steel concerns in Pittsburgh, Chicago, and Philadelphia, which Hadfield described in a notebook,[45] were an important event in his life. He said later: 'I cannot help thinking it was the educative influences brought to bear on my mind in that country which stimulated me in the highest degree and helped me take up what was practically a new line of research and work, the study of special steel alloys.'[46]

During Hadfield's visit to America in 1882 he had toured Pittsburgh with Joseph D. Weeks (1840–96), the distinguished American engineer and technical journalist, who had met Hadfield's father at the Paris Exhibition in 1878. Weeks visited Sheffield in 1883 and during his stay with the Hadfields he was shown the remarkable new alloy. Weeks, who was the editor of the influential Pittsburgh steel and hardware trade journal, the *American Manufacturer*, and was on first-name terms with most of the leading US ironmasters and steelmakers, was a useful business ally and the elder Hadfield quickly enlisted his support in patenting manganese steel in the US and in acting as an agent for its licencing.[47] Weeks publicised the product by reading a paper on the subject at the Chicago meeting of the Institute of Mining Engineers in May 1884 and began looking for suitable customers. In May 1885 Robert A. Hadfield returned to America to expedite the granting of his patent in Washington, DC, opening the way, as he hoped, for the rapid exploitation of his findings.

But disconcertingly, in the US Weeks had little success in attracting licencees. Andrew Carnegie, Weeks reported, was not at all inclined to take the matter up. Negotiations were conducted with William P. Shinn, a leading railway executive and Carnegie's general agent, with the intention of manufacturing car wheels, but little appears to have transpired. Other firms, such as the Solid Steel Co of Alliance, Ohio, and Miller, Metcalf & Parkin, of Pittsburgh, took out options on the product, but no attempt was made to begin large-scale manufacture. Instead, Hadfield found himself in 1889 side-tracked into time-consuming and expensive litigation when a Boston manufacturer, Nathan Washburn, tried to claim manganese additions to steel as his own invention. Thus after several years of laborious experimentation, hundreds of transatlantic letters, and the work of Weeks, Hadfield's manganese steel was largely untried and unknown.

Hadfield grew impatient, but soon other possibilities presented themselves when an American metallurgist, Henry Marion Howe (1848–1922), wrote to Hadfield in 1886 requesting information on manganese steel. 'Who is Henry M. Howe?', Hadfield asked Weeks in 1887, 'He is writing some splendid papers on the metallurgy of steel.'[48] Despite a negative opinion from Weeks, Howe was invited to Sheffield in 1890 and, after being impressed with Hadfield's Steel Foundry and its chairman's energy, agreed to replace Weeks as Hadfield's American representative. Howe was also consultant for the Taylor Co of New Jersey, and eventually Hadfield and the firm were introduced.[49] Hadfield later recalled:

Our first meeting, which I well remember, took place at that prosaic spot known as the Eagle Hotel, Bethlehem. The parties present were Professor Howe, Mr. W. J. Taylor, and later on Mr. Maunsel White, a very famous Metallurgist, who helped make Bethlehem what it is today... Finally an agreement was drawn up, [the Taylors] were to work my patents and this was the introduction of Manganese Steel into the United States.[50]

After a deputation from the American firm had visited Sheffield to learn the processes, the first manganese steel was poured on 29 October 1892, at High Bridge, New Jersey, under the personal supervision of Hadfield and his assistant Sam Mallaband and this was the first casting of an alloy steel in the US. Later, to assist in the trackwork application of the steel, Hadfield and Howe introduced the Taylor Co to William Wharton Jr. & Co, Philadelphia, the two firms eventually merging into the Taylor–Wharton Iron & Steel Co in 1912.

Hadfield's involvement proved to be a limited one. Though the Taylor–Wharton Co pioneered the use of manganese steel for railway equipment in the US and later expanded its output to include the manufacture of projectiles, dredging buckets, and burglar-proof safes, Hadfield later described the firm as 'rather an old-fashioned one; High Bridge, New Jersey, was not, too, at all the best centre for such a works as it was difficult to get a full and proper supply of good labour there, and the development was not as fast as it should have been'.[51] Hadfield was also greatly annoyed that the company, despite its head start, allowed a rival to enter the field which poached his ideas and his staff – an annoyance increased by the fact that the rival in question, Edgar Allen's, was a Sheffield firm.

Founded in 1868 by William Edgar Allen (1837–1915) and his associate, George Rose Jones, Allen's began trading with America in the 1870s in files and small amounts of carbon steel.[52] By the late 1890s the firm began producing manganese steel and in 1904 took over Askham Bros & Wilson Ltd, a well-known name in tramway and mining work with world-wide contacts.[53] No love was lost between Allen's and Hadfields: the manganese steel track structures which Allen's began exporting to America after 1900 were intended to be sold in direct competition with its rival. American representatives were requested to watch prices so that Allen's could 'get into direct touch and compete against Hadfields'.[54]

Clearly, the fact that the foundries stood almost side by side in Sheffield was not taken as a hint that the two companies should work together in America!

In 1910 the Sheffield concern formed the Edgar Allen Manganese Steel Co by taking over the Chicago Heights plant of the American Brake Shoe & Foundry Co. The firm specialised in the manufacture of manganese steel castings of all kinds – frogs, guard rails, switches and special track-work, safes, steam shovel parts and dredger buckets – and Allen's soon had improvements under way to more than double its capacity.[55] Also acquired was the steel casting foundry of the Tropenas Steel Co, at New Castle, Delaware, situated in the heart of the East coast steel casting region.[56]

Edgar Allen's in Chicago imported the necessary knowledge from Sheffield, but followed standard American practice in the use of oil-burning crucibles and American machinery for grinding and rolling. In the Chicago works the management seemed to have taken a good deal of trouble to enlist the utmost co-operation from the workmen. Possibly the American business may have been an attempt by Edgar Allen to overcome a problem which the Sheffield tool steelmakers had highlighted, namely, lower productivity.

One of the Sheffield directors commented in 1899:

(1) We had an [American] employer here about six weeks ago. We showed him some articles we were moulding. One moulder moulds four of these articles per day here: in the United States with a moulding machine, and employing two men and one boy, they would make 220 of the same articles.

(2) Another article, of which there is a considerable sale in this country, we get nine moulded in two days. This is not machine work, but manual labour. This shows that in the States a moulder does about double the work of an Englishman. We may say that we pay 1s 7d each for moulding these articles: they pay 10d each.

(3) Wheels. Of a certain design we get five moulded in a day up to 7 o'clock p.m., at a cost of 1s 10d each for moulding only. In the States they would make 75 on a machine per day, at a cost of 2 to 3d each, plus the cost of the machine.

We had to make several thousands of the wheels referred to in paragraph 3, and anticipating that we should have to compete with America, we had conferences with some of our moulders, and pointed out to them the position of affairs. We asked for their co-operation, and explained to them we should prepare special boxes and patterns to facilitate their work. This we did, and the moulders promised to do their best. When they had been working on these Wheels for three or four weeks, we sent for them and expressed our disappointment at the small quantity of work they were turning out, and their reply was that they could not do any better, and were working very hard indeed to accomplish what they were doing.[57]

Whether Allen's succeeded in solving these problems in the US is a difficult question to answer. Technically, matters went well, and by 1913 Bethlehem Steel was being provided with the largest manganese castings ever made.[58] Edgar Allen was also responsible for introducing the Tropenas converter into America at the end of the century. The process, which the company had developed jointly with its French inventor, was regarded by the firm as one of the cheapest and most efficient of all steel-making methods.[59] Though Allen's complained that Americans were slow to realise the potential of the new system, many US companies invested in the converter in the 1900s.[60] In 1911, however, Edgar Allen informed the Chicago branch that the US trade had lost over £10,000 in the preceding year.[61] It may have been losses such as these which forced Allen's to relinquish its American foundries. By 1918, the Chicago and New Castle branches had been absorbed into a large consolidation of US makers – the American Manganese Steel Co.

Meanwhile, events in America had led to a close liaison between Hadfields and an American firm. In 1911 Hadfield signed an agreement with the US Army Bureau of Ordnance for the use at their Watertown Arsenal of the Hadfield System of manufacturing armour-piercing projectiles – an agreement which underlined Hadfields' technical superiority in a field in which, as one of the leading British producers, it had little trouble in surpassing US makers.[62] The Bureau under this agreement had the right, in a national emergency, to nominate two sub-licencees in order to increase its supplies of shells. In 1917 this option was exercised in favour of the American Clay Machinery Co which acquired the information to make shells by Hadfields' method with a restricted right for its use by the Army. The company operated at Willoughby and Bucyrus, Ohio, for the manufacture of clay-working and sand-lime brick and cement machinery.[63] In December 1919 an agreement was made with Mr R. C. Penfield, proprietor of the firm, whereby a new company was formed, of which Penfield retained 60 per cent of the common stock in consideration of the goodwill and the existing assets, and, in addition to authorising the use of the Hadfield System, Hadfield subscribed $1,166,700 for the remaining 40 percent.[64] After looking over the sites the Hadfield directors selected the Bucyrus plant for the manufacture of manganese steel, with the Willoughby plant producing castings for the company's own use. Preparations were made for Hadfields' staff to make further visits and for members of the Penfield staff to visit Sheffield.[65]

Continuing orders for projectiles after the War were the carrot dangled by the US Government which led Hadfields into the American market.

During the First World War the Sheffield firm had tendered for and won an American Government contract for projectiles, offering substantial savings in price and delivery date over domestic producers.[66] Since he could undercut the Americans from Sheffield, Hadfield would have preferred to manufacture the shells in England, but neither the Army nor Navy chiefs would countenance the shells being made outside their country (though after considerable negotiation the US Government allowed the shell blanks to be made in Sheffield). Once Hadfield became interested the Navy actively encouraged his involvement, since for strategic reasons they were anxious to establish a plant west of the Alleghenies.[67] Hadfields, therefore, had little alternative but to become allied with a US firm, even though the takeover seriously depleted its working capital. When this factor was added to further problems with the US Government over the liquidation of a large war debt to Hadfields (caused by the cancellation of contracts which would have brought the Ohio firm profits of about $1 million), the stage was set for the chequered career of the Hadfield–Penfield Co.

Initially, Sir Robert Hadfield was pleased at the prospect of beginning manufacture in the US. At the back of his mind was the rankling thought that his firm had never derived its just rewards from the discovery of manganese steel, especially since his patents had lapsed. He wrote to one of his co-directors in the US:

It is almost unthinkable that we who introduced Manganese Steel into the World are not deriving one cent of interest or benefit from it in the great country of the United States, into which I introduced the manufacture of Manganese Steel, whereas the rivals who took away our knowledge – you will remember the Sam Mallaband incident and the lowdown tricks of the enemy as regards S.M., his assistants, and some of our staff – are developing.[68]

Hadfield still saw potential for manganese steel in the US, especially with regard to manganese steel rails which Hadfield thought had never had a fair trial in America because makers did not understand the peculiar methods of manufacture.

Hadfield, with his sensitivity to the vast potential of alloy steels in the twentieth century, was not unaware of the advantages that the US offered for English manufacturers. Carefully informed on conditions in the US, he was aware that in 1922 about 600,000 tons of alloy steels were consumed by the burgeoning automobile industry, together with a million tons for sheets and plates.[69] Hadfield himself had no doubt that any firm working on his lines, with the economy of his System (Hadfield virtually guaranteed that every ingot passed would be sound), would find a considerable demand in the US. At this time Hadfields was already sounding out the

Ford Motor Co at Dearborn with a view to supplying it with its own special steels for valves and springs.[70]

In particular Hadfield was pinning his faith on further orders for projectiles. Hadfields had no difficulty competing with American makers on technical grounds. Even the Americans were impressed. Wrote one member of the US Admiralty to a colleague: 'The British Government has the new type of Hadfield shell for all calibres, thus outclassing us completely. The Hadfield American patent ... retains the standard American contour or capacity of the shell, and the same total weight and bursting charge, but with a quality of steel which we have not yet made in America. The Hadfield Company will, however, have the secret.'[71] The ability of Hadfields' shell to penetrate the thickest armour meant that the Navy's guns could be increased in efficiency by as much as 50 percent. Hadfield told a US Vice-Admiral: 'all your Armour-piercing equipment is obsolete'.[72] He believed that, despite the Washington Conference, the US would still require substantial quantities of the Hadfield shell. Entertaining US Admiralty officials at his Cap Ferrat villa in the south of France, Hadfield did all he could to ensure a substantial stream of orders for the Hadfield–Penfield Co. His confidence must have been increased by the fact that the competition had largely evaporated in the early 1920s after Midvale had closed its munitions' plant, the Government had disbanded its factory at Charleston, and Firth Sterling had liquidated the Washington Steel & Ordnance Co.[73]

The main difficulty to Hadfields successfully exploiting the opportunities in America was presented by the company it had taken over. Like many Sheffield firms which decided to enter the US market, the chief problem for Hadfields was how to transfer advanced steelmaking technology to a foreign country and make it work in less than favourable circumstances.[74] Hadfield summarised his doubts to his distinguished American brother-in-law, George W. Wickersham:

As I think you know, I do not feel at all satisfied about its being possible to get any satisfactory future out of the H.P. Co as it is at present constituted. The Penfield crowd know little or nothing about steel questions, and help them as we may they have not got the knowledge to take advantage of our help. Besides, to equip themselves properly means a large expenditure of capital, and the management of such a plant would more or less have to be in our hands, an added burden upon us when we have quite enough to bear and carry on this side.

I am really alarmed when I come to think of the Penfield people undertaking the complete manufacture of an armour-piercing projectile – one of the most difficult operations in the World, requiring in the first place steel knowledge only obtained by long experience, and H.P. have not got that.[75]

The reluctance of Hadfields to sink more capital into the enterprise meant that success could only be achieved by interesting a US company in a joint venture. Hadfield selected the American Rolling Mill Co (ARMCo), in Middletown, Ohio, as a likely candidate.[76] Tentative negotiations were opened with this company in the early twenties with a view to forming some sort of collaboration over the production of projectiles and manganese steel under the Hadfield System. Dr A.S. Cushman, an American metallurgist, was chosen as a go-between to transfer the necessary scientific skill and technical knowledge. In early 1922 Hadfields' directors went to Middletown to see its boss George Verity and to consider a possible partnership. Later in the year ARMCo representatives were in Sheffield and had been suitably impressed. Hadfield himself set great store by some sort of arrangement by which ARMCo would supply the steel blanks under his licence for manufacture by Hadfield–Penfield into shells. '*I believe if this came about*', he told Wickersham, '*I should have done the best piece of work in my life for the Hadfield Company.*' These hopes were not fulfilled. At the end of 1922 Verity informed Hadfield that taking advantage of his approaches would depend very much on whether ARMCo had any surplus managerial or financial capacity to apply to new ventures. Evidently, this was not forthcoming, since the correspondence ceases after that date.

Meanwhile, conditions at Bucyrus had worsened. Since the expected profits from the venture did not materialise, Hadfields had to meet the payment on the three-year common stock bills ($1,166,700) as they matured. The general postwar trading depression, over-capacity in the US manganese steel industry, and plain bad management at the American plant exacerbated the difficulties. The Washington Conference had a disastrous effect on the company and the situation became critical. In 1921 £99,057 projectile blanks had been dispatched from Sheffield with £32,873 in projectiles in progress; whilst the value of shell orders not cancelled was £380,000. In view of this involvement, after visiting Ohio in 1921, the directors concluded that an immediate cash contribution was needed to keep Hadfield–Penfield afloat. This support, totalling £200,908, was provided in 1922 and raised Hadfields' holding in the company from 55 to 75 percent. But this hardly solved the long-term difficulties. The directors were not optimistic about the ability of the firm to carry the high interest charges, unless a shell order for a few million dollars arrived, or the pure steel System was sold to a large concern. One report concluded that the only way to put the foundry at Bucyrus on a working basis was 'to send over a nucleus organisation from home, and to make a clean sweep of the officials'.[77]

Hadfields sized up its opponents and found itself lacking. The directors made several visits to the American Manganese Steel Co at Chicago Heights, the firm which had been run by Edgar Allen. They felt that they had nothing to learn technically from this firm, but in production it was a different story. Hadfield director William E. Parker informed Sheffield in 1924:

The vital piece of information is their, (our principal competitors'), cost of metal in good Manganese Castings at \$220 per ton, i.e. 11 cents per pound. The H.P. Co's costs have always been about 13 cents per pound. We cannot make any profit while this position maintains.

It should be appreciated that the Foundry is considered by everyone in the H.P. Co organisation as peculiarly Hadfields Ltd responsibility, and the heavy losses in this department vitiate criticism of other and smaller losses. Furthermore, the Foundry is the only established unit in the USA of any portion of the Hadfield System, and unprofitable working is a doubtful recommendation of the System as a whole. A thought worthy of serious consideration is the 11 cents per pound of Manganese Steel as made by the AMSCo. If American labour prices, 60 cents an hour for moulders (about double English) were paid in Sheffield, and also the prices of American raw materials interpolated, what is the cost per pound of Mn. steel as made say in the Light Foundry? What is needed is American production methods applied to Hadfield Technical System.[78]

Hadfields did its best to improve matters at Bucyrus by increasing the numbers of technical staff. Electric furnaces were also purchased for the manufacture of castings.[79] The best prospect, however, still seemed to be to interest an American company in the Bucyrus operations.

After the failure to enlist the help of ARMCo, Hadfield turned to his old friends the Taylor–Wharton Iron & Steel Co. Relations with this company had cooled somewhat since the early days of co-operation. After the war, with the proliferation of advanced steelmaking technology, it became increasingly difficult to apply Hadfield's patents, and Hadfield began to suspect that the Taylor–Wharton Co was infringing his rights within the Hadfield System. Nevertheless, the two firms were still in contact (Hadfield remained a shareholder in the American company until his death), and they seemed a likely candidate to help, as Hadfield put it, 'lick Bucyrus into shape'.[80]

The opportunity to open negotiations was presented by Percival Chrystie's letter to Hadfields in 1924, hoping that Hadfield–Penfield would not engage in unfair price-cutting. There were further communications regarding the alleged infringement of Taylor–Wharton patent rights by the Hadfield–Penfield Co with regard to the manufacture of manganese steel. This led to a meeting with Chrystie in New York in 1926 in which Hadfields, represented by (Sir) Peter B. Brown, outlined plans to solve their Hadfield–Penfield differences and also remove the patent problems. Negotiations progressed and the Taylor–Wharton managers visited Bucyrus. However, in 1928 Chrystie vetoed the partnership. He wrote to Hadfield that he regretted that the interests could not be merged: 'For a time it seemed feasible, but developments were such that it was impossible to devise any plan that would be mutually satisfactory... From what I judged the only part of the business at Bucyrus that was at all active was tractors and road scrapers.'[81] Hadfield's reply suggests that he had already resigned himself to the inevitable, and the subject was shelved, though there was still further correspondence between the two companies involving manganese steel, patents, and competition between the two concerns.

The involvement of Taylor–Wharton, however, was probably the last chance for the Hadfield–Penfield Co. In the period 1920–5 the American plant had incurred consistent losses, totalling £545,000; and Hadfields still awaited payment for a further £27,700 in materials. It was felt that the company could only pay its way either if the Government cancelled its debt, possibly in exchange for the Hadfield System, or Hadfields wrote off a quarter of its investment, or there was a complete reorganisation with the closure of excess capacity at the Mansfield and Kensington plants. Major Augustus B. H. Clerke once more stated Hadfields' grievances before the US Government and pointed out the Sheffield firm's technical prowess. After meeting one American official he reported: 'I said that we had a very real claim, if only a moral one, against the Government, and detailed to him the whole story of how we had been led into the mess, and consequent loss of three million [dollars], by the action of the Government.'[82] The Government, however, was not only unsympathetic, but made it clear that the few orders that were available would go to US makers and not to Hadfields.

Hadfields was not prepared to introduce further cash and in the absence of Government co-operation and orders the winding up of the company was clearly envisaged. In 1927, after Major Clerke had made his fourth visit to the plant, he announced to his chairman: 'I feel confident that when you have seen the figures you will agree with me that to attempt to keep the plant in operation could only increase our loss, and that if no fresh development has arisen ... we should resign ourselves to the inevitable.'[83] By then a Receiver had been appointed and production ceased, leaving bad debts of £282,881 and with little chance of salvaging any substantial sum from the sale of the assets.

Denied a direct opening for his firm's products, Hadfield in the late 1920s continued the search for American customers for Sheffield's special steels. In 1925 he hired Albert Sauveur, the famous American metallographer, to push Hadfields' chromium–nickel ('ATV') steels in the US. These alloys had been developed initially by a French firm, Commentry-Fourchambault et Decazeville, at Imphy, which later reached an agreement with Hadfields to pursue research on them with the intention of producing a heat- and corrosion-resistant metal that would improve the efficiency of turbine blades. Again, Hadfield was attracted to the US market and told Sauveur in 1927: 'Just supposing, for example, even one half of the Turbines in the US were to be equipped with Hecla/ATV material, there would be an immense demand.'[84] But the ATV steels were expensive, many turbine makers such as Westinghouse and General Electric were not interested, and, as with manganese steel, overcoming the conservatism of engineers and manufacturers was a slow process. By the early 1930s the British, French and Italian Governments had bought substantial quantities for their respective fleets,[85] but in America, despite a licencing arrangement between Hadfields, Commentry–Fourchambault and Midvale, it was a different story. In 1932 Hadfield was informed that Midvale had found no profit in the agreement: 'It has to be remembered that in our experience of 'ATV' there has been practically no outlet except for marine work ... [and Midvale] have not yet sold a pound to the American Navy.'[86] Once again Hadfield found that Sheffield's great technological advantage was not the road to easy riches.

10

QUALITY PAYS? SHEFFIELD
AND AMERICAN CUTLERY MANUFACTURE

[The Americans] choose a few good popular styles, they invent and use machinery for every process possible, they put in a good blade, neatly ground, splendidly marked, and turn out every knife the precise duplicate of every other. Hence the uniformity, reliability, and general style which is found in *no* Sheffield goods except those of standard makers.

Sheffield Independent's US correspondent, 7 June 1871.

The myriads of safety razors being placed on the market are signs of the times. These are the days when the prevailing demand for all kinds of merchandize is for cheap goods ... Durability is no longer considered so essential; the idea is something that will serve its purpose for a while, even though a short time, and that can be sold at a low popular price.

American Cutler (March 1909), p. 8.

Before 1850 the US market was easily the best, albeit fluctuating, foreign market for Sheffield cutlery. Thus English designs and traditions took precedence over those of continental Europe; and, in fact, the establishment of the American industry owed a good deal to Sheffield workers. Until the mid-1830s Sheffield virtually monopolised the US market: about one-half of the total exports of the British manufactured steel industry went to America. After the '*glorious year of prosperity 1835*',[1] the trade declined: however, the US remained the best foreign buyer until 1860, taking about one-quarter of total English hardware exports. On the eve of the American Civil War Sheffield still accounted for about 90 percent of total US cutlery imports.[2]

The methods, organisation, and location of the Sheffield cutlery trades have been admirably described by Godfrey Lloyd. From him historians derive their familiar portrait of the industry – small-scale, dominated by the guilds and unions, and dependent on the work of numerous craftsmen plying their traditional skills and producing a huge variety of products and styles.[3] The industry was typified by the independence of its workers – the 'little mesters' – products of the domestic industrial system, who provided work for their families, a few apprentices, and sometimes a journeyman. The dominance of the system of outwork, however, should not obscure the growth of large-scale organisations which, in a similar fashion to the bigger crucible steelmaking concerns, had arisen under the stimulus of the American demand. William Greaves' Sheaf Works, established in 1823 in response to the volume of American orders, became the first firm to bring together all the processes of manufacture, from the production of steel to the completion of the finished article. The US trade was reflected in the growth of two other large enterprises – those of George Wostenholm and Joseph Rodgers – names which dominated the American market in the early nineteenth century.

The firm of George Wostenholm & Son, since its founding in 1745, had a distinguished and lengthy record of business with the US. The success was mainly due to the systematic travelling in America by the partners, Stenton and Wostenholm. George Wostenholm (1800–76), who first visited the US in 1836, was the major figure in that market and largely due to his efforts Wostenholm agencies, selling the prestigious I*XL brand-name, were established as far west as San Francisco, with the main office in New York. Wrote Asline Ward, the firm's New York agent: 'The future trade with America must be immense, territories that are now half savage will gradually become desirous of better & better goods & educated to aspirations of *babaric* cost and splendour'.[4] Encouraged by such sentiments Wostenholm undertook thirty visits to America in his lifetime; this gave him the reputation of having visited the country more often than any of his contemporaries and such were his ties with the US that he even cancelled his election as Master Cutler in 1838.[5] He also laid out his Sheffield residence, Kenwood House, on the lines of Kenwood Village, near Oneida Lake, New York, and, more importantly, his 'American zeal for big things' led to the founding of the Washington Works in Sheffield in 1848, where several hundred workers and numerous stages of cutlery production were brought together under one roof.[6] In 1862 the business of the firm was still 'almost exclusively American'.[7]

Wostenholm's reputation was equalled by Joseph Rodgers & Sons, founded in 1724, whose 'razors and penknives', in the words of one American, 'are well known throughout the christian world, wherever chins are shorn or quills are clipped'.[8] The enterprise owed most to John Rodgers (1779–1859), who widened its product range, won a Royal Warrant, and, recognising the value of publicity, established its famous show-room in the 1820s. In the early nineteenth century a member of the firm was sent to New York to exploit fully the transatlantic trade, which was an important factor in Rodgers' expansion into the largest cutlery factory in the world by 1850.[9] In the last week of 1870 it was sending upwards of ten tons of cutlery to America, especially to the Southern states, and accounted for one-seventh of Sheffield's US cutlery trade.[10]

Despite their world-wide prestige these firms were already in retreat to American makers by mid-century. The US cutlery industry, aided by the tariff, which rose gradually from 20 percent ad valorem in 1792 to 35 percent in 1862, was well-established by 1850. At that date, 401 cutlery and edge tool manufacturers, employing 4,275 hands, produced $3.8 million of cutlery and tools; ten years later, 51 cutlery works, with 1,338 hands, turned out $1.3 million of cutlery products; and by 1870, a work-force of 2,111 in 82 workshops had increased production to $2.8 million.[11] The industry became heavily concentrated in Connecticut and Massachusetts where all the country's major manufactories – Ames, Russell, Lamson & Goodnow, and Landers, Frary & Clark – were located.[12]

The pioneers of the American cutlery industry in the years 1830–50 relied heavily upon Sheffield's manual skills and its elementary factory methods, besides employing Sheffield immigrants.[13] Experience as a Sheffield cutler became a useful passport into the American industry. According to one immigrants' guide-book: 'Of foreigners, a Sheffield workman is preferred to all others, and if from the factory of Rogers [sic] it is a sufficient introduction anywhere.'[14] Nathan Ames travelled to England in 1840 to learn about English methods and returned with workers who had been well-trained in the Sheffield techniques.[15] John Russell took up cutlery manufacture after reading Zachariah Allen's 'poetical' description of Sheffield in *The Practical Tourist* (1832) and immediately began recruiting Sheffield workmen and copying English patterns.[16] Amongst Russell's recruits was Matthew Chapman who arrived in the US in 1841 and soon made a name for himself devising cutlery machinery. Joseph Gardner arrived at the Russell Works from Sheffield two years later and also became influential in introducing new techniques and designs. Both men patented methods by which cheaper knives could be drop-forged or stamped out of sheet steel.[17] Gardner's inventions played a major part in the success of Lamson & Goodnow, which by 1860 had become the largest cutlery producer in the US. The firm was an important employer of Sheffield cutlers: in 1848 most of its twenty workers came from Sheffield.[18]

Countless others came to America. Amongst them were the cutlers brought over by the Union Knife Co and the Connecticut Cutlery Co in Naugatuck.[19] The Waterville Manufacturing Co, in Waterbury, Connecticut, also hired Sheffielders: these included James Roberts and his family who were amongst the 61 English-born cutlers enumerated in Waterbury in the 1850 Census.[20] On occasion entire factories were brought to America. In 1879 130 cutlers from B. J. Eyre's establishment in Sheffield, which had been acquired from the New York agency of Wiebusch & Hilger, found work at the Frary Cutlery Co, Bridgeport, Connecticut.[21]

Other Sheffielders founded their own enterprises in the Eastern states. In Pennsylvania Samuel Mason became founder-president of the Beaver Falls Cutlery Co.[22] Camillus, a famous New York cutlery concern, was established by an American and Denton E. Bingham, a Sheffielder.[23] In New Jersey the oldest recorded pocket-knife firm in the state, Booth Bros, was founded in Newark in 1864 by Thomas Booth from Sheffield. In 1853 Sheffield edge toolmakers Charles and Richard Buck set up Buck Bros in Millbury, Massachusetts, later one of the foremost chisel manufacturers in the US.[24] Another Sheffielder, Joseph Turner, who began making razors in Meriden, Connecticut, in 1872, ten years later, with Joseph R. Torrey, founded the Torrey Razor Co in Worcester, Massachusetts.[25] The first documented cutler in the Bay State, Aaron Burkinshaw, was also from the English town, having moved from Connecticut to Pepperell in 1853. One Sheffield man, Charles Hattersley, founded a cutlery business at New Haven, Connecticut, in about 1840, but by the 1850s was involved in pottery manufacture at Trenton, New Jersey, having possibily become interested in the use of china and porcelain as trimmings for knives.[26] A Sheffield cutler, Charles W. Platts, emigrated to Connecticut in the 1860s and he and his descendants played an important part in the establishment of several American cutlery firms, notably W. R. Case, the most famous of the country's pocket-knife makers.[27]

However, not every Sheffielder found the new country's customs to his liking. American attempts to impose a factory discipline of regular hours did not always find favour with workers who valued their independence, had traditionally held 'Saint Monday' as a holiday, and by all accounts were much given to dissipation. At Waterville, for example, many of the new arrivals became discontented and left, the Roberts to participate in the founding in 1852 of a co-operative venture, the New York Knife Co in Walden, Orange County, New York, under Sheffield president Thomas J. Bradley.[28] This was emulated in 1871 by the Co-operative Knife Co, of Ellenville, New York, which before its take-over and renaming in 1876 as the Ulster Knife Co, was managed and staffed by Sheffielders. In Naugatuck the local cutlery industry declined in the 1880s, and at least part of its problems stemmed from labour troubles involving Sheffield workmen, who complained of wages, the cost of living, and the fact that all they saw was the 'shop and house'.[29] The large band of cutlers at the Frary Cutlery Co in Bridgeport, described by one American newspaper as 'splendid material for a workshop, but neither so rapid nor inventive as the American workman', were soon leaving, apparently because 'Colonel Frary made vigorous attempts to compel the men to be in the factory for so many hours every day; but after the free and easy style in which they had worked in Sheffield they resisted his demands.'[30]

In any case, Sheffield's expertise was not the mainspring of American progress – that stemmed from simplified technique. Fine Sheffield knives were first forged and cut to shape; hardened and tempered; ground, sharpened and polished; and finally hafted.[31] Unhampered by craft traditions and able to try new ideas, Americans were able to abandon the more time-consuming processes.[32] The introduction of the trip-hammer, a rapidly running, power-driven device, gave US cutlers their first breakthrough. By 1844 the Russell Co was making a knife in which blade, tang, and bolster were all forged from one piece of steel. In 1848 the same firm was using trip-hammers for drawing out the blades from bars of steel on all its knives. These techniques did not dispense entirely with skilled labour using the older methods,[33] but they did immeasurably speed up production. Eventually heavy dies in power presses were introduced and the era of the mass-produced knife had arrived.

By the 1860s American factory methods were fully evolved. Commented a Sheffield cutler in Meriden, Connecticut, in a memorable description of the US cutlery crafts:

[The Americans] do far more with machinery in all kinds of trades than [Sheffielders] do. Men never learn to do a knife through, as they do in Sheffield. The knives go through thirty or forty hands. One matches and resins all; another pins all; another bores all handles; another glazes all blades; and another buffs all handles... If a Yankee can resin a knife on they call him a cutler; and by doing one thing all the time they become very expert, and they make some very good knives. Not the variety [Sheffielders] make, but such patterns as are done easiest by machinery.[34]

As Habakkuk has suggested the high value of labour seems to have been an important stimulus to labour-saving technology.[35] But at least as influential was the nature of the American demand which proved highly susceptible to, and partly dictated, the introduction of cheap, medium-quality table, butcher, carving, and artisans' knives produced to standard patterns – the type of knives that virtually extinguished Sheffield competition in the second half of the nineteenth century.

Shortly after the Civil War the US imported $1,105,419 of English cutlery, as well as $928,011 of penknives, pocket-knives, and jack-knives; by 1872 total English cutlery imports had fallen to $1,729,154; and five years later the figure was only $654,973.[36] The decline was due not only to the growth of American industry, the tariff, a general trading depression, and the Civil War, which disrupted Sheffield's market in the South and caused many firms to abandon selling there for good,[37] but also Sheffield's inability to supply Americans with the style of cutlery they demanded. It was this factor which commentators identified as the main reason for Sheffield's lack of success.

Sheffield had little difficulty in surpassing its rivals in workmanship and beauty. At the major exhibitions the cutlery of Wostenholm's and Rodgers easily beat the Americans for first place.[38] Wostenholm's, for example, won medals in Philadelphia (1876), New Orleans (1884), Chicago (1893), and San Francisco (1894). But even though such products enjoyed a ready sale in the cities, they were largely irrelevant to the needs of the average American. Hence one spectator, greatly impressed by a Sheffield cutlery display at the Centennial, nevertheless thought that little attention would be given to it since the 'styles [had] so little judgement in regard to the requirements of this market'[39] – a market dictated by the needs of a predominantly agricultural community.

Nor were the knives of Sheffield's more prestigious makers entirely representative of the bulk of the town's output, which was largely in the hands of the 'little mesters'. Viewed through the eyes of a modern buyer, when stainlessness, standardisation, and presentation are taken for granted, the productions of Sheffield's small workshops would appear rather motley. Nineteenth-century observers thought so too. In the 1880s the *Ironmonger* frequently commented on the unfavourable appearance of Sheffield cutlery when compared to American articles, especially from 'the inequality in lengths and breadths of knives, and also in making, grinding, and hafting', whereas the Americans 'always attached the utmost importance to such matters'.[40] The *Sheffield Independent*'s American correspondent, in a detailed review of the reasons for the loss of the town's US trade, went even further, complaining of the 'third-rate quality' of Sheffield exports, and arguing that: 'No country in the world took, for so long a time, anything like the quantity of poor goods ... than the United States did.' The Sheffield trade had, he believed, developed 'a vast mass of patterns, meretricious and gaudy in design, absurdly numerous in variety, and all but useless in quality and strength'.[41] Similar complaints were faced directly by Sheffield agents in the US where faulty workmanship was often compounded by slow deliveries and poor packaging.[42] In these circumstances US manufacturers had little difficulty in displacing their rivals. The 'once all-powerful' Rodgers found its goods pushed aside on the shelves of American stores,[43] whilst Wostenholm's business survived only as a 'tottering wreck', its directors pained to discover that the 'Americans make a knife which is apparently good enough for the average American'.[44]

The reasons for American success were not lost on Sheffield makers, but the introduction of machinery made slow headway. Devices to substitute the hand-forging of steel blades on a commercial scale by using the pressure of revolving dies had been constructed by a Sheffielder as early as 1827.[45] However, labour unrest and the nature of the demand, which favoured the production of an immense variety of type and design, made the adoption of machinery a difficult matter. Even in the large factories of Wostenholm's and Rodgers, though some economies of scale were undoubtedly achieved, there appears to have been no intention to impose a wholesale use of machinery: blades would still be forged by the little mesters and bought in for the final polishing, grinding, and assembling. At Rodgers an American observed: 'they discountenance the use of machinery, except for a few simple operations ... It is certainly amusing to see two men at a fire in a room not larger than a good-sized horse stall, with one anvil, making a knife blade in the same manner, and with the same implements, as their fathers did.'[46]

Towards the 1880s these attitudes changed. By 1862 James Drabble had become the first Sheffield firm to install machinery, expressly to compete with the Americans and Germans, and there were also reports of French attempts at this time to mechanise the town's scissor industry.[47] Rodgers began introducing machinery in the late 1870s, including American polishing machines.[48] Other firms, Atkinson Bros, Matthew Dodworth & Sons, Nixon & Winterbottom, and Boswell & Hatfield, also installed mechanical devices, frequently of US design.[49] But even though machines had become indispensable by the 1890s, particularly for those firms wishing to compete abroad, the transition to factory production was far from complete by the end of the century. The head of the Sheffield Cutlery Council, on a fact-finding visit to the US in 1902, reported that there was still a 'much more extensive use of machinery in the States than in Sheffield for cutlery purposes'.[50] The American cutlery factory was better managed and equipped; there was no outwork, ensuring a more economic use of the worker's time; and American cutlers were more sober.

By this date Sheffield competition was no longer a serious threat to the American manufacturer. US imports of English cutlery fell from

$1,146,272 in 1889 (about 10 percent of US output), to only $285,002 in 1894,[51] largely due to the punitive effects of the McKinley Tariff and the growth of German competition.[52] Henceforth, only pocket-knives, which, with their variety of patterns and complexity proved less suitable for machine production, were able to breach the 50 percent tariff barrier in any quantity.

Correspondence from Wostenholm's American agent in the early 1890s gives an insight into the problems Sheffield cutlers faced at this time. Covering a territory that was evidently his firm's main hunting ground – the South and Midwest – the agent, Edward Beckett, found that it was an uphill struggle to place Wostenholm's goods on the shelves of American stores. Impending tariff changes meant that American retailers were reluctant to buy in any quantity. After visiting the Macon Hardware Co, Beckett told Wostenholm's: 'Since the McKinley Bill these people have not been buying any I*XL goods ... [but] the buyer tells me if a change in the tariff takes place they will commence ordering again.'[53] Cheaper American knives had given domestic purchasers an attractive alternative. The policy of one of Wostenholm's customers in New Orleans was fairly typical. Wrote Beckett: 'Since joining a syndicate in purchasing cheap cutlery in large quantities they appear to have sold less of our goods ... It is evidently a question of profit entirely with them and they are selling Cutlery on price alone, quality not being considered.'[54] Concerning another retailer, he informed Sheffield:

I am quite sure it is not that they cannot sell IXL but [their reluctance to buy] is mainly owing to the fact that they are making a good profit on American goods. They have certainly increased their line of Ulster [US] knives ... 50%. To illustrate to you the difference as to their prices & ours take our knife 16144 as made by the Ulster Knife Co [Ellenville, New York]. [They] buy the Ulster knife for $4.50 per doz. & sell it for $6.75, making a profit of $2.25 per doz. 16144 costs them to import $7.83 and for them to make the same amount of profit they would have to sell them for $10.00 per doz., so you can readily see where our goods are at a disadvantage.[55]

Sheffield exports of scythes and shears were also negligible by the end of the century – a result both of the tariff and the increasing mechanisation of agriculture.[56] In scythe manufacture the Americans had already captured a large share of the market before 1850 with a product that was cheaper and better designed than its English competitor. Sheffield makes were judged too broad and heavy. 'In fact', commented one Sheffield newspaper, 'it is next to impossible to find a man [in America] who will wield the broad, useful, and effective 'Waldron's' or 'Griffin's' scythe among the heavy and extensive fields of grain and grass which this country in some portions produces, and that too under an almost tropical climate.'[57]

Other trades over which Sheffield had traditionally held a monopoly became casualties of changing styles. This was particularly true of razor manufacture where the Americans furnished a classic example of how, if machines could not be adapted to suit the product, then the product and consumer tastes had to be adjusted accordingly. In the nineteenth century the Sheffield straight razor was as much a work of art as the act of shaving itself – an object to be cherished and maintained as a long-term investment.[58] Beginning in 1901, when King C. Gillette, that strange mixture of utopian dreamer and scheming capitalist, pioneered the production of an old idea – the safety razor – these attitudes were turned upside down.[59] Influenced by massive advertising, to which Gillette devoted almost as much attention as production, consumers were taught to throw away their blades, to accept rapidly changing razor designs, and to no longer regard shaving as a predominantly male preserve.[60] US safety razor production rose from virtually nothing in 1900 to $24,554,337 in 1920,[61] with Gillette accounting for a major share of the output. By the mid-1920s the Boston company had set up a world-wide marketing organisation with several European subsidiary firms, including a factory in Slough, England. Sheffield became a mere supplier of razor steel and not until the mid-1920s did the city's own safety-razor industry emerge in its own right.[62]

Despite these developments, it would be wrong to think of the American market as a negligible one. In the early twentieth century the US still took important quantities of Sheffield cutlery; moreover, it remained a significant source of new ideas and technologies.

Wostenholm's maintained its American connection during the period 1914–30, when the firm looked across the Atlantic for both customers and help in introducing modern methods of manufacture. The company records show that a process of rationalisation was instituted by Wostenholm's during and immediately after the First World War which owed much to American practice. This was largely the work of Frank B. Colver (1873–1954), the firm's director, a man with 'progressive ideas', who believed that foreign machine-methods needed to be adopted if Sheffield was to compete.[63] An accountant was appointed in 1915 to examine the organisation of the Washington Works, and with his report Colver was able to show that the efficiency of the office was impaired by lack of accommodation, old-fashioned methods of book-keeping, poor routine, unpunctuality, and absenteeism.[64] It was argued that special attention should be given to the American books and the practice of simply reproducing the American entries on the Sheffield side avoided, so that a more secure method of checking agency transactions could be adopted.[65]

The rationalisation included modernisation of the factory and investment in new plant. In 1932 the company announced that it had carried this through to a large extent and was thus in an excellent position to take advantage of protective duties that the Government had imposed.[66] How had the modernisation been achieved? To begin with, the firm had profited from the introduction of new lines copied from foreign patterns. An agreement was signed with the Solingen cutlery makers to produce scissors under German patents.[67] Also initiated with German help was Wostenholm's belated entry into the safety razor field.

But above all, the Sheffield firm learned from America. Sometime in 1918 Colver made an extensive tour of American pocket-knife factories. Touring all the major US establishments – Camillus, Landers, Frary & Clark, and the New York, Warwick, and Walden Knife companies – the Sheffielder compiled a lengthy report on American techniques.[68] The document reveals an obsession with productivity: exactly how was it, Colver repeatedly seems to have asked, that Americans could produce so much, even in the most labour-intensive area of cutlery manufacture? The attitudes of labour were partly responsible. Colver noted: 'Every encouragement is given to the men to speed up, and those who do so have their wages continually advanced. The men seem very anxious to tell you how much they can do an hour.' He continued: 'I do not think American workmen work any faster than ours but they keep steadily at it and there seems to be little or no idling.' Such attitudes, allied to an extensive use of machinery, accounted for the spectacular output of US firms. At the Walden Knife Co, for example, the 440 men in the pocket-knife section produced 2,800 knives a week.

Colver ended his trip by purchasing several of the American machines which had so impressed him on his tour. In July 1919 it was reported that Thomas R. Moore of the Warwick Knife Co, New York, had received an order from the Sheffield firm covering his entire line of improved cutlery machines, which included blade-squaring, drilling and other modern machinery of his own invention.[69] The German-designed Hemming automatic grinder, which had revolutionised the US industry after its adoption in 1904, and the Schrade pocket-knife shielding machine, were also the subject of Colver's attentions.[70] Negotiations were conducted with a Sheffielder in America, James A. Nell, who had worked in the cutlery trade for some thirty years for such firms as the Walden Knife Co and Landers, Frary & Clark, to come to England to supervise the installation of the machinery.[71]

After the First World War, changing conditions also forced Colver, like other Sheffield makers, to consider the possibilities of manufacture in the US.[72] The Sheffielder may have wished to emulate the highly successful German precedent set by Boker's Valley Forge Cutlery Co in Newark, New Jersey, which was founded in 1899 in response to increasing tariffs.[73] In 1919 detailed discussions began as to whether Wostenholm's should open a New York factory. A memorandum from one of the firm's representatives there, a Mr Bunting, was drawn up to set out the reasons why that time was particularly opportune for the establishment of a Wostenholm cutlery factory in the US: it offers some illuminating comments on the comparative position of the two industries.[74]

The New York agent regarded the ending of the war as a golden chance for Sheffield. Not only had the great German cutlery houses been out of the market for four years, but also there was the possibility of a very great prejudice existing against German cutlery. In short, the time was ripe for Wostenholm's to acquire an 'unassailable' position – in other words, a base to escape the US tariff wall which Bunting thought, correctly, would probably become even higher. The Wostenholm blades were to be drop-forged (by a new method), glazed and marked in Sheffield and then shipped to the American factory. This had the advantage that the duty of 55 percent would not add very materially to the cost of the finished product, as no great value would have been put into the blades, and the steel would have cost less than the comparative American material.

It was not thought advisable for Wostenholm's to start a factory in the US with the methods in use in Sheffield, owing to the scarcity of skilled labour, and the cost which would bar the knives from a large market. Only if the American market was approached in the right way, as had the German cutlers, was success assured. This meant adopting American methods, which ensured low costs and high wages, by using machinery for many operations which in Sheffield were done by hand. In America some of the old New England factories, such as the Northfield Knife Co and Humason & Beckley, had tried to retain the traditional methods, but they were unable to hold their trade. The most successful firms were those which made the most use of machinery. American cutlers had begun to copy German ideas, which reduced costs, and were far removed from the original Sheffield methods. Machinery increased the employment of un-skilled workers; and there were greater numbers of female workers, especially in the assembly of pocket-knives. Factories were cleaner, better lighted, and more comfortable to work in when compared to Bunting's recollections of 'dark, dusty institutions'. Highly accurate blade-squaring machines had removed one of the most laborious jobs. More importantly, great strides had been made in drop-forging, which in the US had virtually superseded the older and more wasteful method of single-band forging. Only if Wostenholm's adopted such methods could trade be successful.

Wostenholm's New York representative envisaged a dual assault on the US market. The fine knives would still be made in Sheffield:

Your fine knives are all that could be desired. In fact, are as fine as the world affords, and will always command their prices, but I have good reason to know that the bulk of the cutlery trade in this country is done in the more moderately priced goods, and with a good selection of these, your line of cutlery would be as complete as any sold in the States.

The more moderately-priced items – jack-knives and flat-back knives (which were lacking in the Wostenholm line) – were to be machined in the US, using German methods. Bunting thought that such knives, stamped with the Wostenholm mark, 'with material prepared by American methods, which had had a little Sheffield skill and experience behind them, and but costing slightly more than ordinary American knives, would command a very wide sale in [the US] market'.

Amongst the likely candidates for the proposed deal were the Schatt & Morgan Co, Titusville, Pennsylvania, the Canton Cutlery Co, Canton, Ohio, and the Schrade Cutlery Co, Walden, New York, with the latter considered as the more attractive option. In 1919 the firm wrote to J. Louis Schrade in New York indicating that Wostenholm's would like to try making some jack-knives at an American factory.[75] Sheffield would supply the blades, drop-forged and marked with the Wostenholm name ready for grinding into the best-quality knives. The goods were to be despatched from Sheffield to Wostenholm's New York agent in Sheffield-style boxes bearing the Sheffield label. The firm was extremely mindful that the name 'Sheffield' would appear on the finished article. Unfortunately, the subsequent business correspondence has not survived – probably because the proposed venture did not succeed in the immediate postwar slump.

At the beginning of the 1920s the state of the city's trade was neatly summarised by a headline in the *American Cutler*: 'Progress Slow in British Cutlery Industry. Need for Machine Methods Understood by Makers but Little is Heard of Scrapping the Old Customs.'[76] The necessity for mechanisation was certainly recognised by Colver, Ibberson's and other cutlery makers, some of whom formed the Cutlery Trades' Technical Society in 1918 to achieve that end. But these manufacturers soon encountered the old craft workers, who bemoaned (not, it must be said, without eloquence) the 'stupid craze for cheapness'.[77] In the interwar years the industry still relied upon the small specialised shop. A Sheffield survey of 1922 listed 220 firms making cutlery and 155 making silver and electroplate; and in 1938 it was estimated that there were still 500 'little mesters' in the trade.[78] Even Wostenholm's factory at about this time had still not fully emancipated itself from the time-honoured arrangements: one cutler recalled that 'it used to be all small shops, it was a big place but all small shops. Each individual person, let's say a father and son would work in a shop on their own and the only time they got visitors was when somebody opened the door and if they didn't want them to see owt they put it away.'[79]

The US industry, on the other hand, was becoming increasingly concentrated. In 1931 a survey of five categories of cutlery concerns showed 33 firms producing 81 percent of the total output. Three producers made 72 percent of the straight razors; eight producers, 86 percent of the pocketknives; and six producers, 90 percent of the pocket-knives with fixed blades.[80] Rare, almost to the point of extinction, was the outworker in America, though some one-man shops still operated in 1935. Grinding, forging, and hafting were all mechanised factory processes, though manual operations were occasionally retained for high-grade cutlery.[81]

In America there was increased interest in the cheaper kinds of stainless alloys with low carbon content and in stainless iron. The quality was poorer; the material was not as hard as forged, heat-treated steel; the grinding process less refined; and the resulting product less sharp and durable. But these knives outsold better products in the 1930s, because they retailed at ten to thirty-five cents. When shown a selection of the cheaper American articles one of Wostenholm's New York agents admitted that if he had his time over again he would sell cheap goods.[82]

The Sheffield horn industry was to be hit by the increasing use of plastics, not only as handles for cheap kitchen ware, but also for some more expensive products.[83] The synthetics were cheaper and easier to make, were more durable, and could be cemented firmly to the blade. Plastics were also being used to make whole knives such as those for fancy bread, fruit and paring.

In the depression the Sheffield cutlers were particularly vulnerable. Table, kitchen and pocket-knife firms were the more seriously threatened, for here cheap goods were more readily substitutable for expensive ones, and the group of consumers involved was less keen in its evaluation of quality. Most Sheffield blades were individually hot-forged after being milled, a process that could require as many as a hundred operations. The extent to which the US had abandoned this kind of handiwork can be gauged from a Tariff Commission Report. By 1935 nearly 90 percent of the pocket-knife producers had substituted cold-rolled, stamped blades for the more expensive forged kinds.[84] Competition was then intensified by the ease with which new firms could enter the market without the traditional techniques. Some munitions firms, such as Remington and Winchester, turned their excess capacity during the immediate postwar recession to the production of pocket-knives and razor blades.[85] Many cutleries began to make their own handles and some handle-makers became cutlers.

Just as the invention of the steel pen in the early nineteenth century had destroyed Sheffield's penknife trade, so economic and social trends in America in the interwar period affected the pocket-knife industry. The Tariff Report highlighted how demand had been affected by changes in personal habits, such as the widespread use of pencil sharpeners, mechanical pencils, and pocket manicure tools. Other factors of importance were the increasing ratio of clerical to manual workers, the changing activities of the youth of the country, and the small replacement demand for the more expensive knives. Colver remarked, in 1931: 'We have a more or less world-wide trade and we find that almost everywhere the ordinary vest pocket-knife has to a considerable extent gone out of fashion.'[86]

So cheap products sold readily, and the selling of them in bulk, often through advertising, weakened the specialised producers. The growth of large wholesaling organisations and chain jobbers, mail-order houses, and large department and retail chain stores further heightened competition, which was to sharpen during the depression. The 1920s also brought systems of cost and inventory control which helped cutlery firms tailor their production to estimated market needs. In the pocket-knife trade, which had the greatest product differentiation, the 300 basic patterns of the industry were reduced to 140 by an agreement sponsored by the Department of Commerce's Division of Simplified Practice, but it is likely that the depression and the nature of the demand would have accomplished this anyway. Whereas a Sheffield firm might boast of holding a stock of 4,000 patterns, at Camillus all but a small fraction of the business at this time was done in knives made from only a dozen designs.[87]

This is the background to Wostenholm's declining New York agency trade in the 1920s. Once the firm's plans for manufacturing knives in America had been abandoned, its ambitions there became decidedly modest. A memorandum from New York in 1932 suggested that it would 'be best to have nothing in America except samples [and] to let the customers import themselves and pay their own duty'.[88]

In 1932 the company admitted that the American turnover was insufficient to justify the maintenance of a New York office (Table 10: 1). 'The

Table 10:1 *Wostenholm's New York agency transactions (£)*

	Sales	Gross profit	Net loss
1922	23,194	4,012	1,153 (profit)
1923	21,802	2,212	134
1923 (Dec)	18,930	2,793	1,748
1924	24,803	5,920	53
1925	19,587	3,959	1,536
1926	18,922	4,466	1,575
1927	16,825	3,797	1,057
1928	17,973	3,692	576
1929	15,230	3,489	969
1930	7,848	1,506	2,093

Source: SCL Wos 145. Summaries Book, pp. 67–8.

duties on our goods are so high, the expenses so heavy and the sales so small that the office has not paid for us for some years', remarked the New York agency.[89]

The Fordney McCumber Tariff undoubtedly played its part (along with other factors) in raising the price of the English product:

Most of our customers are very small buyers, who buy just a small quantity of our goods in order to have an English line if it is asked for. They sell very little because contending our goods bring a slow sale they always put on 100% profit. Now 100% profit on our Sheffield prices, plus 100% duty and plus 20% for New York office or expenses or merchants profit, plus the 100% that the dealer adds makes them, of course, exceedingly expensive.[90]

The reputation of Sheffield cutlery now counted for less. 'I appreciate that your cutlery is of a better grade than anything that has been made over here', wrote one observer, 'but the fact remains that the major part of the users consider that American cutlery serves the purpose.'[91] Wostenholm's products were being increasingly excluded from the US market not only by the tariff but also by the sheer impossibility of producing goods at American prices.

Towards the end of the twenties economic conditions were not on the firm's side. 'American cutlery manufacturers in spite of the protective tariff are having a bad time', reported the New York agency in 1931,[92] and several subsequent communications chronicle the deteriorating business situation. 'The cutlery business is very bad', wrote an agent to Wostenholm's, 'and I doubt whether any of our salesmen are making expenses selling the various cutlery lines they handle.'[93] Added Colver:

General conditions ... are very unsatisfactory, the cutlery business particularly.

Everyone is complaining. In recent years about a dozen fairly large American pocket-knife manufacturers have closed down, and their machinery has been scrapped. In the pocket-knife business the only old manufacturers left seem to be Landers, Castor, Ulster, Schrade, Robeson, Utica and New York Knife Co. Schrade is probably doing best, but he is only working half-time ... [and] although Utica are doing a business, they are making no money, and I am not surprised to hear it. [I was shown] some 2-blade 3¼″ jack-knives, fully polished that sell at $1.50 per doz., some rather larger ones that sell at $3.00 and a 4-blade scout knife they sell at $4.00. We couldn't make knives at these prices in Sheffield. As so few of the old firms are left, one might think the situation would have some hope, but Remington have come into the business and are making a lot of pocket-knives at little or no profit, and in addition two firms have recently started in Providence, the Imperial Cutlery Co and the Colonial Cutlery Co, and they are flooding the country with very poor goods. Very few good pocket-knives are being sold, so few that the New York retail cutlers seem to have ceased to display them in their windows.[94]

By 1931 Wostenholm cutlery was being cleared at a loss and the main question for the firm was how to reduce the stock in New York to a reasonable level and then sell the agency to any interested party.[95] Colver attended to the details on his trip to America in 1931, when he also took the opportunity to tour the Remington and Schrade plants, observing the latest improvements and enquiring about the purchasing and licensing of machines. After attempts through official channels to find another British hardware firm that was interested in sharing a New York office,[96] in April 1931 Wiebusch & Hilger took over Wostenholm's dwindling trade[97] – so ending over a hundred years of American trading.

11

INNOVATION AND ADAPTATION:
THE EVIDENCE OF THE SAWMAKING TRADES

But it was not the mere fact of [Americans] manufacturing those [tools] that so much caused our uneasiness as that, from the first, there was a superior intelligence brought to bear upon the design, shape and finish of the articles manufactured. If, for instance, it was an axe brought under our notice, we observed that it had been constructed with a scientific regard to the purpose for which it would be used; if also the object examined was a hay fork, that strength and neatness of form, combined with the utmost lightness, had been obtained by the use of steel, instead of iron, as a raw material.

> A Sheffield agent quoted in the *Iron Age* 18
> (19 October 1876), p. 17.

Foreign competition is playing – (well, we won't say what) – with the English colonial trade. English agricultural implements, axes, shovels, forks, picks, hoes, etc., 'ain't in it' with the Americans. Disston's saws are preferred – although 20 percent dearer.

> Australian letter quoted in the *Sheffield Daily Telegraph*,
> 10 January 1885.

Despite the importance of iron and steel, wood was America's chief natural resource and major component of all things manufactured or constructed by hand well into the latter half of the nineteenth century.[1] At the Great Exhibition of 1851 the examiners noted: 'In America ... machinery for working wood is even more largely employed than with us ... The style of framing and designing these machines will at once betray their Transatlantic origin, and exhibits great ingenuity, simplicity and fitness for the purpose.'[2] Considerable advances had also been made in American woodworking tools by mid-century.[3] American axemakers such as

144

Douglas and Collins were successfully exporting to foreign markets as early as the 1840s.[4] Later, one Sheffielder remarked that 'the trade in chisels, axes, adzes, and in a great measure in saws, with the exception of one or two descriptions, was leaving Sheffield, and had gone to the United States'.[5]

The first saws of any kind manufactured in the US appear to have been made by William Rowland, who started business in Philadelphia in 1806.[6] Aaron Nichols set up a small plant in Philadelphia in 1823, and in 1828 Richard Hoe in New York City established the manufacture of circular saws from Sheffield steel. In 1836 William Johnson began producing saws in Philadelphia and it was there that Henry Disston learned his trade. Philadelphia emerged as an important sawmaking centre during the 1830s and 1840s, when numerous small industries were founded. In Massachusetts, Charles Griffiths, who had gained experience in England, and arrived in Boston in 1830, established a saw factory in West Cambridge. The firm, later known as Welch & Griffiths, was said to have successfully met the competition from imported goods.[7] In Middletown, New York, Wheeler, Madden & Bakewell, founded in 1853, specialised in machine-ground circular saws and advertised its products as 'at least equal to any manufactured in America or England'.[8] Saw manufacture was conducted in New England by small firms such as the Fisherville Saw Co of Penacook, New Hampshire, and by large ones such as the Simonds Manufacturing Co of West Fitchburg, Massachusetts, which established branch plants throughout the country and in Canada.[9] As population and industry expanded westwards, saw companies were established in the Midwest; E. C. Atkins, of Indianapolis, was an important producer of handsaws for the carpenter and large saws for the lumbering and sawmill industries.

Until American developments the design of the saw had remained virtually unchanged, and its fabrication represented the result of many centuries of experience. The numerous operations involved in the making of a saw – shaping, hardening and tempering, grinding, smithing, and tooth setting – demanded great accuracy of hand and eye, besides great physical strength.[10] The dependence on human skill and the fact that the saws were used under such diverse conditions complicated the manufacturing problem.[11] In its early days, therefore, the American saw industry, as the Hoe correspondence makes clear, relied heavily upon Sheffield's traditional expertise.[12] Some of the smaller firms found it impossible to manage without English sawmakers. James Wood & Sons, at Valley Forge, Pennsylvania, wrote to one customer: 'As regards saws we are not manufacturing any at present, as our saw maker is now in England.'[13] Nevertheless, saw technology in America diverged rapidly from its Sheffield counterpart.

Richard Hoe (1812–86) began by pioneering the mass-production of circular saws from about 1828. By 1840 he was writing to a customer in North Carolina:

We have considerable experience in the use of cir[cular] saws, having an extensive machine shop & foundry as well as saw manufactory. We have used circulars for 15 years passed. The largest circular saw ever made either here or abroad in one plate is 48 in. in diameter; of these we have made several.[14]

Examining the mechanical problems of sawmaking, Hoe had soon developed a device for toothing saws with a steam-powered punch, almost neglecting to have it patented.[15] Shortly afterwards, in 1840, the firm built a machine for grinding long saws in which a leaden wheel was rotated above the saw and fed with a mixture of emery, sand and soapy water. Machines for grinding circular saws were patented in 1842: they held the saws securely to a revolving face-plate whilst a leaden wheel travelled back and forth across the face. These were the first machines ever used for grinding saws in any commercial quantity and gave encouraging results.[16] Hoe informed Sanderson's that the saws were 'all perfectly true and even as it is possible to make anything'.[17] Sanderson's even bought some of the larger circular saws, telling the New Yorkers that they were very much wanted.[18]

Improved machines for grinding circular saws, patented by E. W. Hubbard in 1860 and Stephen D. Tucker in 1868–9, were installed by Hoe's in the 1860s and these were used throughout most of the nineteenth century.[19] They complemented machines designed by Dodge and Blake which ground long saws on revolving cylinders. The latter were in use for many years until their replacement by a system of grinding both sides of the saw simultaneously by passing it between two grindstones.[20]

Hoe's enhanced its reputation with the inserted-tooth saw, which was developed to overcome the drawback that saw steel was not as tough as tool steel. The idea of replacing teeth was an old one, but, as Hoe warned, 'unless the teeth are well inserted ... they are dangerous'.[21] In 1859, however, Nathan W. Spaulding in Sacramento discovered that curved sockets held the teeth securely and firmly.[22] Patents were granted to Warren P. Miller in 1866–8 for a further improvement which made the sockets in the plate a portion of a true circle with V-shaped edges, into which the grooved inserted-tooth slotted. By this method teeth could be fitted together, accurately and cheaply, by machinery. Hoe's bought an interest in these patents in 1869 and the necessary machinery and tools were installed.[23] Sockets and teeth were all made to standard gauges, so that the fitting could be done swiftly.[24] By 1870 Hoe was reporting that inserted-tooth saws 'have proved a great success and are having a large sale'.[25] In the mid-1870s the cutting part of the inserted-tooth saw was again improved by the insertion of expendable chisel-bits. In 1877 such saws were 'being used in all sections of the country with great success'.[26]

By mid-century Hoe's had moved well ahead of most of its rivals and was reaping the benefits of increased mechanisation: annual sales in circular saw blades, mill saws, pit saws, and cross-cut saws, amounted to $140,000 and were still growing.[27]

A similar pattern of invention and mechanisation is also discernible at Disston's, the Philadelphia saw factory founded by English-born Henry Disston (1819–78) in 1840, which became the largest enterprise of its kind in the world.[28] Like Hoe, Disston acquired labour and raw materials from Sheffield. Operatives from Sheffield were hired to superintend the extensive use of machinery in the saw and file departments;[29] and English melters and rollers were on hand when the American built the first important crucible saw steel plant in the US in about 1855.[30]

Henry Disston made other notable contributions. Sometime before 1866 he visited Paris where he learned of French advances in bandsawing machinery. He returned to the US with two of the machines, the first to be installed in America, and later added two more of his own manufacture. The machines were a solution to the problem of turning out enough 'sawed-out' work for handles: two men with the old methods produced about 40 dozen handles per day, whilst with the new device the figure was closer to 165 dozen. The machines were perfected in time for the Philadelphia Centennial in 1876 where the six-inch wide band saws exhibited by Disston were looked upon as great curiosities.[31]

In the late 1860s Disston produced inserted-tooth saws and began re-designing familiar products. In 1874 the skewback saw was introduced by removing a piece from the topside of the tool, which according to Disston gave better balance and lessened weight.[32] It was to be widely imitated. With cross-cut saws Disston used raker teeth, an invention that had striking effects on productivity in the lumber camps.[33]

The new saws were manufactured with a high degree of mechanisation. When Henry Disston began making saws one man produced five dozen blades per day; with a machine the figure was 140 dozen, and the operator also ran two other machines on other work.[34] By the 1880s machines had replaced many of the old hand-processes. In Disston's works small handsaw teeth were rucked out at the rate of 500 per minute by a revolving cutter in an automatic machine. A handsaw with 115 teeth could be toothed in less than two minutes, and an operator could turn out two dozen 24-inch saws in eight hours.[35] In the production of circular saws machinery had equally dramatic results. One man with a circular saw-grinding machine could produce five or six saws a day, while the older, more strenuous methods required two men to do one saw in the same time, and even then it was said the results did not approach the perfection of the machine-ground saw.[36] Machines for hardening, tempering and filing increased Disston's advantages in productivity.[37]

The result was that by the end of the 1870s Disston's was the world leader in sawmaking. So great was the demand that Disston had difficulty in supplying orders and major extensions were necessary at Tacony, in Philadelphia. Increased production led to spin-offs, such as a filemaking plant to supply Disstons grinders. After 1874 one of the Disstons resided permanently in London where he ran a successful hardware business which stocked the firm's goods.[38] By the end of the 1870s, to the consternation of the town's sawmakers, Disston's saws were even selling in Sheffield.[39]

In England's centre of saw manufacture little progress had been made by this date in mechanising the traditional processes or in improving the old designs.[40] During the 1870s and 1880s a few sawmakers installed machinery, largely due, it was said, to workmen returning from the US with fresh ideas.[41] Beardshaw & Sons was the first firm to introduce an American grinding machine, which was later adapted to glazing.[42] Spear & Jackson, which introduced machinery for grinding circular saws in 1851, and Taylor Bros (both prominent American traders destined to suffer severely at the hands of their US rivals) made extensive use of grinding and toothing machines by 1880.[43] Generally, however, hand-techniques held sway, producing goods which, as the Sheffield price lists show, remained very conservative in comparison with those of American competitors.[44]

Why had such a huge gap in technology opened up? Superficially, a good case can be made out for American inventiveness. By mid-century over 300 US saw patents had been issued, especially for shaping and reset-ting saw teeth.[45] Most of the ideas, however, had been around for some time. Benjamin Cummings, of New York, is credited with making the first American circular saw, but England had one dating 1777, the work of Samuel Miller, and it is claimed that similar saws were in use in Holland a century before. Circulars were in regular use by the British Navy for cut-ting ship blocks at the beginning of the nineteenth century.[46] The band-saw, too, owed its origin to European developments. An Englishman, Newberry, designed the first model, though it never progressed beyond a patent specification, and the idea was perfected in France by M. Perin. Bandsaws were taken up in England for cutting metal, but they were not generally adopted, largely because the workmen were, apparently, not disposed to acquire the necessary dexterity.[47] Sheffield was reputed to be supplying the French with steel, though, apart from the notable exception of Moses Eadon & Sons, there does not appear to have been any general attempt to begin manufacturing the bandsaw in the town.[48] Wrote one of the compilers of a Disston history: 'Considering the great extent to which the bandsawing machine is used today, it is curious to note how this important invention, said to have originated in 1808, lay dormant for nearly half a century, and even for some years after that time very little was accomplished towards making it a commercial success.'[49]

The US, however, was particularly suited to mastering saw technology. One Sheffield merchant in the early nineteenth century noted 'how expert the people are with the saw and the axe'.[50] Another Sheffielder, a sawmaker from Spear & Jackson, who visited New York in the 1860s, was impressed 'above all with the vastness of the lumber industry'.[51] These individuals recognised the all-pervading use of wood in the nineteenth-century American economy. By mid-century the drive to exploit these huge resources was well underway and by 1860 about one-quarter of the original forest cover in the eastern half of the US may have been eliminated.[52] As one official American account observed: 'saw making was a particularly favourable business for applying labour-saving machinery to all concerned. Our country was new and the use for this implement in preparing lumber and in building has been enormous.'[53]

Meanwhile, very few sawmills existed in England, and as late as 1825 an American visitor, Zachariah Allen, was struck by the prevalence of hand sawyers and the almost complete absence of sawmills. Steam sawmills, such as the one Allen viewed in Manchester, were the object of violent opposition and repeated incendiary attacks.[54]

The extent of the American market 'led to investigations with respect to saws such as the requirements of [England] were not likely to call forth'.[55] Sheffield makers, therefore, found themselves exporting a product that was imperfectly adapted to the needs of the US consumer.[56] Recalled one American: 'In times gone by the English factories have sent saws into this market which have not been at all satisfactory.'[57] Sheffield criteria for a good saw were entirely different from the American. In England, where high finish and economy were the primary considerations, American saws, even in the 1920s, were described as 'monstrosities'.[58] American inserted-tooth saws, which required a wide saw kerf, were notoriously wasteful. There was also a laxity in the US over technical details in the running of sawmaking machinery, such as 'packing', which resulted in saws of much stouter gauge having to be used, with a consequent loss of power and material. English engineers were as perplexed at this wasteful conservatism, as the Americans were at the tardiness of their counterparts to exploit new ideas.[59]

Machines became an important adjunct to meeting the American demand. The nature of this mechanisation, however, has been frequently misunderstood. It does not appear to have been the case, for example, that US makers like Hoe began using machines primarily to obviate high labour costs. The cost of labour was certainly an important factor, and there was a wide differential between Sheffield and American wages.[60] But developments at Hoe's show that machinery did not dispense with the need for skilled labour, especially skilled Sheffield labour. This was partly due to the nature of sawmaking apparatus. Far from being models 'of early automation for the interrelationship of moving parts',[61] the first American sawmaking machines were remarkably crude. Witness Tucker's description of the Hubbard device for grinding saws:

In machines made by Mr. Hubbard, the saw was placed on the end of a mandrel on a travelling carriage and grasped between a pair of driving rollers which caused it to revolve slowly in front of a grindstone, and as the carriage was moved back and forth, by hand, in contact with the stone, the saw was ground, it being held against the stone by a fixed support behind it.[62]

The key words are, 'by hand'. Productivity was undoubtedly increased, but only the most skilled sawmaker could have worked the machine, even after it was improved by Hoe.[63] As Comparato admits, in the 1840s at the Hoe Works, despite unprecedented mechanisation, there were still eighteen operations in making a saw blade, most of them manual.[64] In 1880, an official report on saw factories observed: 'Often all or nearly all of the operatives are skilled.'[65]

In other words, the technological sophistication of the American saw industry must not be exaggerated; at mid-century many of the smaller factories remained firmly wedded to the old manual techniques.[66] Even in the twentieth century Disston's was still extolling the 'skilled workmanship' put into the material and the product.[67] Photographs of the Philadelphia works taken after 1900 show that the skilled smither, grinder, and toother had still not been dispensed with:[68] hence Disston's commitment to the apprentice system.[69]

As important as the design of American machines was the pace of their introduction. English manufacturers visiting America in the 1900s found that: 'Labour-saving machinery is widely used everywhere and is encouraged by the unions and welcomed by the men, because experience has shown them that in reality machinery is their best friend.'[70] No such attitude prevailed in Sheffield. 'None of your machines here are raising any interest', wrote Charles Sanderson to Hoe in 1839.[71] On other occasions feelings ran higher. When John Wheatman, who had earlier been employed by Hoe, tried to introduce a machine at his Sheffield works for grinding long saws, part of his factory was blown up in 1860 at the instigation of William Broadhead, the infamous secretary of the Saw Grinders' Union.[72] James Chesterman, who founded the Sheffield hardware firm of the same name, also encountered union opposition when he attempted to install a machine for grinding circular saws.[73]

The traditional view is that these problems were not encountered in the US, though, again, the evidence would suggest that some qualifications need to be made. 'None of Mr. Disston's workmen ever destroyed a machine, but no improvement has ever been regarded with favor', commented one official report.[74] On several occasions, notably over his attempts to introduce the steam-hammer and the bandsaw, Henry Disston faced opposition from his men.[75] But labour problems usually proved short-lived, since rapidly rising demand mitigated the difficulties. At Disston's it was said that the demand for saws increased so rapidly that, notwithstanding the labour economised in making them, it had been necessary to increase the number of workmen.[76] Most of the displaced labour was eventually recalled. More importantly, although the price of the product was sharply reduced, wages rose.[77]

Without wishing to underestimate American inventiveness, rapidly rising demand for a cheapening product and increasing wages, which overcame union opposition, seem to have been the critical factors in determining the success of the American saw industry.

Official statistics record the growth of sawmaking in the US. The 1860 Census of Manufactures lists 42 American saw factories in 11 states, with an annual product of $1,237,000; in 1830 the total value of saws manufactured was about $5,000.[78] Despite these advances, in 1866, 17,057 handsaws, 429 dozen back-saws, and quantities of cross-cut and mill saws were imported by the US from England.[79] However, firms such as Hoe's and Disston's rapidly made up the leeway. By 1877 the value of imported saws and other tools from England had dropped to only $8,160 (the 1866 figure was $108,478).[80] Ten years later no saws were tabulated in the US import accounts. Indeed, by 1896, saws and tools exported from the US totalled $2,197,450, and $229,489 of that amount were destined for the UK; only Australasia was a more important American market.[81]

It was in Australasia that Sheffield manufacturers felt the full force of

American competition. The US invasion of these 'neutral' markets generated an enormous amount of comment in the leading English hardware
journal the *Ironmonger* in the late 1870s.[82] Though many of the articles
and editorials expressed confidence in the ability of English makers to
compete with their rivals, there was also the underlying suspicion that
American tools were superior in design and adaptation.[83] The way in
which Americans adapted tool patterns in neutral markets was 'positively
astonishing' declared the *Sheffield Independent*'s US correspondent.[84] One
Auckland dealer, emphasising the superiority of American cross-cut saws,
argued that 'unless the English manufacturers bestir themselves I believe
the time is not far distant when [the Americans] will monopolize [the
trade]. Do you ask how is this, when we can undersell them? It is simply
because their goods are better and more adapted to our requirements.'[85]

Sheffield sawmakers themselves testified to the success of the Americans. Business records relating to Spear & Jackson, one of the city's most
distinguished sawmaking firms, offer illuminating comments on the state
of the American sawmaking art. The company was founded in the eighteenth century, and became known under its present name from about
1830 when Samuel Jackson was taken into partnership by John Spear.[86]
The firm had acquired a large US trade in the early nineteenth century,
built up largely by J. B. Jackson, which declined abruptly in the 1870s.[87]
Thereafter, colonial markets supplied most of the company's custom.

In 1905 Spear & Jackson's managing-director, Major Leslie Jackson
Coombe (1883–1944), made a business trip to Australia. In his diary he
noted: 'Disston and Atkins have done everything possible to wipe out all
other competitors in this line [saws] and have pretty well succeeded.' 'Our
Cross-cuts are not up to the American standard, especially as regards
straightness and tension... Although our Cross-cuts come out cheaper
than the Americans, yet somehow or other the American saws seem to be
better value.' Coombe described the circular saw-grinding machine at
Disston's, which was superior to the one at Spear & Jackson's. The belly
on American handsaws was better, and Spear & Jackson's butcher's bow
saws 'were not as good a shape as Disston's and are dearer'. As regards
interchangeable sets: 'Our set is not quite the same as Disston's, especially
in the width of the blades. I am sending one of Disston's sets home.' Due
to American competition, one retailer told Coombe that Spear & Jackson's goods had gone 'right out of the market'.[88]

By the early twentieth century it was agreed that 'the American makers
have got so firm a hold on the world's markets that the Sheffield makers
cannot hope to overtake them'.[89] Some did try, though, and Tyzack's
were among those firms which mechanised to compete with the Ameri-

cans before 1914.[90] The Spear & Jackson management also made efforts to catch the Americans. The First World War helped the firm expand and rationalise its production and the Ministry of Munitions sanctioned wartime capital expenditure of about £7,000. The most important investment was the electric steel plant, completed in 1918, which included one of the first electric arc furnaces in England to manufacture saw steel.[91] The end of hostilities and the postwar reorganisation ushered in a slump, but the chairman believed that they had 'effectively maintained [their] organisation and extended [their] research facilities for doing a larger trade'.

As well as the extended facilities of the Steel Department, at the end of 1920, after much research, Spear & Jackson had introduced a range of 'Neverbend' tools, spades, forks, and shovels, which had been a striking success. To gear itself for greater output the firm absorbed the sawmakers Sanderson & Drabble; came to an arrangement with the Sheffield Alloy Steel Co, Rotherham, for the supply of steel ingots; and acquired the toolmaking concern of E. & W. Lucas at Dronfield for the expansion of its spade, fork, and shovel department.[92] During 1925 the conversion of Spear & Jackson's rolling mill from steam to electric drive was completed. The company recognised 'the pressing need of manufacturers to increase the country's foreign trade by works efficiency and organisation'. The overhauling of plant and working conditions continued through 1927 and 1928, and the firm looked forward 'with confidence to good results occurring whenever the demand for our goods revives, as we are in a position to cope with greater output'.

With the modernisation went an increased interest in foreign markets. 'The directors are appointing agents and representatives in more of the foreign markets and wherever there is a prospect of trade there will be some representative of our house.' Great success was achieved in the Far East, especially in Japan, where there was a 'splendid trade' in circular and other saws. The demand from Japan became even greater during the reconstruction after the earthquake in 1923. Organisation was maintained and increased in India, and there were business trips by the firm's directors to South Africa and Australasia. In 1930 a Government Trade Mission to South America was headed by Spear & Jackson's chairman, Arthur K. Wilson. American competition was felt in all these areas, but generally the mood was optimistic: 'We believe our buyers will appreciate the good and lasting tools we place at their disposal.'

In 1924 Spear & Jackson, no doubt fondly recalling its once prodigious American West coast trade, acquired a controlling interest in a factory in Vancouver as 'part of a carefully planned scheme for carrying the campaign right into the enemy's country, as the business in saws on the Pacific

coast was formerly entirely in the hands of American-owned concerns'.[93]
For a five-year period from July 1924, Spear & Jackson agreed not to 'sell
or supply circular saws for wood, band saws, frame saws, machine plane
saws and other goods for use in saw mills to any person or firm in British
Columbia other than the Aetna Saw Works Ltd, and will not carry on
business there in competition with [it]'. The Vancouver works was not
merely an agency; it also machined Sheffield sheet steel and executed all
the finishing operations, which allowed the modification of saws to suit
North American tastes.

Spear & Jackson soon made an impact in Canada. 'Its rather amusing
to think', wrote Leslie Coombe, 'what a "how-d'you do" little Aetna
Works has caused'.[94] Sheffield prices were low enough to bring complaints from Canadian and American manufacturers, such as Simonds.
There was a price-cutting war amongst sawmakers in Canada in the
1920s and Spear & Jackson was asked to join an association of mill toolmakers, which would presumably set prices, but the firm held aloof. 'I
think you may take it that we shall not join any association of saw manufacturers over here', wrote Coombe. Instead, more traditional methods
were to be relied upon such as Coombe's personal visits in which he
stressed 'up-to-dateness in plant, patterns and finish'.

It might be presumed that Spear & Jackson, with its modernised plant
and long experience of trading in the US, would be able to meet Canadian
and American manufacturers on something like equal terms. Coombe,
however, on his numerous visits to American sawmaking plants in the
1920s and early 1930s, found to his dismay that the Americans were
moving rapidly ahead in the techniques of mass-production and that Sheffield was still some distance behind.

The differences were not so much in general technique. On a visit to
Simond's factory in Chicago, Coombe was asked about Spear & Jackson's methods. He replied that they were very similar in design – only the
details were different. But as he was to add later: 'The difference between
their practice and ours is evidently one of detail and in that detail they
have it every time.' Coombe filled page after page of his letter-books in an
attempt to provide Sheffield with the 'detail' of American methods.

In the larger works steel sheets came from outside; Atkins and Hoe's,
for example, bought sheets from the old Jessop's branch in Washington,
Pennsylvania. Most of the Americans had also followed Disston's lead in
installing electric furnaces to supplement their output. Extensive use was
made of rolling machinery, enabling firms such as Jessop's 'to get a wonderfully good finish on their sheets'.

But it was the extensive mechanisation of the final stages of production which made the greatest impression on Coombe. At Simond's factory he commented: 'The most important thing I learned here was that they are rapidly developing the tension *Rolling and Machine Hammering of Circular Saws.*' The automatic hammer, which was used for the abnormal places in the saw, where the tension was uneven, could do the major portion of what Spear & Jackson's Vancouver workers did by hand. Productivity was increased. At Simonds:

Already one man can *smith* 32–48" saws a day: Also, their piece work rate for *smithing, hammering and blocking* a 42" shingle saw is 17 cts the lot.
Anyway, I now know it can be done and our plates come out at least as flat as theirs, so we can do it, but I doubt whether any Sheffield saw maker will help us put it through.

At Hoe's factory, New York, there was a similar reliance on machines: 'They have a most complicated M/C which automatically mills 8 shanks per minute and makes a very good job indeed.' But even the work that was done manually was done at a much greater rate than in Sheffield. The Americans changed saw teeth so rapidly that Coombe said he could not see them. The result at Hoe's was an output of 7–8 million teeth a year, of which some 2–3 million were exported.

Machinery reduced the training period for workers. At Atkins plant in Indianapolis: 'a boy who started smithing 8 months ago, smithed 5 saws ... in one day and hammered one repair', whilst 'a man of about 27 years *smithed* 8–42" shingle saws ready for grinding and hammered 1 repair in 8 hours'. These are 'facts' wrote Coombe despondently, and none of the men knew they were being watched – it was just an ordinary day's work. The Sheffielder concluded: 'Our saw makers will have to learn from this side. They seem to me to be hopelessly out of date.' So in 1925, to help reorganise Sheffield methods and start up new lines, Spear & Jackson invited an experienced American grinder from Atkins to travel to England for a possible year's stay.

The success of the Americans explains why Spear & Jackson paid far more attention to the Canadian market. Generally, the firm had difficulty in competing with American prices. The Sheffield products sold well enough on occasions, even attracting a promising demand in Pittsburgh, where Coombe visited Kaufmann's 'Big Store' in 1925. 'We shall get more business from these people', he wrote to Sheffield, 'Our spades sold well and no complaints. So did the rakes, etc.' But the Americans dominated their domestic market. The company considered trading with the eastern states through Montreal, but felt this could only be done if products were sold directly to the retailers, thus bypassing the jobbers.

These difficulties increased during the depression when the firm had to cope with what Coombe described as the 'slaughtered prices' of American makers. Spear & Jackson's New York agency under J. S. McKenzie emphasised that they had only begun to touch the fringe of what could be done if they lowered prices a little. But, as Coombe pointed out, Spear & Jackson's prices in the US were already lower than anywhere else in the world and were barely enabling the firm to recoup its costs. Explained Coombe to his Sheffield directors:

> You have to take 25% and 20% off the prices shown (i.e. 6" – $1,00, 7" $1.25, 8" $1.40, 10" $1.80) to get at the prices at which the Jobbers buy them, because the retailer reckons to make 25% and Jobber 20%.
> After that there is 20% Duty and McK[enzie]'s 10% to say nothing of carriage and freight. We should get about 2/6d for an 8". Sounds hopeless to me.
> I cannot see how McK[enzie] makes our Agency pay.

But it appeared that Spear & Jackson weathered the depression at least as well as its competitors. Coombe reported from Philadelphia in 1934 that 'things are not too bad here, in spite of the exchange and a 20% duty – we are still selling saws to America'.

Spear & Jackson's Vancouver subsidiary also performed well in the early 1930s,[95] and this may have influenced the firm's decision to acquire the controlling interest (about 75 percent of the $13,200 issued capital) in Spear & Jackson (US) Inc, in Tacoma, Washington, in 1935.[96] The company could thus make use of Coombe's extensive range of personal contacts with American sawmakers. He seems to have been allowed complete access to their workshops – a sign perhaps of American confidence – and to have been provided with detailed information as to the processes used. The help was sometimes mutual and at Hoe's Coombe discussed Sheffield's methods of casting and promised to send samples. Other American manufacturers wanted a closer liaison. In 1925 Simonds was interested in some form of amalgamation with Spear & Jackson with a factory at Ecclesfield run on American lines under dual control. In Columbia, Ohlen Bishop Ltd (founded by an Englishman), was also interested in Spear & Jackson as a possible alternative to Jessop's as a supplier of steel sheets. Negotiations were opened with another sawmaker, the Oldham New York Saw Works, in 1925, to discuss the possible takeover by Sheffield of the ailing American concern.[97]

Nothing transpired from any of these proposals.[98] In the twenties, Spear & Jackson contented itself with developing the Canadian market. But the American connection was still crucial to its success, especially when it came to imitating American patterns for the Canadian lumber camps. Like Wostenholm's, the Sheffield firm showed no hesitation in learning from the new masters of the trade. Its success in doing so can be shown by the continued existence of the subsidiaries in Vancouver and Oregon.

12

MEN *VERSUS* MACHINES:
THE STORY OF THE FILE

America must and will for ever be wholly dependent upon the
Sheffield file makers for good workmanship and quality of
files.

> A Sheffield correspondent (John Radley) in the US,
> *Sheffield Independent*, 28 June 1856.

Despite some American success towards achieving a system of interchangeable parts in certain industries, in both the US and Britain in the
early nineteenth century the file remained the major instrument of pre-
cision.[1] At that time file cutting was a purely manual operation – simple in
technique but complicated in operation and extremely laborious. All that
the file-cutter needed was a hammer, chisel, lead block and reasonable
light. The worker sat with his knees at either side of his 'stock', or pillar,
into which was inserted a steel block known as a 'stiddy'. The file was laid
on the stiddy, usually with a block of lead beneath to lessen the recoil and
to prevent the file being damaged. The file was then cut by a series of very
swift blows, the rate of cutting ranging from 70 to 80 strokes per minute.
So practiced were the hand and eye of the file cutter that adjustments
could be made for even the slightest variation in the quality of the steel. As
an example of the Sheffield cutter's skill, one journal in 1844 instanced:

a file about ten inches long, flat on one side and round on the other: the flat side is
cut with a hundred and twenty teeth to an inch, so that there are about twelve
hundred teeth on that side: the round side has such an extent of curvature, that it
required eighteen rows of cuts to compass it: each little cut on this side is not much
above a twentieth of an inch in length: and the number is thus so great, that for the
whole file there are twenty-two thousand cuts, each made with a separate blow of
the hammer, and the cutting tool being shifted after each blow![2]

Once cut, the file was hardened, after prior coating with a saline solution to prevent oxidation. It was then heated to a dull redness in a coke
fire and then plunged perpendicularly into a bath of water. Since the con-

traction was not uniform, further dexterity was required to remedy the twisting of the file. Thorough scouring and washing followed, and a protective layer of oil was added before the final packing and shipment.

There had been numerous attempts to replace hand-techniques with machinery. A file-cutting machine is sketched in Leonardo da Vinci's notebooks, and file-cutting devices were at work in Newcastle upon Tyne in 1765. The French Government, partly to reduce the country's dependence on English and German products, gave encouragement to domestic makers such as Raoul. Swiss manufacturers such as Vautier, Baumer, and Grobet also achieved some success, though their output did little to affect the bulk file trade. Continental developments, however, resulted in the first really practical machine, well designed, and capable of industrial application, invented by Etienne Bernot, of Paris. The machine was built by Greenwood & Batley, of Leeds, and was exhibited in London in 1862.[3]

In the early 1860s there were efforts to find a commercial application for such machines. Amongst the most notable was the Birmingham Patent File Works, which was established to work the Bernot cutting machine. Despite considerable investment the project was abandoned after three years.[4] A similar fate befell the Prestons, who erected a plant near Manchester. The British Patent Hardware Co, of Manchester, with an American mechanic at its head, was also organised at this time, and introduced machines for grinding saws. The devices were soon adapted to manufacture files, initially grinding blanks for handworkers, but they encountered considerable union opposition.

In Sheffield, the centre of file manufacture, little headway was made with machine-cutting. In the 1820s a Sheffield newspaper reported that a 'model of a machine' for reducing the labour in file manufacture had been exhibited to the masters of the local trade, 'but it was neglected'.[5] William Butcher installed an American file-cutting machine in 1852, the invention of Horace Hotchkiss, a Waterbury brass manufacturer, but it was said that the results did not equal those of the hand-cutter, and after spending over £15,000 the experiment was abandoned.[6] In about 1860, Francis Preston of Manchester had invited Sheffield file manufacturers to watch his trials, but they declined his offer of terms.[7] This may have been due to conservatism; on the other hand, Sheffield makers were well aware of the danger to life and property that could result from a confrontation with the unions. So the acknowledged technical success of the Birmingham machines posed an uncomfortable question: 'Can file machines be safely introduced into Sheffield and is there public spirit enough to introduce them; or shall the centres for the trade be allowed to form elsewhere?'[8] That conundrum was answered in 1865, when the first grinding machine

introduced at Turton's Sheaf Works fell foul of the powerful filesmiths'
and filegrinders' societies. Matters reached a head in the great four-month
file strike of 1866 which, although it ostensibly revolved around the
question of a wage advance, was really caused by the threatened installation of machinery.[9] The unions were eventually defeated, but it was a
hollow victory for the employers, since the entrenched attitude against
machinery died hard. In 1884, for example, Osborn's wrote to an American firm: 'We have tried the file grinding machine, but our men here
decline to work at it.'[10] Only after 1890, when it became apparent that
machine-cutting yielded higher wages, did the file unions reluctantly
adapt themselves to new conditions.

'In the United States', wrote the *Iron Age* in 1873, 'file manufacturing,
except such as may be done by the few English outworkers scattered
throughout the country, and who are engaged principally in recutting,
must eventually be done in the peculiarly American way to become a success'.[11] The first file-cutting device was sketched in the *Transactions of the
American Philosophical Society* and several patents were taken out for
filemaking machinery in subsequent years in Massachusetts, New York,
and Pennsylvania.[12] Despite these promising beginnings, however, file
manufacturing made slow progress in the US before the 1860s.[13] In the
Census tables of 1850 and 1860 filemaking did not appear as a distinct industrial item.

In about 1850 the American File Works was erected at Ramapo, New
York, under the direction of a skilled mechanic, and represented the first
American venture into filemaking by machinery. It soon ceased produc-
tion, though. Some years later another file factory was established in
Hartford, Connecticut, with several machines, but this too was a failure.[14]

Sheffielders were involved in these pioneering efforts. John England
founded the Eagle File Works in Pittsburgh in 1840 and so became a pion-
eer of file manufacture west of the Alleghenies.[15] Another experienced
Sheffield mechanic, John T. Cockayne, helped to form King, Cockayne &
Co, which began file manufacture in Middletown, New York, in 1856.[16]
Aaron Chambers, who had been trained in his father's works in Scotland
Street, Sheffield, was introduced by George Chatterton (ca. 1816–1908),
of Providence, Rhode Island, to his first sight of a file-cutting machine.[17]
Chatterton was descended from a long line of English filemakers and had
learned his craft at the Butcher Works. Having begun filemaking in the US
in 1839, he was one of the first manufacturers there to introduce machine-
cut files, which he produced from imported Sheffield cast steel.[18] Due to
its inefficiency and consequent wastage, however, Chatterton's machine
was soon scrapped. Chambers was then employed at the Empire File

Works, Waterbury, Connecticut, as superintendent, where machines designed by Fisher and May were in use. Though an improvement on the Providence devices, they were still too unreliable to compete with the traditional methods.

By 1861 Chambers was involved with a far more significant venture – the Whipple File Co, of Ballardville, Massachusetts, which had been erected in 1858 to house the file-cutting machinery of Milton D. Whipple.[19] Little headway was made initially, but the Civil War, by disrupting English imports, created an upturn in demand and the firm found a ready market without difficulty. The president of the firm, W. P. Pierce, who was characterised as a man of unusual financial ability but lacking practical experience, greatly expanded the works during this period of unnaturally high prices and increased demand.

Machine-cut files by Whipple performed well in trials, though this did not impress Sheffield filers. Wrote one of them:

The idea ... of the Whipple machines being able to produce files equal to those of Messrs. Moss and Gambles, or Greaves and Son, is too much to swallow at once; but, being Yankee buncum, I suppose we must make the attempt. Now, at present, and for some time past, there have been a number of Sheffield file-cutters working at the Whipple Machine Works, and ... I dare pledge my existence that those of the Whipple Co's are hand cut.[20]

The resumption of file imports, however, restored fierce competition to the trade. The Whipple Co responded by erecting steel works (despite the prejudice against American steel) to cheapen costs, and by greatly expanding output. It was here that various technological problems were encountered. According to Chambers the forging machines were a complete failure, and though the cutting machinery was an improvement over previous designs, it did not equal hand-cutting (though Chambers opined that the machines could have been better managed). Despite the large quantity of 'Pembertons' or second-quality files, the company persisted in using the machines until the fall of 1869, when no more capital was available. Production ceased and the capital stock of $700,000 was broken up at public auction at ruinously low prices. The event was greeted with glee by Sheffield filemakers in England and America, where it was seen as a vindication of the superiority of hand-techniques.[21]

Nevertheless, during this period other large companies were erected, the first of which was the American File Co, chartered in the spring of 1863. Substantial brick buildings were constructed at Pawtucket, Rhode Island, under the managership of James S. Brown, a successful manufacturer of cotton machinery. The company obtained file-cutting machines of the Bernot type, and these were operating by the end of 1864. Aaron

Chambers was also employed here and the success of the machines was
such that they, in his words: 'have removed whatever doubts I may have
had as to the practicability of substituting machine for hand labour in the
manufacture of files'. After various improvements, Chambers described
the machines as perfect in use; each machine could produce nine dozen
saw files, of four inches in length, daily, attended by a boy of fourteen
years of age, who was paid 50 cents per day.[22]

In the fall of 1864, however, Brown sold out his interest and withdrew
from the enterprise. Manufacturing continued until 1867 when the uncer-
tainty of the business outlook ended production, the machines being put
into storage and the buildings being adapted to the more lucrative business of cotton cloth manufacture. The firm retained a few hand-workers,
and, when trade improved again some two years later, cheaper wooden
buildings were erected and manufacturing was resumed. The company,
after numerous management changes, was apparently still producing files
in the early 1870s.

The Weed File Co was established in south Boston in the spring of
1866, with large capital. The activities of the enterprise were notable for
the speed and energy with which it put its goods on the market. Cutting
machinery was used extensively, though English workmen were
employed to do the forging and grinding with the old techniques. In April
1868, however, the machinery was sold.

Before the 1860s, then, file manufacture was not amongst American
success stories. A major problem, as the journal *Iron Age* highlighted, was
that the managers had failed entirely to realise the peculiarity of the
file teeth, and the manner in which the files were to be used. The early
file-cutting machines exactly mimicked the actions of the hand-cutter –
except in one important respect. The hand-cutter was able to vary the
distance between the teeth and also their height, whereas the typical
machine-made file had perfect regularity of finish. This had important consequences when the file was passed to the artisan, since
the absence of graduated spacing caused 'chattering' and 'running in
grooves'.

The technical problems were to be overcome by the Nicholson File Co,
of Providence, Rhode Island, which was organised in the spring of 1865
with a capital of $300,000, by William T. Nicholson (1834–93). After
training as a mechanic in Rhode Island, Nicholson had been granted two
patents for file-cutting machinery on 5 April 1864. His lengthy experiments (he is reputed to have completed over forty inventions and produced 400 different kinds of files), like his countryman Henry Disston's,
benefited from European technology: Nicholson travelled to Sheffield

and, after spending some considerable time there, returned with two grinding machines.[23]

The Nicholson File Co grew slowly, but by 1873 it had firmly established itself as the foremost manufacturer of machine-cut files. Nicholson's 'increment-cut file', produced from American steel, which the firm declared was better than the English, began to live down the uncertain reputation of machine-made files. Capacity by 1873 was 700 files per day.[24]

Once the lessons of machine-cutting had been learned, the earlier failures provided a basis for renewed efforts. The Weed and much of the Whipple machinery was purchased by James M. Fessenden, the former superintendent of the Whipple Co, and David Blake, and was used to establish the Western File Works, at Beaver Falls, Pennsylvania, in the fall of 1869. Large buildings were erected and production was inaugurated successfully.[25] Other filemaking centres developed, such as in Paterson, New Jersey, and in Walden, New York.[26]

It was some time, however, before hand-cutting was displaced, even in the US. In the early 1870s it was estimated that three-quarters of American files were hand-cut.[27] Even the more mechanised US factories, such as the New American File Co, Pawtucket, Rhode Island, still retained handcutters in the 1880s for the more difficult files.[28] Again, the Commerce and Navigation accounts are useful in showing the development of the industry. In 1865–6, 1,491,630 files, rasps and floats (valued at $413,505) were imported from England.[29] Ten years later, the Americans had made some progress, since the value of file imports fell to $119,177.[30] But American advances were not quite as impressive as in saw manufacture: in 1885–6, the year in which no tabulations appeared for imported saws, the US continued to import English files to the value of $35,951.[31] By the 1890s, though, American files had conquered the home market, and only small files which required hand-work were imported.[32] Sheffield makers could only compete in some foreign and less developed countries.[33]

In Sheffield it also appeared that machinery had won the day. Well-publicised engineering contests vindicated the machine-cut product and in 1886 a Sheffield newspaper editorial looked forward with certainty to a new era in the file trade; it was indeed unfortunate for the file-cutters, but 'the world cannot stand still for their accommodation'.[34] However, the Sheffield file unions fought a sustained rearguard action in the 1890s to uphold the alleged superiority of hand-cut files. In 1892 the Secretary of the Sheffield File Cutters' Association, appearing before the Royal Commission on Labour, used the occasion to produce a file from his pocket and, to the evident surprise of the chairman, began to denounce the illegal stamping of 'hand-cut' on machine-cut files, which he claimed was destroying the trade.[35] In 1900 there were still 2,300 hand-workers in Sheffield, a number that was to be only gradually reduced in the interwar period. In even the largest of the city's steelworks and toolmaking concerns it was still not unusual to see the old-style file-cutter at work alongside the latest machines in the 1920s.[36]

In contrast, once the early problems were overcome the Americans seem to have applied themselves to the machines with their characteristic vigour.[37] Thus by the early twentieth century, even that most intractable of objects – the file – had succumbed to the American drive for a cheaper, machine-produced article.[38]

13

'HOW SHEFFIELD LOST THE AMERICAN TRADE'*: ASPECTS OF THE MARKETING OF SHEFFIELD PRODUCTS IN AMERICA

the whole success of this business depends on advertising.
King. C. Gillette, memo to directors, 1912. Quoted in
R. B. Adams, *King C. Gillette* (Boston, 1978), p. 85.

advertising on a bold scale is looked upon as a *necessity* in the
States, whereas not a few British firms believe they confer a
favour on the journals they patronise if they advertise at all.
'English and American Advertising',
Ironmonger 29 (28 April 1883), pp. 587–8.

In 1876, at the Centennial Exhibition in Philadelphia, Sheffield manufacturers were presented with dramatic evidence of America's developing skills in the steel and toolmaking arts. Crucible steel ingots and sections by the Pittsburgh makers, such as Park Bro & Co, were judged to be 'creditable in every respect to any establishment in Sheffield'.[1] Magnificent and imaginative displays of axes, saws, and files by Collins, Disston, and Nicholson gave notice that the US was now the world leader in the production of those articles in which Sheffield had previously had a monopoly.[2]

The Exhibition, combined with the decline in the American trade and a general trading depression, occasioned a good deal of soul-searching among Sheffield manufacturers. In March 1877 the *British Trade Journal* published an article, 'Sheffield Industry and the American Trade', in which several of the town's leading makers – Frederick Brittain, Mark Firth, George Wilson, William K. Peace, John Hobson, and Samuel Osborn, many of whom had recently returned from the US – identified the causes of the decline of Sheffield's American trade, blaming:

1st and chiefly. A prohibitive tariff.
2nd The depression of trade.

3rd The folly of manufacturers and workmen in not adapting themselves to the requirements of their customers.
4th The aversion of Sheffield workmen to the use of machinery.
5th The higher wages paid in Sheffield for labour.
6th The presence of Sheffield skilled workmen in the States.[3]

This study has already touched upon some of these points, but the general question of the way in which Sheffield traders approached the US
market remains to be treated. Was it the case, as some historians have as-
serted, that English manufacturers were pushed aside in world markets
because of their inability to sell and advertise their products as successfully as their competitors?[4]

One way of gauging an industry's commitment to a particular country
and the scope of its operations is to look at the industrial shop windows of
the nineteenth century – the exhibitions.

At the Great Exhibition of 1851 Sheffield's triumph had been almost
complete: 'almost every country is a tributary to its works', reported a
Royal Commission.[5] Besides its steel ingots, which compared to the finest
from Krupp's, amongst the cutlery makers none were thought to surpass
the products from Sheffield in extent, variety and excellence. American cutlery was not of the first order, though one disquieting note and portent,
was the excellence of her scythes and the superiority of her axes.

Sheffield soon seems to have fallen away from these high standards.
The town made effective displays at Paris in 1855 and London in 1862,
though so too did German and French makers. At the Great Exhibition of
1862, amongst a large showing by Sheffield, some of the town's most
famous names were absent and its traders complained that the event followed too closely upon those of 1851 and in Paris to warrant the trouble
and expense of exhibiting.[6] At the Paris Exhibition of 1867 a Royal Commission remarked: 'it can hardly escape notice that Sheffield is very badly
represented . . . [and] It is very much regretted that this should be the case,
and that the English manufacturers of cast steel, hammered iron, and
hardware should have declined to take this opportunity of inviting a comparison of which they could not be afraid.'[7] It was reported that the Sheffield cutlers were 'tired of exhibitions, and profess to see no advantage in
appearing at them'.[8] However, though the Sheffield makers were a little
thin on the ground, those that did participate greatly impressed American
ironmasters such as Abram S. Hewitt.[9] These firms appeared again at the
next European exhibition in Vienna in 1873, where Sheffield cutlers and
edge toolmakers such as Brookes & Crookes and Spear & Jackson made a
good showing.[10]

There were some encouraging signs from the Philadelphia Exhibition in 1876. Several Sheffield businesses made the effort to contribute, including Wostenholm's, whose cutlery 'was unsurpassed in quality, finish, and beauty of style',[11] and Jessop's. For the finest American cutlery Sheffield cast steel was said to be the product generally adopted. However, in saws, Parliamentary observers reported that: 'Great Britain has not a single representative, although for years Sheffield supplied not only our own country but nearly all the world'. They concluded that 'in table cutlery, tools, and safes, America was before Great Britain ... A strenuous effort will be required from Sheffield to hold its own in the race of progress. The necessary knowledge exists; what is required is a thorough co-operation between masters and workmen.'[12]

In Paris in 1878, one newspaper reported that Sheffield again was 'not so extensively represented ... as some people desire'.[13] Though some of the special steelmakers, such as Jessop's and Seebohm, mounted impressive displays,[14] one Sheffield sawmaker was:

very much surprised, and greatly disappointed to see old Sheffield so barely represented ... [and] it is the absence of exhibits of some of our best and largest Sheffield firms that I most deplore, though I scarcely need to say they rather ignore than appreciate the utility of the various Exhibitions; [especially since] other countries are making the most of the circumstances, especially the United States, which according to their saw exhibits, as represented by H. Disston, indicates we are a little behind ... [and] we shall have to bestir ourselves, throw off this kind of lethargy which has been too prevalent, be fully alive to improvements, and above all keep pace with the times.[15]

Commercial reasons, though, may have prevented the involvement of some firms. Mounting an exhibit abroad could be costly: Spear & Jackson spent £2,000 in Vienna in 1873.[16] There could also be tariff and transport difficulties – factors which according to the Parliamentary commissioners caused the low English turnout at the Philadelphia Exhibition in 1876. American ineptitude in staging some of the early exhibitions may also have deterred some makers.[17] Some manufacturers also seem to have doubted whether exhibitions actually improved sales. This was certainly the view of some Sheffielders, who, on the eve of the Paris Exhibition of 1878, were reported as being 'tired of these frequent exhibitions, which involve much trouble and expense, and seem to bring little in compensation'.[18]

Criticism of Sheffield traders should be tempered by a reminder that, in terms of travelling time in the nineteenth century, America was a great distance from Sheffield. In the early part of the century letters took a minimum of two weeks to cross the Atlantic, whilst goods could take several months to reach their destination. The advent of steamer services improved matters but shipped goods still had to survive the hazards of the transatlantic journey. Products could be damaged, mis-directed, returned by Customs, or lost in shipwreck.[19] Concerning problems over one shipment of steel, in 1865, Marsh Bros wrote to their New York agent: 'We advised you of the trouble in getting goods to Liverpool; from what we hear it appears we have been quite fortunate; it seems Naylor Vickers Co lost a large parcel for six weeks when the lot turned up in Dublin and J. H. Andrew lost 20 tons of wire rods for West during ten days.'[20] What this meant for American customers can be seen from Hoe's letters to Sanderson's, which were dominated by continual requests for faster service. In a typical letter on 13 November 1843, Hoe began by asking for the utmost speed and then repeated the point at the foot of the page.[21] Any delays resulted in disappointed customers and so Hoe frequently had to explain to them that orders could not be completed because of a lack of steel.[22] When American saw plates did arrive on the scene Hoe must have seized on them with alacrity.

Mistakes, when they did happen, were not so easily rectified when those concerned were separated by the Atlantic. In 1864 a consignment of steel from Marsh Bros was found to be unacceptable by one of its customers in Syracuse, New York. An extended wrangle took place over the shipment which was only settled by the personal intervention of a representative from the Sheffield firm.[23]

To be sure, other traders faced similar problems over long distances, but in some ways Sheffield was a special case. The communications lag had a particularly important relevance for the tool steel trade. Before 1914 such steel was not a standardised item: with any number of exotic ingredients going into the charge, the finished product was never something that was dispatched to the user without an after-thought. Existing specifications often needed to be modified to suit the needs of individual consumers, necessitating a close liaison between the steelmaker and the engineer.[24] In Sheffield it was usual for a steel merchant to hold quantities of a customer's favourite brand until it was required.[25] Where possible this policy was adopted in America. Edgar Allen's in Chicago, for example, not only held samples of stock, but also operated a complete heat-treatment plant for customers who desired such service.[26] Firth Sterling also offered similar facilities at McKeesport where its managers were able to lavish on buyers the 'personal element' that Gerald Firth thought so important.[27] However, these services could not be offered by every Sheffield steelmaker in America, and so as early as 1878 it was reported that US consumers were favouring the domestic product because they could, if necessary, maintain daily contact with the makers.[28]

Nor did circumstances usually allow Sheffield agencies in the US to carry a very heavy stock. This was a difficult problem for exporters and the stock position dominated the thinking of Sheffield's US traders. How much stock dare a manufacturer hold in America without incurring losses? Marsh Bros found that there was no easy answer to this question. The most careful calculations could easily be upset by tariffs, exchange fluctuations, technical developments in the foreign market, or by war. All these factors played a part in influencing Marsh Bros' attitude towards its New York stock in the period 1863–6. The violent fluctuations that resulted have been too well documented by Professor Pollard to need repetition here, but his conclusion can be cited: 'In less than three and a half years ... the policy of the American branch had been changed no fewer than ten times, chiefly on account of external influences on the American market for steel and cutlery goods.'[29] The implication, surely a correct one, was that Marsh Bros could do little to influence events short of entering the American market itself, something which the firm felt was 'entirely out of the question' since it had no capital to spare apart from its current business.[30] The lack of capital was exacerbated by the accumulation of stocks in New York and deficiencies on remittances from the US; in 1857 the deficiency amounted to £12,000 and had increased to over £18,000 by 1864.[31]

Holding a large stock of goods would have circumvented one of the American makers' greatest advantages – the ability to fill orders quickly. American manufacturers carried enormous stocks. 'Hoe's claim to fill any order within 24 hours', noted Leslie J. Coombe of Spear & Jackson in 1925,[32] whilst Sheffield often had difficulty in supplying shipments. Concerning the trade in bandsaws to Vancouver he added: 'It is most unfortunate about deliveries of recent orders and this will make a considerable difference to our sales'; especially since Spear & Jackson was in competition with three rivals who could supply anything 'in a few days or a few weeks at the most'.[33] But the stock position for the Sheffield agencies was to get worse rather than better. Economic conditions in the twentieth century caused a general run-down of Sheffield stock in America and by the 1920s most firms had become reconciled to the idea of selling direct and only holding samples of their goods.

Selling directly had always had its attractions for Sheffield businessmen, especially for the cutlers and toolmakers. The city's first successes in the US had largely been the result of individual effort, typified by the impressive transatlantic journeyings of men such as George Wostenholm.

In the early nineteenth century even the smallest Sheffield enterprises had an office in places such as New York, which was in the closest touch with the American country merchant and traveller. Such personalised selling methods were favoured by Marsh Bros, which, in 1865, sent an old apprentice to the US to tour the manufacturing districts to gain a good connection.[34] Products before 1850 sold on 'name' and a Butcher plane iron, a Marsh knife, or a Spear saw, was the main assurance of quality. This reflected both the unsophisticated nature of the American demand, with its preference for traditional English-style products, and the primitive character of Sheffield marketing, which had only recently evolved from its late eighteenth-century origins in which 'there were no merchants to undertake the useful task of distribution and to place manufacturers in direct communication with distant and foreign markets; and no bankers'.[35]

For a Sheffield firm in the American market much could depend on the talents of its agent. Vickers, whose chief business in the mid-nineteenth century was the export of Swedish bar iron and sheets of steel to the US, made arrangements in 1840 with a young German, Ernst Leopold Schlesinger Benzon, to act as their agent in New York. Wrote Benzon: 'The business we can do in the way of direct orders without outlay of Capital is without end but it requires much personal effort to obtain it.'[36] So successful were Benzon's energetic efforts at promoting the sales of Vickers' products in the US that he later became a partner in the Sheffield firm and eventually chairman. Benzon's business acumen in New York cultivated so much wealth and prestige that, on occasions, there was even some friction between the Sheffield firm and its agency.

There was another side of the coin, though, and agencies could be guilty sometimes of not pushing lines vigorously enough for the liking of the foreign manufacturer. Marsh Bros wrote to its New York representative in 1865: 'We fancy H. G. Wills & Co only sell our steel to those from whom they buy goods; and have travelled little or none at all, for the sole object of placing our steel ... [but] New York is well situated for trading everywhere in the Union and with the expensive store and stuff there it seems incumbent upon us to do all the business thence we can without commission to other parties.' Worse followed in 1866 when Marsh Bros again communicated to its New York office: 'We regret to see the failure of H. G. Wills & Co and must in future be careful how we entrust goods to beginners on little capital ... We have always been surprised what little profit has resulted from consignment even when made to distant new markets that we suppose would be very profitable and almost never consign to any house now.'[37]

But agents too had an interest in their clients' success and a firm could always change to another selling house if it was dissatisfied. Agency agreements, therefore, were something of a compromise. Generally, they functioned well. There is a high degree of continuity in agency arrangements, traced through the technical and periodical literature, and some of them could be long-standing; by 1920 B. M. Jones & Co had been Osborn's American agents for over fifty years.

Before 1860, as the Anglo-American trade expanded, Sheffield's offices in America proliferated. Jessop's, for example, by 1870 had agents in New York, Boston, Philadelphia, Chicago, Cincinnati, Providence, St Louis, New Orleans, and San Francisco. But in the decades after the Civil War the vast expansion of the American market, the emergence of wholesale hardware trade associations and department stores, the practice of selling under advertised brand-names, often through controlled retail outlets, and fierce price competition, all contributed to the erosion of Sheffield's traditional selling methods.

A Sheffield correspondent in America observed in 1875:

it may be said of this old 'factoring' trade of Sheffield to the United States, that fifteen years of protective tariffs, paper money, and high home prices have about killed it. Sheffield men no longer sell the bulk of Sheffield shelf goods, which are sold even yet in this market. Germans, Birmingham men, Jews and Yankees chiefly handle them now; and the bulk of the business is not done of old, by executing specific and properly assorted orders from American importers, who each had a well-defined connection thoroughly understood, but is carried on by the foreigner importing all his goods to his own stock, and then peddling them out at every cross-road store in the country. Any connection, reputation or steady trade is impossible under such a system.[38]

The personal approach by a company's own representative became increasingly anachronistic. Some Sheffielders, on occasions, attempted to cling to the old methods by bypassing the recognised channels of trade, but this brought angry rebukes from Americans. In 1895 Simmons Hardware Co complained to Wostenholm's about their agent who was travelling the country 'calling on trade that heretofore we have left to the jobber'. Simmons opined: 'it is not right for your agent to call upon any trade other than the legitimate jobber. The retail trade should certainly be left to the jobbers in this country. Where are we to get our trade if you propose furnishing the retailers?'[39]

The demise of Sheffield's old-established marketing methods was well-summarised by an official report:

The export trade of Great Britain has been built up by individual effort, and in consequence exhibits a great variety of organisation. In great part the distribution of products in external markets has been the function of merchants who might buy freely from any producer; in some cases the merchants had become attached to a particular manufacturer as his agent or partner; or the manufacturer himself may have built up a strong connection in some particular market. Again, in some branches, the trade of the world was brought together in one great centre. This diversity was well-suited indeed to the conditions under which it grew up. The products of some particular country or individual possessed special qualities or advantages which commended them to the user. Many products of the iron and steel industry have now attained such uniformity that little or no variation is to be found from a standard common to all manufacturers. Price, therefore, and not individual quality has become the dominant commercial factor.[40]

The Report recommended the setting up of an Export Sales Association. The point was stressed again by the National Federation of Iron and Steel Manufacturers in 1919 and by the Iron and Steel Trades Confederation before the Committee on Industry and Trade in 1926. Clearly what was envisaged was an organisation similar to the United States Products Co Ltd, which was one of the main selling agencies for American producers in Britain.

Such a centralised marketing organisation would have helped overcome the poor quality of Britain's official intelligence in the US market. Even in the 1920s commercial intelligence through the British Consular Service in the US was weak. The consul in Portland, Maine, lamented the failure to provide a commercial reference library with up-to-date business files in any of the consulates.[41] In 1920 the British Government toyed with the idea of increasing the number of consuls and of giving them a wide discretion in visiting their district, but it was abandoned because of the cost. Instead, a cheaper system of commercial correspondents, composed of men willing to act either formally or informally as intelligence scouts was to be employed.[42] The net effect, it was felt, was undermanning. The San Francisco consul (whose area included California, Nevada, Utah, and Arizona), despite the help of two subordinates in San Diego and Douglas, had no regular official throughout the whole of Nevada and Utah. Nor did the problem occur only in the West. A consul travelling through Cincinnati, Ohio, was surprised to find that there was no official at such an important centre, despite the openings for high-speed steel.[43]

When questioned by the Committee on Industry and Trade, the Sheffield steelmakers had to admit that they had done little themselves to set up an effective marketing organisation. They regarded the industry as 'emphatically an individualist trade', which needed management 'by individual enterprise and personal knowledge'. One manufacturer, highlighting the fact that 'almost every street in the manufacturing part of the city has little works where really fine articles are being produced and delivered all over the world, and that has been in the past the strength of the Sheffield industry', told the Balfour Committee: 'How those things can all be co-ordinated and managed from any headquarters, I cannot imagine.'[44]

Yet the attempt was surely worth making. It is difficult to see how a concerted selling effort could have helped the producers of high-speed steel after 1918, since the technological and cost advantages of the Americans seem to have been too great. But in cutlery there is a suspicion that some kind of organisation, perhaps headed by Wostenholm and Rodgers or by the Company of Cutlers (which unfortunately confined its activities to trade-mark litigation and honorific functions), would have benefited exports to the US. It would, for example, have enabled resources to be pooled to pay for advertising campaigns.

In the nineteenth century Sheffield trades, especially the light trades, had to cope with American advances in technology; in the twentieth century technology, at least in America, became less crucial than the problems of advertising and promotion. Things became especially difficult for Sheffield manufacturers in the last years of the nineteenth century when developments in the American market began to erode Sheffield's ally – the jobber.[45]

As the Department of Overseas Trade emphasised, by the 1920s advertising had become an almost indispensable factor in selling goods. Yet because of the tariff and American competition, British exporters were unable to compete in the exceedingly expensive business of advertising their products. Furthermore, buyers in America had become so used to attractive offers of 'service', to quick deliveries to conform with the existing 'hand-to-mouth' buying policy, to merchandising under the instalment plan, that the trouble involved in importing foreign goods was often considered scarcely worthwhile. In these conditions collective advertising may have helped. The Commercial Counseller in Washington remarked in his 1926 Report that the merits of Sheffield cutlery were not widely known in the US, adding in 1927, that group advertising of Sheffield goods could scarcely fail to improve matters.[46]

Extremely jealous of its name, Sheffield was remarkably indifferent to advertising it. The 'little mesters' themselves, not surprisingly, had 'made little show in the display of their goods' and other opportunities were limited.[47] 'We have no 'market day' for manufactures', stated one report, 'nor have we, to any large extent, warehouses'.[48] Suggestions in the 1850s that the town should establish a permanent exhibition or 'Museum for Manufactures', both to display Sheffield goods and to witness the innovative designs of American competitors, were ignored;[49] and so, too, was the success of Rodgers' showroom, which seems to have been viewed as a curiosity, rather than as a prototype of successful marketing.

In America there was soon a greater Sheffield commitment to advertising, especially in the pages of the leading steel trade journal *Iron Age*, where by the 1870s everything from clay crucibles to cast steel was on offer. The issue of 2 January 1873 was fairly typical: Sheffield advertisements for cast steel (by Jessop, Sanderson, Wardlow, and Cocker), cutlery (by Rodgers, Wostenholm, Dickinson, and Ward), and saws, files, and edge tools (by Spear & Jackson, Butcher, Wilkinson, and Fisher) dominated the pages, with only one or two American firms such as Singer, Nimick & Co offering any competition. The tone was a confident one. Proclaimed S. & C. Wardlow: 'Half a century of practical experience in all departments of steel manufacture, a long established reputation in England, and the Continent of Europe, and in the Eastern States principally of this country, encourage us to solicit a universal trial of our steel for ... purposes for which a first class material in quality, temper, and durability is needed.' The amount of space gives some indication of Sheffield's involvement with the American market and the progress of the US steel industry, because during the 1870s it declined abruptly. After the 1880s, in fact, Sheffield advertisements in the *Iron Age* became increasingly rare.

Sheffield advertising declined further in the period 1918–30. The *Iron Age* found little patronage from Sheffield's high-speed steelmakers, apart from a solitary advertisement by Balfour's which was run for a few months in 1920.[50] In the *American Cutler* Sheffield steel was more in evidence with firms such as Firth's and Wardlow's trying to tempt the American cutlery manufacturers with their stainless and high-quality steels; but, significantly, there were almost no advertisements by Wostenholm's and Rodgers. Nor were these cutlers devoting their attention to publications with a wider circulation; a cursory sample of the most popular American periodicals in this period failed to reveal a single advertisement for Sheffield cutlery.[51] High-quality Sheffield cutlery and plate were even absent from such journals as *Vogue*, even though other British manufacturers such as Wedgwood were buying space. Instead, advertisements from the Oneida Community dominated the pages, frequently catering for the 'quality' market that, in the past, Sheffield had regarded as its own. Hardly surprising that one man told a Sheffield newspaper in 1922: 'Of one thing I am absolutely certain – our British manufacturers fail miserably to advertise the quality of their products.'[52]

The Sheffield advertisements were all fairly unimaginative – usually simply stating the name of the manufacturer, the product, and the address

of an agent, with no attempt at illustration. But it would be unfair to criti-
cise this since those of most American makers were exactly the same. Only
those for Henry Disston, who began placing advertisements in the *Iron
Age* in the 1870s, consisting of eight full-pages illustrated with over a
hundred wood engravings, were a sign of the more sophisticated selling
techniques to come.

Sheffield manufacturers were certainly aware of these techniques.[53] As
early as the 1850s a Marsh Bros' agent in the US was informed by one
American retailer that Sheffield's style of presentation was 'twenty years
behind the age'. Examining the respective displays, the agent was obliged
to agree:

> Everybody in the trade nearly, now puts up spring cutlery in boxes and, so far as I
> could ascertain, without extra charge. On the shelves our goods in bundles beside
> those of other people in boxes, (making neat square bales) with handsome black,
> gold & green labels, do certainly look ... very 'old fogyish'.[54]

The *Ironmonger* made the same point twenty years later.[55] By then
some Sheffield firms had begun to copy American methods; Spear & Jackson had discarded paper wrappings for its products and was packing them
in neat cardboard boxes.[56] But the lessons seemed to have been imperfectly learned. When Leslie Coombe, visiting Australia in 1905, was asked
by a store-keeper for some advertising material he was unable to provide
it. 'Could we not get up some such thing, either calendar or large show-
card?', he wrote to Sheffield.[57]

Sheffield makers were still making admiring comments about American skill in advertising in the 1930s. Wostenholm's Frank Colver commented on a successful range of American stainless steel kitchen knives,
which were 'being put up in attractive boxes ... There are about a dozen
patterns in the line ... Housewives are being persuaded by advertising to
gradually collect the whole set'.[58] Admitted one Wostenholm man to
Colver: 'The American retailer certainly knows how to display his goods
to the best advantage, and it is a pity that their methods in this particular
department cannot be taken up more extensively by the English retailer.'[59]
Slowly the need to adopt such techniques was recognised in Sheffield
towards the end of the 1920s.[60]

Why, then, was so little achieved? The failure is all the more puzzling
when superficially the prospects seemed so favourable in the 1920s for
Sheffield to reclaim part of its old American trade. The quality of British
manufactures and the belief that Americans would have them at any price
is a constantly recurring theme in trade journals and market surveys in
this period. Sheffield, somewhat complacently, shared these views: 'When

these American cutlers require the highest class pen-knives, hunting-knives and hand-forged table knives they send to Sheffield. They willingly pay heavy freight and import duties in order to obtain goods which they themselves cannot equal.'[61] So, too, did the Department of Overseas Trade, which stressed the diffusion of American prosperity throughout the great industrial centres of the Midwest and Southern states and the large areas of country still untapped by English manufacturers. The journal *Anglo-American Trade* felt that the most troublesome feature about selling British goods to the US was obtaining them – the market was waiting, only the goods were lacking.[62]

Not only quality favoured the Englishman. Despite the distance involved in trading with the US, the vagaries of the transportation networks allowed UK manufacturers to compete favourably with the Americans. Freight rates for steel goods from European to South Atlantic ports, such as Savannah, Mobile, and Pensacola, were approximately $2.00 a ton cheaper than from Atlanta.[63] By shipping through the Panama Canal, English manufacturers could also undercut the Americans on the Pacific coast. The president of the Sheffield Chamber of Commerce assured Vancouver businessmen on their visit to the city in 1923 that the English could supply steel more cheaply to Vancouver by the Panama Canal than could Pittsburgh makers. Spear & Jackson's Canadian trade benefited from the fact that goods sent via the Panama Canal to Vancouver cost 50s per ton, compared to 70s per ton to Montreal.[64]

Unfortunately, Sheffield's contacts with the western half of the US were fading by this time. In the nineteenth century some of the town's cutlers and edge toolmakers had been active around San Francisco.[65] Burgon & Ball, the shear manufacturers, showed some interest in the Californian trade in the 1880s and were told that: 'There is a very large territory here, which will use a great many shears, and the trade only needs working up.'[66] But most Sheffield firms restricted their trade to the East and Midwest. 'I don't think there would be any special advantage in having an office in any of the western cities', wrote a Marsh Bros agent in Cincinnati in 1858: 'If we visit these towns regularly, and at the proper seasons ... I don't think that having an office in any of them would be much of an object.'[67] By the 1920s, apart from vestiges of Wostenholm's California trade, and the presence of Spear & Jackson in British Columbia, the prospects for reviving business in areas west of Chicago were unpromising. Attempts to drum up trade elsewhere also seem to have been unsuccessful, especially when business conditions began to deteriorate. One of Wostenholm's agents terminated a business trip prematurely in the Southern states in 1921 due to lack of interest on the part of American retailers.[68]

The fond hopes of the Department of Overseas Trade that the twenties would witness an upsurge of demand for British products in the West was not realised, at least as regards steel products.

Whatever advantages Sheffield did possess they meant nothing, as two Federation of British Industries' observers made clear, without a close study of the US market.[69] This involved not only studying American selling methods but also adapting products to suit the tastes of US consumers. William K. Peace, president of the Sheffield Chamber of Commerce, had been reported in the *British Trade Journal* in 1877 as arguing that if Sheffielders had met the tastes and styles of American consumers they might have retained them as customers. The inability of the town's sawmakers and cutlery manufacturers to adapt to peculiar American conditions has been noted in earlier chapters in this study. On the other hand, the picture needs balancing with evidence that Sheffield traders did make some attempt to cater for US needs from a very early date. American-style axes and plantation tools were on sale by the 1820s and within a decade the town had found other specialist US markets. In 1836, responding to a request on the frontier for scalping knives, Hiram Cutler wrote to the American Fur Co concerning a knife 'that would probably suit Indians'.[70] In the 1856 edition of the *General Directory of Sheffield* John Askham (formerly Frost, Askham & Mosforth) advertised products 'adapted ... especially for the United States of America'; whilst Alfred Hobson & Sons were listed as makers of 'Fine American Cutlery'. By the mid-nineteenth century Sheffield had begun to produce a variety of American hardware and woodworking tools. 'Drabble has aimed at competing in American styles with domestic manufacturers for some years', wrote Marsh Bros in 1867.[71] Marsh Bros themselves were attentive to the needs of Americans, asking the firm's New York agent to obtain 'leading styles' of American table knives.[72] The company was aware that the speed with which American makers could adapt to their own market gave them an added advantage:

The domestic makers of plough steel cut it into various shapes required by the consumers, and the blacksmiths who use it have very little work left. In that particular I fear it will be hard to compete with them, as plough patterns are all the time changing, and unless we could get orders for the various shapes from plough makers, the sellers of the same material would not feel inclined to order any quantity of any one pattern.[73]

Gradually, 'Yankee notions' and 'American novelties' were adopted by Sheffield makers in the 1870s and 1880s. The American and Canadian owners of the Hardy Patent Pick Co arrived from the US in the early 1870s and began making their pick-axes on the interchangeable principle with detachable heads.[74] The manner in which the cutlery and scissor manufacturers copied American patterns became a feature of the trade.[75] One of the most notable instances of Sheffield adapting itself to the American market was in the Bowie knife trade which was established in the 1830s, expanded during the 1840s, and reached its peak in the 1850s. The legends surrounding James Bowie's Mississippi sand-bar duel, when, armed only with his famous knife, he repulsed the combined attack of four men, are now part of American folklore. As the popularity of the knife grew, Sheffield firms, especially Butcher's and Wostenholm's, soon began to monopolise the trade. Business was particularly heavy in the American South and West, where knives etched and engraved with such delightful mottoes as 'Death to Abolition' (or, conversely, 'Death to Traitors'), 'I Can Dig Gold from Quartz', 'For Stags and Buffaloes', and 'Celebrated Arkansas Toothpick', enjoyed a ready sale. It was a Sheffield weapon which US Congressman 'Bowie Knife' Potter planned to use in his duel with Roger Pryor; a Sheffield knife with which John Wilkes Booth stabbed Major Rathbone after shooting Abraham Lincoln; and a Wostenholm knife that was reputedly found on Bowie's body at the Alamo.[76]

Sheffield adaptation continued in the 1920s. Wostenholm's asked Colver to find out about 'Remington Bakelite knives ... [which] are a line we ought to very carefully consider going in for'.[77] In some cases it was only by imitating the Americans that success could be achieved at all. This was even true in Canada. Coombe, writing to Spear & Jackson from Vancouver, remarked: 'I suppose Rodgers know how well-known and popular their American namesakes brand is out here. The Am'n patterns are wanted.'[78] Spear & Jackson itself could only compete with the US sawmakers, Simonds, by carefully copying its designs. After talks with the lumbermen around Vancouver, Spear & Jackson secured a share of the trade, but only on the understanding that it could deliver the desired article. The development of saw technology meant that there was a new man to please at the lumber camps – the filer. Warned Coombe: 'these men do nothing but file these saws and if there is anything at all they think is not quite right that ends the matter'. Hence his reminder to the Sheffield factory, after a shipment of saws had departed from the regular patterns: 'SIMONDS SAWS MUST BE IMITATED EXACTLY, TO THE SMALLEST DETAIL.'[79]

For Sheffield to be successful in America it would also have to adapt itself to the newer methods of distribution. As one of Wostenholm's New York agents remarked: 'Our national methods of distribution today through mail order houses and chain stores, with department stores, hardware, cutlery and other outlets for our lines, must be considered carefully'.[80] The policies and practices of these distributors had much in common with and often were directly derived from the wholesale jobber. Like the jobber, their basic objective was to assure a high velocity of stock turn. Perhaps the most important of these in the twentieth century was the chain store which was becoming the standard instrument of mass retailing in the US.

Sheffield manufacturers were worried by the low prices and high sales of the chains. In the nineteenth century the purchasing power of such large buyers worked, to a certain extent, in Sheffield's favour: A. J. Jordan (ca. 1846–1929), for example, a St Louis merchant, controlled the kitchen knife-making capacity of Jordan's of Sheffield. However, in the twentieth century American firms were available for bulk contracts, which could often extend for a year or more in advance, and this further depressed the general price-level. To show what this meant, Coombe, in 1934, sent to Spear & Jackson a set of Woolworth's American hacksaws which sold at only twenty cents each, along with a complete handsaw which sold at the same price. 'I never saw a better made Handsaw H[an]dle or a better polished blade', he commented. Woolworth's anticipated selling 200,000 dozen of the saws throughout its 2,000 stores.[81]

The chain stores and mail-order houses were better suited to tapping the demand from rural communities and an increasingly mobile and suburban population. Sheffield appears to have missed out on this. Personalised selling methods meant little in these conditions, and the fact that buyers were usually responsible for private branding and advertising of a product was also essentially alien to Sheffield practice.[82] Some attempt was made to cater for the mass market. Sheffield cutlery and razors featured in the early Sears Roebuck Catalogues. In the 1908 publication, for example, Wostenholm's products were described as 'the standard the world over'. For $1.80 a customer could order a Wostenholm de-luxe carving knife and fork. However, US makers displayed an attractively-boxed 16–piece knife set for only $4.65 – a sign of things to come.[83] Gradually, Sheffield products became too expensive and they were, significantly, beginning to be overshadowed by German products in the 1920s' Catalogues. Sheffield cutlery was also too costly to compete in traditional retail outlets. 'Only stores of the very highest class seem at all interested in our goods', complained Colver and even then demand was limited. He noted after a visit to Wanamakers – 'the finest store I have ever been in' – that although the store was well disposed to Wostenholm's, 'our goods have a very slow sale'.[84]

'Both [in the US] and in Canada people seem to be calling for cheap goods', Colver informed a Sheffield firm.[85] Generally, Sheffield makers

Table 13.1 *US cutlery imports, 1884–1926*

Year	Total (£000's)	UK % of total	Germany % of total
1884–5	296	49	49
1894–5	381	38	59
1904–5	370	24	71
1913–14	588	14	80
1923	339	11	81
1924	301	13	77
1925	254	18	68
1926	282	19	67

Source: Committee on Industry and Trade, *Survey of Metal Industries* (1928), p. 271.

disdained to cater for the cheaper end of the market; but the Germans were more obliging. Wrote one of Wostenholm's agents in New York: 'There are very few people who are interested in English made cutlery, because of the developments that have taken place in this country during the last few years, which have resulted in the production of a better article and also because there is a cheap German product being imported which supplies another class of trade.'[86]

The Germans had a greater variety of goods to sell in the US market, since they produced both the high-grade goods and those at the cheaper end of the scale. These were the kind of blades flooding the market which were noticed by a British consul in Chicago in 1920, where sales were effected mainly by means of excellent samples and prompt deliveries.[87] Though relative to the English proportion of US cutlery imports, the amount of 'cheap German trash', as a Wostenholm agency put it,[88] was diminishing slightly after the high point before the War, the German product still predominated and was ostensibly the main target of the Fordney McCumber Tariff (Table 13: 1).

Sheffield's normally high prices were further inflated by American tariffs. The implementation of import duties punctuated the path of Sheffield's declining American trade in the nineteenth century and, though it would be wrong, as many Sheffielders were fond of doing, to draw a simplistic connection between high tariffs and falling trade, they had severe effects on Sheffield's exports. The subject demands considerably more space than is available here, but the fate of cutlery products under the Fordney McCumber Tariff of 1922 may be cited as an example.

Sheffield's cutlery industry had always been susceptible to US tariff policy. The McKinley Tariff in particular had dealt a severe blow to the trade. Many cutlery manufacturers abandoned the market for good and looked elsewhere, though some were said to have responded to the challenge by reorganising and introducing more modern methods.[89] The changes are neatly summarised by J. G. Elliot, president of the Sheffield Cutlery Manufacturers Association, in evidence submitted to the Committee on Industry and Trade:

Chairman: With regard to adverse effect of tariffs you say that the American tariff has gone up as high as 200 percent? – Yes. The first was the McKinley Tariff, which completely shut us out from the States. There are a few butcher's knives and a few fine pen-knives and some razors which we send there, but the amount of trade done is a mere bagatelle compared with what it was 25 or 30 years ago.[90]

Nevertheless, the American market was still sufficiently important to provoke a response from Sheffield cutlers upon the introduction of the Fordney Tariff. According to Elliot the cutlery trade had once more been 'seriously affected'.

Steel tonnage products were little affected by the tariff,[91] but in cutlery there was a marked decline in the trade after 1922 which was mostly due to the increased duties. The Sheffield Chamber of Commerce's prediction that the rates would be 'prohibitive' proved too pessimistic, since trade continued and there were good years in 1926 and 1927. Nevertheless, adjusted figures for Sheffield cutlery exports to the US show a decline from £41,363 in 1920 to £16,287 in 1923, clearly showing that cutlery was 'one of the imports which suffered most severely under the United States tariff of 1922'.[92] Duties which made Sheffield's American selling prices on good-quality knives about double their English retail price ensured that US volume remained low and the value meagre. This is at least a partial explanation for Sheffield's poor advertising record and US business performance in the 1920s.

The higher rates seemed to have had little effect on other British products, such as woollen and worsted piece goods. But cutlery was less susceptible to the dictates of fashion and by the 1920s American cutlery and silverware manufacturers, such as the Oneida Community, were quite capable of competing successfully with Sheffield's prestige knives and at a price considerably below the imported article. On the store shelves the only thing that distinguished a top-quality American blade from its competitor was the name 'Sheffield' and even that could be easily duplicated.

False branding was a headache for Sheffield traders almost as soon as the American trade began. In about 1825 one of the town's razor manufacturers sent £10 to the US to be 'expended in advertisements and in cautioning the people' against the illegal stamping of his goods.[93] Other firms such as Rodgers placed warnings about spurious trade marks alongside

their normal advertisements.[94] The apathy of such manufacturers to advertising was matched by their obsession with this fraudulent marking of
goods.[95] But even when the culprits were traced, the action a firm could
take was limited, as Rodgers' New York agent found when he tackled one
American retailer, who:

declared most positively he never manufactured a knife or was interested, either
directly or indirectly, in manufacturing knives stamped with [Rodgers'] name, but
acknowledges he has bought them same as any other goods, but, says he never
sold them as genuine; the fact is they are made ... by (as he says) a worthless set of
fellows about a dozen in number, he says they bring the knives to him ... he acknowledges it is wrong and I think we should receive more benefit by keeping good
friends, than taking harsh measures.[96]

Litigation was an option, but this was costly, as the Company of Cutlers discovered in the 1920s when it attempted to prevent an 'unscrupu-
lous' American firm from registering the word 'Sheffield' world-wide.[97] A
special fund had to be instituted to deal with similar cases. So illegal
branding continued into the 1930s, when 'the magic name "Sheffield" ...
still [had] a good reputation amongst the American people.'[98] The shady
practices of American manufacturers provoked sardonic comments from
Sheffield businessmen. In Montreal, Colver saw stainless steel table
knives being retailed at 21 cents each by 'Glen Plate & Cutlery Co, Sheffield'. 'I wonder who they are?', he asked.[99] Coombe came across the
same methods in saw retailing: 'The card has just the word "Sheffield" in
big letters on the top above the saw; below the saw is "E. C. Atkins & Co,
Sheffield Works, Indianapolis", as usual.'[100]

Sheffield makers seem to have regarded these practices with a cynical
weariness – rather than as a back-handed compliment – as yet another
barrier to be overcome in trade with the US. In the 1920s, when psycho-
logical factors in world trade were so important, there seems to have been
a growing belief that perhaps the American market was not worth the
cost. Resignation is discernible in the remarks of Wostenholm's and
Rodgers' directors to Arthur Balfour, concerning the Fordney McCumber
duties: 'With increases of tariff we may take it that the trade will gradually
die out.'[101] By the mid-1930s even Balfour admitted that: 'It is quite useless for us to travel in America today. I remember the time when we used
to stream over there a dozen at a time, and there was plenty of business for
us all, but today it is a waste of time to go to America to sell Sheffield
goods.'[102]

Not surprisingly, Sheffield firms began to look elsewhere. The search
for new markets in substitution for the falling American demand, which
was underway during the American Civil War,[103] gathered pace in the

twentieth century and by the 1920s had become a prominent feature of the Sheffield trade. As Arthur K. Wilson, chairman of Spear & Jackson, commented on an Australian visit in 1923, Britain ought to compensate itself for the loss of old markets by securing bigger ones in Australia, South Africa, India, and the East.[104]

Sheffield's trading record, therefore, needs to be considered in a wider context than simply the American one. Russia (where Firth's, Saville's and Cammell's opened subsidiaries), Japan, South America, and the Colonies provided ample scope for Sheffield's energies before and after the First World War. Here the impression of the city's business performance is more cheerful. The disappointments of Balfour's firm in the US were balanced by the vigour with which it pursued business in other areas, such as South America, where it marketed new lines in high-speed steel milling tools.[105] Spear & Jackson made efforts to break new ground, notably in Japan and South America. Similar efforts were made by Edgar Allen's, Marsh Bros, Hadfields, and Andrew's. This should be borne in mind in any complete assessment of Sheffield's business performance.

CONCLUSION: A CENTURY OF COMMERCIAL AND TECHNOLOGICAL INTERDEPENDENCE IN STEEL

Nothing strikes the American manufacturer more, whom I occasionally conduct through the Sheffield works, than this want of the application of labour saving machinery. For this cause, as well as the superior industry of our people, I apprehend the time is not far distant when we shall be able, not only to dispense with Sheffield goods by our own manufactures, but undersell them in the markets of the world, as we already have done ... in some branches of the Sheffield trades, as for instance, shovels, axes, etc.

USNA T248 American Consul, G. J. Abbott to
Secretary of State, 6 July 1866.

I frequently come across our commercial rivals in law suits, and have been able to gauge accurately the comparative capabilities of America and Germany to produce high-quality steels, and up to the present in that matter, this country has nothing to fear.

SUA VIII/1/27/1. Professor J. O. Arnold to
William Humphrey, 4 June 1915.

The contrast between the light and heavy trades in Sheffield expressed in these two viewpoints, and also emphasised by Godfrey Lloyd in his classic study on cutlery, provides the most illuminating standpoint from which to survey Sheffield's relationship with the American market in the period 1830–1930.

It was in the production of cutlery and edge tools where America showed the kind of striking progress that exemplified the much-discussed 'American System of Manufactures'.[1] Here labour-saving devices were much in evidence with far-reaching effects on productivity. In sawmaking and file manufacture America moved from a position of almost total dependence to one of virtual self-sufficiency during the course of the nineteenth century. In cutlery, progress was equally dramatic: by the 1930s total foreign exports of cutlery to the US amounted to a mere 2 percent of the American output. Diffusion of Sheffield technology to the US was rapid – so swift, in fact, that even before 1850 the flow had been reversed, with Sheffield (albeit tardily and reluctantly) importing American labour and machinery, so restoring a certain symmetry to the transatlantic pattern of technical exchange.

A number of social and economic factors contributed to America's astonishing successes in these light steel trades. Above all, as this study has highlighted, it was the distinctive character of the US market which gave American manufacturers their greatest advantage. The susceptibility of America to standardised goods, the absence of craft traditions which facilitated the introduction of machinery, and the country's enormous resources, which acted as a stimulus to innovation, provided the ideal conditions for American manufacturers to alter completely the design of many of Sheffield's traditional products. The Americans, therefore, concentrated their activities where the nature of demand and the product itself favoured standardised goods and mass-production techniques. In areas where the product was less suited to machinery American progress was rather more uneven. File manufacture is a notable instance of an industry where, largely due to the peculiarities of the product, the Americans made little impact, at least until the 1860s, and remained dependent upon imports.[2]

The nature and extent of American progress in toolmaking were quickly realised in Sheffield. By 1850 the town's newspapers regularly commented on the need for mechanisation and the dire consequences that would result if Sheffield makers failed to adapt. 'Whatever [Sheffield's] customers *want* she must *make*, or towns *will* be found in Germany that will', predicted one correspondent in a review of the declining American trade.[3] But the obstacles that prevented England from following the American example were well known, too. Another commentator, having correctly identified Sheffield's competitive weaknesses and the need for far-reaching changes, ended with the words: '*With regret it must be confessed ... that the jealous constitutions of trade unions make any approach to such a versatility of energies highly problematical.*'[4] Furthermore, the nature of the American market presented the Sheffield cutlery and edge toolmakers with major problems in selling their products. Despite the evidence that some firms were willing to adapt to American styles and advertising techniques, Sheffielders were increasingly out of their depth in America in this period. Small-scale enterprise and individualist products and selling methods, which had proved so useful in opening up the US trade in the early nineteenth century, were exactly the opposite of what was required later. Here there does seem to have been a failure on the part of the Sheffield makers, especially in comparison with their more amenable Swiss and German rivals, not so much to modify the nature of a traditional product (which the Americans could manufacture more cheaply anyway), but to tap the wealthier sections of the US community. Although some allowance must be made for stringent American tariffs, more could have been done by Sheffield manufacturers, especially in advertising.[5]

In the production of special steels American progress was also very impressive. Within the space of about seventy years the crucible steel industry had been successfully established in the US and had almost completely excluded Sheffield imports. Equally noteworthy, however, was the lack of any real progress in the American steel industry until after the mid-nineteenth century. Production of American steel was negligible until the 1860s – a decade when the US industry was founded with Sheffield's help – and even after that the American crucible steel industry remained technically backward compared to its English competitor. So, despite the fact that the city's trade went into an almost inevitable decline, Sheffield steel and technology remained a vital influence in the US well into the twentieth century.[6]

Nor in the production of steel castings, where market conditions, notably the demand from engineering concerns and the shipyards, favoured the English manufacturer, is a comparison with the US to Sheffield's disadvantage.[7] If George Wallis and Joseph Whitworth were impressed by the energy and ingenuity of Americans when they visited the New York Industrial Exhibition in 1854, then it is worth emphasising that Abram S. Hewitt was similarly struck by the abilities of Sheffield makers in handling large steel castings when he journeyed to Europe in the late 1860s. Not until much later in the nineteenth century did the US steel castings industry shake off a series of disastrous failures and begin to equal the efforts of European manufacturers. Even then it is doubtful if American techniques and organisation compared with the best Sheffield practice as evinced at Vickers and Hadfields.[8]

Above all, this study has shown that, although the Americans were more productive, Sheffield's technical lead in special steels was maintained at least until the outbreak of the First World War. It demonstrates that Arnold's expressed belief in English superiority was not mere patriotic drum-beating.[9] For most of the period 1830–1930 Sheffield's sustained progress and innovation, albeit with a superficially archaic technology, had kept it well ahead of its competitors across the Atlantic. Only after Arnold's words were written, when the electric furnace destroyed Sheffield's predominance forever, did a significant gap appear between the levels of the two technologies. Then there was some reluctance in Sheffield in renouncing the older methods, but not as much as has commonly been supposed. Many of the factors which did the most damage to the city's American trade were beyond the control of its steelmakers. It is really, therefore, the First World War which marks the end of Sheffield's Atlantic economy. In the 1920s, the city's manufacturers found themselves in a different world – the interruption of trading links with the US, rapidly rising raw material and labour costs, the problems of implementing a new technology in the face of sluggish demand, presented obstacles which, in the short-term, proved difficult to overcome. The result was that Sheffield lost the American trade.[10]

Sheffield steelmakers appear to have been less successful at transferring their superiority across the Atlantic for their own benefit. There were numerous reasons for this: poor management, bad timing and the defensive nature of the transatlantic ventures can be highlighted from an examination of their performance.[11] Nevertheless, the firms established by Butcher, Sanderson's, Firth's, Jessop's, Allen's, and Hadfields exerted an immense influence on the US special steel industry, exporting not only labour and capital, but also all the most important alloy steels (tool, manganese, silicon, vanadium and stainless).

The final picture is that of the major Sheffield steel firms enjoying a high degree of technological progress, with that progress limited on occasions by labour and market problems.[12] This modifies somewhat the traditional view of the pace and extent of American development and shows that US advances in steelmaking were neither as untrammelled nor as rapid as they have usually been portrayed. It is clear that the Sheffield steel industry at the turn of the century, with its extensive range of contacts with both American and European manufacturers, and its renowned research facilities, was as technically advanced as any of its competitors. It may be true that by the early nineteenth century the US possessed many of the requirements for industrialisation and that comparisons with Britain or Europe became less important.[13] But this study would suggest that there were certain sectors of industry, albeit rather specialised ones, where this is less true, and so the subject of contrasting Anglo-American commercial development and technologies remains a fruitful one.

APPENDIX

US PRODUCTION OF STEEL INGOTS AND CASTINGS BY PROCESSES (GROSS TONS) 1867–1930

Year	Open-hearth	Bessemer	Crucible	All other	Total
1867	–	2,679	16,964		19,643
1868	–	7,589	19,197		26,786
1869	893	10,714	19,643		31,250
1870	1,339	37,500	29,911		68,750
1871	1,785	40,179	31,250		73,214
1872	2,679	107,239	26,125	6,911	142,954
1873	3,125	152,368	31,059	12,244	198,796
1874	6,250	171,369	32,436	5,672	215,727
1875	8,080	335,283	35,180	11,256	389,799
1876	19,187	469,639	35,163	9,202	533,191
1877	22,349	500,524	36,098	10,647	569,618
1878	32,255	653,773	38,309	7,640	731,977
1879	50,259	829,439	50,696	4,879	935,273
1880	100,851	1,074,262	64,664	7,558	1,247,335
1881	131,202	1,374,247	80,145	2,720	1,588,314
1882	143,341	1,514,687	75,973	2,691	1,736,692
1883	119,356	1,477,345	71,835	4,999	1,673,535
1884	117,515	1,375,531	53,270	4,563	1,550,879
1885	133,376	1,519,430	57,599	1,515	1,711,920
1886	218,973	2,269,190	71,973	2,367	2,562,503
1887	322,069	2,936,003	75,375	5,594	3,339,071
1888	314,318	2,511,161	70,279	3,682	2,899,440
1889	374,543	2,930,204	75,865	5,120	3,385,732
1890	513,232	3,688,871	71,175	3,793	4,277,071
1891	579,753	3,247,417	72,586	4,484	3,904,240
1892	669,889	4,168,435	84,709	4,548	4,927,581
1893	737,890	3,215,686	63,613	2,806	4,019,995
1894	784,936	3,571,313	51,702	4,081	4,412,032
1895	1,137,182	4,909,128	67,666	858	6,114,834
1896	1,298,700	3,919,906	60,689	2,394	5,218,689
1897	1,608,671	5,475,315	69,959	3,012	7,156,957
1898	2,230,292	6,609,017	89,747	3,801	8,932,857
1899	2,947,316	7,586,354	101,213	4,974	10,639,857
1900	3,398,135	6,884,770	100,562	4,862	10,188,329
1901	4,656,309	8,713,302	98,513	5,471	13,473,595
1902	5,687,729	9,138,363	112,772	8,386	14,947,250
1903	5,829,911	8,592,829	102,434	9,804	14,534,978
1904	5,908,166	7,859,140	83,391	9,190	13,859,887
1905	8,971,376	10,941,375	102,233	8,963	20,023,947
1906	10,980,413	12,275,830	127,513	14,380	23,398,136
1907	11,549,736	11,667,549	131,234	14,075	23,362,594
1908	7,836,729	6,116,755	63,631	6,132	14,023,247

Year	Open-hearth	Bessemer	Crucible	All other	Total
1909	14,493,936	9,330,783	107,355	22,947	23,955,021
1910	16,504,509	9,412,772	122,303	55,335	26,094,919
1911	15,598,650	7,947,854	97,653	31,949	23,676,106
1912	20,780,723	10,327,901	121,517	21,162	31,251,303
1913	21,599,931	9,545,706	121,226	34,011	31,300,874
1914	17,174,684	6,220,846	89,869	27,631	23,513,030
1915	23,679,102	8,287,213	113,782	70,939	32,151,036
1916	31,415,427	11,059,039	129,692	169,522	42,773,680
1917	34,148,893	10,479,960	126,716	305,038	45,060,607
1918	34,459,391	9,376,236	115,112	511,693	44,462,432
1919	26,948,694	7,271,562	63,572	387,404	34,671,232
1920	32,671,895	8,883,087	72,265	505,687	42,132,934
1921	15,589,802	4,015,938	7,613	170,444	19,783,797
1922	29,308,983	5,919,298	28,606	346,039	35,602,926
1923	35,899,657	8,484,088	44,079	515,872	44,943,696
1924	31,577,350	5,899,590	22,473	432,526	37,931,939
1925	38,034,488	6,723,962	19,562	615,512	45,393,524
1926	40,691,979	6,934,568	15,493	651,723	48,293,763
1927	38,068,335	6,191,727	9,036	666,087	44,935,185
1928	44,113,956	6,620,195	7,769	802,260	51,544,180
1929	48,352,888	7,122,509	6,645	951,431	56,433,473
1930	35,049,172	5,035,459	2,253	612,599	40,699,483

Sources: American Iron and Steel Association, *Annual Statistical Report* (1905), p. 107: American Iron and Steel Institute, *Annual Statistical Reports* (New York, 1918), p. 23; (New York, 1930), p. 25.

NOTES

INTRODUCTION: SHEFFIELD AND THE GENESIS OF THE AMERICAN TRADE

1 See J. Potter, 'Atlantic Economy, 1815–1860: The USA and the Industrial Revolution in Britain', in L. S. Pressnell, ed., *Studies in the Industrial Revolution* (1960), pp. 236–80. By 1830 America was regularly taking one-half or more of total English exports. In the decade before the Civil War England regularly accounted for 90 percent and more of total American cast steel imports. In 1859–60, for example, 93 percent of US imports came from England. *Report of the Secretary of the Treasury ... of the Commerce and Navigation of the United States for the Year Ending June 30, 1860* (Washington, DC, 1860), pp. 230–1. The Atlantic economy is also surveyed in: F. Thistlethwaite, *The Anglo-American Connection in the Early Nineteenth Century* (Philadelphia, 1959), esp., pp. 3–38; N. S. Buck, *The Development of the Organisation of Anglo-American Trade, 1800–1850* (New Haven, 1925).

2 These processes are described more fully in Chap. 2.

3 G. Dodd, *British Manufactures. Metals* (1845), vols. 3 & 4, p. 35.

4 J. Holland, *The Picture of Sheffield* (Sheffield, 1824), pp. 232–3, lists 62 distinct Sheffield products and manufactures. For a visual display of this variety, see J. Smith, *Explanation or Key, to the Various Manufactories of Sheffield*, ed. J. S. Kebabien (Vt., 1975). This diversity is beyond the scope of a single book and so, despite their strong links with America, the precious metal trades are excluded. Interested readers can consult: W. H. G. Armytage, 'A Sheffield Quaker in Philadelphia 1804–1806', *Pennsylvania History* 17 (July 1950), pp. 192–205; F. Bradbury, *History of Old Sheffield Plate* (1912); G. S. Gibb, *The Whitesmiths of Taunton* (Cambridge, Mass., 1943); J. and J. Hatfield, *The Oldest Sheffield Plater* (Huddersfield, 1974); J. G. Timmins, ed., *Workers in Metal Since 1784 ... W. & G. Sissons* (Sheffield, 1984); J. W. Torrey, *Old Sheffield Plate* (Boston & New York, 1918); D. D. Waters, 'The Workmanship of an American Artist', Philadelphia's Precious Metal Trades and Craftsmen, 1788–1832 (Delaware PhD, 1981); R. E. Wilson, *200 Precious Metal Years* (1960).

5 Sir R. Phillips quoted in T. Allen, *A New and Complete History of the County of York* (1831), vol. 3, p. 34.

6 For a meticulous survey, see S. Pollard, *A History of Labour in Sheffield* (Liverpool, 1959).

7 For an early American view of Sheffield and its manufactories, see J. Griscom, *A Year in Europe* (New York, 1823), vol. 2, pp. 547–8.

8 Z. Allen, *The Practical Tourist* (Providence, 1832), vol. 1, pp. 288–9. For other American comments on Rodgers' 'brilliant' display, see N. H. Carter, *Letters from Europe* (New York, 1827), vol. 1, p. 97.

9 Samuel Jackson, *PP* 1833, VI, SC on Commerce, Manufactures, etc, p. 187, argued that America was unable to compete with fine English cutlery, due to its high labour costs, though he admitted that it had made some progress in the heavier edge tools, largely owing to the high import duty. The *Sheffield Iris*, 15 December 1829, showed some awareness of America's potential but comforted its readers with the belief that: 'The Sheffield trades cannot be taken up by inexperienced individuals, nor is machinery applicable to the production of our staple wares.'

10 See Chap. 10.

11 A. Gatty, *Sheffield: Past and Present* (Sheffield, 1873), p. 197.

12 A. Young, *A Six Months Tour Through the North of England* (1770), vol. 1, pp. 131–6. J. Holland, *The Picture of Sheffield*, pp. 232–3, dates the US trade from 1760. One firm which began trade with America in the 1760s was John Kenyon & Co. See *Bi-Centenary Celebration, 1710–1910* (Sheffield, 1910), p. 7. Cf. also: J. T. Dixon, 'Aspects of Yorkshire Emigration to North America, 1760–1880' (Leeds PhD, 1982), vol. 3, pp. 1301–28; G. C. Neumann, *Swords and Blades of the American Revolution* (Newton Abbot, 1973).

13 *The Local Register and Chronological Account ... of Sheffield* (Sheffield, 1830), pp. 53–4.

14 On the American liking for Sheffield tools, see: W. L. Goodman, 'Tools and Equipment of the Early Settlers in the New World', *CEAIA* 29 (September 1976), pp. 40–51; idem, 'Gabriel & Sons, Stock Inventories', *CEAIA* 36 (September 1983), pp. 53–61; C. F. Hummel, 'English Tools in America: The Evidence of the Dominys', *Winterthur Portfolio* 2 (1965), pp. 27–46; idem, *With Hammer in Hand* (Charlottsville, 1968); P. B. Kebabien and W. C. Lipke, *Tools and Technologies* (Burlington, Vt., 1979), pp. 13–63; D. M. Semel, 'A First Look at Duncan Phyfe's Tool Chest', *CEAIA* 29 (December 1976), pp. 56–60. See also W. L. Goodman, *British Plane Makers from 1700* (Needham Market, Suffolk, 2nd. edn., 1978).

15 *PP* 1812, III, Reports from Committees. Orders in Council, pp. 132, 145–52, 155.

16 J. Hunter, *Hallamshire* (Revd. edn. by A. Gatty, Sheffield, 1869), p. 174. Quoted remarks are from the *Sheffield Independent*.

17 W. Cobbett, *Rural Rides*, (1853 edn.), pp. 557–8.

18 Hunter, *Hallamshire*, p. 175.

19 Gatty, *Past and Present*, p. 202. The evidence for this remark can be found in numerous accounts: A. B. Bell, ed., *Peeps into the Past* (Sheffield, 1909), p. 218; G. I. H. Lloyd, *The Cutlery Trades* (1913), pp. 338–43; S. Pollard, *Three Centuries of Sheffield Steel* (Sheffield, 1954), pp. 22–7, 37–41; A. C. Marshall and H. Newbould, *The History of Firth's (1842–1918)* (Sheffield, 1924), p. 11; J. D. Scott, *Vickers* (1962), pp. 9–11. Samuel Osborn, the Sheffield steelmaker, remembered 'the time when, if the American trade with Sheffield was bad, the whole town was thrown into a state of distress. The trade with America was a very capricious one; at one time we would have an immense pressure of work, and at another time nothing'. *PP* 1886, XXI, RC Appointed to Inquire into the Depression of Trade and Industry, C. 4621, p. 105.

20 P. L. Smith, 'The Sheffield and South Yorkshire Navigation', *Transport History* 11 (1980), pp. 228–43; M. W. Flinn and A. Birch, 'The English Steel Industry Before 1856, with Special Reference to the Development of the Yorkshire Steel Industry', *Yorkshire Bulletin of Economic and Social Research* 6 (1954), pp. 163–77.

21 R. Adamson, 'Swedish Iron Exports to the United States, 1783–1860' *Scandinavian Economic History Review* 17 (1969), pp. 58–114; E. W. Fleisher, 'The Beginning of the Transatlantic Market for Swedish Iron', *Scandinavian Economic History Review* 1 (1953), pp. 178–92.

22 J. G. Timmins, 'Concentration and Integration in the Sheffield Crucible Steel Industry', *Business History* 24 (March 1982), pp. 61–78; *idem*, 'The Commercial Development of the Sheffield Crucible Steel Industry' (Sheffield MA, 1976). Using rate-book evidence, Timmins identifies major cycles of investment activity and relates them to the overseas demand for steel, especially the US demand. The relationship became particularly close after the mid-1830s.

23 Four examples will give an idea of the riches accumulated by merchants trading with America. George Wostenholm, cutler, left an estate of £250,000 in 1876; Thomas Jessop, steelmaker, £656,000 in 1887; Mark Firth, steelmaker, £600,000 in 1880; and Frederick T. Mappin, cutler and steelmaker, £946,263 in 1910. These represented enormous sums for the time, especially since all these men had made substantial investments in property besides endowments to the town during their lifetimes. See: *DBB passim*; G. Tweedale, *Giants of Sheffield Steel* (Sheffield, 1986).

24 *Sheffield Daily Telegraph*, 1 December 1887. Besides Jessop's, other firms which opened up a US trade during 1820–60 were Wilson, Hawksworth, Moss & Ellison (*Histories of Famous Firms* (1957–8), vol. 18, No. 6, p. 4); W. K. Peace (*Implement and Machinery Review* 36 (1 May 1910), pp. 71–2); and Frost, Askham & Mosforth (M. Chesworth, *Nineteenth Century Sheffield Through its Billheads and Related Documents* (SCL, 1984), n.p.). Other companies – Butcher's, Sanderson's, and Greaves – are mentioned in SCL Marsh 14. Extracts of Letters from the United States 1833–40.

25 J. R. Grabb, 'Shear Steel. A Forgotten but Useful Metal', *CEAIA* 28 (March 1975), pp. 8–11. On steel in colonial tools, see C. Bridenbaugh, *The Colonial Craftsman* (New York, 1950), pp. 46, 55, 59, 84.

26 H. J. Kauffman, 'Cast Steel', *CEAIA* 22 (December 1969), pp. 49–50; J. Gardner, 'Cast Steel', *CEAIA* 23 (March 1970), pp. 6, 16.

27 See Chap. 11.

28 BLCU, Hoe Papers, esp. Box 21; F. E. Comparato, *Chronicles of Genius and Folly* (Culver City, Ca., 1979), pp. 111–29.

29 EMHL Acc 1567, 'The Disston History', vol. 2, p. 15.

30 G. Porter, ed., *Asher and Adams' Pictorial Album of American Industry 1876* (New York repr., 1976), p. 98.

31 H. J. Kauffman, 'Some Notes on Axes', *CEAIA* 7 (April 1954), pp. 18–20; *idem.*, *American Axes* (Vt., 1972), p. 45.

32 J. S. Kebabien, 'The Douglas Axe Manufacturing Company, East Douglas, Mass.', *CEAIA* 25 (September 1972), pp. 43–6.

33 Connecticut Historical Society, Ms. 72190, 'The Collins Company Historical Memoranda, 1826–1871', by S. W. Collins, 14 February 1868, folios 194–7, 195 (I am grateful to Dr K. C. Barraclough for a copy of this Ms.); R. B. Gordon, 'Material Evidence of the Development of Metalworking Technology at the Collins Axe Factory', *I.A.: The Journal of the Society for In-

dustrial Archeology 9 (1983), pp. 19–28; P. Uselding, 'Elisha K. Root, Forging, and the "American System"', *Technology and Culture* 15 (October 1974), pp. 561–2.

34 K. D. and J. Roberts, *Planemakers and Other Edge Tool Enterprises in New York State in the Nineteenth Century* (Cooperstown, N.Y., 1971), p. 7 and *passim.*

35 J. A. Moody, *The American Cabinetmaker's Plow Plane* (Evansville, Ind., 1981); K. D. Roberts, *Wooden Planes in Nineteenth Century America* (2 vols., Fitzwilliam, N.H., 1978/83), pp. 42–3; A. Sellens, *Woodworking Planes* (P.p., 1978); R. K. Smith, *Patented Transitional Metallic Planes in America 1827–1927* (Lancaster, Mass., 1981); P. C. Welsh, 'The Metallic Woodworking Plane: An American Contribution to Hand-Tool Design', *Technology and Culture* 7 (1966), pp. 38–47.

36 C. P. Russell, *Firearms, Traps, and Tools of the Mountain Men* (New York, 1967), pp. 122–44, 352, 369–72.

37 See M. Van H. Taber, *A History of the Cutlery Industry in the Connecticut Valley* (Northampton, Mass., 1959), p. 21.

38 See R. D. Hurt, *American Farm Tools* (Manhattan, Kans., 1982), esp. appendix, 'Metallurgy and Technological Change in American Agriculture', pp. 113–16.

39 R. L. Ardrey, *American Agricultural Implements* (Chicago, 1894), pp. 5–20, 164–8; W. G. Broehl, *John Deere's Company* (New York, 1984), p. 125; 'The History of the Steel Plow', *Iron Age* 68 (18 July 1901), pp. 26–7; N. M. Clark, *John Deere. He Gave to the World the Steel Plow* (Moline, Ill., 1937), 32–8, 42.

40 F. J. Deyrup, *Arms Makers of the Connecticut Valley* (Northampton, Mass., 1948), pp. 79–81; K. T. Howell and E. W. Carlson, *Men of Iron: Forbes & Adam* (Lakeville, Conn., 1980).

41 The decline in the quality of Salisbury iron has been confirmed by analysis of surviving samples. See: R. B. Gordon, 'The Metallurgical Museum of Yale College and Nineteenth Century Ferrous Metallurgy in New England', *Journal of Metals* (July 1982), pp. 27–33 (Dr K. C. Barraclough supplied me with this reference); *idem*, 'Materials for Manufacturing: The Response of the Connecticut Iron Industry to Technological Change and Limited Resources', *Technology and Culture* 24 (October 1983), pp. 602–34.

42 The Colt Co. from its founding made all its revolver barrels of steel, ordering substantial quantities from Naylor & Co. of Sheffield in the late 1840s. (Naylor & Co., based in Boston and New York, was the American agency of Naylor Vickers – later Vickers – and should not be confused with Naylor Sanderson, the forerunner of Sanderson Bros.) See J. E. Parsons, *Saml. Colt's Own Record* (Conn., 1949), pp. 35–6, and *passim*. (The Sanderson Booth referred to in this book is presumably Sanderson Bros., Sheffield.) On the early use of steel in guns, see M. L. Brown, *Firearms in Colonial America* (Washington, DC, 1980), pp. 240–1, 243–5.

43 Whitney imported Sanderson's steel. See C. C. Cooper, R. B. Gordon and H. V. Merrick, 'Archeological Evidence of Metallurgical Innovation at the Eli Whitney Armory', *I.A.: The Journal of the Society for Industrial Archeology* 8 (1982), pp. 1–12. The Whitney Arms Co. Papers, Yale University, contain several letters to Sanderson's. I am grateful to Professor R. B. Gordon for copies, which show that the American firm also relied on the Sheffielders for high-quality bar iron.

John H. Hall, the renowned superintendent of the Harpers Ferry Armory, in his personal account book recording his dealings as a craftsman in Maine, refers to cast steel rifle barrels as early as 1817. If Hall's nomenclature was correct (unfortunately, the term 'cast steel' was often used carelessly at that time) it would be the earliest reference to crucible steel in American guns. I am grateful to Ron Kley, Curator of the Maine State Museum for this information. See also *idem*, 'Researching Early Maine Craftsmen: John H. Hall and the Gunsmith's Trade', *Maine Historical Society Quarterly* 24 (Spring 1985), pp. 410–15, 414.

44 The Springfield Armory, for example, besides importing English bar iron, relied upon Jessops's and Sanderson's steel by 1850. See letter, 8 February 1850, from Springfield Armory Superintendent Roswell Lee to Superintendent James Burton at the Harpers Ferry Armory, in the Burton Papers, Yale University. Again, I am grateful to Ron Kley for this information.

45 Taber, *Cutlery Industry*, p. 38.

46 G. Bathe, *An Engineer's Notebook* (St Augustine, Fla., 1955), p. 11.

47 R. G. Hall, 'Datable Characteristics of Anvils', *CEAIA* 29 (June 1976), pp. 21–4; J. Lasansky, *To Draw, Upset and Weld* (Lewisburg, Pa., 1980), p. 7.

48 *Ibid.*, pp. 14–15; H. R. Bradley Smith, *Blacksmiths' and Farriers' Tools at Shelburne Museum* (Shelburne, Vt., 1966), *passim*.

49 BL Ms. 596, Washburn & Goddard, 1822–ca.1848. W314. Vol. 1, Letters to England 1843–45; Ms. 596, C. Goodrich, 'Story of the Washburn & Moen Manufacturing Company 1831–1899' (1935), pp. 5–9.

50 C. H. Bailey, *Two Hundred Years of American Clocks and Watches* (Englewood Cliffs, N.J., 1975), p. 156; T. R. Crom, *Horological Shop Tools 1700 to 1900* (Melrose, Fla., 1980); D. S. Landes, *Revolution in Time* (Cambridge, Mass., 1983), p. 232.

51 Cast steel was crucial for the emergence of the steel pen trade in the early nineteenth century. See: M. Daniels, 'The Ingenious Pen: American Writing Implements from the Eighteenth Century to the Twentieth', *American Archivist* 43 (1980), pp. 312–24; S. Howard, 'The Steel Pen and the Modern Line of Beauty', *Technology and Culture* 26 (October 1985), pp. 785–98.

52 'Best cast steel' was the basis for Jacob Perkins' experiments with bank-note engraving plates. See D. & G. Bathe, *Jacob Perkins: His Inventions, His Times, & His Contemporaries* (Philadelphia, 1943), pp. 24, 61, 182–5. In the 1820s cast steel plates reduced printing costs, while bank-note printers both in Britain and America found them useful in preventing forgery by allowing a superior ornamental quality in engraved notes. See *The Penny Cyclopaedia of the Society for the Diffusion of Useful Knowledge* (1842), vol. 23, pp. 4–7.

53 D. J. Jeremy, *Transatlantic Industrial Revolution* (Cambridge, Mass., 1981), p. 187.

54 T. G. Lytle, *Harpoons and Other Whalecraft* (New Bedford, Mass., 1984), pp. 4–5 and *passim*. In Herman Melville's *Moby Dick* (Chap. 5, 'The Counterpane'), Ishmael sees Queequeg shaving with a harpoon: 'Afterwards I wondered less at this operation when I came to know of what fine steel the head of a harpoon is made'.

55 *Abstract of the ... Seventh Census, 1850* (Repr. 1970, New York), pp. 5, 45, 73.

56 Timmins, 'Commercial Development', p. 78. Expansion in the 1850s was phenomenal. The number of melting holes is said to have increased from 1,333 to 2,437 in 1851–62 (an increase of about 82½ percent). See *Inter-*

national Exhibition 1862. Reports by the Juries (1863), Class XXXII, Section A, pp. 2–3.

57 *Ironmonger* 28 (2 September 1882), pp. 326–9, describing Albert A. Jowitt. Sheffield merchants congregated particularly around Cliff, Gold, John, and Pearl Streets. See R. G. Albion, *The Rise of New York Port 1815–1860* (Hamden, Conn., 1961), pp. 67–8.

58 *Scientific American* 14 (30 October 1858), p. 61. Issue 3, n.s. (10 November 1860), p. 313, made similar remarks.

59 *Sheffield Independent*, 6 August 1859. The favourable US trade in this year was reported almost every week. See for example *ibid.*, 21 May 1859; 4 June 1859.

60 *Ibid.*, 21 November 1857. Even the mighty Naylor Vickers suspended payment.

61 *Ibid.*, 1 June 1861; 29 June 1861; 28 September 1861.

62 Letter signed E.B., *ibid.*, 10 September 1853, in reply to the Master Cutler's remarks on US competition. Another communication from E.B., *ibid.*, 24 September 1853, argued that American scissors and tailor's shears 'beat us entirely'. On the superiority of American tools, see also *ibid.*, 2 January 1858.

63 Letter from 'A Sheffield Agent' in NY, *ibid.*, 29 October 1859. Some disagreed with this assessment of American quality (see *ibid.*, 24 September 1859), but generally opinion expressed in the *Sheffield Independent* was that the town was increasingly unable to compete. See *ibid.*, 10 September 1859; 28 April 1860, 3 November 1860.

64 Letter signed H.T., *ibid.*, 17 September 1853. On Sheffield complacency contrasted with Yankee efficiency and sobriety, see letter by 'Anglo-Saxon', *ibid.*, 14 January 1854.

65 *Ibid.*, 31 March 1855 (letter on 'Manufacture of Steel in America' signed DEMEZY); 27 November 1858.

66 *Scientific American* 8, n.s. (14 March 1863), p. 166; (21 March 1863), p. 182.

67 *Sheffield Independent*, 30 August 1856.

1. THE BIRTH OF THE AMERICAN CRUCIBLE STEEL INDUSTRY

1 As a comparison, Sweden had begun copying the Sheffield methods by 1769, Switzerland by 1804, Germany by 1814, and France by 1815. See J. R. Harris, 'Attempts to Transfer English Steel Techniques to France in the Eighteenth Century', in S. Marriner, ed., *Business and Businessmen* (Liverpool, 1978), pp. 199–233.

2 F. H. Taylor, *History of the Alan Wood Iron and Steel Company, 1792–1920* (n.d., p.p.), p. 7.

3 B . F. French, *History of the Rise and Progress of the Iron Trade of the US from 1621 to 1857* (New York, 1858), pp. 50–3.

4 The best source on the American crucible steel industry is James M. Swank, Secretary of the American Iron and Steel Association, who collected information when compiling a report for the 1880 Census (Manufactures). See *History of the Manufacture of Iron in All Ages* (Philadelphia, 1884). EMHL Acc 322 and HSP F–33 contain some of Swank's letters, but they add nothing to the above account. On early steelmaking attempts see also: A. C. Bining, *Pennsylvania Iron Manufacture in the Eighteenth Century* (Harrisburg, 1938), *passim*; *idem.*, *British Regulation of the Colonial Iron Industry*

(Philadelphia, 1933), p. 89 and *passim*; V. S. Clark, *History of Manufactures in the United States* (New York, 1929), vol. 1, pp. 516–17.

5 During the 1820s the Franklin Institute offered awards for the production of blister steel and bar iron. See B. Sinclair, *Philadelphia's Philosopher Mechanics* (Baltimore, 1974), pp. 87–8. Satisfactory blister steel was manufactured at competitive prices in the 1820s, according to the New York press; it sold for 10 cents per lb compared to 14 cents for the English product. See *Sheffield Iris*, 27 October 1829.

6 Swank, *Iron*, pp. 292–6; *BAISA* 18 (13 February 1884), p. 41.

7 Information and quotations are from B. Seely, 'Adirondack Iron and Steel Company, "New Furnace", 1849–1854' (1978), pp. 68–9, 83–4, to whom I am indebted for the loan of the typescript.

8 See Chap. 7.

9 Though not identified by Seely this may have been Charles Pickslay (1781–1852), a Sheffield manufacturer who also worked with Faraday on his experiments with alloy steels. See R. A. Hadfield, *Faraday and His Metallurgical Researches* (1931), pp. 132–6.

10 On Dixon see: *DAB; NCAB; Mechanical Engineers in America Born Prior to 1861* (New York, 1980), pp. 118–19. For descriptions of Dixon's Crucible Co see: G. Porter, ed., *Asher & Adams' Pictorial Album of American Industry 1876* (New York repr., 1976), p. 155; *Scientific American* 37, n.s. (20 October 1877), p. 242; 40, n.s. (18 January 1879), pp. 31, 34. Dixon was awarded the Elliot Cresson Medal by the Franklin Institute for a product 'about equal to the average quality of imported steel', produced by partly decarbonising pig or cast iron in an oven stratified with pulverized oxide of iron and then melting it in graphite crucibles. See: A. M. McMahon and S. A. Morris, *Technology in Industrial America* (Wilmington, Del., 1977), p. 165; *Journal of the Franklin Institute* 20 (1850), p. 41.

11 J. P. Templeton, 'Jersey City: Early American Steel Center', *Proceedings of the New Jersey Historical Society* 79 (1961), pp. 169–77.

12 Seely, 'Adirondack Co', p. 93.

13 *Ibid.*, pp. 114–15. See also: *Hunt's Merchant's Magazine and Commercial Review* 20 (1849), pp. 678–9; *Scientific American* 4 (15 July 1849), p. 341; 5 (17 November 1849), p. 66. Partly in a further attempt to attract British capital, the company sent cast steel and iron to the Great Exhibition 1851, where it received favourable mention. See C. T. Rodgers, *American Superiority at the World's Fair* (Philadelphia, 1852), p. 46.

14 Swank, *Iron*, p. 299.

15 *Ibid.*, p. 298.

16 *Ibid.*, p. 296. The 1850 Census makes no mention of steelmaking in any other state than Pennsylvania, but Swank argues that this is inaccurate. In contrast, Sheffield's production of blister steel was approaching 40,000 tons by 1853. For an analysis of the patchy Sheffield data, see K. C. Barraclough, 'The Production of Steel in Britain by the Cementation and Crucible Processes', *Historical Metallurgy* 8 (1974), pp. 103–11.

17 Again, Swank is the best source. He based much of his account on an anonymous study, *Pittsburgh, Its Industry and Commerce* (1870), and G. H. Thurston, *Pittsburgh and Allegheny in the Centennial Year* (Pittsburgh, 1876). Cf. also: Thurston, *Pittsburgh's Progress, Industries and Resources* (Pittsburgh, 1886); and Swank, 'The Manufacture of Iron and Steel in Beaver County', in J. H. Bausman, ed., *History of Beaver County, Pennsyl-*

vania and Its Centennial Celebration (New York, 1904), vol. 2, pp. 1265–69. Also useful, though derivative of Swank, is H. Gilmer, 'Birth of the American Crucible Steel Industry', *Western Pennsylvania Historical Magazine* 36 (1953), pp. 17–36. I consulted at least a dozen books and unpublished theses, of varying quality, on Pittsburgh's economic and social history; none mentioned the city's crucible steel industry, even in passing.

18 Broadmeadow later designed a novel converting furnace which allowed the bars to be taken out hot for tilting, so avoiding reheating them. Like many short-cuts in converting and crucible melting it was probably not a success. See 'Improvement in the Manufacturing of Steel', 25 May 1844 (Pat. No. 3,596), *Journal of the Franklin Institute* 8, 3rd s. (1844), pp. 122–4. For other furnace 'improvements' see: *ibid.* 21. n.s. (1838), pp. 46–7; *ibid.* 7, 3rd s. (1849), pp. 23–4.

19 J. S. Jeans, *Steel. Its History, Manufacture, Properties and Uses* (1880), p. 140. According to Thurston, *Pittsburgh's Progress*, it was Patrick and James Dunn who commenced production. Interestingly, Edward Dunn (steelmaker) appears in the 1850 Ms. Census of Population for Pittsburgh.

20 Swank, *Iron*, p. 299, quoting Thomas S. Blair of Pittsburgh. For further details on the Schoenbergers, see: BL Ms. 596, E. P. Loy, 'History of the Various Schoenberger Iron & Steel Companies' (typescript, 1914); *ibid.* A. G. Warren, 'Centenary of Schoenberger Works. American Steel & Wire Company, Pittsburgh, Pa. 1824–1924' (typescript, n.d.).

21 G. H. Thurston, *Pittsburgh As It Is* (Pittsburgh, 1857), p. 113. 'It is ... the iron-works of Pittsburgh that usually attract the stranger first, astonish him most, and detain him the longest', remarked J. Parton in *Atlantic Monthly* 21 (January 1868), p. 28. For similar comments, see *Daily Pittsburgh Gazette*, 30 November 1861. A useful account of the locational factors affecting Pittsburgh's iron industry, not without relevance to the steel industry, is L. C. Hunter, 'Influence of the Market upon Technique in the Iron Industry in Western Pennsylvania up to 1860', *Journal of Economic and Business History* 1 (1928–9), pp. 241–81. See also J. L. Bishop, *A History of American Manufactures from 1608 to 1860* (Philadelphia, 3rd edn., 1868), vol. 3, pp. 96–112.

22 *Pittsburgh Gazette*, 18 June 1867.

23 Swank, *Iron*, p. 300.

24 Jeans, *Steel*, p. 141.

25 USNA, US Bureau of the Census Ms. Population Schedules (microfilm), M432 (745–6), M653 (1058–60), M593 (1290–1, 1295–8). It is easy to identify crucible steel workers, because no Bessemer converters were built in Pittsburgh until after 1870. The number of English steel men was negligible before that date. Two 'steel makers' (Henry Roberts, Edward Dunn) and one 'steel manufacturer' (John Wilkinson) were enumerated in 1850, alongside over 50 English-born ironworkers. In 1860 there were still only two English steelmakers listed in Pittsburgh.

26 J. S. Jeans, ed., *American Industrial Conditions and Competition* (1902), p. 169; *Ironmonger* 25 (26 March 1881), p. 408; E. Young, *Labor in Europe and America* (Washington, DC, 1875), pp. 325, 765. For a fuller discussion see Chap. 2.

27 *Magazine of Western History* 3 (1885/6), p. 630; C. Robson, ed., *The Manufactories and Manufacturers of Pennsylvania in the Nineteenth Century*

(Philadelphia, 1875), p. 218. For further evidence of Pittsburgh firms recruiting Sheffield labour, see C. J. Erickson, *American Industry and the European Immigrant 1860–1885* (Cambridge, Mass., 1957), p. 40. One Sheffield steelmaker (George Senior) who later visited Park's Black Diamond Works found a number of workmen 'almost as familiar to me as my own men, including moulders, rod rollers, tilters, and others'. See *Journal of the Sheffield Technical School Metallurgical Society* (1892), p. 90.

28 *Daily Pittsburgh Gazette*, 2 October 1865. An engraving in H. R. Miller. *Fleming's Views of Old Pittsburgh* (Pittsburgh, 1932), shows a view of the works with two converting furnaces.

29 Davy's was a Sheffield firm, founded in 1830, which specialised in making machinery for steel works. For brief details, see: *The Anvil* 4 (1956), pp. 9–10; 4 (1957), pp. 14–16; *Industries of Sheffield and District* (Sheffield, 1905), pp. 94–101. Fort Pitt Iron & Steel Works, Pittsburgh, also imported Davy's hammers. Cf. *American Manufacturer*, 28 May 1874, p. 13.

30 *Iron Age* 15 (4 February 1875), p. 9. On Crescent see also *American Journal of Mining* 20 (18 December 1875), p. 594. The Sheffield-style layout can be clearly seen in the plan of the Works in *Engineering* 24 (23 November 1877), pp. 394–6.

31 *Engineering* 23 (4 May 1877), p. 337; 'Park, Brother & Co, Black Diamond Works, Pittsburgh, Pa.', unpublished typescript from the archives of the Crucible Steel Co of America, kindly loaned to me by K. C. Barraclough; *Scientific American* 12, n.s. (1 April 1865), pp. 207–8.

32 *History of Allegheny Co., Pennsylvania* (Philadelphia, 1876), pp. 110–11.

33 Thomas S. Blair, quoted in Swank, *Iron*, p. 300.

34 N. Rosenberg, ed., *The American System of Manufactures* (Edinburgh, 1969), p. 336. There are also echoes of bad labour relations in H. M. Howe, *The Metallurgy of Steel* (New York, 1891), p. 307, who reported 'the experience of an American crucible steel works whose manager, discharging imported steel men in disgust, hired a sailor and a butcher, neither with any knowledge of steel-making, as a melter and as puller-out. He certainly keeps his works running, though with much waste of his own issue'.

35 'Sheffield Steel Makers in America', *Sheffield Independent*, 28 March 1865. For another letter in a similar vein, see *ibid.*, 28 January 1879.

36 A fairly typical response was that of Dr C. B. Webster, American Consul in Sheffield, quoted in *BAISA* 17 (11 April 1883), p. 98: 'The workmen here do not have the same ambition that our artisans at home have. They have no desire to rise. If they can earn enough to keep them in bacon, bread and beer, they are content. They indulge in betting and drinking … they seem to have little care for the future.' See also Webster's remarks in E. Young, *Labor*, pp. 408–9, and *Sheffield Independent*, 11 January 1876, where he emphasises the fact that in Sheffield Monday was often taken as a holiday. S. Pollard, *A History of Labour in Sheffield* (Liverpool, 1959), is the standard account of working life in the town. On the importance of social factors in technological development, see J. E. Sawyer, 'The Social Basis of the American System of Manufacturing', *Journal of Economic History* 14 (1954), pp. 361–79.

37 'How Sheffield Workmen in America Act Towards Their Masters', letter by R.T.B., *Sheffield Independent*, 10 May 1865.

38 *Sheffield Independent*'s US correspondent, 2 December 1871. 'There are a great number of skilled workmen who have returned from America during the last two or three years very much dissatisfied', testified Samuel Osborn:

PP 1886, XXI, RC Appointed to Inquire into the Depression of Trade and Industry, C. 4621, p. 107.

39 American Iron and Steel Association, *The Ironworks of the United States. A Directory* (1874), pp. 96–100; *idem, Directory to the Iron and Steel Works of the United States* (1880), pp. 114–22. See also *The Iron and Steel Institute in America in 1890* (1892), pp. 427–9.

40 Pittsburgh Chamber of Commerce, *The Mercantile, Manufacturing and Mining Interests of Pittsburgh* (Pittsburgh, 1884), p. 38. See also: Thurston, *Pittsburgh's Progress*, pp. 6–17; *BAISA* 18 (1 October 1884), p. 250; 'Natural Gas in the United States', *Ironmonger* 26 (16 October 1886), pp. 154–8.

41 C. W. Siemens, 'On the Regenerative Gas Furnace as Applied to the Manufacture of Cast Steel', *Journal of the Chemical Society* 6 (1868), pp. 279–308.

42 W. F. Durfee, 'The Development of American Industries since Columbus. VIII, The Manufacture of Steel', *Popular Science Monthly* (New York, October 1891), pp. 729–49. The *American Journal of Mining* 6 (28 November 1868), p. 338, stated that Anderson's 24-pot furnace could produce 10,800 lbs of steel in twenty-four hours.

43 On American gas furnace technology, see Chap. 2.

44 American Adirondack iron cost about one-third of the price of imported iron, according to the *Journal of the Franklin Institute* 17, 3rd s. (1849), p. 405. Even East coast manufacturers sometimes had to wait up to a year for supplies of Swedish iron. See Connecticut Historical Society, Ms. 72190, 'The Collins Company Historical Memoranda, 1826–1871', by S. W. Collins (1868), Folio 197.

45 *Daily Pittsburgh Gazette*, 2 October 1865.

46 *Pittsburgh Gazette*, 28 November 1866; *BAISA* 1 (26 September 1866), pp. 18–21.

47 Bishop, *American Manufactures*, p. 108

48 Ironmonger 25 (25 March 1881), p. 293.

49 *Iron Age* 15 (4 February 1875), p. 9.

50 *Ibid.*, 18 (17 August 1876), p. 5.

51 Swedish iron imports correspond closely to US crucible steel production until the 1870s, when the amount of iron imported fell markedly. Data on Swedish iron imports to the US can be found in A. Attman, *Fagerstabrukens Historia: Adertonhundratalet* (Uppsala, 1958), pp. 20–1, 255–6. See also: R. Adamson, 'Swedish Iron Exports to the United States, 1783–1860', *Scandinavian Economic History Review* 17 (1969), pp. 58–114; E. G. Danielsson, *Anteckningar om Norra Amerikas Fri-Staters Jerntillverkning Samt Handel Med Jern-Och Stalvaror* (Stockholm, 1845); E. W. Fleisher, 'The Beginning of the Transatlantic Market for Swedish Iron', *Scandinavian Economic History Review* 1 (1953), pp. 178–92.

52 Vickers exported £200,000–£300,000 a year in Swedish iron in the 1850s. See *Engineer* 4 (13 November 1857), p. 359.

53 On Pittsburgh's manufacturing advantages, see *Annual Report of the Secretary of Internal Affairs of the Commonwealth of Pennsylvania. Pt. III. Industrial Statistics.* Vol. 4 (1875–6), pp. 109–14.

54 *History of Allegheny Co., Pennsylvania* (Philadelphia, 1876), p. 110; EMHL Acc 1191. Ninth Census of Manufactures, 1870, shows Hussey, Wells & Co capitalised at $1,145,000. An attempt to derive total capital invested in the Pittsburgh steel industry failed because the firms were only partly enumerated in every Census between 1850 and 1880.

55 *BAISA* 17 (2 May 1883), p. 116.
56 Cf. L. C. Hunter, 'Financial Problems of the Early Pittsburgh Iron Manufacturers', *Journal of Economic and Business History* 2 (May 1930), pp. 520–44.
57 *ACAB*; Bishop, *American Manufactures*, vol. 3, p. 107; *DAB; Magazine of Western History* 3 (1885/6), pp. 329–48; *NCAB; Pittsburgh Gazette*, 26 April 1893; Robson, *Manufactories*, pp. 177–8; E. Wilson, *Standard History of Pittsburgh, Pennsylvania* (Chicago, 1898), pp. 1001–3. Hussey was in Sheffield in 1862, apparently attracted by the Bessemer process, which he eventually decided was too risky to undertake. Cf. *History of Allegheny Co., Pennsylvania* (Chicago, 1889), pp. 254–8.
58 *Magazine of Western History* 2 (1885), pp. 550–6; Wilson, *Standard History*, pp. 1004–5.
59 Hussey, Wells & Co., *Steel Memorial, December 1, 1865* (Pittsburgh, 1865); *In Memoriam Calvin Wells* (Philadelphia, 1910); *Magazine of Western History* 3 (1885/6), pp. 626–35; Robson, *Manufactories*, p. 178.
60 *ACAB; BAISA* 17 (2 May 1883), p. 116; *DAB; Magazine of Western History* 4 (1886), pp. 524–8. Park was a frequent visitor to Sheffield, where he was often a guest at Jessop's steel works. See 'What Mr. William Jessop thinks of America', *Ironmonger* 29 (23 June 1883), pp. 863–4.
61 *BAISA* 9 (23 April 1875), p. 115; *History of Allegheny Co., Pennsylvania* (Philadelphia, 1876), pp. 179–80, 187, 190; Robson, *Manufactories*, pp. 218, 219, 253, 268–9.
62 On the social origins of Sheffield steelmakers see: *DBB* (cf. Brown, Cammell, Firth, Hadfield, Vickers); C. J. Erickson, *British Industrialists* (Cambridge, 1959); W. Odom, *Hallamshire Worthies* (Sheffield, 1926); J. H. Stainton, *The Making of Sheffield 1865–1914* (Sheffield, 1924); G. Tweedale, *Giants of Sheffield Steel* (Sheffield, 1986).
63 See generally: P. A. David, 'The Mechanization of Reaping in the Antebellum Midwest', in H. Rosovsky, ed., *Industrialization in Two Systems* (New York, 1966), pp. 3–39; J. Kuuse, *Interaction Between Agriculture and Industry* (Upsalla, 1974); L. Rogin, *The Introduction of Farm Machinery in its Relation to the Production of Labor in the Agriculture of the United States During the Nineteenth Century* (California, 1931). This is not to underestimate the importance of Civil War armaments' demand, which coincided with the rise of the Pittsburgh steel industry. However, in view of American armsmakers' conservatism in adopting domestic steels, agriculture seems the critical influence. The impact of the Civil War on the American economy has been much debated by economic historians.
64 *Daily Pittsburgh Gazette*, 12 September 1860. Thurston, *Pittsburgh's Progress*, p. 81, states that Hussey's firm was formed expressly to supply steel for edge tools.
65 *Daily Pittsburgh Gazette*, 2 October 1865. For further details on this firm and the rapidly rising demand, see: *Pittsburgh Gazette*, 25 September 1867, 28 July 1868, 22 September 1868; *Scientific American* 43, n.s. (14 August 1880), pp. 94, 100. An 1863 Price List for the Pittsburgh Steel Works (see n. 72) shows agricultural steels very much in evidence.
66 *Iron Age* 15 (4 February 1875), p. 9.
67 *Ibid.*, 18 (17 August 1876), p. 5.
68 SCL Marsh 248. Mollison to Woodcock, Cincinnati, 11 June 1858. Most of

Marsh Bros' letters to its New York agent, W. N. Woodcock, are in SCL MD
1485. The company's history is related in S. Pollard, *Three Centuries of Sheffield Steel* (Sheffield, 1954).

69 MD 1485. Marsh Bros to Woodcock, New York, 1 April 1865.
70 *Ibid.*, 27 January 1866.
71 *Ibid.*, 24 June 1864.
72 Sheffield and American prices compared in Table 1: 2 are from price lists collected by a Marsh Bros' agent in the US. The steel tariff and the influence of
the highly protectionist American Iron and Steel Association are described in
P. H. Tedesco, 'Patriotism, Protection, and Prosperity: James Moore Swank,
the American Iron and Steel Association, and the Tariff, 1873–1913'
(Boston PhD, 1970).
73 *Scientific American* 15, n.s. (15 September 1866), p. 187; (6 October 1866),
p. 6; 20, n.s. (9 January 1869), pp. 22–3. 'Red-shortness' was a fault in
wrought iron caused by impurities, especially sulphur, which made it brittle
at high temperatures.
74 HSP. Baldwin Locomotive Papers. New York Office Letters, Incoming
Letter Book Oct.–Dec. 1865. Letter, 9 October 1865. The file contains
numerous letters from Hussey's firm, relating mostly to orders for low-grade
steel plates and locomotive parts.
75 *Sheffield Independent*, 17 June 1875. Trade with America in the 1870s is
reviewed, with the aid of US Consular Returns, in *ibid.*, 2 October 1880.
76 PP 1886, XXI, RC Appointed to Enquire into the Depression of Trade and
Industry. C. 4621, p. 108. Albert Vickers crossed the Atlantic 34 times
during his lifetime. See my Vickers' entry in *DBB*.
77 *Sheffield Independent*, 30 October 1879.
78 C. H. Fitch, 'The Manufacture of Saws and Files', *Tenth Census*, II, 'Manufactures' (Washington, DC, 1883), p. 724.
79 BLCU, Hoe Papers, Box 27, Steel Order Book, 15 April 1862–7 April 1869.
80 Marsh 249 (1–77). Misc. letters ca. April/March 1867.
81 PP 1877, XXXIV, Reports on the Philadelphia International Exhibition of
1876, I, p. 127. It is interesting to note that Disston advertised his products
as being made from 'London Spring Steel' at this time – a testimony to the
continued popularity of English steel.
82 F. E. Comparato, *Chronicles of Genius and Folly* (Culver City, Ca., 1979),
pp. 127–9.
83 Marsh 249 (1–77).
84 *American Manufacturer*, 26 February 1874, p. 4.
85 *BAISA* 1 (17 October 1866), pp. 42–3.
86 See *75 Years of Business Progress and Industrial Advance, 1832–1907*
(Cambridge, Mass., 1907), p. 9. Simonds' steel plant is described in *Iron
Trade Review* 54 (17 April 1919), pp. 1009–16; the manager A. T. Simonds
had been trained in Sheffield.
87 *Imperial Trade Journal* (January 1926), p. 81. E. C. Atkins, who established
his firm in 1857, built the reputation of his 'Silver Steel Saws' on Jessop's
steel. See also *Reports of the Committee of the Senate ... for the 2nd Session
of the 53rd Congress. Replies to Tariff Inquiries. Schedule C. Metals and
Manufactures of* (Washington, DC, 1894), No. 1686, pp. 32–5.
88 *BAISA* (26 March 1874), p. 97; (23 April 1874), pp. 129, 132. The Boston
pamphlet opposing the steel duties was published in eleven parts by the

American Manufacturer (1874), which then issued a long-winded rebuttal, 28 May 1874, p. 11.

89 See: G. Porter, ed., *Pictorial Album*, pp. 98, 144; 'The Collins Company Historical Memoranda'; E. L. Klinger, 'The Douglas Axe', *CEAIA* 27 (June 1974), p. 31; K. D. and J. Roberts, *Planemakers and Other Edge Tool Enterprises in New York State in the Nineteenth Century* (Cooperstown, N.Y., 1971), p. 52. A. S. Bolles, *Industrial History of the United States* (Norwich, Conn., 1878), pp. 270–4, describes the cutting parts of the finest American axes as 'being composed of nearly a pound of the best Jessop steel'. Even as late as 1939 the Stanley Plane Co of New Britain, Connecticut, advertised its products as being made of English cast steel. Eventually, the Stanley Works' Great Britain was formed in 1936 by renaming the purchased firm of J. A. Chapman of Sheffield. Cf. A. Sellens, *The Stanley Plane* (Burlington, Vt., 1975), pp. 14, 27; F. Wright, *Stanley 1936–1986* (1986). On English steel in plane cutting irons, see K. D. Roberts, *Wooden Planes in Nineteenth Century America* (Fitzwilliam, N.H., 2nd edn., 1978), pp. 42–3.

90 M. Van H. Taber, *A History of the Cutlery Industry in the Connecticut Valley* (Northampton, Mass., 1959), pp. 40–1, 44.

91 H. Barnard, ed., *Armsmear: The Home, The Arm, and the Armory of Samuel Colt* (1866, repr. 1976), pp. 224–5. Colt's steel came from Firth's. See generally F. J. Deyrup, *Arms Makers of the Connecticut Valley* (Northampton, Mass., 1948), pp. 139, 192.

92 This subject receives detailed consideration in Chap. 9.

93 Hadfield's US notebook, American Notes, Plants, etc., SCL Hadfield Papers.

94 See Barraclough, 'Production of Steel', and J. G. Timmins, 'The Commercial Development of the Sheffield Crucible Steel Industry' (Sheffield University MA, 1976), pp. 66–72, 186–99. Barraclough revises his figures in *Steelmaking before Bessemer* (1984), vol. 2, Appendix 19, pp. 322–31.

95 H. Bessemer, *An Autobiography* (1905), pp. 213–15; *idem.*, 'On the Manufacture and Uses of Steel with Special Reference to Its Employment for Edge Tools', Paper read at Cutler's Company of London, 1 December 1880. Bessemer's claim met with a sagacious rebuke in H. Seebohm, *On the Manufacture of Crucible Cast Steel* (Sheffield, 1884), p. 3.

96 A useful summary of these developments is J. McHugh, *Alexander Holley and the Makers of Steel* (Baltimore, 1980). Holley was one of a number of American engineers and steelmakers who travelled to Sheffield after about 1860 to see Bessemer operations there. Interestingly, Holley's father had manufactured pocket-knives in Lakeville, Connecticut, in about 1842, importing Sheffield cutlers for the task. Holley himself wrote articles on the subject for *Poor's American Railroad Journal* (May–July 1850).

97 *Iron Age* 60 (12 August 1897), p. 15.

98 See *Reports of the United States Commissioners to the Paris Exposition 1867–'68* (Washington, DC, 1868), vol. 2, pp. 1–183. Hewitt's report is reproduced in A. Nevins, ed., *Selected Writings of Abram S. Hewitt* (New York, 1937). Holley came to the same conclusion: 'The crucible seems destined, however, to hold its place for the production of fine tools and other very fine steels, because the whole of the material it employs may be selected from the most highly refined direct process or puddled products, while the Bessemer and the open-hearth must use more or less crude cast iron'. *Metallurgical Review*, vol 1, p. 332.

99 Apparently, Sheffield crucible steel was considered for parts of the Brooklyn

Bridge, until Alexander Holley intervened to ensure that American open-hearth steel was used instead. See McHugh, *Holley*, pp. 295–6; D. McCullough, *The Great Bridge* (New York, 1972), pp. 372–96.

100 J. C. Danziger, 'High-Grade Steel', *Journal of the Association of Engineering Societies* 19 (July–December 1897), pp. 20–1; W. Metcalf, 'Revolution in Steel Making', *American Manufacturer* 57 (20 September 1895), p. 404; G. Porteus, 'High Carbon Open-Hearth Steel *versus* Crucible Steel in the Manufacture of Miscellaneous Tools', *TASST* 1 (1920), pp. 238–44; 'Crucible Steel's Hard Struggle', *American Manufacturer* 68 (16 May 1901), pp. 637–8.

101 F. H. Rowe, *History of the Iron and Steel Industry in Scioto County, Ohio* (Columbus, Ohio, 1938), pp. 50–1.

102 T. W. Bradley, Walden, N.Y., *Tariff Hearings Before the Committee on Ways and Means. 1st Session. 53rd Congress 1893*, p. 417.

103 Robert Holmshaw, *Mosely Industrial Commission to the United States of America* (Manchester, 1903), p. 104.

104 American Axe & Tool Co, *Trade Catalogue* (Glassport, Pa., 1907); *Illustrated Catalogue 1894* (repr., 1981).

105 W. S. Casterlin, *Forty Years at Cast Steel and Tool Making* (Scranton, Pa., 2nd edn. 1895), pp. 5–6.

106 T. R. Navin, *The Whitin Machine Works Since 1831* (Cambridge, Mass., 1950), pp. 120–1.

107 Jeans, *American Industrial Conditions*, p. 169. On English *v.* American tool steels, see M. T. Richardson, *Practical Blacksmithing* (New York, 1889), vol. 2, pp. 16–17.

108 Lord Riverdale (Arthur Balfour), *Quality* 7 (May 1936), p. 300.

109 J. Sheldon, *The Founders and Builders of Stocksbridge Works* (Stocksbridge, 1922), pp. 57–8, which reproduces a letter from the *Philadelphia Record*, 8 April 1882. See also: S. Moxon, *A Fox Centenary. Umbrella Frames, 1848–1948* (Stocksbridge, 1948), pp. 15–16; H. Stansfield, *Samuel Fox and Company Limited 1842–1967* (Stocksbridge, 1967). See generally: *Pawson and Brailsford's Illustrated Guide to Sheffield and Neighbourhood* (Sheffield, 1862), pp. 163–5; J. B. Smith, *A Treatise upon Wire* (1891), p. 15; *Ironmonger* 24 (17 July 1880), p. 78. On Andrew's see Chap. 8.

110 *Lee of Sheffield. A Family Enterprise* (Sheffield, 1962), p. 6. Arthur Lee first visited the US in 1863 as a salesman for Moss & Gamble. He later served on the Northern side in the Civil War, became a member of the Grand Lodge of New York in 1867, and returned to Sheffield in 1870. His firm later developed contacts with the American Steel & Wire Co and at time of writing still enjoys a New York trade in high-grade steel products. See: M. Brailsford, *Lee Steel 1874–1974* (Sheffield, 1974); *Men of the Period* (1896), p. 114; *Sheffield and Neighbourhood* (Sheffield, 1899), pp. 223–6.

111 H. Shaw (Magnets) Ltd, *Magnets and Memories* (Sheffield, 1983), p. 11; *Sheffield and Rotherham 'Up-to-date'* (1897), p. 140.

112 *American Manufacturer* 67 (19 July 1900), p. 50; (26 July 1900), p. 69; (16 August 1900), p. 126; (28 November 1900), p. 421. The combine included: the Pittsburgh firms of Park (1861), Singer, Nimick (1848), Howe, Brown (1865), Crescent (1865), La Belle (1863); Anderson, DuPuy of McKees Rocks, Pa. (1845); the steel dept. of Cumberland Steel & Tin Plate Co, of Cumberland, Md. (1873); Burgess Steel & Iron Works of Portsmouth, Ohio (1871); the steel dept. of the Benjamin Atha & Illingworth Co, of Harrison,

N.Y. (1864); Spaulding & Jennings of Jersey City (1880); Sanderson Bros of Syracuse, N.Y. (1876); Beaver Falls Steel Works of Beaver Falls, Pa. (1875); Aliquippa of Aliquippa, Pa. (1892).

113 Crucible Steel Co of America, *President's Report and Balance Sheet* (1901); idem., *50 Years of Fine Steelmaking* (1951); W. H. Colvin, *Crucible Steel of America* (New York, 1950); *Iron Age* 67 (21 February 1901), p. 17; 69 (20 March 1902), pp. 14–18. Generally, the combine avoided publicity and, without manuscript sources, its early history is difficult to reconstruct in detail. But cf. A. D. Chandler, *The Visible Hand* (Cambridge, Mass, 1977), esp. pp. 361, 369.

114 EMHL Acc 1613. Mimeographed book (incomplete) on the history of the iron and steel industry, p. 49.

2. SCIENCE AND ART: SHEFFIELD AND AMERICAN CRUCIBLE STEEL TECHNOLOGIES CONTRASTED

1 J. S. Jeans, ed., *American Industrial Conditions and Competition* (1902), p. 171.

2 See K. C. Barraclough, 'The Development of the Cementation Process for the Manufacture of Steel', *Post-Medieval Archaeology* 10 (1976), pp. 65–88; F. Giolitti, *The Cementation of Iron and Steel* (New York, 1915). Some firms such as Doncasters specialised in the production of converted steel. See *Daniel Doncaster & Sons Ltd 1778–1978* (Sheffield, 1978).

3 Tradition has it that the word shear was originally derived from the fact that the blades of shears, formerly used for cropping woollen cloth by the Yorkshire clothiers, were always made by this method.

4 See: T. S. Ashton, *Iron and Steel in the Industrial Revolution* (Manchester, 2nd edn., 1951), pp. 24–59; idem., *An Eighteenth Century Industrialist* (Manchester, 1939), pp. 37–40; E. S. Dane, *Peter Stubs and the Lancashire Hand Tool Industry* (Altrincham, 1973), pp. 76–81, 181–3; M. W. Flinn and A Birch, 'The English Steel Industry before 1856, with Special Reference to the Development of the Yorkshire Steel Industry', *Yorkshire Bulletin of Economic and Social Research* 6 (1954), pp. 163–77; R. A. Hadfield, 'Benjamin Huntsman of Sheffield. The Inventor of Crucible Steel', *Cassier's Magazine* 7 (1894–5), pp. 78–84; E. W. Hulme, 'The Pedigree and Career of Benjamin Huntsman', *Transactions of the Newcomen Society* 24 (1943–5), pp. 37–48; R. Jenkins 'Notes on the Early History of Steel Making in England', *Transactions of the Newcomen Society* 3 (1922–3), pp. 16–32; C. Sanderson, 'On the Manufacture of Steel as Carried on in This and Other Countries', *Journal of the Society of Arts* 3 (1854–5), pp. 450–8, and repr. in the *Journal of the Franklin Institute* 30, 3rd s. (1855), pp. 133–6, 203–9; S. Smiles, *Industrial Biography* (1863, repr. Newton Abbot, 1967), pp. 102–11.

5 The best accounts are by Sheffielders. Harry Brearley, famous for his discovery of stainless steel, gives a superb account of the process from the shopfloor level in *Steel-Makers* (1933). Also useful are: R. A. Hadfield, 'The Early History of Crucible Steel', *JISI*, 1894, ii, pp. 224–38; H. Seebohm, 'On the Manufacture of Crucible Cast Steel', *JISI*, 1884, ii, pp. 372–96 (Sheffield, 1884, cited hereinafter). These descriptions can be supplemented with the excellent illustrations in K. C. Barraclough, *Sheffield Steel* (Buxton, 1976), who has also produced the definitive account of the Sheffield methods in *Steel-*

making Before Bessemer (2 vols., 1984). Also worth consulting are the classic contemporary account by F. Le Play, 'Mémoire sur La fabrication de l'Acier en Yorkshire', *Annales des Mines*, 4s., 3 (1843), pp. 583–714; and the detailed description of methods and costs in D. Carnegie (with S. G. Gladwyn), *Liquid Steel* (1913), pp. 51–115.

6 C. S. Smith, *Sources for the History of the Science of Steel 1532–1786* (Cambridge, Mass., 1968); *Réaumur's Memoirs on Iron and Steel. A Translation from the Original Printed in 1722*, by A. G. Sisco with an introduction and notes by C. S. Smith (Chicago, 1956); R. F. Tylecote, *A History of Metallurgy* (1976).

7 J. Percy, *Metallurgy* (1864), p. 764. Percy enlisted the help of E. F. Sanderson of Sanderson Bros, Sheffield, in writing the crucible steel section. There are a few of E. F. Sanderson's letters to Percy amongst the notes and clippings collected by the latter for an unrealised revision of the book. The papers, which were on temporary loan to SCL, are in possession of the Institute of Metals, London.

See generally G. Tweedale, 'Science, Innovation and the 'Rule of Thumb', The Development of British Metallurgy to 1945', in J. Liebenau, ed., *The Challenge of New Technology* (Aldershot, 1987).

8 See J. Percy, 'On the Cause of the Blisters on "Blister Steel"', *JISI*, 1877, i, pp. 460–63; J. O. Arnold, 'The Micro-Chemistry of Cementation', *JISI*, 1898, ii, pp. 185–94. For the debate over the relative merits of Swedish and other irons, see below.

9 Seebohm, *Crucible Cast Steel*, p. 14. See generally R. A. Hadfield, *The Work and Position of the Metallurgical Chemist* (1921). Brearley, *Steel-Makers*, pp. 75–8, commented on the uncanny ability of the 'adept' to judge carbon content by sight alone. This ability was not rendered obsolete by the development of chemical analysis. Remarked Dr J. A. Mathews, one of America's foremost special steelmakers: 'There are many skilled in the handling of tool steel whose judgement of quality based upon visual examination of a fracture is more to be depended upon than an analysis report'. See *TASST* 7 (1925), p. 160.

10 Professor C. S. Smith summarises it thus: 'Metals are simple aggregates of innumerable small crystals, packed more or less randomly against each other to fill the space. This simple fact was not clearly understood until nearly the end of the nineteenth century, yet long before this the existence of variable granularity was known to the philosopher and used by the artisan'. See *History of Metallography* (Chicago, 1960), p. xvi; and *idem*, 'The Discovery of Carbon in Steel', *Technology and Culture* 5 (1964), pp. 149–75; *idem.*, *A Search for Structure* (Cambridge, Mass., 1981).

11 H. C. Sorby, 'On the Application of Very High Powers to the Study of the Microscopical Structure of Steel', *JISI*, 1886, i, pp. 140–7; 'On the Microscopical Structure of Iron and Steel', *JISI*, 1887, i, pp. 255–88. See also: C. H. Desch, 'The Work of Sorby and the Development of Metallography', *Journal of the West of Scotland Iron and Steel Institute* 29 (March 1921–22), pp. 62–68; C. S. Smith, ed., *The Sorby Centennial Symposium on the History of Metallurgy, Cleveland, 1963* (New York, 1965), pp. 1–58; N. Higham, *A Very Scientific Gentleman* (1963); R. H. Nuttall, 'The First Microscope of Henry Clifton Sorby', *Technology and Culture* 22 (April 1981), pp. 275–80.

12 See A. Sauveur, *Metallurgical Reminiscences and Dialogue* (Ohio, 1981), pp. 5–8, 18–19.

13 Seebohm, *Crucible Cast Steel*, p. 2. Not until 1905 did the Iron and Steel Institute visit Sheffield.

14 The Sandersons, who, amongst others, entertained J. C. Fischer, were an exception. One of them told a visitor: 'The great secret is to have the courage to be honest – a spirit to purchase the best material, and the means and disposition to do justice to it in the manufacture.' See D. Lardner, *The Cabinet Cyclopaedia* (1831), vol. 1, p. 243.

15 SCL Os 14. Letter to Thos. F. Stevenson, New York, 2 February 1882. The distinguished American metallurgist Samuel Hoyt was surprised to find, even in the 1920s, that he was refused access to Hadfield's melt shop. See *Men of Metals* (Ohio, 1979), p. 83.

16 Arthur Balfour & Co, *A Centenary 1865–1965* (Nottingham, 1967), p. 12.

17 Hadfield, 'Early History', p. 233, mentions that it was not unknown for Sheffield water to be shipped to America. This caused some amusement to Americans. See: 'Sheffield Water for Tempering Steel', *Engineering and Mining Journal* 30 (10 July 1880), p. 26; *Iron Age* 16 (22 July 1880), p. 14, 20. According to the *Ironmonger* 27 (11 March 1882), p. 358: 'The water in the alien atmosphere lost its inimitable magic'. Apparently, the source for these articles was the *New York Sun*. See *Sheffield Independent*, 6 September 1879.

18 Huntsman was a clockmaker, Sorby an amateur philosopher, and Bessemer an inventor and engineer. Henry Seebohm, one of the most lucid writers on crucible steel manufacture, was a world-famous ornithologist and eventually gave up steel manufacture to concentrate on his collections. See 'Chemical Analysis of Steel', *Ironmonger* 26 (5 November 1881), pp. 655–7.

19 The *Sheffield Independent*, 24 January 1862, reported the details of a meeting at the Council Hall which discussed plans for a School of Science and Metallurgy. See also: A. W. Chapman, *The Story of a Modern University* (1955), pp. 40–1; J. O. Arnold, 'The Department of Iron and Steel Metallurgy at the University of Sheffield', *JISI*, 1905, ii, pp. 13–26; B. W. Thwaite, 'The Metallurgic Department of Sheffield's Technical School', *JISI*, 1891, ii, pp. 93–111.

20 The connections between the Sandersons, Faraday, and Percy should be emphasised in this context. See R. A. Hadfield, *Faraday and His Metallurgical Researches* (1931), pp. 73–5. Edward F. Sanderson was said to have taken a very keen interest in science, and was a member of scientific bodies in New York and Sheffield. He was the President of the Sheffield Literary and Philosophical Society in 1857. See: *Sheffield Literary and Philosophical Society. Portraits of Presidents*, vol. 2, 1856–88; Lord Sanderson (Henry Sanderson Furniss), *Memories of Sixty Years* (1931), p. 2. The links between science and industry are stressed by A. E. Musson and E. Robinson in *Science and Technology in the Industrial Revolution* (Manchester, 1969), cf. pp. 147–53. See also: W. H. G. Armytage, 'Science and Industry in Sheffield: Some Historical Notes', *Chemical Society. Anniversary Meetings. Sheffield, 2–5 April 1962*, pp. 6–10; C. S. Smith, 'The Interaction of Science and Practice in the History of Metallurgy', *Technology and Culture* 2 (1961), pp. 357–67.

21 See R. F. Mehl, *A Brief History of the Science of Metals* (New York, 1948), p. 17, who notes that the *Transactions of the American Institute of Mining Engineers* 'for the early years display but little interest in physical metallurgy – indeed, it is striking how thoroughly process metallurgy absorbed attention until quite recent years. The first volume [1871] carries no article that can be strictly described as physical metallurgy'. Similarly, in a review of the Iron and Steel Institute's achievements, another authority remarks, *JISI* 211 (July–Dec

1973), p. 834: 'The papers in the first volume [1871] ... were concerned with production processes and few related to metallurgy as we understand it today.' On the growth of metallurgy as a profession in England with some international comparisons, see R. S. Hutton, 'The Training and Employment of Metallurgists', *Supplement to His Recollections* (1966), pp. 325–36.

22 See *The Emporium of Arts and Sciences*, n.s. 1 (June–October 1813) (Philadelphia, 1813–14).

23 G. H. Makins, *A Manual of Metallurgy* (Philadelphia, 1865); H. S. Osborn, *The Metallurgy of Iron and Steel* (Philadelphia, 1869); F. Overman, *The Manufacture of Steel* (Philadelphia, 1851); idem., *A Treatise on Metallurgy* (New York, 1852); M. M. Coste and Perdonnet, 'Note on the Fabrication of Blister, and Cast Steel, at Sheffield, in Yorkshire', *Journal of the Franklin Institute* 6, n.s. (1830), pp. 402–5; 'Account of Steel-Making at the Fitzalan Steel and File Works, Sheffield', *Journal of the Franklin Institute* 8, 3rd s. (1844), pp. 52–8 (originally printed in the *Penny Magazine* 13 (1844), pp. 121–8).

24 One Swedish visitor to Sheffield refused to divulge the crucible process because 'it may be of some advantage to keep this art to ourselves'. See *Svedenstierna's Tour of Great Britain 1802–3* (Newton Abbot, 1973), p. 93. Another important visitor to Sheffield who was more forthcoming, was Gustaf Broling. See *Anteckningar under en Resa i England aren 1797, 1798 och 1799* (3 vols., Stockholm, 1811–17). Cf. M. W. Flinn, 'The Travel Diaries of Swedish Engineers of the Eighteenth Century as Sources of Technological History', *Transactions of the Newcomen Society* 31 (1957/8), pp. 95–109.

25 See D. Lardner, *Cabinet Cyclopaedia*, vol. 1, pp. 219–47; R. Hunt, ed., *Ure's Dictionary of Arts, Manufactures and Mines* (1867), vol. 3, pp. 760–4; J. Nicholson, *The Operative Mechanic and British Machinist* (Philadelphia, 1826), vol. 1, pp. 348–52; Sir J. A. Phillips, *A Manual of Metallurgy* (1852), pp. 304–23; A. Rees, ed., *The Cyclopaedia* (1802–20; Philadelphia, 1810–24), cf. 'Steel' (vol. 34) and 'Tilting of Steel' (vol. 35); J. Scoffern *et al.*, *The Useful Metals and Their Alloys* (1857); C. Tomlinson, *The Useful Arts and Manufactures of Great Britain* (1861), pp. 1–16.

26 R. B. Gordon, 'The Metallurgical Museum of Yale College and Nineteenth Century Ferrous Metallurgy in New England', *Journal of Metals* (July 1982), pp. 26–33, 30. See also R. H. Chittenden, *History of the Sheffield Scientific School of Yale University, 1846–1922* (New Haven, 1928), Chaps. 2 and 13. The School was named after Joseph E. Sheffield, a benefactor, and not the English town.

27 Le Play, 'Mémoire', p. 603. Firth Sterling, a Sheffield subsidiary in Pittsburgh, was still stressing the 'human element' in steelmaking in 1925. See *Firth Sterling Tool Steels* (McKeesport, Pa., 1925), kindly loaned to the author by K. C. Barraclough.

28 Seebohm, *Crucible Cast Steel*, p. 13; C. H. Desch, *The Steel Industry of South Yorkshire* (1922), p. 136.

29 For comments on the slow transmission of metallurgical techniques, see: N. Rosenberg, *Perspectives on Technology* (Cambridge, 1976), p. 182; W. P. Strassmann, *Risk and Technological Innovation* (New York, 1956), pp. 52–4.

30 Brearley, *Steel-Makers*, p. 28. On crucibles and mixes, see A. B. Searle, *Refractory Materials* (3rd edn., 1950), pp. 582–631. See also G. H. Davenport, 'Firebrick. A History of Refractories Technology and its Applications to Iron and Steel Processes in Britain from 1750 Onwards' (Open University PhD, 1979),

vol. 1, pp. 136–52, 166–7; G. Harrison, 'The Stourbridge Fire Clay', in S. Timmins, ed., *The Resources, Products, and Industrial History of Birmingham and the Midland Hardware District* (1866), pp. 133–7.

31 A visiting American manufacturer, Zachariah Allen, witnessed 'a poor fellow … employed in treading out the cold wet clay with his bare feet, in a cellar as dark and damp as the vault of a dungeon … Forlorn appeared the condition of this man, who was engaged in this uncomfortable employment, with damp cellar walls around him, and with only a modest share of the light of heaven. He exhibited, however, no lack of cheerfulness, and continued to trudge around whilst I talked to him.' *The Practical Tourist* (Providence, 1832), vol. 1, pp. 287–8.

32 Searle, *Refractory Materials*, p. 605; J. F. Kayser, 'Practical Crucible Steel Melting', *ICTR* 114 (November 3, 1927), p. 396.

33 Hadfield, 'Early History', p. 234. Enormous numbers of pots were therefore expended: according to Hadfield the figure once approached 14,000 a week in Sheffield; but one source highlights that Vickers alone used over a thousand crucibles daily by about 1870. See *MPICE* 42 (1874–5), p. 61.

34 'Crucible Steel; Its Manufacture and Treatment', *Proceedings of the Staffordshire Iron and Steel Institute* 17 (1901–2), pp. 55–76, 62. Another Sheffielder remarked: 'The amazing skill in teeming was taken for granted, but just think of being able to pour 50 odd pounds of molten steel into a 2½ in square mould about 30 in deep without catching the sides! A "catched" ingot was a black mark!' Quoted in Barraclough, *Steelmaking*, Appendix 18, p. 319. Since the moulds were made of an inferior metal any 'catching' resulted in a degrading of the final ingot.

35 *Journal of the Franklin Institute* 50, 3rd s. (1865), p. 358. On the production of large castings at Firth's, see *Scientific American* 23, n.s. (8 October 1870), p. 226.

36 *Engineering* 4 (25 October 1867), p. 384.

37 Seebohm, *Crucible Cast Steel*, pp. 14–17, is particularly emphatic on the care and skill needed in these finishing stages.

38 On American crucible steelmaking see: A. O. Backert, ed., *The ABC of Iron and Steel* (Cleveland, 1st edn., 1915), pp. 103–20; Carnegie, *Liquid Steel*, pp. 99–105; M. A. Grossman and E. C. Bain, *High-Speed Steel* (New York, 1931); H. M. Howe, *The Metallurgy of Steel* (New York, 1890), pp. 296–316. Two particularly noteworthy accounts of American practice are: J. A. Coyle, 'Making High-Grade Steel', published in 13 parts in the *Iron Trade Review* 77–79 (10 December 1925–15 July 1926); and T. Holland Nelson, 'Comparison of American and English Methods of Producing High-Grade Crucible Steel', *TASST* 3 (1922–3), pp. 279–98.

39 *Magazine of Western History* 3 (1885/6), p. 341.

40 Howe, *Metallurgy*, p. 297. According to Coyle, *Iron Trade Review* 77 (10 December 1925), p. 1457, the last few converting furnaces in Pittsburgh were demolished in 1905. They had been conserved for a time in case the traditional methods were resurrected.

41 British pat. 26 August 1839 (8129).

42 This was facilitated by reversal of Swedish Government policy in 1855, which thereafter permitted the direct export of Swedish cast iron. See Barraclough, 'Cementation Process'. See also 'Is it Preferable to Carburise Iron in the Cementation Furnace or in the Crucible?', *Journal of the Sheffield Technical School Metallurgical Society* 2 (1892), pp. 50–8, 75–9.

43 See 'Gas and Steel', *Pittsburg Gazette*, 29 December 1870. The layout of American crucible furnaces can be seen in the numerous photographs in Backert, *ABC*, and Coyle, 'Making High-Grade Steel'.

44 There was a record-run of over three years by a furnace of the Columbia Tool Steel Co. See: *Bulletin of the American Institute of Mining Engineers*, No. 81 (1913), pp. 2379–81; *Iron Age* 91 (15 May 1913), p. 1167.

45 Grossmann and Bain, *High-Speed Steel*, p. 8.

46 Holland Nelson, 'Comparison', p. 292.

47 Brearley, *Steel-Makers*, p. 87, who added: 'A Sheffield teemer would think the casting of such ingots a sloppy process, and be prepared to find as many men engaged in removing defects from ingots and cogged bars as were engaged in melting the steel.'

48 *Iron Age* 107, Pt. 1 (10 February 1921), p. 372.

49 K.-G. Hildebrand, 'Foreign Markets for Swedish Iron in the 18th Century', *Scandinavian Economic History Review* 6 (1958), pp. 31–2.

50 F. H. Hatch, *The Iron and Steel Industry of the UK Under War Conditions* (1919), p. 16.

51 Barraclough has calculated overall American usage of Swedish bar iron in crucible steel production at about 42 percent in the period 1872–1913; selective evidence for Sheffield shows a figure of around 60 percent. See 'The Production of Steel in Britain by the Cementation and Crucible Processes', *Historical Metallurgy* 8 (1974), pp. 107–9.

52 *JISI*, 1904, ii, p. 170. The argument for the use of Swedish iron was essentially one between believers and disbelievers. Robert A. Hadfield told R. F. Mushet (letter, 11 June 1884): 'there is no necessity whatever for using these [Swedish] irons, but equal results can be obtained without the use of foreign irons at all, but to persuade steel-makers generally of this fact would be about as difficult a task as you undertook when you first introduced your valuable triple-metallic alloy to the world'. But Mushet was unconvinced and stated (12 July 1884): 'We must agree to differ as to Swede Iron – No substitute has yet been found for the best tool steel.' The correspondence is in the Weeks' volumes, Hadfield Papers, SCL.

53 K. C. Barraclough and J. A. Kerr, 'Metallographic Examination of Some Archive Samples of Steel', *JISI* 211 (July-December 1973), pp. 470–4; 'Steel From 100 Years Ago', *Historical Metallurgy* 10 (1976), pp. 70–6. W. H. Hatfield found a similar purity and uniformity when analysing old Sheffield knives. See Hatfield, *The Application of Science to the Steel Industry* (Cleveland, 1928), pp. 146–9.

54 Carnegie, Liquid Steel, pp. 79, 101. The differential had increased by the 1920s. See F. M. Parkin, 'Gas *versus* Coke Melting in Crucible Steel Making'. Verbatim copy of notes before the Sheffield Society of Metallurgists and Metallurgical Chemists, 19 April 1921, p. 8, who quotes figures of £23 8s 11d per ton of topped ingots for coke; £12 3s 6d for gas. (Copy loaned to the author by K. C. Barraclough.)

55 'Sheffield and its Steelworkers', *BAISA* 17 (11 April 1883), p. 98.

56 See reply of Park, Bro & Co, *Reports of the Committee of the Senate ... for the 2nd Session of the 53rd Congress. Replies to Tariff Inquiries. Schedule C. Metals and Manufactures of* (Washington, DC, 1894), p. 10. See also 'Wages in Sheffield and Homestead', *BAISA* 26 (24 August 1892), p. 241; 'Mr. Cleveland Answered by Mr. D. B. Oliver', *BAISA* 26 (12 October 1892), p. 297.

57 P. M. Tyler, 'High-Speed Steel Manufacture in Sheffield', *Iron Age* 107, Pt. 1 (10 February 1921), pp. 372–3.

58 *Ibid.*

59 H. Brearley, *Talks about Steel Making* (Cleveland, 1946), p. 45.

60 'Comparison', p. 298. Nelson was a Sheffield-trained manager at Disston's, the Philadelphia sawmakers.

61 See Connecticut Historical Society, Ms 72190, 'The Collins Company Historical Memoranda, 1826–1871', by S. W. Collins, for comments on the variable quality of domestic ores.

62 *MPICE* 42 (1874–5), p. 62. In the regenerative gas furnace 1½ tons of coal per ton of steel and furnace repairs cost 21s 6d; the corresponding figure for the 2½ tons of coke in the ordinary furnace, plus repairs, was 57s.

63 Sanderson Bros & Newbould, *400 Years of Iron and Steel* (Sheffield, 1969–71), p. 13.

64 T. A. Seed, *Pioneers for a Century, 1852–1952* (Sheffield, 1952), p. 27.

65 A. C. Marshall and H. Newbould, *The History of Firth's (1842–1918)* (Sheffield, 1924), p. 81.

66 *JISI*, 1905, ii, p. 496.

67 Brearley, *Steel-Makers*, p. 14.

68 Carnegie, *Liquid Steel*, p. 54.

69 *Ibid.*, pp. 54–69.

70 Morgan Crucible Co Ltd, *Battersea Works 1856–1956* (1956). See also *Scientific American* 10, n.s. (18 June 1864), pp. 388–9. Graphite crucibles were in use at the Vickers River Don Works in the 1860s, though this was mainly for larger castings. Careful consideration seems to have been given to plumbago pots at this time. See *Engineering* 4 (8 November 1867), p. 438. In England the usefulness of graphite as a crucible material had been recognised by 1828. See Davenport, 'Firebrick', vol. 1, p. 151.

71 Carnegie, *Liquid Steel*, p. 91; *JISI*, 1919, ii, p. 47.

72 F. W. Harbord, *The Metallurgy of Steel* (1904), p. 258. It was calculated that if gas was used throughout the crucible steel industry in Sheffield it would mean savings of from £100,000 to £120,000 per annum (*ibid.*, p. 260). On gas furnaces see also *PIME* (1891), pp. 47–66.

73 SCL MD 3970. Directors' Letter Book, 1892–96, pp. 8–11, letter to Allen, 18 July 1892, from A. E. Wells. See also *Edgar Allen News* 5 (June 1926), pp. 801–2.

74 F. M. Parkin, 'Gas *versus* Coke Melting', p. 12.

3. THE RESPONSE TO A NEW TECHNOLOGY: ELECTRIC STEELMAKING

1 A. O. Backert, ed., *The ABC of Iron and Steel* (Cleveland, 1st edn., 1915), pp. 253–64; Canada, Dept. of the Interior, *Report … to Investigate the Different Electro-Thermic Processes … in Europe* (1904); D. Carnegie, *Liquid Steel* (1913), pp. 418–76; E. B. Clarke, 'Electric Furnaces for Steelmaking', *TAES* 25 (1914), pp. 139–44, disc. pp. 145–59; G. I. Finch, 'Some Industrial Applications of Electro-Thermics', *Journal of the Society of Arts* 75 (1927), pp. 1081–128, 1132–51; E. F. Lake, 'Steels Made in the Electric Furnace', *Cassier's Magazine* 42 (May 1912), pp. 99–112; A. Den Ouden, *Electric Steelmaking up to 1930* (Nederland, 1981); J. N. Pring, *The Electric Furnace*

(1921); W. Roden-Hauser, J. Schoenawa, and C. H. Vom Baur, *Electric Furnaces in the Iron and Steel Industry* (New York, 2nd edn., 1913); F. T. Sisco, *The Manufacture of Electric Steel* (New York, 1924); A. Stansfield, *The Electric Furnace* (New York, 1907); *idem.*, *The Electric Furnace for Iron and Steel* (New York, 1923); US Dept. of Interior. Bureau of Mines, Bulletin 77, D. R. Lyon, R. M. Keeney, and J. F. Cullen, The *Electric Furnace in Metallurgical Work* (1914).

2 No attempt will be made to describe the different types of electric furnace. Readers are referred to the works by Stansfield, above, and to the enormous technical literature generated by the advent of electric steelmaking in such publications as the *JISI*.

3 Canada, Dept. of Interior. *Report*, p. 31.

4 It was calculated that, expressed in terms of fuel-produced heat, the cost of making one ton of steel from cold scrap in the electric furnace lay between 7,740,000 and 9,288,000 cals., as against 12,000,000 to 16,000,000 cals. required per ton of steel made by the crucible process. See Finch, 'Industrial Applications' (n. 1), p. 1135.

5 Carnegie, *Liquid Steel*, p. 443. For further information on electric steel melting costs, see 'Electric Steel Furnaces in Sheffield', *Electrical Review* 73 (25 July 1913), pp. 156–7, where costs are given for the production of steel in Darwin & Milner's electric furnace of between £2 15s 8d and £3 2s 6d per ton (depending on the price of electricity).

6 The figures for UK electric steel production are, however, reproduced for comparison with the US in Table 3: 2.

7 W. H. Hatfield, *TASST* 16 (1929), p. 278.

8 Finch, 'Industrial Applications', p. 1135.

9 'High-Speed Steels', *TASST* 11 (1927), pp. 711–25, 712.

10 J. F. Kayser, 'Practical Crucible Steel Melting', *ICTR* 114 (11, 18 March 1927), pp. 396–7, 438–9.

11 For comments on the rarity of electric furnaces in America, see *Journal of Society of Arts* 61 (22 August 1913), p. 910. No official statistics are available for the number of electric furnaces in Sheffield. For the purpose of this study the UK figures are taken as a close approximation, since Sheffield was by far the largest electric steel producer in the UK. In 1924, out of a national electric furnace production of 64,500 tons, Sheffield produced 52,100 tons (80 percent). (*NFISM Statistics* (1924), p. 8.)

12 See: L. W. Spring, 'The Story of Iron and Steel', in *A Popular History of American Invention*, ed. W. B. Kaempffert (New York, 1924), vol. 2, pp. 3–46; J . A. Mathews, 'The Electric Furnace in Steel Manufacture', *Yearbook of the American Iron and Steel Institute* (1916), pp. 73–85, 74.

13 R. Szymanowitz, *Edward Goodrich Acheson* (New York, 1971), cf. Chap. 9.

14 *NCAB.*

15 In a review of these developments, Mathews, 'Electric Furnace', remarked: 'I mention these early achievements because they make more conspicuous our neglect of electric furnaces for steel making'.

16 EMHL Acc 1567. 'History of the Works', p. 88; *Iron Age* 77 (7 June 1906), pp. 1811–13.

17 Mathews, 'Electric Furnace'; *TAES* 51 (1927), pp. 95–9.

18 Mathews, 'Electric Furnace', p. 78. See also *Iron Age* 99 (4 January 1917), p. 99, for details on Halcomb's four 24-pot crucible steel furnaces.

19 Disston 'History of the Works', p. 119.

20 SCL SJC 82. L. J. Coombe to A. K. Wilson (Spear & Jackson), Philadelphia, 14 July 1925.

21 American Iron and Steel Institute, *Directory* (1930), p. 152.

22 M. A. Grossmann and E. C. Bain, *High-Speed Steel* (New York, 1931), p. 1; Sisco, *Electric Steel*, p. 7. See also 'Crucible or Electric Steel', *Edgar Allen News*, No. 3. (November 1919), p. 38; *TAES* 37 (1920), pp. 319–28.

23 J. H. Hall, a leading American metallurgist at Bethlehem, remembered: 'We kept ourselves advised of [electric furnace] progress abroad, watched when one was installed at Halcomb's in Syracuse ... and went into action with them just before the world war'. Cf. A. D. Graeff, ed., *A History of Steel Casting* (Philadelphia, 1949), p. 141.

24 *NCAB*.

25 See Mathews, 'Electric Furnace', p. 75; and F. Rawlinson, 'The Present and Future Scope of the Electric Furnace in the Manufacture of Tool Steel', read before W. Yorks. Metallurgical Society, *ICTR* 104 (14 April 1922), p. 526. As Brearley put it in his inimitable fashion: 'the electric furnace has claimed to be able to make anything from anything – silk vanity bags from cast-off socks'. *Talks about Steel Making* (Cleveland, 1946), p. 46.

26 *Electrical Review* (n. 5), p. 157.

27 *Ibid.*

28 *ICTR* 105 (11 August 1922), p. 180.

29 US Dept of Interior, *Electric Furnace*, p. 70. The *Electrical Review* quotes the cost of Norwegian electricity at 0.05d per unit (£1.75 per KW-year); England at 0.33d per unit (£12 per KW-year). The high price of electricity in Sheffield meant that some firms sited their furnaces in Tyneside, where costs were lower. See *Journal of Society of Arts* 60 (15 November 1912), p. 1146.

30 B. W. Thwaite to Hadfield, 21 June 1893, Hadfield Papers, SCL.

31 Hadfield to J. F. Hall, 12 May 1893. Hadfield Papers.

32 *Engineering* 75 (15 April 1903), pp. 650–2. Paul Héroult had visited Allen's at about this time. See SCL Aurora 541 (a). R. Woodward to A. Tropenas, 10 March 1903.

33 R. S. Hutton, *Recollections of a Technologist* (1964), p. 48; *Supplement to His Recollections* (1966) pp. 27–48.

34 See SCL SUA VIII/1/10. Steel Research Committee. Minutes. See also SCL Marsh 198. Papers relating to High-Speed Steel Technology. Arnold to H. P. Marsh, 12 September 1906.

35 *Engineering* 87 (22 January 1909), pp. 118–20; J. B. C. Kershaw, 'Methods of Refining Steel in the Electric Furnace', *Cassier's Magazine* 36 (1909), pp. 237–48.

36 See remarks of W. F. Beardshaw, *Ironmonger* 126 (6 February 1909), p. 257.

37 *Edgar Allen News* (November 1927), p. 69. See also *Ironmonger* 112 (22 July 1905), pp. 174–5, for details on the Héroult furnace in Sheffield.

38 Wm. Jessop & Sons, *Visit to a Steel Works* (Sheffield, 1913), p. 58, pronounced electric steel melting commercially successful.

39 *Engineering* 93 (9 February 1912), p. 191.

40 *Iron Age* 99 (4 January 1917), pp. 105–7. Hadfields' total had increased to 12 by 1919, the largest group of electric furnaces in the world. See *AGM* 1919, p. 8.

41 T. A. Seed, *Pioneers for a Century, 1852–1952* (Sheffield 1952), p. 42.

42 See SCL Directors' Minute Book, 17 February 1905–24 February 1916. The meeting of 29 July 1915 discussed the erection of a 3- or 7-ton electric fur-

nace. Cf. also Brown Bayleys Ltd, *Brown Bayleys 1871–1971. A Centenary* (Sheffield, 1971), p. 16.

43 *Histories of Firms* 18 (1957–8), pp. 4–6.

44 Stansfield, *Electric Furnace* (1923), p. 357. Electro Metals Ltd was the designer of the other well-known English make of electric furnace. America in turn exported electric furnaces to England, such as the Snyder design.

45 A. Balfour & Co, *A Centenary 1865–1965* (Nottingham, 1967), p. 42. On Balfour's experiences with electric steelmaking, see pp. 27, 36. Balfour's had an arc furnace in operation during the First World War. Lord Riverdale recalled: 'In general this was not as good as the crucible, and after the 1914–18 War I remember a pile of ingots that was difficult to dispose of'. Private communication to the author, 19 March 1984.

46 R. M. Ledbetter, 'Sheffield's Industrial History from about 1700, with Special Reference to the Abbeydale Works' (Sheffield MA, 1971), p. 213. Wardlow's had enjoyed a strong American business in the nineteenth century built up by Marmaduke Wardlow. The firm had a New York branch office in the 1890s from where 'a heavy trade' was conducted. See *Men of the Period* (1896), pp. 109–10.

47 La Belle Works, Pittsburgh, was described as the only remaining US crucible melting shop in a superb photographic essay in 'Crucible Steel Made in America', *Metal Progress* 37 (May 1940), pp. 543–51.

48 A. L. Levine, *Industrial Retardation in Britain, 1880–1914* (1967), p. 40. This book shows little grasp of either the technology or the history of the steel industry. See also T. H. Burnham and G. O. Hoskins, *Iron and Steel in Britain 1870–1930* (1943), pp. 185–6, for similar remarks.

49 *Edgar Allen News* 6 (January 1928), pp. 99–101; (March 1928), pp. 129–31. See also *Edgar Allen News* 8 (January 1930), pp.534–5. The *Sheffield Daily Telegraph*, 7 December 1927, referred to it as making 'Steel by Wireless'. The first American high-frequency induction furnace was installed in the following year. See J. A. Succop, 'High-Frequency Induction Furnaces', *Metal Progress* 18 (December 1930), pp. 40–4.

50 On the advantages of high-frequency induction melting, see *Edgar Allen News* 8 (October 1929), p. 479.

51 On uniformity in steels, see G. Burns, 'The Quality of Toolsteel – Recent Developments and Future Predictions', *Metal Progress* 65 (March 1954), pp. 75–8.

4. THE RISE OF ALLOY STEELS

1 H. C. H. Carpenter, 'Alloy Steels, Their Manufacture, Properties and Uses', *Journal of Royal Society of Arts* 76 (27 January 1928), p. 251. See generally: P. S. Bardell, 'The Origins of Alloy Steels', in N. Smith, ed., *History of Technology, 9th Annual Volume* (1984), pp. 1–29; S. Keown, 'A History of Alloy Steels with Particular Reference to Sheffield Contributions', *Historical Metallurgy* 19, No. 1 (1985), pp. 126–33.

2 See T. A. Wertime, *The Coming of the Age of Steel* (Leiden, 1962), pp. 280–3.

3 See R. A. Hadfield, *Faraday and His Metallurgical Researches* (1931); L. Pearce Williams, 'Faraday and the Alloys of Steel', in C. S. Smith, ed., *The Sorby Centennial Symposium on the History of Metallurgy, Cleveland, 1963* (New York, 1965), pp. 145–62.

4 *Obituary Notices of Fellows of the Royal Society* 3 (1939–40), pp. 647–64;

DBB; G. Tweedale, 'Sir Robert Hadfield FRS (1858–1940), and the Discovery of Manganese Steel', *Notes and Records of the Royal Society* 40 (November 1985), pp. 63–73. See also Hadfield, *Metallurgy and Its Influence on Modern Progress* (1925). Most of Hadfield's papers appear to have been lost, though a few important items survive from the company's files (now in SCL), including a typescript history by a close collaborator of Sir Robert, Dr S. A. Main, 'The Hadfields of Sheffield. Pioneers in Steel'. See also Main, 'The Contributions of Sir Robert Hadfield to Metallurgical Science and Technology', in Smith, ed., *Sorby Centennial*, pp. 81–98.

5 Hadfield's 'Scribbling' diaries in SCL, 1876–78.

6 In SCL. The frontispiece of the 60-page notebook reads: 'This translation from the French original was prepared by Robert A. Hadfield, for his father, in the year 1878, his age then being nineteen years. Paris Universal Exhibition of 1878. Terre-Noire, La Voulte, & Bésséges. Foundry and Ironworks Company. History and Statistics of the Co, Catalogue of Exhibits, etc.'

7 Bound notebook, 'Early Experiments', SCL. Hadfield quoted this entry in *Metallurgy and Its Influence*, p. 74, but subtly changed the emphasis by substituting the words 'entirely revolutionise' for 'quite alter'. Nevertheless, it was a remarkable discovery for a twenty-three-year-old.

8 Hadfield donated his experimental specimens of manganese steel to the Science Museum, London, where they are presently on display.

9 British pats. 12 January 1883 (200), 27 May 1884 (8,268). The first patent covered manganese additions of 7–20 percent, the second additions of 7–30 percent. See 'Letters From/To Bowden 1885–1890', a bound volume of Hadfield's correspondence to his London patent agent in SCL. Also in SCL is Hadfield's bound notebook, 'Experimental Books 1 & 2', dated 1882; 300 pages of analyses document his alloy steel work until about 1889.

10 Letter to Weeks, 27 March 1884. For details of the Weeks' correspondence, see Chap. 9.

11 See 'Hadfield's Steel Foundry', *Engineering* 59 (8, 22 February 1895), pp. 165–6, 233–6.

12 'Manganese Steel. I, Manganese in its Application to Metallurgy; II, Some Newly Discovered Properties of Iron and Manganese', *MPICE* 93, iii (1887–8), pp. 1–126; 'On Manganese Steel', *JISI*, ii (1888), pp. 41–82. Hadfield's paper before the Civil Engineers earned him the first of his many awards, the Telford Medal and Premium. Hadfield's work on manganese steel was published in the following American journals: *Engineering and Mining Journal* 37 (1 March, 14 June 1884), pp. 159, 440; *TASME* 12 (1890–1), pp. 955–74; *Institute of Mining Engineers* 23 (1893), pp. 148–96. In America in 1891 Hadfield was awarded the Scott Medal by the Franklin Institute for his work on manganese steel. See A. M. McMahon and S. A. Morris, *Technology in Industrial America* (Wilmington, Del., 1977), p. 198.

13 Letter to Weeks, 19 August 1885.

14 Letter to Weeks, 29 May 1884. Hadfield's patent of 1883 had described the steel as 'suitable for guns, armour plates, railway and tramway wheels, rolls, toys, etc.'.

15 Hadfield to Weeks, 17 April 1884. Robert F. Mushet, for example, was decidedly unimpressed. He told Hadfield, 26 June 1884: 'There is nothing new to me, expressed in your patent claim, but I have no doubt it is new to the many who have not possessed the advantages or the leisure for steel investigations.' For details of the subsequent exchange of letters, see Tweedale, 'Discovery'.

16 See Chap. 9.

17 'The Hadfield System, Its Application and Advantages', ca. 1897. Hadfield Papers. The take-off in manganese steel demand is reflected in the growth of Hadfields Ltd: between 1894 and 1914 capital grew from £135,750 to £700,000, the work-force from 530 to 5,980.

18 F. Bland, *Tramway Track, 1883 to 1923; or 40 Years of Tramway Practice* (Sheffield, 1923), p. 26; D. Brooke, 'The Advent of the Steel Rail 1857–1914', *Journal of Transport History*, 3rd s., 7 (March 1986), p. 27; Hadfields' Directors' Minute Book (1 & 2).

19 *Metallurgy and Its Influence*, pp. 102–39.

20 'On Alloys of Iron and Silicon', *JISI*, 1889, ii, pp. 222–55. Hadfield's patent (no. 15,949) for silicon additions of from 1.5 to 5 percent was registered in 1884.

21 'On the Electrical Conductivity and Magnetic Permeability of Various Alloys of Iron', *Scientific Transactions of the Royal Dublin Society* 7, iii, pp. 67–126; and 'Researches on the Electrical Conductivity and Magnetic Properties of Upwards of One Hundred Different Alloys of Iron', *Journal of the Institution of Electrical Engineers* 31, pp. 674–729.

22 W. Jones, 'Electrical Steel – A Triumph of Steelmaking, Heat Treatment and Scientific Metallurgy', *Metal Progress* 65 (February 1954), pp. 70–4.

23 In 1929 the city electrical engineer, Samuel Fedden, returned a 60 KW transformer to Hadfield, for which the latter had supplied the silicon steel sheets free of charge. (It was being removed to make way for a larger one.) Fedden remarked: 'It may be interesting to add that the construction of this 60 KW transformer with your silicon steel sheets followed the successful results obtained with a small experimental transformer of about 0.5 KW capacity, for the construction of which in 1903 you also supplied us with your Silicon Steel sheets ready for use. This small transformer showed energy losses of only 15 watts as compared with 22.5 watts obtained with its previous core of ordinary transformer iron.' Letter, 3 May 1929. Hadfield Papers.

24 J. W. Hammon, *The Story of General Electric* (Philadelphia, 1941), pp. 330–1. Hadfield later had to contest the payment of royalties with the GE Co. There is a small file of patent litigation concerning this in the Hadfield Papers. A Westinghouse engineer calculated that the total world saving in the seventeen years since Hadfield filed his US patent in 1903 amounted to $340 million – enough to build the Panama Canal. See T. D. Yensen, 'The Development of Magnetic Materials', *Electric Journal* 18 (March 1921), pp. 93–5.

25 See Letter re 'Silicon Steel and the US Steel Corporation, 11 July 1907'; 'Agreement between Hadfields and the American Sheet and Tin Plate Co, N.J., 14, 30 December 1911'. Hadfield Papers.

26 F. B. Howard-White, *Nickel: An Historical Review* (1963), pp. 97–100. The manufacture of armaments, of course, was closely intertwined with many alloy steel developments. See repr. presidential address by L. Baclé, 'Armour Plate, – Its Influence on the Metallurgy and Manufacture of Steel', Société des Ingénieurs Civils de France (British Section), 18th OGM, London, 24 November 1926.

27 M. Sanderson, 'The Professor as Industrial Consultant: Oliver Arnold and the British Steel Industry, 1900–14', *Economic History Review* 31, 2nd s. (November 1978), pp. 585–600. See also: *Engineering* 129 (4 April 1930), pp. 450–1; *Royal Society of London. Proceedings* 130 (1930–31), pp. xxiii–xxvii. For a negative view of Arnold, see Smith, ed., *Sorby Centennial*, pp. 99–108, though it is only based on a handful of secondary sources.

28 'Record of the Discovery of the Influence of Vanadium on Steel. Introductory Note', Arnold Letter Book, SUA VIII/1/27/1, pp. 120–1. SUA Ms 72, Letter Book (1) 1904–6, has several letters by Arnold on the subject of chrome-vanadium steel, which he 'suggested to steel makers as the most suitable [material] for Motor Car Work'. See letter to E. Grainger, 7 March 1905.

29 *Engineer* 98 (1 July, 2 September 1904), pp. 18–19, 235; 99 (9 June 1905), p. 565.

30 See Capt. Riall Sankey and J. Kent Smith, 'Heat Treatment Experiments with Chrome-Vanadium Steel', *PIME*, Pts. 2–3 (1904), pp. 1235–82. Arnold pointed out during the discussion (p. 1301) that the 'first ingot of chrome-vanadium steel ever melted was made in the crucible steel department of the Sheffield University College in March 1902'. See also L. Guillet, 'The Use of Vanadium in Metallurgy', *JISI*, 1905, ii, pp. 118–65, and disc. 190–203. For details on the Ford connection see: H. Ford, *My Life and Work* (New York, 1924), pp. 65–7; A. Nevins and F. E. Hill. *Ford. The Times, the Man, the Company* (New York, 1954), pp. 348–9. Eventually manganese carbon steel proved better suited to Ford's needs.

31 Letter to W. Howard Head, 9 July 1915. SUA VIII/1/27/1, p. 286.

32 For a description of Arnold's department, which included Siemens, Tropenas, Kjellin, gas and coke-fired crucible furnaces, and various forging and testing machines, see *Colliery Guardian* 97 (11, 18 June 1909), pp. 1161–3, 1213–14. See also, B. B. Argent, '100 Years of the Department of Metallurgy in Sheffield', in *Perspectives in Metallurgical Development* (1984), pp. 15–25.

33 In fact, so modest was Arnold's fee that he described it as 'farcical'. When he resigned his retainer he wrote: 'It may well be that in some law case the amount of my retainer in Sheffield will come out and would make the Sheffield manufacturers and myself a laughing stock'. Letter to Col. Hughes, 12 June 1916. Arnold Letter Book, SUA VIII/1/27/2, p. 19.

34 Some idea of the vigour with which Arnold defended Sheffield's reputation against lesser mortals can be gauged by his letter to the *Ironmonger*, 9 November 1915, in which he contested the claims of a German, Otto Vogel, concerning the discovery of tungsten and vanadium steels. Arnold was not fond of Germans. See SUA VIII/1/27/1, pp. 286–93.

35 Amongst the first papers presented was W. Tozer, 'Notes on a Visit to the United States with the Iron and Steel Institute', *Journal of the Sheffield Technical School Metallurgical Society* 2 (1892), pp. 66–74, 81–7.

36 Letter, 11 October 1915. SUA VIII/1/27/1, pp. 354–7.

37 *The Brown-Firth Research Laboratories* (Sheffield, 1937). The American metallurgist, Samuel L. Hoyt, was highly impressed by these facilities in the mid-1920s. After a visit to the Laboratory he wrote: 'we had nothing like it in the United States, because our steel industry hardly recognized the significance of research and development as a separate function. I was surprised to witness such a large-scale program even though it was supported by two firms.' See Hoyt, *Men of Metals* (Cleveland, 1979), p. 83.

38 For Arnold's own account (with A. McWilliam) of Sheffield and its metallurgical research, see 'The Iron and Steel Industries of Sheffield', in *British Association Handbook & Guide to Sheffield* (Sheffield, 1910), pp. 209–57.

5. THE EVOLUTION OF HIGH-SPEED STEEL

1 On the development of self-hardening and other tool steels, see: J. L. Gregg,

The Alloys of Iron and Tungsten (New York, 1931); F. M. Osborn, *The Story of the Mushets* (1952); G. A. Roberts, J. C. Hamaker, and A. R. Johnson, *Tool Steels* (Cleveland, 3rd edn., 1962); L. T. C. Rolt, *Tools for the Job* (1965), O. Thallner, *Tool Steel* (Philadelphia, 1902). Background information on tungsten can be found in K. I. Rigby, 'Tungsten Ore in the United States Economy 1900–1929' (London School of Economics MSc, 1979).

2 See esp. *Engineer* 26 (25 December 1868), p. 481, repr. in *Scientific American* 20, n.s. (30 January 1869), p. 68; and 'Tool Steel', *Ryland's Iron Trade Circular* (9 April 1870), p. 228.

3 Osborn, *Mushets*, p. 79.

4 T. A. Seed, *Pioneers for a Century 1852–1952* (Sheffield, 1952). For brief details of the Works see: *Ironmonger* 25 (26 February 1891), p. 276: PIME, 1890, pp. 457–8. On Samuel Osborn, see: *Sheffield Independent*, 8 July 1891, p. 5; *Men of the Period* (1896), pp. 77–8.

5 Osborn, *Mushets*, p. 80.

6 *Ibid.*, p. 81; 'Mushet's Special Steel', *Engineering and Mining Journal* 15 (1 April 1873), p. 200.

7 *Sheffield Independent*, 16 April 1874.

8 SCL Os 14. Osborn Letter Book. Letter to T. F. Stephenson, New York, 3 July 1875.

9 Os 14. Letter to F. Farish, Chicago, 5 January 1876.

10 Os 14. Letter to [?], New York, 1 December 1875.

11 Os 14. Letter to J . W. Branch, St Louis, 15 December 1875: Os 14 also contains several other letters in 1876 relating to America dated 5, 15 January; 7 April; 9 May; 18 May.

12 Os 14. Letter to C. Bathe, New York, 9 June 1876; to T. F. Stephenson, New York, 3 July 1876; to J. W. Branch, St Louis, 14 August 1876.

13 Os 14. Letter to Jones, Boston, 17 October 1877, Osborn, *Mushets*, pp. 96–8.

14 Os 16. Letter, 4 April 1883. Further letters to Jones in Os 16 are dated 5, 26 January 1883; 9 March 1883; 30 August 1883; 2, 26 April 1884.

15 Os 16. Letter to T. S. Stephenson, New York, 7 March 1888; Seed, *Pioneers*, pp. 24, 28.

16 Gregg, *Alloys*, pp. 274–6.

17 F. W. Taylor, *On the Art of Cutting Metals* (New York, 1907), p. 191. This was a published version of an address before the American Society of Mechanical Engineers (see vol. 28 of the *Transactions*) in 1906.

18 On these developments see: F. B. Copley, *Frederick W. Taylor, Father of Scientific Management* (New York, 1923), vol. 2, pp. 79–118; Gregg, *Alloys*, pp. 272–83; D. Nelson, *Frederick W. Taylor and the Rise of Scientific Management* (Madison, Wis., 1980), pp. 31–8; Roberts et al., *Tool Steels*, pp. 5–9; Rolt, *Tools*, pp. 192–200; Taylor, *Cutting Metals*, passim.

19 Manchester Association of Engineers, *Report on Past Experimental Work on Cutting Tools, March 13, 1915*. See also J. M. Gledhill, 'The Development and Use of High-Speed Tool Steel', *JISI*, 1904, ii, pp. 127–82.

20 *Iron Age* 68 (19 September 1901), pp. 10–13. An American metallurgist reported that Maunsel White 'when giving [him] his first knowledge of these tools in 1899 or early in 1900, said that a young man in the Bethlehem shop had lighted a cigarette with the newly cut chip, a statement that seemed almost unbelievable at the time'. See H. D. Hibbard, *Manufacture and Uses of*

Alloy Steels (New York, 1919), p. 68. One of B. M. Jones' contacts in the US was also disbelieving, stating that a tool that: 'may become red hot in the working [and] will still hold its edge ... sounds like a Fairy tale'. See Os 103. Letter from Einwechter & Wyeth, Philadelphia, to Jones, 26 November 1900.

21 G. W. Alling, *Points for Buyers and Users of Tool Steel* (New York, 1903), p. 72. See also: O. M. Becker, *High-Speed Steel* (New York, 1910), pp. 275–318; N. Rosenberg, 'Technological Change in the Machine Tool Industry, 1840–1910', *Journal of Economic History* 23 (1963), pp. 441–2; H. D. Wagoner, *The US Machine Tool Industry from 1900 to 1950* (Cambridge, Mass., 1966), pp. 9–10. In English shipyards it was noted: 'The British machines used in our Works in almost all cases are those used for general all round work, and in the majority of cases they become obsolete ... because they have insufficient driving power to take the heavy cuts, or alternatively to stand the high speeds which improved tool steel has rendered possible'. Evidence of Mr Thomas Bell. PRO BT 55/112. Shipping and Shipbuilding Committee. Precis of Evidence and Memoranda on the Position during the Period of Economic Reconstruction. 1916.

22 Taylor, *Cutting Metals*, pp. 191–2.

23 See Chap. 4.

24 H. A. Brustlein, *JISI*, 1886, ii, 'On Chrome Pig Iron and Steel', pp. 770–8.

25 See Chap. 6.

26 J. W. Langley, *TASCE* 27 (1892), 'Some Chemical and Physical Properties of Steel and Alloy Steels', pp. 385–405.

27 The best scholarly treatment of these developments is A. S. Townsend, 'Alloy Tool Steels and the Development of High Speed Steel', *TASST* 21 (1933), pp. 769–95. S. Keown, 'Tool Steels and High-Speed Steels 1900–1950', *Historical Metallurgy* 19, No. 1 (1985), pp. 97–103, also contains useful information, but based as it is on published accounts, gives far too much prominence to American developments and ignores Sheffield contributions. On Sanderson's see also J. A. Mathews, 'Modern High Speed Steel', *PASTM* 19 (1919), ii, pp. 142–56, who refers to the extraordinary results obtained by one tool user with a bar of old Sanderson self-hardening tool steel, and quotes the comments of a former associate of his at the Sanderson Works, Dr E. L. French, who predicted prior to 1900 that the tendency would be to rely on chromium and tungsten rather than upon carbon in order to secure red hardness. It should be mentioned that Elwood Haynes, the American discoverer of stainless steel, had also experimented with chromium and tungsten alloys. Cf. R. D. Gray, *Alloys and Automobiles* (Indianapolis, 1979), p. 151.

28 See Chap. 7. Before 1900 Sanderson's Syracuse Works had produced tool steels with 1.0 percent carbon, 1.5 percent manganese, and a substantial chromium content. Sanderson Kayser Ltd, *400 Years of Iron and Steel* (Sheffield, 1967–71), p. 13.

29 F. M. Osborn, *Tool Steel* (1908), p. 20. (Copy in Os 136.) See also *Engineering* 76 (1903), pp. 590–5, 639–44, 654–8. In these articles, relating to the Manchester Association of Engineers' experiments, F. M. Osborn stated that 'with proper heat treatment the results of Mushet steel would approximately be those of high-speed steel'. (p. 658.)

30 Technical treatises recommended Mushet steel for roughing-out but not general work. Cf. 'Practical Mechanism' series in *Scientific American* 31, n.s. (11 July 1874), p. 21; J. Rose, *The Complete Practical Machinist* (Philadelphia, 1890), p. 220.

31 *Times Engineering Supplement*, 22 November 1911, p. 9.
32 SCL Marsh 108. High Speed Steel Association 1907. The file contains private and confidential memos relating to the combination of Sheffield steelmakers which was organised to lend support to Niles-Bement-Pond.
33 *Ibid.*
34 EMHL Acc 1770. Archibald Johnston Collection. Series I, Box 9. Patent Infringement – Niles-Bement-Pond 1905–9. Folder 47. C. P. Byrnes to T. Bakewell, 15 August 1907. Other letters relating to the Taylor-White litigation are in Folders 44, 45, 46. Sir Robert Hadfield, who was a close friend of Maunsel White (the American was best man at his wedding in Philadelphia in 1894), was sympathetic to Bethlehem's case, but felt he could do nothing to help.
    The formation of the Sheffield steelmakers' combination was underway by 1903, when Edgar Allen's was asked to join. See SCL Aurora 541 (a). Letter from R. Woodward to R. H. Radford, 21 August 1903. Woodward believed that Mushet steel 'always [was] a High-Speed Steel, although not capable of running at such high speeds as the modern High-Speed Steels'.
35 Osborn, *Mushets*, pp. 102–3; Seed, *Pioneers*, p. 36. Unfortunately, apart from a passing reference to Taylor-White in SUA VIII/1/27/1, pp. 483–4, Arnold's correspondence concerning the case has been lost. He lent his formidable talents to the Sheffield cause by briefing the city's legal expert, Col. Herbert Hughes.
36 *Ironmonger* 126 (6 February 1909), p. 256; (13 February 1909), p. 309.
37 Copley, *Taylor*, vol. 2, pp. 114–16; *Iron Age* 66 (2 August 1900), p. 19. The Bethlehem correspondence in the Archibald Johnston Collection (EMHL Acc 1770) shows that interested parties were allowed from the beginning to view the Taylor-White investigations. See Memo to R. P. Linderman, 25 January 1900. Series II, Box 17, Folder 2. It is interesting to note that Vickers paid $100,000 for the patent rights as early as 1900, so at least one Sheffield firm believed the Americans had discovered something new.
38 *Quality* 7 (May 1936), p. 301. See also A. Balfour & Co Ltd, *A Centenary 1865–1965* (Nottingham, 1967), p. 23; *Engineering* 72 (2 August 1901), p. 145; *Ironmonger* 94 (March 30, 1901), p. 583. Balfour's production of high-speed steel in 1901 was 64 tons. See SCL BDR 97. Steel Melting Records.
39 SCL MD 7063. Letter, 18 December 1901. The steel cost 1s 8d per lb.
40 *British Steelmaker* 25 (April 1959), pp. 126–8; *Engineering* 74 (8 August 1902), p. 190. On Jonas & Colver, see also *Men of the Period*, pp. 71–5; *Illustrated London News Supplement* (1 May 1909), p. xviii.
41 *Engineering* 75 (16 January 1903), pp. 81–2; A. C. Marshall and H. Newbould, *The History of Firth's (1842–1918)* (Sheffield, 1924), pp. 81–3.
42 Os 103. 'Report of a Visit to Paris Exhibition Oct. 1900'. Pye-Smith asked, perceptively: 'How are [Bethlehem] to ensure a man who knows the secret at one works not taking it to another as an asset of his own – just as in the States a man who can't work RMS is of no account.' This report is pasted into a clippings book, which was used by Fred Osborn for his study of the Mushets. There are also what appear to be cuttings from the company minute book, referring to letters from B. M. Jones about the impact of Taylor-White steel on RMS. On 18 September 1900, for example, Jones reported: '[Taylor-White steel] may be fine in the main but *entirely impractical*. Even if successful RMS would still be wanted.' Jones added, on 5 October 1900: 'Large Railroad under nose of Bethlehem told me genuine RMS good enough for them.'
43 Os 86. Mixtures Meetings 1903–7. See esp. entries marked 'T. W. Process' on

6 November, 10 December 1906. Seed, *Pioneers*, p. 76, details the chemical evolution of RMS into Super Mushet 723.

44 *American Machinist* 29, Pt. 1 (5 April 1906), pp. 438–44; *Engineering* 82 (26 October 1906), pp. 563–4; Seed, *Pioneers*, pp. 33–6; *Implement and Machinery Review* 32 (1 September 1906), pp. 561–9.

45 *Engineering* (n. 29). Armstrong-Whitworth of Manchester also took part in the trials. A Vickers' analysis book shows intense experimentation into high-speed steels after 1903, with attempts to duplicate the composition of various Sheffield and American steels. See SCL LD 1878, 'VS & M Ltd, Crucible Steel, No. 2'.

46 *JISI*, 1905, ii, pp. 460–504; *Industries of Sheffield and District* (Sheffield, 1905), *passim*. Beardshaw's, for example, produced their 'High Velocity Steel' and reported: 'Three good firms have tested our make, and in each case the upshot is that it is equal to Messrs Firth's make; another firm have found it to be superior, and they have promised to supply ... full details as to speeds and cuts.' See SCL MD 7081 (5) 1893–1906, London office report, 20 January 1902.

47 *Times Engineering Supplement* (n. 31).

48 See Chap. 8.

49 Lengthy coverage was granted to English steels in the pages of this journal during the 1900s. See: *American Machinist* 25 (8 May 1902), pp. 666–7; 27 Pt. 1 (11 February 1904), pp. 190–1; 28, Pt. 1 (8 June 1905), p. 777; 30, Pt. 2 (12 December 1907), p. 922; 32, Pt. 1 (2 February 1909), p. 241; 32, Pt. 1 (11 March 1909), p. 414; 32, Pt. 1 (13 May 1909), p. 791; 32, Pt. 1 (17 June 1909), p. 1024.

50 E. T. Clarage, 'English *v.* American High-Speed Steels', *American Machinist* 32, Pt. 1 (17 June 1909), pp. 1031–2.

51 Becker, *High-Speed Steel*, pp. 51–2. See also M. A. Grossmann and E. C. Bain, *High-Speed Steel* (New York, 1931).

52 F. Foster, *Engineering in the United States* (Manchester, 1906), p. 80.

53 Jonas & Colver introduced its 'Novo Superior' steel as an insurance policy in case Bethlehem won its action. See *Ironmonger* 126 (6 February 1909), pp. 268–9.

54 *Engineering* 95 (31 January 1913), p. 162. According to Arnold the copyrighted reports issued from Sheffield University during the years 1900–2 had been unconscious plagiarisms of a series of American patents in 1904–8.

55 Os 86. Mixtures Meetings 1903–7, reports initial trials with vanadium on 23 October 1905. On 27 November 1905, the first trial was reported to be good 'but nothing worth the extra cost'. Further trials in 1906, however, brought vanadium into regular use. Seed, *Pioneers*, p. 36, claims that Osborn's made the first commercial use of vanadium in high-speed steel.
   John Brown's also experimented with vanadium at this time. See K. C. Barraclough, *Steelmaking Before Bessemer* (London, 1984), vol. 2, p. 141.

56 *Iron Age* 91 (30 January 1913), p. 339; *NCAB*; J. A. Mathews, 'Comments on the Making and Use of Alloy Tool and Special Steels', *TASST* 7 (1925), pp. 147–67, 158; *Metal Progress* 27 (February 1935), pp. 40–1; G. A. Roberts, 'Vanadium in High-Speed Steel', *Transactions of the Metallurgical Society of AIME* 236 (July 1966), pp. 950–63. On vanadium generally see G. Burns, 'The Quality of Toolsteel – Historical Development', *Metal Progress* 65 (February 1954), pp. 97–100.

57 *Metal Progress* 65 (June 1954), p. 128. Kuehnrich, who committed suicide in

1932, had also pioneered high-carbon, high-chromium die tool steels and experimented with molybdenum. A letter in *Metal Industry* 16 (2 January 1920), p. 11, describes him as having 'the reputation of having carried out more tool steel alloying experiments than any living man'. It is a comment on the obscurity of many tool steel developments that little is known about his work.

58 Osborn's recognised this: 'There is no doubt that MHS [Mushet High Speed] is very good steel, but it does not occupy the place in relation to other steels that RMS did a few years ago to its imitators'. Os 17. Letter to Jones, Boston, 3 June 1903.

6. CONTRARY TO NATURE: THE DISCOVERY OF STAINLESS STEEL

1 C. A. Zapffe, 'Who Discovered Stainless Steel?', *Iron Age* 191 (14 October 1948), pp. 122–8. See also: A. S. Darling, 'Metallurgical Developments Between 1900 and 1939', *Transactions of the Newcomen Society* 55 (1983–4), pp. 41–7; R. A. E. Hopper, 'Stainless Steels – Past, Present and Future', *Metals and Materials* 2 (January 1986), pp. 10–12; Zapffe, *Stainless Steels* (Cleveland, 1949), pp. 5–26.

2 'Alloys of Iron and Chromium', *JISI*, ii, pp. 49–175.

3 Cf. H. S. Osborn, *The Metallurgy of Iron and Steel* (Philadelphia, 1869), pp. 132–3; *Scientific American* 13 (2 September 1865), p. 152; 31, n.s. (19 September 1874), pp. 376–78. For further details on Baur and chrome steel, see Chap. 9.

4 For a survey of these contributions see: J. H. G. Monypenny, *Stainless Iron and Steel* (2nd edn., 1931), pp. 18–27; E. E. Thum, ed., *The Book of Stainless Steels* (Cleveland, 2nd edn., 1935), pp. 1–8.

5 Brearley has provided us with two accounts of his life and his work with stainless steel. See *Knotted String* (1941); *Stainless Steel: The Story of Its Discovery*. Repr. from the *Sheffield Daily Independent*, 2 February 1924. In 1931 Brearley also deposited a sworn declaration, 'History of Stainless Steel Cutlery', at the Company of Cutlers in Hallamshire, with instructions that its contents should remain a secret until the Cutlers' Feast in 1960. The date was awaited with some eagerness, but when the report was read it disclosed little that was not already known. However, the account, dated 14 December 1931, does reproduce a number of interesting letters that are cited below.

6 *Stainless Steel*, p. 10.

7 Brearley declaration. James Dixon & Sons also had difficulty in forging the steel. The knives made by Ibberson and Dixon's were presented by Brearley to the Company of Cutlers, where they are presently displayed. On the problems involved in the working of stainless steel, see R. G. Hall, 'Stainless Steels and the Making of Cutlery', *TASST* 2 (1921/2), pp. 561–8.

8 Brearley declaration. The word 'stainless' apparently came into use in about 1915. Stain-resisting, or rust- or corrosion-resisting are more correct terms, for no variety of stainless steel resists every corroding substance.

9 *Knotted String*, p. 157.

10 *Stainless Steel*, p. 17. This account was Brearley's attempt to set the record straight. At the end of his account (p. 23) Brearley reproduced an affidavit from the Firth directors, containing statements fully crediting his work, to protect 'other young men who may find themselves at variance with powerful

manufacturing interests'. See also 'Messrs. Firth's Reply to Mr Brearley', *Sheffield Daily Telegraph*, 4 February 1924, which also has information by Ernest Stuart on the same page. One of Sheffield's leading manufacturers and technologists commented on the affair: 'Having known some of the directors of Thomas Firth and Sons whom he criticized, I have always felt that they did not deserve Brearley's strictures. It is perhaps difficult, looking back, to realize how a conservative craft industry, like cutlery, might be expected to react to a revolutionary material for knife blades. At the time I remember being surprised that Brearley succeeded in persuading one or two cutlers to make trials and with his help overcome early teething troubles.' R. S. Hutton, *Recollections of a Technologist* (1964), p. 60.

11 *Brown Bayleys 1871–1971: A Centenary* (1971), p. 16.

12 *Sheffield Daily Telegraph*, 20 March 1915; 25 September 1915. G. Ethelbert Wolstenholme, a Firth director, also publicised the product in his address, 'Stainless Steel: Its Development and Uses', to the Manchester Federated Ironmongers' Association in 1915.

13 Statement forwarded by Brearley to E. Gadsby, 5 September 1917, contained in the Firth–Brearley Stainless Steel Syndicate (FBSSS) files, in possession of Johnson Firth Brown, Sheffield. On Firth's Pittsburgh steelworks, Firth Sterling, see Chap. 7. An early application of the material was in Westinghouse turbine blades. See: *Engineering* 117 (1924), p. 604; *ICTR* 103 (28 October 1921), pp. 626–7.

14 The Syndicate files show that Brearley was paid £10,000 and held 7,000 shares, the same number as his friend Maddocks.

15 *Knotted String*, p. 137.

16 FBSSS, Minute Book, No. 1, 12 October 1917, p. 57; Wolstenholme's letter of introduction, F. Best to J. Kinnear, 30 August 1917 (in possession of Mrs Celia Bobby, Repton). Best told Kinnear: 'There is no doubt ... that stainless steel cutlery has come to stop, and will revolutionise the cutlery trade'. Wolstenholme also demonstrated the value of stainless steel aero-engine valves to various US firms with the aid of electric arc furnaces. See Wolstenholme, 'A Survey of Engineering and Metallurgical Progress', Institution of Mechanical Engineers (Yorkshire Branch), 12 December 1934.

17 R. D. Gray, *Alloys and Automobiles* (Indianapolis, 1979), pp. 145–55.

18 R. D. Gray, *Stellite; A History of the Haynes Stellite Company, 1912–1972* (Kokomo, Ind., 1974); and Haynes, 'Stellite and Stainless Steel', *Proceedings of the Engineers' Society of Western Pennsylvania* 35, pp. 469–70.

19 Gray, *Alloys*, p. 149.

20 FBSSS, Minute Book, No. 1, 21 February 1918, p. 76.

21 In 1920 capital was increased to $250,000 and the Midvale Steel Co, which was threatening the manufacture of a 15–20 percent chromium and 1–2 percent carbon steel, was admitted to the combine. Firth director Frederick Best recommended this (letter, 11 July 1919) because 'it will complete the full range of limits [and] it will be preferable to bring them into line rather than legal action'.

22 One contentious issue was the 'mark' question, which surfaced in 1928. Brearley was annoyed that Firth's were selling stainless steel stamped 'Firth Stainless' instead of 'Firth–Brearley Stainless' and demanded that the Syndicate discuss the question. The chairman, though, felt it had been discussed 'ad nauseam' and another board member argued that the mark question was 'obstructing the business of the syndicate'. See FBSSS, Minute Book, No. 3, 13

June 1928, pp. 117–19. I am grateful to Mr W. G. Ibberson, whose father was involved in the production of the first stainless steel knives, for helpful comments on the operation of the Syndicate.

23 See the Firth publications: *Stainless Steel* (McKeesport, Pa., 1923); *The Development of Stainless Steel* (Sheffield, 1922).

24 FBSSS, Best file, letter to Syndicate, 11 July 1919.

25 FBSSS, Minute Book, No. 2, 9 October 1922, pp. 74–5. On 18 December 1922, pp. 89–90, it was further decided to send data to the American Co 'to emphasize the manner in which Stainless Steel is being developed in England for miscellaneous purposes'.

26 FBSSS, Brearley to Gadsby, 4 February 1921. See also Brearley's account in *Knotted String*, pp. 39–42, where he omits to mention that the case was won only on appeal; nor does he refer to Haynes, though it seems that the two men never met. Whilst in the US, though, Brearley did take the opportunity to make some melts of stainless steel at Firth Sterling, to urge the development of rustless iron, to tour New England cutlery factories, to talk to manufacturers about the product, and to lecture at the Massachusetts Institute of Technology.

As might be expected English and American manufacturers followed closely Ludlum's attempt to manufacture without a licence a low-carbon chromium steel with silicon. There is a file of correspondence regarding the case in the Hadfield Papers in SCL. Hadfield, after his chromium researches in 1892, was undoubtedly irked that stainless steel had been discovered and patented by someone else. He told his directors on 12 March 1920: 'B[rearley] has not discovered any new material; my Paper showed this long ago. He might have taken something I showed and obtained certain qualities from it which are now found useful, but he is no more the discoverer of the product than the man in the moon.' Brief details on Ludlum's early history can be found in J. H. Ransom, *Vanishing Ironworks of the Ramapos* (New Jersey, 1966), pp. 117–18.

27 Gray, *Alloys*, p. 165.

28 Monypenny, *Stainless Iron*, p. 23.

29 W. H. Hatfield, *Pamphlets* (in SCL); *JISI*, 1946, i, pp. 369–75; *Obituary Notices of the Fellows of the Royal Society* 4 (1944), pp. 617–27.

30 Thum, *Book of Stainless Steels*, p. 387. See also another Firth booklet, *The Development of 'Staybrite' Steel* (n.d.).

31 W. H. Hatfield, 'The Fabrication of Acid-Resisting Steel Plant', repr. from *Transactions of the Institution of Chemical Engineers* 7 (1929), p. 16. Hatfield's emphasis on American dependence is justified, though he should perhaps have highlighted Krupp's pioneering work.

32 J. Truman, 'The Initiation and Growth of High Alloy (Stainless) Steel Production', *Historical Metallurgy* 19, No. 1 (1985), pp. 116–25, 119. For details of Hatfield's visits to America in the 1920s, which show his general admiration for that country, see Hatfield, *Sheffield Burns* (Sheffield, 1943), pp. 167–92.

33 Thum, *Book of Stainless Steels*, p. 67.

34 Quoted in Monypenny, *Stainless Iron*, p. 19. The US National Bureau of Standards, even after the First World War, believed stainless steel had only a limited usefulness! See R. C. Cochrane, *Measures for Progress* (Washington, DC, 1966), p. 172. On the slowness of the US cutlery makers to take up stainless steel, see *American Cutler* (March 1920), p. 40. In contrast, Vickers began experimenting with stainless steel only a year after its discovery. See K.

C. Barraclough, 'A Crucible Steel Melter's Logbook', *Historical Metallurgy* 12 (1978), pp. 98–101.

35 See S. A. Main, 'The Properties, Characteristics and Uses of Stainless Steel', *Journal of the Royal Society of Arts* 83 (7 June 1935), pp. 673–700. Stainless steel has become so ubiquitous that listing all its uses would be an endless task. But Main cites three American examples to illustrate the metal's versatility: the structural parts of the Chicago, Burlington & Quincy RR 'Burlington Zephyr' train, which cut maintenance costs by almost a third; the deck fittings of the America's Cup defender, the 'Enterprise', in 1930; and the ornamental sheathing of the Empire State and Chrysler buildings.

Truman's study, 'Initiation', of the introduction of stainless steel has no counterpart in the American literature, though Thum, *Book of Stainless Steels*, contains a wealth of information on the early use of the alloy in US industries.

7.TRANSATLANTIC SPECIAL STEELS I:
THE CRUCIBLE STEELMAKERS

1 See J. G. Timmins, 'The Commercial Development of the Sheffield Crucible Steel Industry' (Sheffield MA, 1976), pp. 200–1; 'Concentration and Integration in the Sheffield Crucible Steel Industry', *Business History* 24 (March 1982), pp. 61–78.

2 Sanderson Kayser Ltd, *400 Years of Iron and Steel* (Sheffield, 1969–71), pp. 2–9.

3 J. Percy, *Metallurgy* (1864), pp. 768–73; R. A. Hadfield, *Faraday and His Metallurgical Researches* (1931), pp. 73–5, 114, 132.

4 W. O. Henderson, *J. C. Fischer and His Diary of Industrial England 1814–51* (1966), pp. 65, 156–60.

5 T. Allen, *A New and Complete History of the County of York* (1828–31), vol. 3, pp. 40–1, quoting Sir Richard Phillip's *Personal Tour* (1828); J. Hunter, *Hallamshire*. Revd. edn. by A. Gatty (Sheffield, 1869), p. 216; *Iron Age* 18 (14 August 1876), p. 14. An early reference to the firm's steel is found in the records of the Philadelphia merchant, Nathan Trotter, who turned to Naylor & Sanderson after the War of 1812. See E. Tooker, *Nathan Trotter, Philadelphia Merchant, 1787–1853* (Cambridge, Mass., 1955), p. 97.

6 F. Thistlethwaite, *The Anglo-American Connection in the Early Nineteenth Century* (Philadelphia, 1959), p. 17. For brief biographical details on E. F. Sanderson, see H. S. Furniss (Lord Sanderson), *Memories of Sixty Years* (1931), p. 2. E. F. Sanderson was one of New York's wealthiest citizens, with a fortune estimated, in 1846, at $200,000. See M. Y. Beach, *The Wealth and Biography of the Wealthy Citizens of the City of New York* (New York, 11th edn., 1846), p. 25.

7 Z. Allen, *The Practical Tourist* (Providence, 1832), vol. 1, p. 286. Allen had visited Sheffield and his account of the town included a description of the crucible process (pp. 286–8). On Sanderson's, see also D. Lardner, *The Cabinet Cyclopaedia* (1831–4), vol. 1, p. 243.

8 SCL Misc. Papers. 'To the Importers and Consumers of Steel', March 1832. The original included a testimonial from various American firms regarding the excellence of Sanderson's steel.

9 B. Seely, 'Adirondack Iron and Steel Company, "New Furnace". 1849–54' (1978), quoted p. 39. Seely does not identify the Sanderson brother involved, but it was almost certainly Edward.

10 K. C. Barraclough believes that the plans may refer to a type of slagging bloomery patented by Charles Sanderson on 11 October 1838 (British Pat. No. 7,828).

11 See Hoe Papers, BLCU.

12 See Sanderson letters (indexed) in Letter Book, 1 September 1834–15 April 1835; and Letter Book, 11 December 1839–15 February 1841. Hoe Papers, Box 20.

13 F. E. Comparato, *Chronicles of Genius and Folly* (Culver City, Ca., 1979), p. 114. Comparato examines the Sheffield connection in some detail in Chap. 3, pp. 111–29.

14 Letter Book, 15 September 1842–15 April 1846. Hoe Papers, Box 21. See also letter of 26 April 1843, which contains similar remarks.

15 Hoe to Sanderson, 31 March 1843.

16 Comparato, *Chronicles*, pp. 118, 419–20.

17 Letter Book 15 December 1842–15 April 1846. Letters, Hoe to Sanderson, 30 January, 24 February 1844. Hoe Papers, Box 21.

18 Comparato, *Chronicles*, p. 122. After his employment by Hoe, Wheatman returned to Sheffield and began manufacturing saws at the Russell Works in 1845 with a partner, John Smith. See *Ironmonger* 33 (28 February 1885), p. 282; and Chap. 11.

19 See Steel Order Book. Hoe Papers, Box 27; and Box 34, Hoe to Sanderson, 19 March 1877.

20 Quoted in *400 Years*, p. 11. On Sanderson's problems at US customs, see *Sheffield Independent*, 2 November 1869. The US tariff also severely damaged the fortunes of the firm which Sanderson's later took over – Kayser Ellison. See 'The Story of Kayser Ellison & Co Ltd', *Sanderson Kayser Magazine* 1 (1961), pp. 2–8.

21 *British Trade Journal* 15 (1 October 1877), p. 544. One of these directors may have been Edward Tozer (1820–90), who managed Sanderson's US business after 1866.

22 W. M. Beauchamp, *Past and Present of Syracuse and Onondaga County New York* (New York, 1908), vol. 2, pp. 22–5; D. H. Bruce, ed., *Memorial History of Syracuse, N.Y.* (Syracuse, 1891), pp. 618–19; W. W. Clayton, *History of Onondaga County, New York* (Syracuse, 1880), pp. 216–18; *Engineering and Mining Journal* 8 (16 November 1869), p. 305; H. Perry Smith, *Syracuse and Its Surroundings* (1878), pp. 111–16; and newspaper clippings and typescript notes supplied by Richard N. Wright.

23 *American Manufacturer*, 6 February 1873, p. 6, states that Sweet used Jessop's best saw plate because the Pittsburgh makers had not succeeded in producing steel good enough for the toughest mower knives.

24 SCL MD 1485. Letter, 11 November 1864. Other letters relating to Sweet in the file are dated 1, 4, 15, 22 October 1864.

25 *Ibid.*, 12 November 1864.

26 *Ibid.*, 19 November 1864.

27 SCL Os 14. Osborn to Sweet, 29 November 1878; 8 November 1881. Vickers had earlier refused to allow Sweet to tour their works, informing Osborn that 'we and other Sheff'd houses have done too much of that in former times and we have given it up'. Since Samuel Osborn, besides producing Mushet steel, also manufactured finger-bars and knives for reaping and sowing machines, his friendship with Sweet is not surprising. Osborn's US visits were undertaken partly to make himself 'perfectly acquainted with the requirements of

the implement makers'. See *Implement and Machinery Review* 5 (2 February 1880), p. 2726.

28 *American Manufacturer*, 10 August 1876, p. 11; 14 September 1876, p. 11; *Iron Age* 18 (14 August 1876), p. 14; *Ironmonger* 18 (1 November 1876), pp. 414–15.

29 *Sheffield Independent*, 30 September 1876. See also *ibid.*, 27 September 1876.

30 American Iron and Steel Institute, *Directory to the Iron and Steel Works of the United States* (New York, 1880), p. 94; Halcomb Steel Co, *Catalogue and Hints on Steel* (1906), preface. Two converting furnaces can be seen in the engraving of the works reproduced in *400 Years*, p. 20.

31 *Sheffield Independent*, 30 September 1876.

32 *Ironmonger* 25 (18 June 1881), p. 859.

33 *Ibid.*, 40 (2 July 1887), p. 25.

34 *400 Years*, p. 13. This brief company history states that: 'Records left by members of the firm who went out to Syracuse are still in existence'. Unfortunately, despite repeated approaches, Sanderson Kayser would not cooperate in the writing of this study and told me that searching for old documents had 'no priority' with them.

35 F. H. Chase, *Syracuse and Its Environs* (New York, 1924), vol. 1, pp. 443–4; vol. 3, pp. 167–8, 404–5.

36 This information has been gleaned from the yearly American Iron and Steel Institute *Directory*.

37 *Ironmonger* 93 (6 October 1900), p. 34. The directors reported that the whole of the US assets had been released 'on very advantageous terms'. The take-over allowed Sanderson's to absorb Samuel Newbould & Co Ltd, which had also had an extensive American trade. Samuel Newbould Jr. (1787–1851) went to America early in the nineteenth century and set up a warehouse in New York, where he acted as resident agent. See *400 Years*, p. 16.

38 Beauchamp, *Past and Present*, vol. 1, p. 507, vol. 2, pp. 789–80; Chase, *Syracuse and Its Environs*, vol. 1, pp. 443–4.

39 See Firth–Brown, *100 Years in Steel* (Sheffield, 1937); A. C. Marshall and H. Newbould, *The History of Firth's (1842–1918)* (Sheffield, 1924). For an account of the works see *Ironmonger* 13 (28 February 1871), pp. 101–2. Further information can be found in the black-edged edition of the *Sheffield Independent*, 29 November 1880, which contains an obituary of over seven columns on Mark Firth; *DBB*; *Engineer* 50 (3 December 1880), p. 417; *Illustrated London News* 67 (28 August 1875), p. 193, 209–10; *Practical Magazine* 6 (1876), pp. 289–92.

40 *DNB*; R. E. Leader, 'The Rise and Growth of the Trades of Sheffield', in G. W. Hastings, ed., *Transactions of the National Association for the Promotion of Social Science* (1866), p. 495; Marshall and Newbould, *History of Firth's*, pp. 3, 9, 11.

41 *Sheffield Independent*, 7 September 1880.

42 Information and quotations for this section have been derived from Thomas Firth & Sons, Directors' and General Meetings' Minute Books (see esp. No. 1, pp. 85–97), and the directors' files for those meetings, 1902–14. The documents are in the possession of Johnson Firth Brown plc. On the founding of Firth Sterling, see also: Marshall and Newbould, *History of Firth's*, pp. 71–2; and the relevant years of the *American Manufacturer*.

43 The Sterling Steel Co was originally the Fort Pitt Steel Works, established in 1874. See *History of Allegheny County Pennyslvania* (Chicago, 1889), pp. 739–40. On Wheeler see: *American Manufacturer* 65 (14 September 1899), p. 225; *NCAB*.

44 On the Carpenter Steel Co, see E. M. Brumbach, *Fifty Years of Progress 1889–1939* (1939). Much of this firm's technology came from England, possibly from Firth's. Robert A. Hadfield wrote in his Notes on American & Other Trips, pp. 130–1, 18 November 1890, that Carpenter had recently been to France and Sheffield and had 'given $60,000 for secrets'. Hadfield Papers.

45 *American Manufacturer* 68 (2 May 1901), p. 571.

46 See Chap. 6.

47 In the 1920s Firth Sterling had an interest in the largest producer of tungsten ores in the US, the Wolf-Tongue Mining Co in Colorado. See K. Rigby, 'Tungsten Ore in the United States Economy 1900–1929' (London School of Economics MSc, 1979), p. 38.

48 Personal information from Sir Eric Mensforth. Firth Sterling was purchased by the bankers Lehman Bros, on behalf of their American clients. Firth Brown held at this date 2,515 of the 5,000 preferred shares and 40,652 of the 80,000 common stock shares; prior to their sale these were expected to realise $251,500 and $1,524,450, respectively.

49 SCL BDR 77. Directors' Minute Book, p. 30 (27 July 1900), p. 44 (14 November 1900), p. 76 (7 January 1902). See also *Iron Age* 66 (25 October 1900), p. 15, (22 November 1900), p. 31; *Ironmonger* 93 (27 October 1900), pp. 153–4.

50 J. H. Stainton, *The Making of Sheffield 1865–1914* (Sheffield, 1924), p. 273. The *Sheffield Daily Telegraph* devoted a six-column obituary to Thomas Jessop on 1 December 1887.

51 Saw plates were a speciality of Jessop's, which by the 1870s was said to be making the largest circular saw plates in existence (87 inches diameter). See *Sheffield Independent*, 13 October 1873.

52 *Ibid.*, 1 December 1887.

53 *Pawson and Brailsford's Illustrated Guide to Sheffield and Neighbourhood* (Sheffield, 1862), p. 124. Jessop's St Louis agent from 1869 was a Sheffielder, Ezra Hounsfield Linley (d. 1911), who besides sending in large orders for mining steel also built up his own railway supply business and was reputed to have become a millionaire. See W. Odom, *Hallamshire Worthies* (Sheffield, 1926), pp. 90–1.

54 The Works contained 3 steel melting furnaces with an annual capacity of 5,000 gross tons of ingots, 18 melting holes capable of holding 108 pots, and a fully equipped rolling mill with annealing furnaces. See American Iron and Steel Institute, *Directory* (New York, 1901), p. 398; *Engineer* 95 (8 May 1903), p. 482.

55 *Industries of Sheffield and District* (Sheffield, 1905), p. 56. A photograph of the Washington plant is reproduced in Wm. Jessop & Sons, *Visit to a Steelworks* (Sheffield, 1913), p. 5. See also *Engineer* 99 (10 March 1905), p. 253. Sydney Jessop Robinson supervised the building of the Washington works. See *Ironmonger* 112 (12 August 1905), p. 307.

56 Quoted in *Iron Age* 67 (28 March 1901), p. 19. See also: *ibid.*, 67 (21 February 1901), p. 14; 68 (25 July 1901), p. 37; *Engineer* 93 (14 March 1902), p. 271.

57 Wm. Jessop mentioned the case of an American consumer who was threatened with a virtual boycott if he did not buy his steel exclusively from the Crucible Steel combine. See *Engineer* 91 (15 March 1901), p. 262.

58 *Ibid.*

59 American Iron and Steel Institute, *Directory* (New York, 1920), p. 190.

60 SCL SJC 83. L. J. Coombe to Spear & Jackson, 12 July 1925.

61 A few miscellaneous items relating to Jessop's can be found in the records of the Birmingham Small Arms Co (University of Warwick Modern Records Centre). See MSS 19A/1/2/43 Pollen Report. Cf. also B. Ryerson, *The Giants of Small Heath* (Yeovil, 1980), pp. 37, 42.

62 BSA Papers, *loc.cit.*, MSS 19A/1/2/52. Letter to Chase Fosdick Machine Tool Co, Cincinnati, 26 June 1922.

63 *Sheffield Daily Telegraph*, Industrial Supplement, 31 December 1925. Lantsberry died in Scarsdale, New York, in 1939. See *Journal of the Institute of Metals* 66 (1940), p. 441. Brief financial details on Jessop's US trade can be found in BSA Papers, *loc.cit.*, 19A/2/45/1–7. Balance Sheets.

8. THE RISE AND DECLINE OF SHEFFIELD'S HIGH-SPEED STEEL TRADE WITH AMERICA, 1900–30

1 SCL Os 17. Letter to B. M. Jones & Co, 18 November 1902.

2 The output of A. Balfour & Co averaged only 300 tons p.a. between 1901–14, though there was a rise to over 1,000 tons p.a. in 1916–18. See BDR 97. Steel Melting Records.

3 Os 17. Letter to Jones, 3 June 1903.

4 Os 86. Mixtures Meetings 1903–7. For a detailed description of Osborn's factory at this time, see *American Machinist* 29, Pt. 1 (5 April 1906), pp. 438–44.

5 Mixtures Meetings. See notes by Stanley Pye-Smith concerning a personal visit to one of Osborn's best customers at Ramapo, New York, and also the meeting on 13 February 1906, which mentions a very satisfactory letter from Jones.

6 Os 17. Letter to Jones, 7 February 1906. See also letter, 25 April 1906.

7 *Steel and Iron (American Manufacturer)* 40 (1 September 1906), p. 399, quoting a Sheffield newspaper. See also *Ironmonger* 110 (14, 28 January 1905), pp. 77, 187–8.

8 The Association met 'from time to time to discuss and consider matters of general interest pertaining to the manufacture of High-Speed Steel and to agree on such selling prices for the same as may be decided by a majority of members'. See Papers relating to the Association in SCL Marsh 108. See also SCL BDR 77, Meeting of Directors, 26 July 1907, p. 212.

9 Os 17. Letter to Jones, 24 September 1907.

10 Os 17. Letter to Jones, 25 July 1907.

11 *Ibid.*

12 Os 17. Letter to Jones, 21 January 1909; 14 July 1909. Osborn's had for many years been worried about the stock position in the US, asking Jones in 1906: 'supposing some other steel came out to supersede existing High-Speed Steels, where would we be with our enormous stocks?'. See Os 17. Letter, 25 April 1906. On the declining US demand for Sheffield steel, see *Sheffield Daily Telegraph*, 28 December 1911.

13 Os 150 & 151.

14 *Ironmonger* 166 (1 March 1919), p. 68.

15 *Iron Age* 107, Pt. 1 (10 February 1923), p. 374.
16 On higher costs, see *Minutes of Evidence Taken Before the Committee on Industry and Trade 1924–1927*, vol. 1, pp. 334–5. On US costs, which almost doubled in the postwar period, see *Iron Trade Review* 77 (10 December 1925), p. 1459.
17 PRO FO 371/5673. 'Memo on the effect of the proposed Tariff No. HR 7456 of June 29th 1921 on the Trade of Sheffield and District.' The file also contains letters to Balfour from Sheffield steel and toolmakers. See also F. Stones, *The British Ferrous Wire Industry 1882–1962* (Sheffield, 1977), p. 118.
18 PRO FO 371/5692. 'Formation of American Tungsten Steel Importers Commission to Protect British Trade Interests in the US.' The organisation was a logical extension of the High-Speed Steel Alloys Ltd of Widnes, of which Balfour was also chairman, which was formed to safeguard supplies of tungsten during the First World War. The Commission included: Balfour; J. H. Andrew; Kayser Ellison; Osborn; Jessop; Firth; Jonas & Colver; Armstrong-Whitworth (Manchester); Watson Savile; Walter Spencer; Edgar Allen; Sanderson Bros & Newbould; Henry Rossell; J. J. Saville; Wm. Atkins; John Nicholson; T. Inman; Spear & Jackson; Samuel Warren.
19 PRO FO 371/5692. 'Postponement of diplomatic action respecting US Tariff treatment of imported high-speed steel.' Memo by R. H. Hadow, 7 April 1921.
20 *Ibid.* Memo by Hadow, 20 August 1921.
21 PRO FO 371/7306. 'Representations to US Government on behalf of Messrs. A. Balfour & Co.'
22 *Ibid.* Memo, 25 May 1922, p. 2–3.
23 PRO FO 371/7306. *Aide-mémoire* No. 2 from the Commercial Counsellor, 21 June 1922, p. 6.
24 *Senate Docs. Vol. 5, Pt. 3, Tariff Act of 1921. Hearings before the Committee of Finance, 67th Congress, 2nd Session*, pp. 1752–61.
25 *Ibid.*, pp. 1756, 1758. See also Balfour, 'Effect of the World War on the Iron and Steel Business', *TASST* 8 (1925), pp. 621–34.
26 *Sheffield Daily Telegraph*, 15 September 1922.
27 A. Balfour & Co, *A Centenary 1865–1965* (Nottingham, 1967), p. 14. In Pittsburgh Seebohm admitted 'that in the practical part of [steel] manufacture I might have something to learn, but could have nothing to teach'. *Ironmonger* 25 (5 March 1881), p. 293.
28 *Centenary*, pp. 16–17. Balfour made 73 sea voyages to America and remembered when 'the heads of many of the Sheffield firms went once or twice a year regularly on personal visits to their customers [in the US]. We used to meet on the boats going out and coming back, and had the closest possible touch with our customers.' See Lord Riverdale, 'Sheffield Steel. Memories of 50 Years', *Quality* 7 (May 1936), pp. 300–1. Cf. my entry in *DBB*; and his son's reminiscences, 'Lord Riverdale Remembers', *Quality* (May-December 1984).
29 BDR 134, which contains Accounts Reports summarising the state of the trade. Unless stated, all information and quotations are from this source. Arthur Balfour Steel Co was incorporated in Delaware in 1920 with a nominal capital of $60,000. See BDR 95.
30 Balfour's was already losing £230 on its US account in 1921 and also incurring serious losses in Canada (BDR 130. Minute Book). On over-capacity in the US tool steel industry, see *Iron Age* 102 (5 September 1918), p. 577.
31 *Centenary*, pp. 30–6. Bad trading conditions are reflected in Balfour's steel

output which fell from 2,311 tons in 1920 to 526 tons in 1921 and 659 tons in 1922. See BDR 97.

32 On the decreasing profitability of high-speed steel manufacture at this time, see J. A. Coyle, *Iron Trade Review* 78 (14 January 1926); pp. 136–7, who remarks that profits in America were down 40 percent compared with the prewar period.

33 BDR 79. Company Minutes, 14 September 1923; 15 December 1931; 11 November 1932. The loss of the American market was described in *Centenary*, p. 32, as the 'biggest blow' to Balfour's export trade in this period. The Tariff had 'slammed the door tight shut on Sheffield's exports'.

34 SCL MD 2333. US Order Book, 1924–34. Subsequent information in the text is from comments written alongside the orders.

35 On these developments, see *ICTR* 115 (9 December 1927), p. 869.

36 *Iron Age* 102 (19 September 1918), p. 730; 103 (12 June 1919), p. 1574. On reductions in the price of high-speed steel, see *Iron Age* 103 (9 January 1919), p. 156.

37 On the performance of Allen's steel in America, see *Edgar Allen News* 5 (September 1926), p. 842; 7 (July 1928), p. 203.

38 *Ibid.* 7 (1928), p. 327; 8 (January 1930), p. 533.

39 *Ibid.* 8 (September 1929), p. 647. See also MD 2336, Journal, containing brief details on the liquidation of the Chicago stock, which appears to have occurred about 1928–9.

40 E. N. Simons, 'The Story of a Great Steel Firm', *Edgar Allen Magazine* (February 1957), p. 114.

41 *Sheffield and Neighbourhood* (Sheffield, 1899), pp. 206–8; J. H. Stainton, *The Making of Sheffield 1865–1914* (Sheffield, 1924), p. 260; *Times Engineering Supplement*, 22 November 1911, p. 15. John H. Andrew (1824–84) is said to have visited the US on over sixty occasions. See *JISI*, 1884, i, p. 554. His son, Henry H. Andrew (b. 1850), also crossed the Atlantic several times, before his sudden death in New York in 1903. See *Sheffield Daily Telegraph*, 14 October 1903.

42 This section is based on SCL Aurora 56. Minute Book, 1914–27; and Aurora 60. Minutes of General and Shareholders Meetings 1898–1926.

9. TRANSATLANTIC SPECIAL STEELS II: STEEL CASTING ENTERPRISES

1 W. O. Henderson, *J. C. Fischer and His Diary of Industrial England 1814–51* (1966), p. 7. There is no general survey of the European steel castings industry, but on Fischer see: G. Fischer Ltd, *The Metallurgist Johann Conrad Fischer 1773–1854 and His Relations with Britain* (Schaffhausen, 1947); K. Schib and R. Gnade, *Johann Conrad Fischer 1773–1854* (Schaffhausen, 1954); and on Krupp's: *Engineer* 22 (17 August 1866), p. 111; 64 (29 July 1887), p. 85. Cf. generally A. E. Musson, 'Continental Influences on the Industrial Revolution in Great Britain', in B. M. Ratcliffe, ed., *Great Britain and Her World, 1750–1914* (Manchester, 1975), pp. 71–85.

2 Descriptions of the foundries and processes of these firms can be found in: *Sheffield and Neighbourhood* (Sheffield, 1899); *Sheffield and Rotherham 'Up-To-Date'* (1897); *Ryland's Iron Trade Circular* (12 February 1876), pp. 239–40 (Cammell's); *Sheffield Independent*, 1 January 1867 (Firth's); *Ironmonger* 34 (14 November 1885), pp. 790–1 (Jessop's); *Sheffield Indepen-*

dent, 16 January 1858 (Shortridge, Howell & Jessop). On Vickers see: J. D. Scott, *Vickers* (1962); C. Trebilcock, *The Vickers Brothers* (1977); Vickers, Sons & Maxim Ltd, *Their Works and Manufactures* (1898). For Hadfields, see below.

3 In a standard textbook, *Steel and Iron* (3rd edn., 1887), p. 518, W. H. Greenwood refused to divulge any details of the manufacture of steel castings. For a fascinating insight into the tribulations of steel casting, see the typescript notes of John Mallaband (who worked at Vickers before joining Hadfields) to R. A. Hadfield, 6 May 1895. SCL Hadfield Papers. Mallaband highlighted in particular the problems with mechanical defects in steel castings in the early days, telling Hadfield: 'Ah! but your old friend honeycomb was there. I may say that [in the late 1850s] he was in his prime, monarch of all he surveyed, and he made a most thunderous mess whenever it suited him ... so much so that there was very little satisfaction to anyone about the job'. See also R. A. Hadfield's presidential address, *JISI*, 1905, i, pp. 91–2.

4 F. Kohn, *Iron and Steel Manufacture* (1869), pp. 175–8.

5 *Engineering* 4 (25 October 1867), p. 384. Vickers' expertise was largely due to the technical genius of T. E. Vickers: see my entry in *DBB*. At the River Don Steel Works at this time Vickers was using 288 melting-holes, each capable of taking two pots of either 60 lbs or 100 lbs, and 40 tons of Swedish and English bar iron were often melted in a single day.

6 A. Nevins, ed., *Selected Writings of Abram S. Hewitt* (New York, 1937), p. 51. The remarks are from *Reports of the United States Commissioners to the Paris Exposition 1867–'68* (Washington, DC, 1868).

7 There is a printed leaflet of testimonials from American customers in the Vickers Papers, Cambridge University Library (Doc 720). See also C. Sherlock, 'Cast Steel Bells', *Special Steels Review*, No. 2 (Spring 1970), pp. 25–31. For details of the casting of a San Francisco fire-bell at Naylor Vickers, see *Illustrated London News* 36 (7 January 1860), p. 12. (According to a Sheffield newspaper the firemen found the bell unsuitable and it was to be re-located at the church of St Ignatius at Parker Avenue and Fulton St.) See generally on the advantages of steel castings, *Griffith's Guide to the Iron Trade of Great Britain* (Newton Abbot, 1967 repr. of 1873 edn.), pp. 201–3.

8 On the substitution of steel tyres for iron, see Nevins, *Hewitt*, p. 31. As a comparison of steel tyre costs, Hewitt quoted crucible steel tyres at £45 per ton, Bessemer at £28.

9 J. H. White, *American Locomotives: An Engineering History*, 1830–1880 (Baltimore, 1968), pp. 32, 182–3; *idem.*, *The American Railroad Passenger Car* (Baltimore, 1978), p. 539. Sheffield heavy steelmakers also supplied many of the rails on which the wheels ran. See: J. Austin and M. Ford, *Steel Town* (Sheffield, 1983); K. Warren, 'The Sheffield Rail Trade, 1861–1930; An Episode in the Locational History of the British Steel Industry', *Institute of British Geographers Transactions* 34 (1964), pp. 131–57.

10 *Iron Age* 13 (1 January 1874), p. 3.

11 *Ibid.* Mr W. Bailey Lang had extensive works in Jersey City for rolling tyres from blooms imported from Cammell's of Sheffield.

12 On Krupp's and cast steel tyres see: W. Berdrow, *The Krupps: 150 Years Krupp History 1787–1937* (Berlin, 1937), pp. 113–16; W. Manchester, *The Arms of Krupp 1587–1968* (London, 1964), pp. 102–3. Baldwin's imported Sheffield cast steel tyres, besides fire-box steel and axles, from Vickers, Cammell's, and Butcher. Numerous letters document the transactions in the Bald-

win Locomotive Co Papers (HSP 1485); see Letters from N.Y. Office January 1861–October 1861; Incoming Letter Book October–December 1865. The letter books are listed under 'New York Office Letters 1865–1867'.

13 *History of the Baldwin Locomotive Works 1831–1920* (Philadelphia, 1920), p. 58. On Justice cf. obituary *BAISA* 35 (10 May 1901), p. 78. Letters from Justice to Baldwin's are contained in HSP 1485, Letter Book April–June 1865. Justice was also involved in the importation of guns for the North. See W. B. Edwards, *Civil War Guns* (Harrisburg, 1962), pp. 60–4.

14 HSP 1485, Incoming Letter Book July–September 1865, Letter from Justice to Baldwin's, 5 September 1865. This was probably an attempt to interest Baldwin's in the plan. Justice puffed up the venture further in another letter ('The exceedingly profitable results are beyond any doubt'.) on 12 September 1865.

15 G. Tweedale, *Giants of Sheffield Steel* (Sheffield, 1986), pp. 20–8. An American merchant's reminiscences of the two brothers were published in the *Sheffield Independent*, 4 January 1871; while the *Ironmonger* 13 (31 March 1871), p. 195, described the Sheffield Works (employed 800–1200 skilled men; produced weekly 12 tons of files, 800 doz. razors, 600 doz. chisels and gouges, and 400 doz. planes, from its own steel made at the Philadelphia Works in Sheffield).

16 *Sheffield Independent*, 4 January 1871. According to a source in the *Sheffield Independent*, 2 October 1852, Butcher was second only to Turton's as a file-maker (the latter had 40 hearths, Butcher 29) and led in edge tool capacity with 26 hearths.

17 SCL MD 1485. Letter to Marsh's New York agency, 30 September 1865. See also HSP Claude W. Unger Collection, Invoice of Tools to Longstreth & Baldwin, 2 April 1836; S. W. Burchard, 'Butcher Blades in America', *CEAIA* 31 (December 1978); p. 61. Butcher also supplied steel to US toolmakers. See Baldwin Tool Co, *Illustrated Supplement [of] Arrowmammett Works, Middletown, Conn.* (Middletown, 1857, repr. 1976), pp. 50–1. There is an early Butcher catalogue, ca. 1830, in the Winterthur Museum, Delaware.

18 C. J. Erickson, *American Industry and the European Immigrant 1860–1885* (Cambridge, Mass., 1957), p. 42; R. W. Hunt, 'A History of the Bessemer Manufacture in America', *American Institute of Mining Engineers* 5 (1876/7), p. 207; *Daily Pittsburgh Gazette*, 2 December 1865. Wrote Marsh Bros to its New York agent: 'We fancy Wm. Butcher is to be the manager of a steel works near Harrisburg, Pa., he has been to the US this autumn and soon returns ... We fancy Wm. Butcher won't have much money invested in Harrisburg.' (MD 1485, 17 December 1865.)

19 EMHL Acc 1191. US Bureau of Census, 'Manufactures, 1870', shows the works capitalised at $750,000. Presumably, much of this capital came from the Philadelphia capitalists, such as Justice, William Sellers, and the directors of the Philadelphia & Reading Railway Co, who backed the venture.

20 The best account of the early history of the Butcher Works is by G. A. Aertsen in the Midvale Steel Co's journal, *The Safety Bulletin* 1 (December 1914)–2 (March 1915). See also: *Journal of the Franklin Institute* 84, 3rd s. (1867), pp. 293–4; E. T. Freedley, *Philadelphia and Its Manufactures* (Philadelphia, 1867), pp. 360–3; Midvale Steel Co, *The Seventy-Fifth Anniversary of the Midvale Steel Company* (1942); R. T. Nalle, *Midvale and Its Pioneers* (New York, 1948); C. Robson, ed., *The Manufactories and Manufacturers of Pennsylvania in the Nineteenth Century* (Philadelphia, 1875), pp. 236–7.

21 For a plan and description of the Works, see *Engineering* 23 (30 March 1877), p. 239. The Ms. Census of Manufactures adds that the plant included 3 steam hammers, 1 rolling mill and 5 boring machines; nearly 200 were employed; annual production of cast steel was 3,000 tons, produced from 2,500 tons of bar iron, 750 tons of scrap, and 50 tons of pig.

22 *Scientific American* 18, n.s. (18 January 1868), p. 42. There is a report of crucible steel castings being made by the Buffalo Malleable Iron Works in 1861, but Butcher's venture appears to have been the more significant. See W. H. Moriarty, *A Century of Steel Castings* (New York, 1961), p. 8. Butcher's success was later corroborated by none other than Robert A. Hadfield who, in the 1890s, visited the New Jersey Central Railway and made the following observation: 'Saw here 4 remarkable wheels of cast steel made by William Butcher & Co, Philadelphia (now Midvale). It appears the wheels were made (some 30 or 40) 10 to 12 years ago & those I saw had been running 10 years ... Certainly remarkable wheels & vindicate cast steel for car wheels.' See Notes on American and Other Trips, ca.1890+. Hadfield Papers.

23 A. D. Graeff, ed., *A History of Steel Casting* (Philadelphia, 1949), p. 8; R. P. Lamont, 'Manufacture of Steel Castings', *Iron Age* 99 (31 May 1917), pp. 1353–7.

24 Aertsen, *Safety Bulletin* 2 (January 1915), p. 8.

25 J. A. Kouwenhoven, 'The Designing of the Eads Bridge', *Technology and Culture* 23 (October 1982), pp. 561–4, has emphasised that various Philadelphia businessmen were instrumental in pushing the contract in Butcher's direction.

26 C. M. Woodward, *A History of the St Louis Bridge* (St Louis, 1881), p. 68, and *passim*, provides a detailed account of Butcher's involvement with the bridge.

27 Whether Eads and Baur fully realised the implications of the use of chromium and, indeed, whether the bridge eventually contained chromium at all, is a subject of some debate. See Q. Scott and H. S. Miller, *The Eads Bridge* (Columbia, 1979), pp. 112–17, who are sceptical of Eads and Baur, and J. A. Kouwenhoven, 'Eads Bridge', who believes Eads 'knew a good deal about chrome steel'. A recent analysis suggests that at least some of the bridge staves are of unusually high-grade chromium. Cf. E. E. Thum, 'Alloy Bridge Steel Sixty Years Old', *Iron Age* 122 (20 September 1928), pp. 683–6, 733–4; R. Dirscherl, 'Eads Bridge Pioneered New Era in Steel Usage', *Metal Progress* 120 (8 December 1981), pp. 28–33.

28 Aertsen, *Safety Bulletin* 2 (1915), p. 8.

29 Woodward, *Bridge*, p. 88.

30 *History of the Baldwin Locomotive Works 1831–1920* (1920), pp. 149–50; *The Story of Standard Steel Works 1795–1945* (1945), pp. 7–8. Descendants of these men were said to be still employed by the Freedom Works (later Standard Steel, a Baldwin subsidiary) in 1920.

31 The date of Butcher's death raises an interesting question concerning his personal involvement with the St Louis Bridge. All the authorities on the history of the Eads Bridge assume that Butcher himself directed operations. However, it should be noted that he died only a month after the Eads contract was signed. The *Sheffield Independent*, 21 April 1869, reported that he was unwell, presumably in Sheffield, and later stated in his obituary, 9 November 1870: 'Partly from delicate health, and partly from choice, Mr Butcher led a very retired life, more particularly since the death of Mrs Butcher in 1867.' (Alongside many of Sheffield's famous steel and toolmakers, Butcher is buried

in Ecclesall Churchyard.) It is therefore unlikely that the septuagenarian was in America during 1870. Possibly the management problems stemmed from this fact; if so, they may have been exacerbated by the death of the other brother, Samuel, the year before.

32 On Sellers see *Mechanical Engineers in America Born Prior to 1861* (New York, 1980), pp. 273–4. Sellers seems to have been brought into the company through stock payments for his machine tools.

33 *Iron Age* 42 (2 August 1888), p. 161.

34 J. L. Cox and F. B. Foley, 'Pioneering at Midvale', *Metal Progress* 18 (November 1930), pp. 51–5.

35 See Chap. 5.

36 In 1898–1903 Vickers was engaged in negotiations with several US concerns, including Midvale, with a view to the creation of a huge naval arsenal on the East Coast of America. See Trebilcock, *Vickers Brothers*, pp. 135–9. Vickers' correspondence concerning the proposed US base is on Microfilm R307, Vickers Papers, Cambridge University Library. Hadfields collaborated with Midvale in the twentieth century on chromium–nickel alloys (known as ATV) for steam turbine blades and automobile exhausts. See this Chap., below.

37 The history of the US steel castings industry is well treated in: W. P. Conway, *Cast to Shape* (Ohio, 1977); Graeff, *History*; Lamont, 'Manufacture' (n. 23); Moriarty, *Century*; F. M. Reck, *Sand in Their Shoes* (Ohio, 1952).

38 BL Ms. 596, Case 12, J. M. Camp, 'Hainsworth Steel Co', unpublished typescript, n.d.

39 *History of Allegheny Co, Pennsylvania* (Philadelphia, 1876), p. 111; *Iron Age* 16 (18 November 1875), p. 17. Brief notes on the rapid rise of the firm can be found in: *Iron Age* 22 (5 December 1878), p. 24; 25 (27 May 1880), p. 1; *American Manufacturer* (24 April 1873), p. 4, (30 July 1874), p. 4, (20 August 1874), p. 4, (10 September 1874), p. 3.

40 Quoted in D. C. Allard, 'The Influence of the United States Navy upon the American Steel Industry, 1880–1900' (Georgetown MA, 1959), p. 42. See also W. I. Brandt, 'Steel and the New Navy, 1882–1895' (Wisconsin PhD, 1920).

41 Lamont, 'Manufacture', p. 1354.

42 On the development of moulding sands, see Reck, *Sand*, pp. 2–7.

43 Lamont, 'Manufacture', p. 1354. See also: 'Steel Castings', *TASME* 12 (1890–1), pp. 710–24; 'Recent Progress in the Manufacture of Steel Castings', *ASME* 15 (1893–4), pp. 260–76.

44 On Hadfield's Steel Foundry Co's history and its perfection of manganese steel, see: my entry in *DBB*; *Engineer* 97 (22 April 1904), p. 414; *Engineering* 59 (8, 22 February 1895), pp. 165–6, 233–6; *Hadfield's Steel Foundry Company Ltd* (1905); *A Short Description of Hadfields Ltd* (1938); *Visit of HM the King to the East Hecla Works of Hadfields Ltd* (1915). SCL also has three unpublished and undated typescript histories: 'A Record of 50 Years Progress (1888–1938)'; S. A. Main, 'The Hadfields of Sheffield: Pioneers in Steel'; A. W. McKears, 'The Hadfields of Sheffield'.

45 American Notes, Plants, etc., subtitled American Industry, July and August 1882. Hadfield Papers. Hadfield was not over-impressed with American efforts at steel casting; however, Bessemer production at the Edgar Thomson Steel Works made an enormous impact on him and his breathless description ('[I] could have easily done with twenty instead of one pair of eyes') runs to several pages (copy in author's possession). Hadfield also recorded details of

his first American trip in a diary, which is reproduced as an appendix in Main, 'Pioneers'. A second American notebook, Notes on American and Other Trips, ca.1890+, also survives and has details on visits to numerous Eastern engineering and steel concerns, besides notes on the early application and manufacture of manganese steel in the US.

46 Quoted in Main, 'Pioneers', Chapter 3, p. 13. Between 1882 and 1914 Hadfield made eleven visits to the US.

47 On Weeks see *DAB*. Hadfield's voluminous correspondence with Weeks has been bound in three volumes in the Hadfield Papers, SCL.

48 Letter to Weeks, 23 May 1887. On Howe, who became Professor of Metallurgy at Columbia University, New York City, see: *DAB*; M. Gensamer, 'Henry Marion Howe's Contributions to Metallurgy', in C. S. Smith, ed., *The Sorby Centennial Symposium on the History of Metallurgy, Cleveland, 1963* (New York, 1965), pp. 59–66. (A full list of Hadfield's American contacts appears in his *Metallurgy and Its Influence on Modern Progress* (1925), p. 363.)

Hadfield became dissatisfied with Weeks and later recalled (letter to W. E. Parker, 23 March 1924): 'Mr Weeks ... did nothing but talk and got very little done. I do not mean that he was not an able man but he had not just the right flair for dealing with technical matters.' Weeks, for his part, had little time for Howe, and told Hadfield, 5 March 1889: 'I can hardly agree with you that [Howe] would be a good man to get interested in manganese steel. He is a splendid fellow in some respects, but he is one of those people who know it all, and others can teach him but little.'

49 See EMHL Acc 1292. Taylor–Wharton Iron & Steel Co Papers, 1742–1950, which contain drafts for the company's published histories and patents. See also: Taylor–Wharton Iron & Steel Co, *Historically Speaking 1742–1917: 175th Anniversary*; H. J. Parish and T. J. Ross, *200th Anniversary, 1742–1942* (1942).

50 'Statement Regarding Taylor–Wharton Company and Manganese Steel', 29 January 1924. T–W Files. Hadfield Papers.

51 *Ibid*. Information on Taylor–Wharton's performance is contained in a typescript, 'The Hadfield System: Its Application and Advantages' (ca. 1897), in the Hadfield Papers. Despite a depression when the process was introduced, the Hadfield licencees were said to be 'operating very successfully, and have in the comparatively short time of 2½ years turned out no less than £58,000 of steel castings on the Hadfield system. Their output of manganese steel has amounted to £23,700, and, according to their last returns, they are now turning out manganese steel at the rate of £27,000 per annum, and their profits, estimated upon the basis of their April, 1895, output, are at the rate of over £9,000 per annum.' The firm was helped by a £30,000 American Government order for projectiles: apparently, not one shell was rejected.

52 On Allen's history, see E. N. Simons, 'The Story of a Great Steel Firm', *Edgar Allen Magazine*, No. 28 (December 1953) – No. 58 (October 1958). The Works is described and illustrated in *ICTR* 104 (14 April 1922), pp. 515–17; *Engineering* 112 (1921), pp. 272–4, 304–7, 335–8; *Implement and Machinery Review* 20 (1 December 1894), pp. 18571–3.

53 On Askham Bros & Wilson, see *The Century's Progress* (1893), p. 115. The earliest mention of manganese steel in the Edgar Allen records is in SCL MD 3971. Directors' Letter-Book, 1896–1900, pp. 286–8. J. C. Hand to directors, 24 November 1897.

54 *Ibid.*
55 *Iron Age* 85 (30 June 1910), p. 1574. A detailed illustrated description of the Chicago plant was published in *Iron Trade Review* 52 (19 June 1913), pp. 1404–11. According to the *Implement and Machinery Review* 36 (1 May 1910), p. 103, the company was incorporated with a capital of $300,000.
56 Graeff, *History*, p. 88.
57 MD 3971, pp. 923–4. R. Woodward to T. Biggart.
58 *Iron Age* 91 (19 June 1913), p. 1487.
59 *Engineering* 65 (14 January 1898), pp. 43–6; E. N. Simons, 'The History of the Tropenas Process', *Engineer* 201 (9 March 1956), pp. 247–9.
60 'Why Steel Founders in your country have not adopted the process long ago, we cannot understand', wrote Allen to the editor of *Engineering News*, New York, 5 October 1897 (MD 3971, pp. 245–6). See also letter, 25 November 1897 (p. 282). There are a score of letters from Allen's to US customers concerning the Tropenas process in SCL Aurora 541 (a), Letter Book, January 1899–July 1904. In America the design of the Tropenas converter was greatly improved by the eminent American metallurgist Bradley Stoughton. See G. E. Doan, *Bradley Stoughton* (Ohio, 1967), pp. 5–6.
61 Simons, 'Story', No. 43 (April 1956), p. 274.
62 See 'Articles of Agreement between Hadfield's and the Bureau of Ordnance, United States Navy Department, to Produce Projectiles under the "Hadfield System"', 24 April 1914. This was probably a revision of an earlier agreement. The Hadfield System was a general term used to describe the company's secret manufacturing process, defined in the agreement as 'a system of making steel projectiles by pouring molten metal into moulds together with the necessary and suitable material for projectiles'. This was probably the episode C. H. Desch had in mind when he commented on the US importing Sheffield steel technology during the First World War. See *The Steel Industry of South Yorkshire* (1922), pp. 136–7. On the Hadfield Co's involvement with projectiles, which had resulted in its first large British Government order in 1888, see Main, 'Pioneers', Chap. 9; *Engineer* 127 (7 March 1919), p. 231; *The Hadfield System as Applied to War Material* (Sheffield, confidential booklet, n.d.).
63 Manganese steel was of great importance in the manufacture of crushing and digging machinery and here America offered a huge potential market. See: G. B. Anderson, *One Hundred Booming Years* (South Milwaukee, 1980); H. F. Williamson and K. H. Myers, *Designed for Digging* (Evanston, Ill., 1955). For general background see W. T. W. Miller, *Crushers for Stone and Ore* (1935). This book, written by a Hadfield manager, has a short foreword by Sir Robert Hadfield.
64 Hadfield also had investments in the American Equipment Co, the Era Steel Co, the Pacific Tractor Co, the Cahl Truck Co, the Bucyrus Building Co, and the ACM Co, Del. This and subsequent information is from the Hadfield-Penfield files in the Hadfield Papers, with additional material from the Midvale, ARMCo, Taylor–Wharton, and Ludlum Steel Co correspondence.
65 See Folder relating W. E. Parker's Reports of Visits to USA. Draft notes 1920, 'Interchange visit between Hadfields' Staff and the Hadfield-Penfield Company's Staff', 9 September 1920.
66 On Hadfields' US shell contracts, see *Annual General Meeting*, 28 March 1919, pp. 12–17. *Scientific American* 116 (3 February 1917), p. 116, reported: 'Hadfields Ltd offered to build the 16-inch projectiles at from $237 to

$387 less per shell (than US makers) and that in the case of the 14-inch projectiles the prices were from $144 to $194 less per shell. The time for delivery was in some cases as much as 23 months less.' See Hadfields' Directors' Minute Book (2), p. 151, 10 July 1917, re. US Navy contract for 4,494 14-inch armour-piercing shells at $356 each.

67 The US Government attitude was stated as early as 1890, when it wrote to Weeks: 'The Bureau does not desire to purchase armour piercing shells made abroad, but if arrangements are made by which the Hadfield shells can be manufactured in the United States from domestic material, the Bureau would be pleased to purchase and test some of them.' Letter, 10 March 1890, from Wm. Folger, Chief of Bureau of Ordnance.

Before the First World War only one American plant was engaged in the production of projectiles. See *Iron Age* 99 (4 January 1917), pp. 41–4. On US inferiority in shell manufacture, see S. L. Hoyt, *Men of Metals* (Ohio, 1979), p. 35. On Hadfields' product Hoyt remarked, p. 83: 'During the war their cast armor-piercing projectiles were as good as our best wrought product and better than those of our second and third producers.'

68 Memo from R. A. H. to W. E. Parker (US), 1 January 1924. The rivals were the Edgar Allen Co. Hadfield had netted gross royalties of £107,360 from Taylor–Wharton during 1891–1918; total US royalties on Hadfield's patents to 1918 were £216,890, which also included £100,470 on low hysteresis steel and £9,060 on various others. Total British royalties over roughly the same period were £135,170; German £47,750.

Hadfield was contemplating an American base in 1905. In a letter to G. W. Wickersham, 9 October 1905, he talked of a firm capitalised at $2–3 million – like Jessop's only bigger – and thought 'there ought to be an immense future for a Company of this kind in America'.

69 R.A.H. to Mr Hook (ARMCo), 26 June 1923. Commenting on the potential demand in America to Albert Sauveur, Hadfield wrote, 17 August 1925: 'all this makes one's mouth water as they say, when over here we can only get contracts after terrific scrambling and cutting of prices to the bone, in fact into the bone! There ought, however, to be a niche or corner in your big country where the Hadfield System could usefully find employment with profit and advantage to all concerned!! that is, if we have specialities to suit American requirements, and I believe we have.'

70 See 'Ford' memo by R.A.H., 7 July 1925, which refers to Parker's visit to Detroit. Hadfield thought the best idea would be 'an arrangement with us to let us put before them all our information in a confidential way, so that they could make a thorough and proper trial at their own Works'. For background on the alloy steel market, see W. T. Hogan, *Economic History of the Iron and Steel Industry in the United States* (Lexington, Mass., 1971), vol. 3, pp. 993–1087.

71 Letter of introduction for P. B. Brown: Vice-Admiral A. P. Niblack to Admiral Coontz, 17 March 1922.

72 Hadfield to Niblack, 17 March 1923.

73 In this period Bethlehem Steel 'literally turned from the manufacture of guns to plowshares'. EMHL Acc 1770. Archibald Johnston Collection, Series II, Box 20, REPORTS & TESTS – MISC. Folder 2, 'Decline in Ordnance Production 1924', 3 January 1924. On the Washington Steel & Ordnance Co, see Chap. 7.

74 Hadfields was also heavily involved in a major reorganisation at home at this

time. See *Iron Trade Review* 71 (10 August 1922), pp. 370–8. It had also acquired an interest in Harper–Bean, a Dudley-based car firm, another investment which was to turn out badly. See author's, 'Business and Investment Strategies in the Interwar British Steel Industry: A Case Study of Hadfields Ltd, Sheffield, and Bean Cars', *Business History* (1987).

75 R.A.H. to Wickersham, 4 December 1922. (For details on Hadfield's marriage – like E. F. Sanderson and Albert Vickers, he married an American – see *DBB*. On Wickersham, who was Attorney-General under Taft, and became Hadfield's legal adviser in the US, see *DAB, Supplement 1 & 2*.) In a further communication to his directors, 4 April 1922, R.A.H. added: 'I should like to see the whole of the H.–P. crowd, as far as the Steel side is concerned, put in a railway truck and sent off to Nova Scotia.'

76 See ARMCo, *The First Twenty Years* (Middletown, Ohio, 1922). ARMCo became famous in 1926 for successfully pioneering the continuous rolling of steel strips for mass-produced durables, particularly the automobile.

77 J. B. Thomas' Report. 9th Visit. May 1926.

78 8th Visit, W.E.P.'s Report, 1 October 1924. See also Report of a Visit of Mr P. B. Brown and Mr W. E. Parker to the American Manganese Steel Company, Chicago Heights, on 17 May 1921. A Firth's representative also commented on higher American productivity: 'The American workman is out to earn all the dollars he possibly can, and consequently he works hard, and my observations led me to conclude the output per man was double that of the moulder on this side.' See *The Bombshell* 3 (October 1919), p. 374.

79 In 1921 the firm was in contact with the president of the Electric Furnace Construction Co, Mr Hodson, a Sheffielder who had graduated at Sheffield University in about 1908 and settled in the US in 1918. See Brown and Parker Visits to USA.

80 R.A.H. memo to Brown (N.Y.), 1 June 1926.

81 Chrystie to R.A.H., 25 February 1928.

82 Major Clerke's Report of 4th Visit to the USA, April 1927.

83 *Ibid.*

84 R.A.H. to Sauveur, 3 August 1927. A large correspondence concerning ATV steels is extant in the Hadfield Papers.

85 *AGM*, 20 April 1933, pp. 25–6. See also 'ATV Turbine Blading', *Engineering* 135 (10 March 1933), pp. 289–92.

86 Hadfield directors to R.A.H., 26 April 1932. This was not quite the end of Hadfields' involvement with the US; further technical and commercial interchange took place during and after the Second World War. See Directors Private Minute Book, reports of Special Meetings on 24 September, 15 October 1946, 4 February 1947.

10. QUALITY PAYS? SHEFFIELD AND AMERICAN CUTLERY MANUFACTURE

1 Letter, *Sheffield Iris*, 25 February 1843. The correspondent remarked that in 1835 Sheffield exported £1,104,356 of goods to America from total exports of £2,096,970; in 1840 the respective figures were £1,183,705 and £3,177,658.

2 In 1859–60, for example, US cutlery imports totalled $2,240,905, England supplying $2,070,241 (92 percent) of this figure. See *Report of the Secretary of the Treasury ... of the Commerce and Navigation of the United States for*

the Year Ending June 30, 1860 (Washington, DC, 1860), pp. 226–7. See J. Potter, 'Atlantic Economy, 1815–1860: The USA and the Industrial Revolution in Britain', in L. S. Pressnell, ed., *Studies in the Industrial Revolution* (1960), pp. 236–80. Cf. also P. C. Garlick, 'The Sheffield Cutlery and Allied Trades and Their Markets in the 18th and 19th Centuries' (Sheffield MA, 1951), pp. 142–95.

3 G. I. H. Lloyd, *The Cutlery Trades* (1913). See also: J. F. Hayward, *English Cutlery* (1957); D. Hey, *The Rural Metalworkers of the Sheffield Region* (Leicester, 1972); J. B. Himsworth, *The Story of Cutlery* (1953); A. McPhee, 'The Growth of Cutlery and Allied Trades to 1914', unpublished typescript (SCL, 1939); C. Pagé, *La Coutellerie Depuis L'Origine Jusqu'à Nos Jours* (Chatellerault, 1896), esp. vol. 6, pp. 1449–504; C. A. Turner, *A Sheffield Heritage* (Sheffield, 1978).

4 SCL Wos 168. Letter, Ward to Wostenholm, 3 March 1858. Asline Ward (1821–1905), the son of the well-known Sheffield merchant and local figure, was Wostenholm's New York agent for fifty years. Cf. *Ironmonger* 111 (13 May 1905), p. 261. On Wostenholm generally see: my entry in *DBB*; H. Bexfield, *A Short History of Sheffield Cutlery and the House of Wostenholm* (Sheffield, 1945); *Sheffield Independent*, 19 August 1876; *Ironmonger* 18 (1 September 1876), p. 8; J. H. Stainton, *The Making of Sheffield 1865–1914* (Sheffield, 1924), pp. 246–7; G. Wostenholm & Son, *Trade Catalogue 1885* (Louisville, 1975).

5 R. E. Leader, *History of the Company of Cutlers in Hallamshire in the County of York* (Sheffield, 1905), vol. 1, p. 286.

6 PP 1865, XX, 'Report upon the Metal Manufactures of the Sheffield District', by J. E. White, pp. 46–7. Wostenholm's became a limited company in 1875 (capital £100,000).

7 *Pawson and Brailsford's Illustrated Guide* (Sheffield, 1862), p. 140.

8 Z. Allen, *The Practical Tourist* (Providence, 1832), vol. 1, p. 288.

9 For descriptions of Rodgers' Works see: T. Allen, *A New and Complete History of the County of York* (1828–31), vol. 3, pp. 33–6, quoting Sir Richard Phillips' *Personal Tour* (1828); F. Bland, 'A Brief History of Joseph Rodgers & Sons Ltd', repr. from *Edgar Allen Works & Sports Magazine* (May 1930); *Penny Magazine* 13, n.s. (1844), pp. 161–68; *Scientific American* 36, n.s. (31 March 1877), p. 197. The *Ironmonger* 13 (31 January 1871), pp. 5–6, adds further details and remarks that the work-force was 1,200. The firm was made a limited liability company in 1871 (capital £130,000). Brief historical details can be found in J. Rodgers & Sons Ltd, *Under Five Sovereigns* (1911); *A Royal Record* (1930).

10 *Ironmonger* (n. 9). The *British Trade Journal* 14 (1876), p. 98, reported: 'An American [cutlery] manufacturer ... solicited an order at Delmonico's [New York], and was met with the reply – "The fact is we are famed for our rump steaks here, and if we did not use Roger's [sic] we should lose [our custom]".'

11 *Seventh Census*, 'Abstract of the Statistics of Manufactures' (repr. New York, 1970), p. 138; *Eighth Census*, III, 'Manufactures of the United States in 1860' (Washington, DC, 1865), p. 735; *Ninth Census*, III, 'The Statistics of the Wealth and Industry of the United States' (Washington, DC, 1872), p. 431.

12 See M. Van. H. Taber, *A History of the Cutlery Industry in the Connecticut Valley* (Northampton, Mass., 1955); P. Pankiewicz, *New England Cutlery* (Gilman, Conn., 1986).

13 R. T. Bertoff, *British Immigrants in Industrial America, 1790–1950* (Cam-

bridge, Mass., 1953), pp. 70–1; J. T. Dixon, 'Aspects of Yorkshire Emigration to North America, 1760–1880' (Leeds PhD, 1982), vol. 3, pp. 1329–426; C. J. Erickson, *American Industry and the European Immigrant 1860–1885* (Cambridge, Mass., 1957), pp. 41–2.

14 *British Mechanic's and Labourer's Handbook, and True Guide to the United States* (1840), p. 234.

15 Taber, *Cutlery Industry*, p. 96.

16 Russell must have had a romantic imagination, Allen's account (vol. 1, pp. 288–93) being somewhat pedestrian. See also R. L. Merriam *et al.*, *The History of the John Russell Cutlery Company 1833–1936* (Greenfield, Mass., 1976). One design Russell copied was the 'Barlow' – a cheap, one-blade pocket-knife marketed by the Sheffield cutlers, which became very popular in the US in the nineteenth century. See: L. A. Johnson, 'The Barlow Knife', *CEAIA* 12 (June 1959), pp. 17–21; D. J. Struik, 'The Story of the Barlow Knife', unpublished typescript, n.d., SCL (MP 1703 M). References to the Barlow can be found in: James Fenimore Cooper, *The Pioneers* (1823), Chap. 8; and Mark Twain, *The Adventures of Tom Sawyer* (1876), Chap. 4, and *The Adventures of Huckleberry Finn* (1885), Chap. 9. One Sheffield maker recalled: 'We used to send [barlows] to the United States in casks. We made little or no profit on them, and ... were always behindhand with the orders.' SCL Wos R13 (f). Colver to L. D. Bement, American Cutlery Manufacturers' Association, 17 September 1952.

17 *CEAIA* 37 (September 1984), p. 55; Merriam, *Russell Cutlery Co*, p. 13; Taber, *Cutlery Industry*, pp. 36, 96.

18 Taber, *Cutlery Industry*, p. 96.

19 C. McL. Green, *History of Naugatuck, Connecticut* (New Haven, Conn., 1948), pp. 62, 136–7.

20 See SCL MD 2027. Roberts Correspondence. The Roberts' letters are annotated and reproduced in C. J. Erickson, *Invisible Immigrants* (1972), pp. 319–28. For further details on cutlery manufacture in Waterbury, see: J. Anderson, ed., *The Town and City of Waterbury, Connecticut* (New Haven, 1896), vol. 2, pp. 29–30; H. Bronson, *The History of Waterbury, Connecticut* (Waterbury, 1858), p. 563.

21 *Sheffield Independent*, 20 August 1879; 6 September 1879.

22 Mason returned briefly to Sheffield to scold his townsmen on their antiquated methods. See *American Manufacturer*, 20 July 1876, p. 6.

23 A. Lief, *Camillus* (New York, 1944), p. 15.

24 J. S. Kebabien, 'Buck Brothers, Millbury, Mass.', *CEAIA* 25 (March 1972), pp. 10–11; Buck Bros, *Trade Catalogue 1890* (repr. with notes by K. D. Roberts, 1976).

25 *American Cutler* (May 1921), p. 19; *Scientific American* 43, n.s. (23 October 1880), p. 266.

26 A. McG. Lamb, 'A History of the American Pottery Industry; Industrial Growth, Technical and Technological Change and Diffusion in the General-ware Branch 1872–1914' (London PhD, 1985), p. 205.

27 H. Platts, *The Knife Makers Who Went West* (Longmont, Colo., 1978). With more research at a state level this listing of Sheffield immigrants could undoubtedly be increased. Much useful information can be found in American cutlery collectors' magazines, newsletters and guide-books. It is impossible to cite all this literature, but I have found B. Levine, *Levine's Guide to Knives and Their Values* (Northbrook, Ill., 1985) esp. useful.

28 Erickson, *Invisible Immigrants*; E. M. Ruttenber and L. H. Clark, eds., *History of Orange County, New York* (Philadelphia, 1881), p. 403. T. J. Bradley's son, Thomas W. Bradley, was later one of the driving forces in pushing through the cutlery duties in the McKinley Tariff.

29 See letters in the *Sheffield Independent*, 14 March 1870; 2 April 1870; 5, 6 April 1870.

30 *Sheffield Independent*, 25 September 1880. Further information on disgruntled Sheffielders in the US can be found in: *Sheffield Independent*, 10 May 1865; *Ironmonger* 23 (6 March 1880), p. 336. It is interesting to note that production also ceased at the Beaver Falls Cutlery Co in 1886, after labour problems had caused the owners to hire 400 Chinese workers as an experiment. It is possible that Sheffield immigrants were at the root of the problem. See J. H. Bausman, *History of Beaver County Pennsylvania and its Centennial Celebration* (New York, 1904), vol. 2, p. 670.

31 Lloyd, *Cutlery Trades*, esp. Chap. 2; and Turner, *Heritage*. For a description of the Sheffield methods in a work setting, see the account of Mappin Bros, *Ironmonger* 5 (30 May 1863), pp. 122–7.

32 Taber, *Cutlery Industry*, esp. Chap. 3.

33 At Lamson & Goodnow's, for example, despite the use of machinery, grinding and polishing were still done in the Sheffield manner. See J. L. Bishop, *A History of American Manufactures from 1608 to 1860* (Philadelphia, 3rd edn., 1868), vol. 3, pp. 338–41.

34 *Sheffield Independent*, 14 February 1865. Similar comments are made in another letter from Meriden Sheffielders in *Ryland's Iron Trade Circular*, 3 July 1869. I am grateful to Charlotte J. Erickson for both references. On American cutlery manufacture, cf. also *Sheffield Independent*, 26 December 1871.

35 H. J. Habakkuk, *American and British Technology in the Nineteenth Century* (Cambridge, 1967). A discussion of the Sheffield trades is lacking in this work, even though they would have illustrated the arguments very well.

36 Statistics from the *Annual Reports ... on the Commerce and Navigation of the United States, Year Ending June 30, 1867* (Washington, DC, 1868), p. 152; *June 30, 1872* (Washington, DC, 1873), p. 56; *June 30, 1877* (Washington, DC, 1878), p. 54. Lloyd, *Cutlery Trades*, pp. 482–3, provides a complete series of Sheffield cutlery exports to the US (£) from 1868–1910 based on US Consular Returns.

37 Ibbotson's was one firm which gave up the US market. See *Ironmonger* 24 (27 November 1880), p. 641.

38 See, for example, the Paris Exhibition 'Supplement' in the *Ironmonger* 20 (19 October 1878).

39 *Sheffield Independent*, 6 June 1876. Remarked the *British Trade Journal* 14 (1 August 1876), p. 469: 'The English have highly polished works that add much to the expense, but nothing to the service. The high finish of American work is applied only to where it has utility, not where it is a useless expense.' Earlier in the century Sheffield cutlers had been criticised for ignoring the more utilitarian aspects of display and manufacture in *The Sheffield Mechanics' Exhibition Magazine*, No. 9 (1 August 1840), pp. 99–100: 'Our mechanics pride themselves too much on making the largest, the most diminutive, the most costly, or the most complex articles. This is a false idea of excellence ... [and] must necessarily fail of giving the pleasure that an union of the *useful* with the *beautiful* always affords.'

40 *Ironmonger* 37 (15 January 1887), pp. 88–9; and cf. also 34 (25 July 1885), pp. 171–2, 37 (22 January 1887), pp. 124–5.

41 'How Sheffield Lost the American Trade', *Sheffield Independent*, 17 June 1875. *Ibid.*, 21 March 1878, is also critical of English cutlery.

42 The post-1865 Marsh Bros correspondence, particularly SCL M 241–9, is filled with references to complaints from American retailers.

43 *Sheffield Independent*, 20 March 1878.

44 Quoted in W. R. Williamson, *I*XL Means I Excel* (1974), pp. 15–17.

45 *London Journal of Arts and Sciences* 2, 2nd s. (1829), pp. 153–4.

46 *Sheffield Independent*, 13 October 1873. The traditional methods are also in evidence in the description of Rodgers in *British Trade Journal* 15 (1 February 1877), pp. 91–2.

47 'Machine-Made Table Knives', letter by Drabble, *Sheffield Independent*, 29 May 1862; *International Exhibition of 1862. The Illustrated Catalogue of the Industrial Department. British Division. Vol. II* (1862), Class XXXII, p. 158; 'The Manufacture of Scissors', *Sheffield Independent*, 22 May 1863.

48 *Ironmonger* 24 (21 August 1880), pp. 208–9; *Iron Age* 19 (22 February 1877), p. 9. Again, Rodgers' aim was to augment hand-work rather than replace it. See *Pawson & Brailsford's Illustrated Guide* (Sheffield, revised edn., 1879), p. 256–7, which also reported that the firm 'now make large quantities of medium and cheaper wares, which are a great improvement upon American designs, and are intended for use in that country'.

49 *Implement and Machinery Review* 24 (1 October 1898), p. 23290; *Ironmonger* 23 (15 May 1880), p. 660; 24 (16 October 1880), pp. 412–13; 91 (21 April 1900), p. 95; 95 (11 May 1901), p. 242. Atkinson Bros was said to have halved its costs by installing machinery and was therefore able to compete successfully with the Americans. Thus, remarked the *British Trade Journal* 8 (1880), p. 575, 'the introduction of machinery has effected a revolution in the cutlery trade'.

50 Robert Holmshaw, *Mosely Industrial Commission to the United States of America* (Manchester, 1903), pp. 103–7. The state of the Sheffield art can be seen in the photographs in Thos. Turner & Co and Wingfield Rowbotham & Co, *Handicrafts That Survive* (Sheffield, 1902), which show some mechanisation in this firm's processes, but the emphasis – epitomised by the title of this centenary souvenir – was still on the older craft methods. At any one time the firm had in stock or 'to order' 2,000 to 3,000 different cutlery patterns. See also S. Pollard, *A History of Labour in Sheffield* (Liverpool, 1959), pp. 202–8.

51 *Annual Reports ... on the Commerce and Navigation of the United States, Year ending June 30, 1889* (Washington, DC, 1890), p. 120; *Year ending June 30, 1894* (Washington, DC, 1895), p. 117.

52 See Chap. 13.

53 SCL Wos R12. Letter, 11 March 1893.

54 *Ibid.*, letter, 1 June 1893.

55 *Ibid.*, letter, 18 July 1893.

56 D. H. Blackwell, 'The Growth and Decline of the Scythe/Sickle (Shear) Trade in Hallamshire' (Sheffield PhD, 1973), vol. 1, pp. 173–4; *Ironmonger* 23 (31 January 1880), pp. 164–5; R. M. Ledbetter, 'Sheffield's Industrial History from about 1700, with Special Reference to the Abbeydale Works' (Sheffield MA, 1971), pp. 118–66; Wm. Tyzack Sons & Turner Ltd, *Centenary Souvenir 1812–1912* (Sheffield, 1912); *Implement and Machinery Review* 5 (1

June 1879), pp. 2266–7; J. Wiss & Sons, *A Story of Shears and Scissors 1848–1948* (Newark, 1948).

57 *Sheffield Times*, 7 April 1849.

58 B. Kingsbury, *A Treatise on Razors* (1797); H. T. Lummus, 'Old Sheffield Razors', *Antiques* (December 1922), pp. 261–7; E. Rhodes, *Essay on the Manufacture, Choice, and Management of a Razor* (Sheffield, 1824).

59 R. B. Adams, *King C. Gillette* (Boston, 1978); G. B. Baldwin, 'The Invention of the Modern Safety Razor: A Case Study in Industrial Innovation', *Explorations in Entrepreneurial History* 4 (1951–2), pp. 73–102; I. Coster, *The Sharpest Edge in the World* (1948); Gillette Safety Razor Co, *25th Anniversary* (1926); *Iron Age* 77 (1 February 1906), p. 470.

60 Feminine use of the razor was referred to, delicately, as 'smoothing'.

61 *Abstract of Fourteenth Census of the United States* (Washington, DC, 1923), pp. 1178–9.

62 James Neill & Co and George Butler & Co seem to have been amongst the first Sheffield firms to engage in safety razor manufacture. See *Quality* 5 (May 1934), p. 181; *Sheffield Daily Telegraph*, Industrial Supplement, 31 December 1925. Paul R. Kuehnrich, the Sheffield metallurgist (see Chap. 5), also became involved in safety razor manufacture, when he bought the Simplex Motor Works for that purpose in 1924. He later visited America on sales trips.

63 R. S. Hutton, *Recollections of a Technologist* (1964), p. 61. Besides the US, Colver visited Solingen and Thiers. See Colver, 'British and German Practice Compared', *Metal Industry* 16 (16 February 1920), pp. 105–7; *Sheffield Independent*, 9 February 1922.

64 SCL Wos R6. Colver memo, 18 November 1915.

65 Wos R6. Memo re. proposed revision, n.d.

66 Wos R16. Memo 1932.

67 Wos R11.

68 Wos R7. (no pagination). Marmaduke Wardlow also toured US cutlery factories at this time. See *American Cutler* (December 1920), p. 33.

69 *Ibid.* (July 1919), p. 4.

70 Colver noted that the Hemming and Moore's grinding machines cost $1,000 and $625, respectively. The purchasing and importing of the Schrade device, which cut out the shield holes in pocket-knife handles, would have been ironic: George Schrade, founder of the Walden Co in 1904, had tried to install such a machine in Sheffield at Thos. Turner & Co in 1910, but had been defeated by the unions. See *American Cutler* (August 1921), pp. 31–3.

It might be mentioned here that before the First World War the Americans had revolutionised the grinding trade with the invention of an artificial abrasive wheel. Such wheels, which were tougher and safer than sandstone, were imported by George Jowitt, a Sheffield firm, which by the 1950s had a small plant in Philadelphia. See *George Jowitt & Sons Ltd. A History* (Sheffield, 1966).

71 Wos R7. Copy of Mr Geo. Quirck's letter, 4 December 1918.

72 'English Cutlers Look to US', *American Cutler* (October 1920), p. 32.

73 *Ibid.* (February 1921), pp. 40–1. Boker is still in production at Maplewood, New Jersey. The other important German cutler in the US was Henckels, though it never opened an American subsidiary. See H. Kelleter, *Geschichte der Familie. J. A. Henckels in Verbinding mit einer Geschichte der Solinger Industrie* (Solingen, 1924).

74 Wos R8. Report, 6 May 1919.

75 Wos R12. Letter to Schrade, New York, 8 August 1919.

76 *American Cutler* (February 1921), pp. 14–17; and (July 1920), p. 28, (November 1920), pp. 35–7.

77 P. Shirtcliffe, 'Fine Quality Cutlery – Quality before Price', *Armourers' & Brasiers' Journal* 8 (1938), pp. 16–27, 17. This was a paper read before the Sheffield Trades' Technical Society, the Minutes (1918–39) of which are in SCL, LD 1803. Colver was one of its presidents.

78 See: Pollard, *Labour*, p. 293; Board of Trade, Safeguarding of Industries, Cutlery Committee, *Report 1925*, Cmd. 2540; *Report Respecting Cutlery 1928–29*, Cmd. 3180; Ministry of Labour, Report by the Cutlery Wages Council, *Industrial Conditions in the Cutlery Trade 1945*. There are now (1986) only two 'little mesters' in Sheffield: Graham Clayton and Stan Shaw. Ironically, their beautiful hand-made 'workback' pocket-knives find a ready sale, particularly amongst Americans. Even more ironic, is that American collectors 'Scavenging in Sheffield's Ruins' (the phrase is Bill Adams' from an article in K. Warner, ed., *Knives '86* (Northbrook, Ill., 1985), pp. 12–21) have done a profitable business buying up cheaply knives from the nineteenth-century trade that the Americans crippled by tariffs and mechanisation.

79 V. Answer, *Sheffield's Traditional Craftsmen* (Sheffield, 1980), p. 68. While machinery produced the cheaper pocket-knives, 'mesters' like Stan Shaw were employed by Wostenholm's for the higher qualities. Author's conversation with Stan Shaw, 1986.

80 US Tariff Commission, *Cutlery Products* (Washington, DC, 1938), p. 19.

81 See description of Lamson & Goodnow, *Iron Trade Review* 71 (13 July 1922), pp. 111–16.

82 Wos R12. N.Y. agents to Sheffield, 13 March 1931. Sheffield attitudes on cost cutting are illustrated by L. Du Garde Peach, *The Company of Cutlers in Hallamshire in the County of York 1906–1956* (Sheffield, 1960), p. 76, who cites the views of a Master Cutler who saw little point in the cheapening of a product which the average householder bought once in a lifetime.

83 W. Taylor, *The Sheffield Horn Industry* (Sheffield, 1927), p. 71.

84 US Tariff Commission, *Pocket Cutlery* (Washington, DC, 1939), p. 10.

85 *American Cutler* (July 1921), pp. 9–15, 42; A. P. Hatch, *Remington Arms in American History* (New York, 1956), p. 227; *Iron Trade Review* 72 (29 March 1922), pp. 954–6; H. F. Williamson, *Winchester. The Gun that Won the West* (Washington, DC, 1952), p. 288.

86 Wos R13a. Letter to Dwight Divine & Sons, Ellenville, N.Y., 19 February 1931. On Sheffield's short-lived penknife trade (as distinct from that of pocket-knives, with which it is often confused), see M. Pearce, 'Sheffield Penknives' (Sheffield, 1976). Another trend in the 1920s which reduced the demand for Sheffield goods was the introduction of the refrigerator: no longer would ice firms or households need crucible steel slicers and picks for blocks of ice.

87 Lief, *Camillus*, pp. 50–1.

88 Wos R12. Memo, February 1932.

89 *Ibid*. Wostenholm's office was at 258 Broadway.

90 *Ibid*.

91 Wos R12. Letter from Swedish Steel Mills, N.Y., to J. B. Thomas, 10 December 1931.

92 *Ibid*. Letter, 26 February 1931.

93 *Ibid*. Frank Holroyd to A. S. Keeton, Sheffield, 13 April 1930.
94 *Ibid*., Colver to Wostenholm's, 13 March 1931.
95 This seems to have been done by selling cutlery at knockdown prices. Wos R13a. Colver to A. Field & Co, 3 March 1931.
96 *Ibid*. Colver to British Consulate, 6 March 1931.
97 Wos R12. Wostenholm's, N.Y., to Sheffield, 17 March 1931. Wostenholm's, after merging with Rodgers, had become part of the Imperial Knife Co of New York by 1982. See *Quality* 29 (May/June 1982), pp. 35–7. The Rodgers Wostenholm Group has now ceased production.

11. INNOVATION AND ADAPTATION: THE EVIDENCE OF THE SAWMAKING TRADES

1 B. Hindle, ed., *America's Wooden Age* (New York, 1975); P. B. Kebabien, *American Woodworking Tools* (Boston, 1978); P. B. Kebabien and W. C. Lipke, *Tools and Technologies* (Burlington, Vt., 1979).
2 *RC Report of the Juries, Great Exhibition 1851*, p. 201.
3 *Ibid*., p. 488; C. T. Rodgers, *American Superiority at the World's Fair* (Philadelphia, 1852), p. 42.
4 On Collins see: J. L. Bishop, *A History of American Manufactures from 1608 to 1860* (Philadelphia, 3rd edn., 1868), vol. 3, pp. 212–13; Collins Co, *One Hundred Years* (Collinsville, 1926), pp. 24–8; H. Greeley *et al.*, *The Great Industries of the United States* (Hartford, 1872), pp. 124–33; J. S. Kebabien, 'The Collins Company', *CEAIA* 12 (March 1969), pp. 9–10; *Scientific American* 1, n.s. (16 July 1859), pp. 36–7. On Douglas see: W. A. Emerson, *History of the Town of Douglas (Massachusetts)* (Boston, 1879), pp. 268–74; J. S. Kebabien, 'The Douglas Axe Manufacturing Company, East Douglas, Mass.', *CEAIA* 15 (September 1972), pp. 43–6.
5 J. Wilson, 'On the Manufacture of Articles from Steel, Particularly Cutlery', *Journal of the Society of Arts* 4 (11 April 1856), p. 365. See also Wilson's letter, *Sheffield Independent*, 24 May 1856. For evidence of the consternation aroused by American competition in axes and hay forks, see letters: *Sheffield Independent*, 13 June 1857; 27 June 1857; 18 July 1857. American superiority in woodworking tools was treated at length in Joseph Hutton, 'Condition and Future Prospects of the Staple Trades of Sheffield', *Sheffield Times*, 31 March 1849.
6 H. Disston & Sons, *The Saw in History* (Philadelphia, 1915). On Rowland cf. E. T. Freedley, *Philadelphia and Its Manufactures* (Philadelphia, 1867), pp. 303–4; J. S. Kebabien, 'An Early Philadelphia Pit-Saw', *CEAIA* 26 (March 1973), pp. 13–14; C. Robson, ed., *The Manufactories and Manufacturers of Pennsylvania in the Nineteenth Century* (Philadelphia, 1875), p. 31.
7 Bishop, *American Manufactures*, vol. 3, pp. 300–1; *Professional and Industrial History of Suffolk County, Massachusetts* (Boston, 1894), vol. 2, p. 452.
8 *Illustrated Price List 1860* (Vt., 1976 repr.); E. M. Ruttenber and L. H. Clark, eds., *History of Orange County, New York* (Philadelphia, 1881), pp. 478, 489–91, 494–6.
9 Simonds Manufacturing Co, *75 Years of Business Progress and Industrial Advance, 1832–1907* (Cambridge, Mass., 1907). The firm was founded in 1832 by Abel Simonds, of north of England descent, for the manufacture of scythes.

10 For descriptions of the techniques of saw manufacture, see: *Ironmonger* 12 (30 November 1870), pp. 1009–11; 13 (25 October 1871), p. 912; *The Working Man* (1866), vol. 1, pp. 65–6.

11 C. Holtzappfel, *Turning and Mechanical Manipulation* (London, 1846), vol. 2, pp. 682–816.

12 BLCU, Hoe Papers. See also: *British Mechanic's and Labourer's Handbook, and True Guide to the United States* (1840), p. 233; F. E. Comparato, *Chronicles of Genius and Folly* (Culver City, Ca., 1979), pp. 111–29. Sawmakers in other parts of New York state, such as Rochester, were usually Englishmen. See K. D. and J. W. Roberts, *Planemakers and Other Edge Tool Enterprises in New York State in the Nineteenth Century* (Cooperstown, N.Y., 1971), pp. 58, 75, 110–18.

13 EMHL Acc 333, item 15. Letter, 12 March 1846.

14 Letter Book 11 December 1839–15 February 1841. Hoe to J. G. Elliot, 5 December 1840. Hoe Papers, Box 20. See also S. D. Tucker, 'History of R. Hoe & Co', p. 16, typescript in Box 1, Hoe Papers.

15 Comparato, *Chronicles*, p. 115; Hoe to Halsey & Pettigrew, N. Carolina, 10 December 1840: 'We manufacture a most excellent gumming or toothing machine for $75 which is very much approved of'. Letter Book 11 December 1839–15 February 1841. Hoe Papers, Box 20.

16 Comparato, *Chronicles*, pp. 115–16; Tucker, 'History', pp. 20–1.

17 Letter, 29 June 1843. Hoe Papers, Box 20. On the interest generated by Hoe's circular saws, see Hoe Letters (in-coming) 1850–5 in EMHL Acc 1477.

18 Sanderson to Hoe, 11 January 1853. Hoe Papers, Box 3.

19 Tucker, 'History', pp. 99–100.

20 *Ibid.*, pp. 102–3.

21 Letter to J. G. Elliot (n. 14).

22 Disston, *Saw in History*, p. 14; *NCAB*. James E. Emerson, who later manufactured saws in Beaver County, Pa., is also credited with the invention of the inserted-tooth circular saw in the 1850s. See *DAB*; *NCAB*.

23 With reference to inserted-tooth saws, Hoe's wrote to C. & J. Cooper & Co, 8 April 1869: 'We are just starting new machines for their [?] extensive manufacture, and shall be prepared to fill orders promptly.' Hoe Papers, Box 27.

24 Comparato, *Chronicles*, p. 120; Tucker, 'History', pp. 109–10.

25 Letter to Thomas Young, [?] April 1870. Hoe Papers, Box 27.

26 Letter to Ryan Johnson & Co, 2 April 1877. Hoe Papers, Box 34; Tucker, 'History', (n. 14) p. 122.

27 Comparato, *Chronicles*, p. 122.

28 Disston's business records have not survived. However, an unpublished typescript history (2 vols., EMHL Acc 1567) covers the period up to 1920. For published sources see: *ACAB*; Bishop, *American Manufactures*, vol. 3, pp. 40–2; *DAB*; J. Disston, *Henry Disston (1819–78)* (New York, 1950); Freedley, *Philadelphia*, pp. 600–1; Greeley, *Great Industries*, pp. 363–78; J. S. Kebabien, 'The Disston Factory, Philadelphia, Pa.', *CEAIA* 23 (September 1970), pp. 39–40; P. W. Morgan, 'The Henry Disston Family Enterprise', *CEAIA* 38 (June–December 1985); L. L. Nelson, 'A Disston Hand Saw Made for President Rutherford B. Hayes, April 26, 1878', *CEAIA* 38 (June 1985), pp. 21–2; Obituary, *Iron Age* 11 (21 March 1878), p. 1; 'The Keystone Saw, Tool, Steel and File Works', *Annual Report of the Secretary of Internal Affairs of the Commonwealth of Pennsylvania. Pt. III, Industrial Statistics* 15

(1887), doc. no. 12; Robson, *Manufactories*, pp. 119–22; J. T. Scharf and T. Westcott, *History of Philadelphia* (Philadelphia, 1884), vol. 3, pp. 2267–8.

29 *Implement and Machinery Review* 6 (2 November 1880), p. 3213. There are also references to Sheffielders employed at Disston's in: J. H. Cox, *Diary and Report of a Visit to Paris and the French Exhibition* (Sheffield, 1878), p. 19; R. Grimshaw, *Saws; The History, and Development etc.* (Philadelphia, 1882), p. 97. The Ms. Population Census 1860 (USNA M653 [1166]) enumerates several Englishmen in Philadelphia's 16th ward, the site of Disston's factory: 5 saw grinders, 5 sawmakers, 2 apprentice sawmakers, 2 saw manufacturers (one of whom was Henry Disston), and one saw polisher.

Disston's imported grindstones from the Sheffield area: see *Ironmonger* 26 (24 September 1881), p. 413. It may be added that Robert A. Hadfield, and representatives from Marsh Bros and Spear & Jackson also visited Disston's; and in the twentieth century, T. Holland Nelson, a Sheffield steelmaker, became manager there. According to W. L. Goodman, *The History of Woodworking Tools* (1964), p. 151, Henry Disston was trained at Spear & Jackson, Sheffield. However, the fact that Disston was born in Tewkesbury and arrived in the US when he was fourteen makes this assertion rather questionable. Disston, though, was certainly apprenticed to two English sawmakers, Charles and William Johnson. See EMHL Acc 1567. The Disston History. vol. 1, 'Family', pp. 27–8.

30 In the Marsh Bros correspondence (SCL MD 1485) there is the following comment in a letter, 5 April 1867, to a New York agent: 'we hear that Mr Henry Diston [sic] of Phila. has built a melting furnace and one of our melters "South" sails next Wednesday to make cast steel at Diston's and will be friendly towards us'. *Ryland's Iron Trade Circular* (30 December 1876), pp. 954–5, also refers to an English steel roller at Disston's. Apparently, the prejudice against domestic steel was so strong that when he began to produce his own steel Disston was compelled to conceal the fact. See The Disston History, vol. 2, 'History of the Works', pp. 11, 15–16; *Iron Age* 42 (27 September 1888), p. 461.

31 The Disston History, 'History of the Works', pp. 21–3.

32 *Ibid.*, p. 14; Disston, *Saw in History*, pp. 54–5.

33 Two sawyers with a cross-cut raker saw could fell twice as much wood in a day as two axemen. See D. MacKay, *The Lumberjacks* (Toronto, 1978), p. 80.

34 'History of the Works', p. 44. On Disston's productivity, see also *BAISA* 24 (3 September 1890), p. 251.

35 Grimshaw, *Saws*, p. 97.

36 'History of the Works', p. 46. A Sheffielder commented upon the prevalence of machinery in American saw works in the *Iron Age* 11 (4 April 1878), p. 5.

37 The 1860 Pennsylvania Census of Manufactures (EMHL Acc 1191) shows 175 men at Disston's producing 10,000 doz. saws and tools. The 1870 Census lists 315 machines at the factory; 555 people produced 52,000 doz. saws and 13,000 doz. tools per annum, from 1,000 tons of steel. For further information, see *Scientific American* 28, n.s. (12 April 1873), p. 227.

38 'History of the Works', p. 65.

39 For references to Disston's invasion of Sheffield and English markets, see: *American Manufacturer*, 29 October 1874, p. 9; *Ironmonger* 17 (1 October 1875), p. 1219; 19 (1 March 1877), p. 106; 19 (1 December 1877), p. 474; 20 (14 September 1878), pp. 952–3; 21 (17 May 1879), p. 69; *Sheffield Indepen-*

dent, 22 February 1873; 26 June 1877; 15 January 1879. According to the *British Trade Journal* 14 (1 June 1876), pp. 351–2, Disston was sending saws to England in 1876 to be sold at $10.50 per dozen, as much as 50 percent less than the price of English saws sold in the US in 1840.

After the 1880s, one Sheffield manufacturer and agency began selling a selection of American woodworking tools, including Disston saws, alongside its own products. See William Marples & Sons, *1909 Price List of American Tools* (Fitzwilliam, N.H., 1980 repr.); *Price List. 1907 Edition* (Repr., 1979); *Implement and Machinery Review* 8 (2 January 1883), pp. 4821–2. Marples also acted as sole agents for the revolutionary Russell Jennings wood drill, which, as K. D. Roberts has pointed out, was perhaps the first US product to achieve prominence in Sheffield. See *Price List of Russell Jennings Mfg. Co, c. 1899 with Supplementary Data by K. D. Roberts* (Fitzwilliam, N. H., 1981). Cf. also D. L. Burn, 'The Genesis of American Engineering Competition, 1850–1870', *Economic History* 2 (1931), pp. 292–311.

40 On Sheffield's growth as a sawmaking centre, see R. M. Ledbetter, 'Sheffield's Industrial History from about 1700, with Special Reference to the Abbeydale Works' (Sheffield MA; 1971), pp. 152–5.

41 *Ironmonger* 27 (17 June 1882), p. 824.

42 *Ibid.*, 36 (18 August 1886), pp. 294–5.

43 *Implement and Machinery Review* (1 November 1878), pp. 1869–70; 7 (3 October 1881), pp. 3886–8. Spear & Jackson also installed an American device for manufacturing shovels: see *Ironmonger* 34 (25 July 1885), p. 168.

44 Disston's extensive US advertisements in the *Iron Age* and *American Manufacturer* can be contrasted with English goods in the *Sheffield Standard List* (1871).

45 Comparato, *Chronicles*, p. 126. According to Grimshaw, *Saws*, pp. 275–6, 166 patents alone were issued from 19 October 1880 to 7 March 1882. Disston's name had appeared on 20 patents by 1868 (Bishop, *American Manufactures*, vol. 3, p. 41). See EMHL Acc 1675. Henry Disston & Co, Patent and Design Drawings for Saws, ca. 1835–75. For a breakdown of the number of saw patents by year in the nineteenth century, see J. Schmookler, *Patents, Invention and Economic Change*, eds., Z. Griliches and L. Hurwicz (Mass., 1972), pp. 176–9. A good guide to saw types is R. A. Salaman, *Dictionary of Tools Used in the Woodworking and Allied Trades, c. 1700–1970* (1975).

46 C. C. Cooper, 'The Portsmouth System of Manufacture', *Technology and Culture* 25 (April 1984), pp. 182–225; Disston, *Saw in History*, p. 13; P. d'A. Jones and E. N. Simons, *The Story of the Saw* (Sheffield, 1961), pp. 42–4. Spear & Jackson exhibited five-foot circulars at the Great Exhibition 1851. See *RC Report*, p. 486.

47 M. P. Bale, *Woodworking Machinery* (3rd edn., 1913), pp. 4–6; W. S. Worssam, *History of the Bandsaw* (Manchester, 1892), pp. 7–14.

48 On Eadon's and bandsaws, see *Ironmonger* 27 (18 February 1882), p. 260; 27 (25 February 1882), p. 269; 28 (18 November 1882), pp. 705–6. Atkin & Peace seem to have been the only other maker of the bandsaw. See *Sheffield Independent*, 23 April 1859.

49 'History of the Works', p. 22. On American use of the bandsaw, cf. *Scientific American* 16, n.s. (27 January 1872), p. 65.

50 R. Sutcliffe, *Travels in Some Parts of North America in the Years 1804, 1805, & 1806* (York, 1815), p. 281. Similarly, William Cobbett remarked in *A*

Year's Residence in the United States of America (New York, 1818), p. 227: 'Every man can use an *ax*, a *saw*, and a *hammer*'.

51 The Sheffielder was so impressed that he stayed and established his own factory, the New York Saw Works. See SCL SJC 73. Facts regarding the Oldham Saw Works, ca. 1925.

52 See M. Williams, 'Clearing the United States Forests: Pivotal Years 1810–1860', *Journal of Historical Geography* 8 (1982), pp. 12–28, 25.

53 'Keystone Saw Works' (n. 28). On the development of lumbering in the US, see: J. E. Defebaugh, *History of the Lumber Industry of America* (2 vols., Chicago, 1907); J. Illick, 'The Story of the American Lumbering Industry', in W. B. Kaempffert, ed., *A Popular History of American Invention* (New York, 1924), vol. 2, pp. 150–98; McKay, *Lumberjacks*, pp. 80–8. Some idea of the size of the US lumbering trade can be obtained by simply sampling the statistics for one state. The Ninth US Census enumerates 3,922 lumbering establishments in Pennsylvania alone. See *Ninth Census*, III, 'Statistics of the Wealth and Industry of the United States' (Washington, DC, 1872), p. 453.

54 Z. Allen, *The Practical Tourist* (Providence, 1832), vol. 1, p. 159. On the damage done to sawmills, see also D. Lardner, *The Cabinet Cyclopaedia* (1831), vol. 1, pp. 332–3.

55 Rev. A. Rigg, 'Tools used in Handicraft – Saws', *Journal of Society of Arts* 23 (3 September 1875), p. 865. Disston saws were used as exhibits during the lecture. Rigg's remarks were echoed by the Rev. R. Willis who commented on the diversity of American woodworking contrivances, 'which the peculiar conditions of that country have called into existence, by creating a market for them'. See Royal Society, *Lectures on the Results of the Great Exhibition of 1851* (1852), p. 316.

56 Bishop, *American Manufactures*, vol. 3, p. 300. Noted a correspondent in the *Sheffield Times*, 21 April 1849, p. 6: '[American timber] needs a wide toothed, peculiarly ground saw, to work easily and free itself rapidly, far different from those most suitable at home. Now, for a long time, Sheffield makers either could not or would not understand and supply this alteration'.

57 SJC 73. Letter, G. V. Oldham, N.Y., to W. W. Woodbridge, Sheffield, 5 March 1924.

58 Drabble & Sanderson, *The Saw Doctor's Handbook* (1925), p. 33. (Copy in SJC 105.)

59 Bale, *Woodworking Machinery*, p. 328. See also S. W. Worssam, 'On Mechanical Saws', *Transactions of the Society of Engineers* (1867), pp. 196–230. Worssam believed that American machines were unsuitable for the English market: see *MPICE* 7 (1857–8), p. 45.

60 Wages for the English and American sawmaking trades can be compared in: *BAISA* 17 (11 April 1883), p. 98; C. D. Wright, *Comparative Wages and Prices, 1860–1883. Massachusetts and Great Britain* (Boston, 1885), p. 39. These sources show that the wages of skilled Sheffield sawmakers and English toolmakers were about half those of American workers.

61 The phrase is Comparato's, *Chronicles*, p. 115, describing Hoe's 1840 saw grinder.

62 Tucker, 'History' (n. 14), p. 99.

63 Grimshaw, *Saws*, p. 97, in an impressive account of a saw machine at Disston's, noted that the operator was a Sheffielder.

64 *Chronicles*, p. 116.

65 *Tenth Census*, II, 'Manufactures' (Washington, DC, 1883), p. 725. On

American sawmaking techniques, see also the account of the Cayadutta Saw Works, N.Y., in *Scientific American* 26, n.s. (30 March 1872), p. 212.

66 In a study of the Ms. Census of Manufactures for the Philadelphia region, two historians conclude, perceptively: 'Pockets of hand techniques and labor-intensive work, survivals of the past and creations of the industrial revolution, could be found in the most advanced work settings.' See B. Laurie and M. Schmitz, 'Manufacturing and Productivity: The Making of an Industrial Base, Philadelphia, 1850–1880', in T. Hershberg, ed., *Philadelphia: Work, Space, Family, and Group Experience in the Nineteenth Century* (New York, 1981), pp. 43–92, 52.

67 'History of the Works', p. 87.

68 See H. Disston & Sons, *Lumberman Handbook* (Philadelphia, 1912).

69 [Henry Disston] 'knew that the best executive management would fail without skilled hands ... Through his life he maintained the apprentice system'. 'History of the Works', p. 20.

70 *Mosely Industrial Commission to the United States of America* (Manchester, 1903), p. 6.

71 Comparato, *Chronicles*, p. 117.

72 *Ironmonger* 24 (16 October 1880), pp. 412–13; *PP* 1867, XXXII, Report Presented to the Trades Unions Commissioners ... Appointed to Inquire into Acts of Intimidation ... in the Town of Sheffield, p. 225. This Report is repr. in S. Pollard, ed., *The Sheffield Outrages* (Bath, 1971). When he laid down a circular saw grinding machine in 1856, Wheatman had employed a watchman for a year. See *Sheffield Independent*, 21 January 1860.

73 *Ironmonger* 24 (28 August 1880), p. 218. On Chesterman, see also D. J. Hallam, *The First 200 Years. A Short History of Rabone Chesterman Limited* (Birmingham, 1984).

The mechanisation of saw manufacture appears to have progressed a little more rapidly in Birmingham where the unions were weaker, though that city had also lost its US trade by the 1860s. See S. Timmins, *The Resources, Products, and Industrial History of Birmingham and the Midland Hardware District* (1866), pp. 659–61.

74 'Keystone Saw Works' (n. 28).

75 On labour difficulties at Disston's, see 'History of the Works', pp. 4, 21–2, 26. For details of a wage dispute at Disston's steelworks, cf. *Ironmonger* 36 (4 December 1886), pp. 391–2.

76 'Keystone Saw Works' (n. 28).

77 At Disston's back saws fell in price from $11.54 per doz., in 1870, to $8.08 per doz. in 1888; over the same period 60-inch circulars were reduced from $147.00 each to $64.60 each. Machinists' wages rose from $2.33 per day, in 1872, to $2.75 per day, in 1877; the corresponding figures for long saw smithers were $2.00 and $2.66, for circular saw grinders $2.50 and $2.75. The figures are reproduced in greater detail in the 'Keystone Saw Works' report and also quoted in The Disston History (EMHL), pp. 71–2. Mechanisation also increased wages in Sheffield. Spear & Jackson (SJC 42. Machinery & Wages Notebook, ca. 1871–93) noted that one of the firm's circular saw grinders had earned 39s 5d for 51 hours work in 1886; the same grinder had earned 34s for the same hours without a machine. But results such as this did not overcome the sawmakers' dislike of machinery.

78 *Eighth Census*, III, 'Manufactures of the United States in 1860' (Washington, DC, 1865), p. cxciv.

79 *Report of the Secretary of the Treasury ... on the Commerce and Navigation*

of the United States for the Year Ending June 30, 1866 (Washington, DC, 1867), pp. 266–8.

80 *Annual Report ... on the Commerce and Navigation of the United States for the Fiscal Year Ended June 30, 1877* (Washington, DC, 1878), pp. 54–5.

81 *The Foreign Commerce and Navigation of the United States for the Year Ending June 30, 1896* (Washington, DC, 1897), vol. 1, pp. 306–7.

82 See for example: *Ironmonger* 17 (1 October 1875), p. 1214; 18 (1 May 1876), p. 169; 18 (1 June 1876), p. 210; 21 (17 May 1879), p. 638; 25 (21 May 1881), pp. 693–4.

83 'American Axes', *British Trade Journal* 15 (1 May 1877), p. 279; A. S. Bolles, *Industrial History of the United States* (Norwich, Conn., 1878), pp. 272–3; C. A. Heavrin, 'The Felling Axe in America', *CEAIA* 35 (September 1982), pp. 43–53; *Ironmonger* 33 (10 January 1885), pp. 67–9. The English *v.* US axe debate continued in the 1890s. See 'The Axe Trade in Australia. Position of Sheffield Manufacturers', *Implement and Machinery Review* 23 (2 February 1898), pp. 22443–4. The views of Birmingham axemakers were elicited in the same journal on 1 April, 2 May, 2 July, and 1 August 1898. For a recent view, see V. Foley and R. H. Moyer, 'The American Axe. Was it Better?', *CEAIA* 30 (June 1977), pp. 28–32. Cf. also I. W. McLean, 'Anglo-American Engineering Competition, 1870–1914: Some Third-Market Evidence', *Economic History Review* 29, 2nd s. (August 1976), pp. 452–64.

84 *Sheffield Independent*, 8 April 1878. For similar remarks, see *ibid.*, 15 November 1877.

85 Quoted, *Iron Age* 14 (20 November 1879), p. 20.

86 *Ironmonger* 22 (6 September 1879), pp. 338–41; *Pawson and Brailsford's Illustrated Guide to Sheffield and Neighbourhood* (Sheffield, 1862), pp. 154–6; *PIME* (1890), pp. 463–4; Spear & Jackson Ltd, *Continual Progress Since 1774* (n.d.).

87 An American Letter Book survives for the period 1852–8 (SJC 68); unfortunately it is faded and illegible. Spear & Jackson's trade appears to have been satisfactory before the Civil War (see *Sheffield Independent*, 8 May 1858), but the decline of the US trade is signified by the fall in the value of its New York stock from £2,901 in 1874 to £163 in 1878; after that date it ceased to hold any New York stock. See SJC 24. Partnership Ledger.

88 SJC 79. Coombe also noted that in hay forks the 'trade is *entirely* in the hands of the Americans'.

89 E. A. Pratt, *Trade Unionism and British Industry* (1904), p. 138.

90 Tyzack Sons & Turner Ltd, *Centenary Souvenir 1812–1912* (Sheffield, 1912), no pagination.

91 Narrative and quotations in this section are based largely on SJC 8. Minute Book of Directors' Meetings, November 1905–December 1936.

92 These developments can be traced in SJC 97–106. Papers relating to subsidiaries.

93 *Sheffield Daily Telegraph*, Industrial Supplement, 30 December 1927. See also SJC 8. 19th AGM, 20 May 1924.

94 The following material and quotations are derived from Coombe's overseas letter books to S & J in SJC 79–88.

95 In the three years ending 1936 the Vancouver operations made profits totalling $47,000. See Times, *Prospectuses* 94 (1937), p. 113.

96 The firm made a loss of £920 in its first year, but presumably business improved thereafter since the company still has (1986) an American subsidiary in Eugene, Oregon.

97 SJC 73.

98 'Fear not interested in American market at present', Coombe told Oldham Saw Works, 30 May 1925. Ibid.

12. MEN *VERSUS* MACHINES: THE STORY OF THE FILE

1 D. Hounshell notes that what dominated the Singer Sewing Machine Co's expenditures in the early 1850s were vast quantities of British-made files and files re-cut by a New Jersey firm. See *idem, From the American System to Mass Production 1800–1932* (Baltimore, 1984), p. 85.

2 *Penny Magazine* 13 (March 1844), p. 128. On filemaking see: C. Holtzappfel, *Turning and Mechanical Manipulation* (1846), vol. 2, pp. 817–93; D. Lardner, *The Cabinet Cyclopaedia* (1831), vol. 1, pp. 297–315; G. Taylor, 'Some Points in the Manufacture of Files', *JISI*, 1919, i, pp. 345–78; C. A. Turner, *A Sheffield Heritage* (Sheffield, 1978); H. Turner, *The Manufacture of Files* (Sheffield, 1862). Good accounts of filemaking enterprises are: 'Agenoria Works of Messrs. Peace, Ward, and Co, Savile-Street East', *Ironmonger* 5 (31 August 1863), pp. 212–15; *Scientific American* 25, n.s. (9 August 1871), pp. 111–12 (Beardshaw, Stevenson & Co); *Implement and Machinery Review* 4 (2 October 1878), pp. 1829–30 (J. R. Spencer & Co).

3 See: C. Fremont, *Files and Filing* (1920), pp. 25–34; T. Greenwood, 'On File-Cutting Machinery', *PIME* (1859), pp. 134–40; R. C. Ross, 'Description of a New Machine for Cutting and Forging Files', *PIME* (1856), pp. 226–30; 'The File Trade on the Continent', by a 'Sheffielder', *Sheffield Independent*, 28 September 1867, 1 October 1867. Cf. also: R. Hunt, ed., *Ure's Dictionary* (1867), vol. 2, pp. 289–94; *Scientific American* 6, n.s. (5 April 1862), p. 218; J. R. Harris, 'First Thoughts on Files', *Tools & Trades* 3 (1985), pp. 27–35.

4 *Ironmonger* 1 (30 September 1859), p. 87; 1 (30 November 1859), p. 124; 6 (31 August 1864), p. 116; 8 (31 December 1866), pp. 181–2; 9 (31 January 1867), p. 10. For a detailed account of file-cutting in Birmingham, with information on costs and productivity, see *Sheffield Independent*, 3 July 1863.

5 *Sheffield Iris*, 16 February 1827, which told its readers: 'The *cutting* of files ... is not likely, we believe, ever to be successfully effected by any other than the present method, although machines for this purpose have been made and consigned to the oblivion of longitudinal instruments and perpetual motions.'

6 *Ironmonger* 13 (31 March 1871), p. 195; J. Anderson, ed., *The Town and City of Waterbury, Connecticut* (New Haven, 1896), vol. 2, pp. 326–7. Labour hostility may also have been involved, since newspaper sources at this time indicate that on one occasion William Butcher and his wife were awoken one night by someone throwing a bomb through their bedroom window!

7 *Sheffield Independent*, 25 September 1858; 11 December 1858; 28 March 1862.

8 Letter from 'Americus', *Sheffield Independent*, 31 October 1863.

9 *Ironmonger* 8 (31 March 1866), pp. 38–9; 8 (31 May 1866), p. 69; 8 (30 June 1866), p. 92; S. Pollard, *A History of Labour in Sheffield* (Liverpool, 1959), pp. 127–8; *Sheffield Independent*, 11, 12 October 1865. According to C. Tomlinson, ed., *Cyclopaedia of Useful Arts* (1866), vol. 1, pp. 640–7, Turton's worked the file-cutting machines of John Ericsson, who had patented such a device in 1836. See W. C. Church, *The Life of John Ericsson* (1890), vol. 1, p. 80.

10 SCL Os 16. Letter to Weed & Co, Philadelphia, 15 August 1884.

11 'File Making by Machinery', *Iron Age* 12 (25 December 1873), p. 3.

12 G. Bathe, *An Engineer's Note Book* (St Augustine, Fla., 1955), p. 11. Cf. also: H. Greeley *et al.*, *The Great Industries of the United States* (Hartford, 1872), pp. 445–55; J. Nicholson, *The Operative Mechanic and British Machinist* (Philadelphia, 1826), vol. 1, pp. 320–1.

13 C. H. Fitch, 'The Manufacture of Saws and Files', *Tenth Census*, II, 'Manufactures' (Washington, DC, 1883, pp. 724–5. *Scientific American* 14 (25 September 1858), p. 22, laments the dependence on Sheffield files and steel.

14 Information from the *Iron Age* article (n. 11). See also H. Disston & Sons, *The File in History* (Philadelphia, 1920).

15 The Ms. Census of Manufactures (EMHL Acc 1191) shows his works to have operated on a modest scale: in 1850, with capital of $400 and two hands, production was 160 doz. files p.a.; in 1870 six men were producing 800 doz. p.a. See also C. Robson, ed., *The Manufactories and Manufacturers of Pennsylvania in the Nineteenth Century* (Philadelphia, 1875), pp. 274–5.

16 E. M. Ruttenber and L. H. Clark, eds., *History of Orange County, New York* (Philadelphia, 1881), p. 478.

17 See Chambers' letter, *Sheffield Independent*, 30 June 1866. Charlotte Erickson first brought this letter to my attention.

18 J. L. Bishop, *A History of American Manufactures from 1608 to 1860* (Philadelphia, 3rd edn., 1868), vol. 3, pp. 395–6. Chatterton became an important Rhode Island figure. See *Sheffield Daily Telegraph*, 11 February 1908. The area seems to have been an important centre for early attempts at machine-cutting files. See *English Mechanic* 1 (11 August 1865), pp. 229–30; 3 (25 May 1866), p. 165.

19 On Whipple see *Scientific American* 6, n.s. (19 April 1862), p. 243; 10 (13 February 1864), p. 105.

20 'Machine-Made *v.* Hand-Made Files', letter by Mr H. Cutts, *Sheffield Independent*, 16 December 1865.

21 See letter of George Outram, a Sheffield file grinder in the US who was busy organising a union there, *ibid.*, 5 May 1866; and Outram's reply to Chambers, *ibid.*, 14 August 1866. On the Whipple collapse, see *ibid.*, 3, 17 April 1866; 9 May 1866.

22 Chambers (n. 17) added: 'It makes file blanks of any size, of perfect finish and uniformity, and turns out in one day more than Mr. Outram and his striker ever made in two weeks' time.'

23 See: *DAB*; Nicholson File Co, *A Treatise on Files and Rasps* (Providence, 1878); *TASME* 14 (1892–3), pp. 1451–2.

24 *Iron Age* (n. 11); *Practical Magazine* 7 (1877), pp. 36–7.

25 *American Manufacturer*, 21 September 1876, p. 4; Robson, *Manufactories*, p. 162; J. H. Bausman, *History of Beaver County Pennsylvania and Its Centennial Celebration* (New York, 1904), vol. 2, p. 675.

26 L. R. Trumbull, *A History of Industrial Paterson* (Paterson, 1882), pp. 108–9; Ruttenber and Clark, *Orange County*, p. 404.

27 *Iron Age* 13 (16 April 1874), p. 7. See also D. A. Lyle, *Report on the Manufacture and Uses of Files and Rasps* (1881), which states that hand-cutting was still in operation at the National Armory, Springfield, Mass. There was still a place for the immigrant Sheffield hand-cutter, though he was soon to become extinct. A good example was Augustus Rothery, who established a small file-cutting business in Auburn, New York. See D. L. Parke, Jr., 'Augustus Rothery – File Cutter', *CEAIA* 36 (September 1983), pp. 49–52.

28 See *Scientific American* 47, n.s. (9 September 1882), pp. 159, 165, for a description of the New American File Co. Sheffield steel was used in the firm's

machine chisels. According to the *Sheffield Independent*, 1 October 1878 (quoting an American source), the seven leading US makers produced 1,500 doz. machine-cut and 200 doz. hand-cut files per day.

29 *Report ... on the Commerce and Navigation of the United States for the Year Ending June 30, 1866* (Washington, DC, 1867), pp. 266–8.

30 *Annual Report ... on the Commerce and Navigation of the United States for the Fiscal Year Ended June 30, 1877* (Washington, DC, 1878), pp. 54–5.

31 *Annual Report ... on the Commerce and Navigation of the United States for the Fiscal Year Ending June 30, 1886* (Washington, DC, 1887), p. 91.

32 See *Reports of the Committee of the Senate ... for the 2nd Session of the 53rd Congress. Replies to Tariff Inquiries. Schedule C. Metals and Manufactures of* (Washington, DC, 1894), No. 1645, Reply to Montgomery & Co, N.Y., p. 113; No. 1639, Reply of Peter A. Frasse & Co, N.Y., pp. 104–6. Remarked the *Ironmonger* 34 (18 July 1885), p. 120: 'The buyers of the States only rely upon the Sheffield houses for a few classes of the more elaborate and difficult hand-cut files.'

33 See 'Files in Spanish America', *Special Consular Reports* (Washington, DC, 1890), vol. 1, pp. 239–68. J. W. Merriam remarked, p. 243: 'There is no demand for American files in this district [Chile], for the reason that dealers find that they can buy files from Sheffield much cheaper.'

34 *Sheffield Independent*, 5 August 1886.

35 Evidence of S. Uttley, *PP* 1892, XXXVI, RC on Labour (1892–4). C. 6795, pp. 558–68. Uttley also appeared before the RC Appointed to Inquire into the Depression of Trade and Industry, *PP*, 1886, XXI. C. 4621, p. 12, where he argued that some Americans would 'give almost anything for a good hand-made Sheffield file'.

36 G. I. H. Lloyd, *The Cutlery Trades* (1913), p. 199. See account of Cocker Bros' Fitzalan Works, *PIME* (1890), p. 449, where file-cutting machines designed by Ambrose Shardlow did not preclude the employment of hand-cutters. Cf. 'Ambrose Shardlow & Co Ltd', typescript history (n.d.), SCL; *Ironmonger* 37 (26 March 1887), p. 508. Osborn's also did not entirely renounce the old techniques. See *American Machinist* 29, Pt. 1 (5 April 1906), pp. 438–44.

37 According to E. A. Pratt, *Trade Unionism and British Industry* (1904), p. 141: 'Even now the Americans obtain a very much better output from the file-cutting machines in proportion to the wages paid than [Sheffielders] ... [because of] a lack of ambition on their part, and to a spirit of contentment which prompts them to be satisfied with the wages they get.'

38 One manufacturer noted: 'The American file is made of the poorest material ... [and] It is not the habit of the Americans to re-cut a file. The American throws it away when it is done with, and then uses another one, but it is the habit in [England] to re-cut it twice or three times till there is nothing left.' Evidence of C. W. Kayser, 5 May 1904. British Library of Political and Economic Science. Tariff Commission Papers. TC 3 1/12.

13. 'HOW SHEFFIELD LOST THE AMERICAN TRADE'*: ASPECTS OF THE MARKETING OF SHEFFIELD PRODUCTS IN AMERICA

1 US Centennial Commission, *International Exhibition 1876, Reports and Awards: Group I* (Philadelphia, 1878), pp. 32–3.

* Headline from *Sheffield Independent*, 17 June 1875.

2 The displays by Collins and Nicholson were seen by the author in 1983 in the '1876' Exhibition at the Smithsonian Institution, Washington, DC. The collection of polished axe-heads by Collins was particularly impressive. See R. C. Post, ed., *1876: A Centennial Exhibition* (Washington, DC, 1976), p. 134.

3 *British Trade Journal* 15 (1 March 1877), pp. 139–40. See also 'American Competition in Sheffield Goods', *British Trade Journal* 15 (1 October 1877), pp. 543–5.

4 The debate over the alleged failings of English businessmen is explored in P. L. Payne, *British Entrepreneurship in the Nineteenth Century* (1974).

5 *RC Report of the Juries, Exhibition of 1851*, p. 10. Over 90 Sheffield firms exhibited at the Crystal Palace. For descriptions of the various displays, see: *Illustrated Exhibitor*, No. 12, 23 August 1851; *Sheffield Independent*, 5 April 1851; 19 April 1851; 10 May 1851.

6 On Paris see *Sheffield Independent*, 14 April 1855; 28 July 1855; August 4, 1855. On the Great Exhibition in 1862, see: *Ironmonger* 3 (31 May 1861), p. 14; and the extensive reports in the *Sheffield Independent*, 15 April–3 June 1862.

7 *PP* 1867/8, XXX, Reports on the Paris Universal Exhibition, 1867. Pt. II, vol. IV, p. 258.

8 *Sheffield Independent*, 9 February 1867. On the poor Sheffield presence at Paris, especially in the light trades, see: *Sheffield Independent*, 29 December 1866; 14 January 1867; 22 February 1867.

9 *Reports of the United States Commissioners to the Paris Exposition 1867–'68* (Washington, DC, 1868), vol. 2, pp. 1–183. Repr. in A. Nevins, ed., *Selected Writings of Abram S. Hewitt* (New York, 1937), pp. 19–85. The impressive quality of the British exhibits and their limited number is also mentioned by F. Kohn, *Iron and Steel Manufacture* (1869), p. 193. See also *Reports of Artisans Selected by a Committee Appointed by the Council of the Society of Arts to Visit the Paris Universal Exhibition 1867* (1867), pp. 37–51 (saws and tools), pp. 52–63 (cutlery).

10 See *Sheffield Independent*, 3 April 1873; 6 June 1873; 10 June 1873; *PP* 1874, LXIII, Reports on the Vienna Universal Exhibition of 1873.

11 *PP* 1877, XXXVI, Reports of the Philadelphia International Exhibition, p. 120. For favourable comments on Sheffield steel exhibits by two US experts, A. L. Holley and Lenox Smith, see 'Iron and Steel at Philadelphia', *Engineering* 23 (9 February 1877), p. 115. Sheffield participation is also described in the *Sheffield Independent*, 14 March 1876; 17 March 1876; 11 April 1876.

12 *PP* 1877, Philadelphia Exhibition, 'Edge Tools, – etc.', by D. McHardy, p. 133; and p. 153.

13 *Sheffield Independent*, 22 August 1878.

14 *Sheffield Independent*, 14 May 1878. The US Commissioner thought the British steel display 'extensive, varied, and exceedingly suggestive of mechanical excellence'. See Secretary of State, *Reports of the United States Commissioners to the Paris Universal Exposition, 1878* (Washington, DC, 1880), vol. 3, p. 16.

15 J. H. Cox, *Diary and Report of a Visit to Paris and the French Exhibition* (Sheffield, 1878), pp. 17–18. Cox thought Disston's saws 'unequalled'. See also *PP* 1880, XXXII–XXXIII, Report of HM Commissioners for the Paris Universal Exhibition of 1878 C. 2588; and the detailed 'Supplement' in the *Ironmonger* 20 (19 October 1878).

16 *Sheffield Independent*, 10 June 1873.
17 M. E. Calvert, 'American Technology at World Fairs 1851–1876', (Delaware MA, 1962), p. 156.
18 *Sheffield Independent*, 22 August 1878.
19 Apparently, one of the factors which influenced the US plough maker, John Deere, in his decision to patronise Pittsburgh suppliers was that Sheffield steel became heavily rusted during the Atlantic crossing. See N. M. Clark, *John Deere: He Gave to the World the Steel Plow* (Moline, Ill., 1937), p. 42. L. J. Coombe (Spear & Jackson) mentions a large consignment of garden tools returned to England by US Customs because they were not marked with the place of manufacture. Another store received the firm's goods by mistake. See SJC 83. Coombe to S. & J., Pittsburgh, 4 July 1925. On goods damaged in a steamship collision, see Wos R3. Letter to F. B. Gurney, New York, 14 February 1896.
20 MD 1485. Letter to Woodcock, New York, 18 November 1865.
21 BLCU, Hoe Papers. Letter Book 15 December 1842–15 April 1846. Hoe to Sanderson, 13 November 1843. Box 21.
22 See esp. Letter Book 25 February–19 September 1850, letter to E. Pratt & Bros, Baltimore, 11 March 1850; letter to [?], 18 March 1850; letter to Albany customer, [?] March 1850.
23 See Chap. 7.
24 'Tool Steel from a Salesman's Point of View', *Iron Age* 91 (20 March 1913), pp. 706–8.
25 See the *Edgar Allen News* for the amount of attention devoted to this. Helpful handbooks, published to ensure that steel consumers obtained the best results from their steel, were also issued. See for example A. Balfour, *Hints to Practical Users of Tool Steel* (Sheffield, ca. 1920). The Americans produced similar handbooks. See: Crescent Steel Co, *The Treatment of Steel* (Pittsburgh, 1884); *idem, Condensed Suggestions for Steel Workers* (Pittsburgh, 1890); W. Metcalf, *Steel: A Manual for Steel-Users* (New York, 1911).
26 *Edgar Allen News* 2 (November/December 1921), p. 231.
27 *Firth Sterling Tool Steels* (McKeesport, Pa., 1925), p. 65.
28 *BAISA* 12 (30 October 1878), p. 251.
29 S. Pollard, *Three Centuries of Sheffield Steel* (Sheffield, 1954), p. 40, and cf. pp. 22–7, 35–40.
30 MD 1485. Letter to New York, 11 December 1865.
31 One cause of these deficiencies was the extended credit that firms such as Marsh Bros felt obliged to give to Americans who sold the company's goods. To compete with other Sheffield houses in St Louis, one Marsh Bros agent noted that credit arrangements that extended up to a year were necessary. See Marsh 248. Letter from J. Mollison to Marsh Bros, 4 June 1858.
32 SJC 82. 14 July 1925, New York; SJC 80. 26 May 1925.
33 SJC 82. 16 July 1925, New York.
34 MD 1485. Letter to New York, 25 August 1865.
35 See R. E. Leader, *Sheffield in the Eighteenth Century* (Sheffield, 2nd edn., 1905), p. 89. For an insight into trading at this time, see B. A. Holderness, 'A Sheffield Commercial House in the Mid-Eighteenth Century: Messrs Osborne and Gunning around 1760', *Business History* 15 (1973), pp. 32–44.
36 Cambridge University Library, Vickers Papers, Lehmann Letters (602), Benzon to Frederick Lehmann, Boston, 14 September 1853. See also J. D.

Scott, *Vickers* (1962), pp. 7–13. Benzon was heavily involved in the import of Swedish bar iron into the US through agencies in Boston and New York and the 'Norway Iron Works' in Boston. See: A. Attman, *Fagerstabrukens Historia: Adertonhundratalet* (Uppsala, 1958), pp. 257–8; R. Adamson, 'Swedish Iron Exports to the United States, 1783–1860', *Scandinavian Economic History Review* 17 (1969), pp. 112–14. An engineering firm which owed its success in the US to its agent was Lockwood & Carlisle Ltd. The firm's American trade in the 1920s was opened up by the Kearfott Engineering Co Inc. See E. N. Simons, *Lockwood and Carlisle Ltd of Sheffield* (Sheffield, 1962), p. 30.

37 MD 1485. Letters to New York, 21 October 1865; 3 November 1866.

38 *Sheffield Independent*, 17 June 1875. See also *ibid.*, 5 October 1872; 17 June 1875. Wiebusch took over Butcher's stock; Hermann, Boker & Co that of Wostenholm's. There are hints in the literature that New York importers such as Wiesbusch & Hilger had acquired enough buying power in the late nineteenth century to actually control Sheffield factories.

39 Wos R3. Letter, 8 March 1895. The correspondence in Wos R12, esp. letter, 18 July 1893, shows that the agent was Edward Beckett (see Chap. 10) who was anxious to bypass the jobbers because they were more interested 'in selling [American] cutlery by which they can make more money'.

40 *PP* 1918, XIII, Report of ... the Board of Trade to Consider the Position of the Iron and Steel Trades After the War. Cd. 9071, pp. 16–17. A point repeated by T. H. Burnham and G. O. Hoskins, *Iron and Steel in Britain, 1870–1930* (1943), pp. 210–12.

41 PRO FO 115/2578. 8 January 1920.

42 FO 115/2581. FO Circular, Washington, 16 April 1920.

43 *Ibid.*, Report from W. S. Paul, 23 July 1920.

44 Testimony of J. H. Doncaster, Committee on Industry and Trade. *Minutes of Evidence*, vol. 1, p. 323.

45 W. H. Becker, 'American Wholesale Hardware Trade Associations, 1870–1900', *Business History Review* 45 (1971), pp. 179–200; G. Porter and H. C. Livesay, *Merchants and Manufacturers* (Baltimore, 1971).

46 Dept. of Overseas Trade, J. J. Broderick, *Report on the Finance, Industry and Commerce of the United States of America* (1926), p. 26; (1927), p. 91.

47 A. Gatty, *Sheffield: Past and Present* (Sheffield, 1873), p. 209.

48 *Sheffield Independent*, 5 June 1858.

49 *Ibid.*, 9 September 1854; 12 July 1856; 26 July 1856.

50 'We have run no advertisements in trade papers, or any other publications except the Boston City Directory, in which we have run a small one in order to secure such listing as is likely to do us some good ... the bulk of the advertising expense is accounted for by the lettering on our office windows ... [and by] an advertisement in the *Iron Age*'. SCL BDR 134. Reports & Accounts, 13 December 1921.

51 Periodicals sampled included: *Colliers; Forbes; House and Garden; The Independent; Ladies Home Journal; McCall's Magazine; Saturday Evening Post; Vogue; Woman's World.*

52 *Sheffield Daily Telegraph*, 28 August 1922.

53 Disston's advertisements were mentioned in the *Sheffield Independent*, 26 June 1877.

54 Marsh 248. J. Mollison to Marsh Bros, New York, 22 January 1858.

55 'We know very well, and all British manufacturers and merchants must also be aware of the fact, that the headway made by the American exporters is largely owing to the superior way in which their wares are sent out', remarked the *Ironmonger* 22 (2 August 1879), pp. 173–4. See also 'The Secret of Yankee Success', *British Trade Journal* 18 (1 December 1880), p. 615.

56 *Ironmonger* 22 (6 September 1879), pp. 338–41.

57 SJC 79. 30 June 1905.

58 Wos R13a. Letter to B. W. Nixon, Wostenholm's, 27 March 1931.

59 *Ibid.*, H. Bexfield to Colver, 17 March 1931.

60 'Advertising Sheffield: The Chamber's Scheme', *Sheffield Chamber of Commerce Journal* (August 1927), pp. 6–7. See also SCL LD 1803. Minutes of the Sheffield Cutlery Trades' Technical Society, 5 November 1925.

61 *Sheffield Development Department, Town Hall, 1922: The Metal Industries of Sheffield*, pp. 8–9. In 1890, the cutlers, Christopher Johnson & Co, had expressed the same view more succinctly: 'Americans *will* have *best* English goods, no matter what the price may be.' MD 2369. Letter to Weatherby Jardine & Co, 12 May 1890.

62 *Anglo-American Trade* 4 (January 1920), p. 9.

63 The Atlantic Steel Co was one firm which felt the effect of English competition because of the lower freight rates. See H. R. Kuniansky, *A Business History of Atlantic Steel Company 1901–1968* (New York, 1976), pp. 114–15. See also *Tariff Hearings. Senate Docs. Vol. 5. Pt. 3. Tariff Act of 1921*, pp. 1633, 1721.

64 *Anglo-American Trade* 7 (July 1923), p. 277; SJC 86. Memo to J. E. Whitten, 23 October 1933.

65 For occasional references to Wostenholm's West coast trade see Wos R3. Letters, 18 March 1895; 28 October 1895; 28 November 1895. The Letter Book (MD 2369) of the cutlers, Christopher Johnson & Co, also mentions the West coast in letters 10, 14 May 1889; 12 May 1890.

66 SCL B & B 69. Letter from Baker & Hamilton Hardware Co, San Francisco, 12 April 1881. A further letter (B & B 68, 1 June 1876) promised a good demand for the firm's shears, with the familiar proviso that goods must be adapted to American conditions. Mostly, Burgon & Ball, along with other Sheffield shear makers, such as Ward & Payne, concentrated on the Australasian market. See *Implement and Machinery Review* 3 (3 October 1877), pp. 1189–90; 4 (1 June 1878), p. 1595; 17 (1 August 1891), pp. 14486–7.

67 Marsh 248. Mollison to Woodcock, New York, 11 June 1858. Mollison noted that Jessop's, Sanderson's, Naylor's, and Ellison's, all had agencies in St Louis (letter to Woodcock, 4 June 1858).

68 Wos R13 (a). E. J. Newey, New Orleans, to Wostenholm's, 19 March 1931.

69 F. V. Willey and G. Locock, *Report on a Visit to the USA* (FBI, 1925).

70 C. P. Russell, *Firearms, Traps, and Tools of the Mountain Men* (New York, 1967), p. 191. In the 1837 *Sheffield Directory* Unwin & Rodgers also advertised 'American & Indian Hunting, and Self-Defence Knives'.

71 MD 1485. Letter to New York, 19 April 1867. See also Charles Cammell & Co, *Illustrated List of Files & Rasps, Saws, etc.* (ca. 1860), which shows 'American' hammers, trowels, wedge axes, and tomahawks.

72 MD 1485. 13 May 1867.

73 Marsh 248. J. Mollison to Woodcock, Cincinnati, 11 June 1858.

74 'Sheffield Cutlery at the Centennial', *Iron Age* 17 (13 April 1876), p. 24.

Hardy's Centennial exhibit resulted in a large number of US orders. See *Implement and Machinery Review* 3 (1 March 1878), pp. 1439–40.

75 On Sheffield copying US patterns, see: *Ironmonger* 15 (1 June 1873), p. 676; 24 (28 August 1880), p. 239; 26 (3 December 1881), p. 816; 27 (7 January 1882), p. 40. Brookes & Crookes' Atlantic Works was one firm which was heavily involved in the manufacture of American 'novelties'. See *Implement and Machinery Review* 8 (1 July 1882), pp. 4425–6.

76 R. Abels, *Classic Bowie Knives* (New York, 1967); H. L. Petersen, *American Knives* (New York, 1958), pp. 25–70; C. P. Russell, *Mountain Men*, pp. 190–6; R. W. Thorp, *Bowie-Knife* (New Mexico, 1948); R. Washer, *The Sheffield Bowie Knife and Pocket-Knife Makers 1825–1925* (Nottingham, 1974); W. R. Williamson, *I*XL Means I Excel* (1974), p. 10. Sheffield City Museum has a particularly fine Butcher Bowie (ca. 1860). Etched around an American eagle are the words: 'The United States, The Land of the Free and the Home of the Brave. Protected by Her Noble and Brave Volunteers.'

77 Wos R13a. Letter, 9 March 1931. Wostenholm's was also interested in copying Remington's display case. Wos R12. F. Holroyd to A. S. Keeton, 13 April 1930.

78 SJC 86. 17 August 1934.

79 SJC 86. Undated letter 1934; letter, 24 May 1934.

80 Wos R12. Letter from G. Walter Davis, 4 December 1931. A good summary of these developments is A. D. Chandler, *The Visible Hand* (Cambridge, Mass., 1977), esp. pp. 207–39.

81 SJC 88. Letter, 4 October 1934. For comments on cheap cutlery sold through the chains, see Wos R13. Colver letter, 31 March 1931.

82 The stores devoted particular attention to the promotion and display of cutlery. See R. R. Williams, *The American Hardware Store* (New York, 1897), pp. 284–308.

83 Sears Roebuck Catalogue, *1908 Edition*, ed. J. J. Schroeder Jr. (repr., Illinois, 1971), p. 767. See also *1887 Edition* (repr., New York, 1968); *1927 Edition*. A. Mirken, ed. (New York, 1970).

84 Wos R13. Colver to Wostenholm's, 3 March 1931. Added Colver: 'In 1930 Wanamaker's, Philadelphia, and New Y[ork] stores only had $500 worth of goods from us, (£50 at Sheffield prices).'

85 Wos R13a. Colver to Boswell Son & Naylor, 26 February 1931.

86 Wos R12. Letter from Swedish Steel Mills, New York, to J. B. Thomas, 10 December 1931.

87 FO 115/2580. A. H. King, Chicago, 11 September 1920.

88 Wos R3. Letter from San Francisco agents, 21 January 1896. See generally R. J. Hoffman, *Great Britain and the German Trade Rivalry 1875–1914* (Philadelphia, 1933).

89 One Sheffielder regarded high US duties as 'very far from an unmixed evil. It has driven our merchants and manufacturers to seek "fresh fields and pastures new", and instead of confining their attention to the home, the American, and a few other markets, their representatives roam the world over seeking orders'. See F. Callis, *Sheffield Under Free Trade* (Sheffield, 1903), p. 11. For an international survey of comparative tariff rates, including the US, see F. Brittain, *Address … on the Results of Foreign Tariffs, especially with Reference to Sheffield* (Sheffield, 1875).

90 Committee on Industry and Trade. *Minutes of Evidence*, vol. 1, p. 345.

91 A Brookings study by A. Berglund and P. G. Wright, *The Tariff on Iron and*

Steel (Washington, DC, 1929) concluded, p. 130: 'from about 1896 on the [American] industry, so far as concerns the manufacture of tonnage products, was independent of the tariff'.

92 Committee on Industry and Trade, *Minutes of Evidence*, vol. 1, p. 338; *idem, Survey of Metal Industries* (1928), pp. 271–2.

93 N. H. Carter, *Letters from Europe* (New York, 1827), vol. 1, p. 96.

94 See Rodgers' advertisement in the *Iron Age* 11 (2 January 1873), p. 10, which declared that the firm would 'thankfully receive from the trade information touching any such or other violation of their name and trademarks'. In 1871 Rodgers was involved in a court case with a Washington government stationers which was selling Prussian knives as Rodgers. See *Ironmonger* 13 (30 December 1871), pp. 5–6; *Sheffield Independent*, 13 October 1871.

95 Anyone reading the nineteenth-century Sheffield trade press and the minutes of the Sheffield Chamber of Commerce or its published journal cannot but be impressed by the enormous attention devoted to this problem. It continues to this day. For numerous references, see S. Pybus *et al.*, *Cutlery: A Bibliography* (SCL, 1982).

96 MD 6209. New York, 30 January 1844. On counterfeiting see also: MD 6213/i, letter, New York, 15 November 1843; Wos R3, letters, 28 October, 28 November 1895; Wos R4. Correspondence with Thos. Firth & Sons about improper use of Wostenholm's and Firth's names in advertising matter by the Empire Knife Co, Winsted, Conn., 1895–1911.

97 L. Du Garde Peach, *The Company of Cutlers in Hallamshire in the County of York 1906–1956* (Sheffield, 1960), pp. 61–2. See Company of Cutlers, *Extracts from the Records of the Company of Cutlers in Hallamshire in the County of York* (Sheffield, 1972), Plate 55 reproduces a label used by a non-existent American firm (the Sheffield Cutlery Co) in 1889 on boxes of cutlery offered for sale in Denmark. It should be mentioned that Sheffield was an important influence on international business law. Col. Herbert Hughes (1853–1917), for example, the Secretary of the Sheffield Chamber of Commerce, was an acknowledged expert on trade marks and patent law.

98 SJC 88. Coombe to S. & J., 4 October 1934, Philadelphia.

99 Wos R13a. Letter to Boswell Naylor & Co, Sheffield, 26 February 1931.

100 SJC 86. Letter, 4 October 1934. Ironically, Sheffield cutlers themselves had once been adept at illegal branding, frequently copying London marks in the seventeenth century. See J. F. Hayward, *English Cutlery* (1957), pp. 9–11.

101 FO 371/5673. Letter, 10 August 1921.

102 *Quality* 6 (February 1935), p. 165.

103 *Sheffield Independent*, 1 January 1863; 2 January 1864.

104 SJC 90. Clipping from *Australasian Manufacturer*, 29 September 1923. Neutral and colonial markets may have represented a 'soft' option for some firms, and some areas seem to have become too popular. Remarked R. S. Hutton, *Recollections of a Technologist* (1964), p. 54: 'At that time [ca. 1910] the competition for Sheffield trade in Canada was quite ridiculous considering its limited extent. In Vancouver I found from the hotel register that thirteen travellers from Sheffield in electro-plate, etc., had been there within about a month of one another.'

105 A Balfour & Co, *A Centenary 1865–1965* (Nottingham, 1967), p. 40.

CONCLUSION: A CENTURY OF COMMERCIAL AND TECHNOLOGICAL INTERDEPENDENCE IN STEEL

1 H. J. Habakkuk, *American and British Technology in the Nineteenth Century* (Cambridge, 1962); N. Rosenberg, ed., *The American System of Manufactures* (Edinburgh, 1969). For excellent recent discussions of the 'American System', see: O. Mayr and R. C. Post, eds., *Yankee Enterprise* (Washington, DC, 1981); and D. Hounshell, *From the American System to Mass Production 1800–1932* (Baltimore, 1984).

2 The file trades provide evidence for S. B. Saul's assertion that the speed of America's nineteenth-century technical advance has been exaggerated by some writers and that progress varied greatly between industries. See Saul, ed., *Technological Change* (1970), pp. 1–21, 13.

3 *Sheffield Times*, 30 June 1849.

4 *Ibid.*, 7 April 1849.

5 The view presented here and in my 'English *versus* American Hardware: British Marketing Techniques and Business Performance in the USA in the Nineteenth and Early Twentieth Centuries', in R. P. T. Davenport-Hines, ed., *Markets and Bagmen* (Aldershot, 1986), differs from a recent interpretation, which suggests that 'the traditional picture of the British industrialist employing amateurish marketing techniques and outdated selling institutions is misleading'. See S. J. Nicholas, 'The Overseas Marketing Performance of British Industry, 1870–1914', *Economic History Review* 37 (November 1984), pp. 489–506, 505.

   On recent visits to America the author noticed that Swiss pocket-knives and German table cutlery are still on prominent display. The French have also achieved recent success in America, largely with the help of clever marketing. See Vincent Beaufils, 'Opinel: Un Succès à Double Tranchant', *L'Enterprise*, No. 5 (October 1985), pp. 84–5. Sheffield goods in the US, however, appear to have completely disappeared – the end result, it would appear, of the neglect of marketing.

6 G. Tweedale, 'Metallurgy and Technological Change: A Case Study of Sheffield Specialty Steel and America, 1830–1930', *Technology and Culture* 27 (April 1986).

7 'The Market and the Development of the Mechanical Engineering Industries in Britain, 1860–1914', in Saul, *Technological Change*, pp. 141–70.

8 A. Shadwell, *Industrial Efficiency* (1906), vol. 2, pp. 68–70.

9 See also Arnold, *British and German Steel Metallurgy* (1915), pp. 9–10.

10 Some countries did survive changing conditions. Sweden, for example, continued to sell tool steel in the US in the 1930s and afterwards, basing its competitive position, as Sheffield had done, on a superiority in uniformity and surface finish. See E. C. Bain, *Pioneering in Steel Research* (Ohio, 1975), pp. 192–4.

11 G. Tweedale, 'Transatlantic Specialty Steels: Sheffield High-Grade Steel Firms and the USA, 1860–ca. 1940', in Geoffrey Jones. ed., *British Multinationals: Origins, Management and Performance* (Aldershot, 1986).

12 It should be noted that despite the loss of the US market Sheffield did not become technologically moribund after 1920. Many important metallurgical advances emanated from the city in the interwar period, and Sheffield was to supply the special steels for the first jet engine. See G. Tweedale, 'Science, Innovation and the 'Rule of Thumb': The Development of British Metallurgy

to 1945', in J. Liebenau, ed., *The Challenge of New Technology* (Aldershot, 1987).

13 This is the view of T. C. Cochran, who quotes approvingly the following remarks of Jefferson written in 1826: 'Our manufactures are now very nearly on a footing with those of England. She has not a single improvement which we do not possess, and many of them better adapted by ourselves to our ordinary use.' See *Frontiers of Change* (New York, 1981), p. 77.

BIBLIOGRAPHY

Place of publication of works cited is London unless otherwise stated.

I: MANUSCRIPTS AND UNPUBLISHED SOURCES
(a) Manuscripts

Baker Library, Harvard University, Boston
  Ms 596. American Steel and Wire Collection
British Library of Political and Economic Science, London
  Tariff Commission Papers. TC 3 1/12. Evidence of C. W. Kayser
Butler Library, Columbia University, New York City
  Richard M. Hoe & Co Papers, 1833–1901
  Stephen D. Tucker, 'A History of R. Hoe & Co'. Typescript, n.d.
Cambridge University Library
  Vickers Papers: esp. 602, Lehmann Letters; Microfilm R307
Company of Cutlers in Hallamshire, Cutlers' Hall, Sheffield
  Declaration of Harry Brearley, 'History of Stainless Steel Cutlery', 14 December 1931
Connecticut Historical Society, Hartford, Connecticut
  Ms 72190. 'The Collins Company Historical Memoranda, 1826–1871', by Samuel W. Collins
Eleutherian Mills Historical Library, Wilmington, Delaware
  Accession 322. James M. Swank Collection. Letters. (Microfilm)
  Accession 333. Alan Wood Steel Co Papers, 1728–1937
  Accession 1191. US Bureau of Census. Pennsylvania Census Records: Seventh–Tenth Census of Manufacturers, 1850–80
  Accession 1292. Taylor–Wharton Iron & Steel Co Papers, 1742–1950
  Accession 1477. Robert Hoe & Co. In-correspondence, 1850–5
  Accession 1567. The Disston History, 1920. 2 vols
  Accession 1631. American Iron and Steel Institute Collection
  Accession 1675. Henry Disston & Co. Patent and Design Drawings for Saws, ca. 1835–75
  Accession 1770. Archibald Johnston Collection. Bethlehem Steel Trade Catalogue Collection
Historical Society of Pennsylvania, Philadelphia
  1485. Baldwin Locomotive Co Papers
  F–33. James M. Swank Collection
Johnson Firth Brown plc, Smithfield House, Blonk Street, Sheffield

Thomas Firth & Sons, Directors' Minute Books, Reports, 1881–1945
Firth–Brearley Stainless Steel Syndicate Records, 1917–51
Modern Records Centre, Warwick University
Mss 19A. Records of the Birmingham Small Arms Co
National Archives, Washington, DC
T 248. Despatches from US Consuls in Sheffield, 1864–1906
M 432 (745–6); M 653 (1058–60); M 593 (1291–2, 1295–8); M653 (1058–60, 1166). US Bureau of the Census. Eighth, Ninth and Tenth Census of Pittsburgh and Allegheny Co. Population Schedules
Public Record Office, Kew
FO 371. Political Correspondence. US
FO 115. Correspondence. US Consular Reports
Sheffield City Library, Archives Division
Allen, Edgar & Co (Aurora 541 (a); MD 2333, 2336, 3970–1)
Andrew, J. H. & Co Ltd (Aurora 56, 60)
Andrews, Thos. & Co Ltd (MD 7063)
Balfour Darwin Ltd (BDR 77, 79, 95–6, 134–5)
Beardshaw, J. & Son Ltd (MD 7081 (5))
Brown, Bayley's Ltd (Directors' Minute Book, 1905–16, uncatalogued)
Burgon & Ball Ltd (B & B 68–9)
Hadfields Ltd (uncatalogued; see G. Tweedale, 'The Records of Hadfields Ltd, Sheffield', *Business Archives*, forthcoming)
Johnson, Christopher & Co (MD 2367–9)
Marsh Bros (M 14, 19, 108, 198, 241–49; MD 1485)
Osborn, Samuel & Co (Os 1–17, 85–94, 100–26, 136, 150–1)
Roberts, James. Correspondence (MD 2027)
Rodgers, Joseph & Sons (MD 6209, 6213)
Sheffield Cutlery Trades' Technical Society (LD 1803)
Spear & Jackson Ltd (SJC 8, 24, 42, 68, 73, 79–88, 97–106)
Vickers, Sons & Maxim (LD 1878)
Wostenholm, George & Son Ltd (Wos R3–4, R6–8, R12–13; 168)
Sheffield University Archives
Department of Metallurgy Letter Books (Ms 72)
Arnold Letter Books (SUA VIII/1/27/1–2)
Steel Research Committee (SUA VIII/1/10)
Winterthur Library, Winterthur, Delaware
Trade catalogue collection

(b) *Unpublished typescripts*

Allard, Dean C. 'The Influence of the United States Navy upon the American Steel Industry, 1880–1900'. Georgetown MA, 1959
Blackwell, D. H. 'The Growth and Decline of the Scythe/Sickle (Shear) Trade in Hallamshire'. 2 vols., Sheffield University PhD, 1973
Brandt, W. I. 'Steel and the New Navy, 1882–1895'. Wisconsin PhD, 1920
Calvert, Monte E. 'American Technology at World Fairs 1851–1876'. Delaware MA, 1962
Davenport, Geoffrey H. 'Firebrick. A History of Refractories Technology and its Application to Iron and Steel Processes in Britain from 1750 onwards'. 2 vols., Open University PhD, 1979

Dixon, John T. 'Aspects of Yorkshire Emigration to North America, 1760–1880'. 4 vols., Leeds PhD, 1982

Garlick, Peter C. 'The Sheffield Cutlery and Allied Trades and Their Markets in the 18th and 19th Centuries'. Sheffield MA, 1951

Lamb, Andrew McG. 'A History of the American Pottery Industry: Industrial Growth, Technical and Technological Change and Diffusion in the General-ware Branch, 1872–1914'. London PhD, 1985

Ledbetter, R. M. 'Sheffield's Industrial History from about 1700, with Special Reference to the Abbeydale Works'. Sheffield MA, 1971

McPhee, Allan. 'The Growth of Cutlery and Allied Trades to 1814'. 1939, SCL

'Park Brother and Co, Black Diamond Works, Pittsburgh, Pa.'. Archives of the Crucible Steel Co of America, ca. 1880

Parkin, F. M. 'Gas *versus* Coke Melting in Crucible Steel Making'. Verbatim copy of notes before the Sheffield Society of Metallurgists and Metallurgical Chemists, 19 April 1921

Rigby, Karen I. 'Tungsten Ore in the United States Economy 1900–1929'. London School of Economics MSc, 1979. Economic History Dept

Seely, Bruce. 'Adirondack Iron and Steel Company: "New Furnace", 1849–1854'. Historic American Engineering Record of the Heritage Conservation and Recreation Service, 1978

'Ambrose Shardlow & Co Ltd'. n.d., SCL

Struik, D. J. 'The Story of the Barlow Knife'. n.d., SCL

Tedesco, Paul Herbert. 'Patriotism, Protection, and Prosperity: James Moore Swank, the American Iron and Steel Association, and the Tariff, 1873–1913'. Boston PhD, 1970

Timmins, John G. 'The Commercial Development of the Sheffield Crucible Steel Industry'. Sheffield MA, 1976

Waters, Deborah D. '"The Workmanship of an American Artist": Philadelphia's Precious Metal Trades and Craftsmen, 1788–1832'. Delaware PhD, 1981

II: OFFICIAL PUBLICATIONS

(a) Canada

Department of the Interior. *Report of the Commission Appointed to Investigate the Different Electro-Thermic Processes for the Smelting of Iron Ores and the Making of Steel in Operation in Europe.* 1904

(b) UK

Board of Trade. Committee on Industry and Trade (Balfour Committee), *Minutes of Evidence; Survey of the Metal Industries.* 1927–8

Board of Trade. *Report Respecting Cutlery.* 1928–9, Cmd. 3180

Board of Trade Safeguarding of Industries, Cutlery Committee. *Report 1925*, Cmd. 2540

Department of Overseas Trade. *Reports. USA.* 1920+

Ministry of Labour. Report by the Cutlery Wages Council (Great Britain). *Industrial Conditions in the Cutlery Trade.* 1945

PP 1812. III. Reports from Committees. Orders in Council

PP 1833. IV. SC on Commerce, Manufactures, etc.

PP 1851. RC Report of the Juries. Exhibition of 1851

PP 1865. XX. 'Report upon the Metal Manufactures of the Sheffield District', by

J. E. White. Appendix to Fourth Report of Children's Employment Commission

PP 1867. XXXII. Report Presented to the Trades Unions Commissioners ... Appointed to Inquire into Acts of Intimidation, Outrage, or Wrong ... in the Town of Sheffield

PP 1867/8. XXX. Reports on the Paris Universal Exhibition of 1867

PP 1874. LXIII. Reports on the Vienna Universal Exhibition of 1873

PP 1877. XXXIV–XXXVI. Reports on the Philadelphia International Exhibition.

PP 1880. XXXII–XXXIII. Report of Her Majesty's Commissioners for the Paris Universal Exhibition of 1878. C. 2588

PP 1886. XXI–XXIII. RC Appointed to Inquire into the Depression of Trade and Industry, C. 4621

PP 1892. XXXVI. RC on Labour (1892–4). C. 6795

PP 1918. XIII. Report of the Departmental Committee Appointed by the Board of Trade to Consider the Position of the Iron and Steel Trades after the War. Cd. 9071

(c) US

Bureau of the Census. *Seventh*, 'Compendium' (1854); *Eighth*, III, 'Manufactures of the United States in 1860' (1865); *Ninth*, III, 'Wealth and Industry' (1872); *Tenth*, II, 'Manufactures' (1883)

Department of the Interior. Bureau of Mines. Bulletin 77. *The Electric Furnace in Metallurgical Work*. D. R. Lyon; R. M. Keeney; and J. F. Cullen

Pennsylvania. Department of Internal Affairs. *Annual Reports of the Secretary of Internal Affairs of the Commonwealth of Pennsylvania*. Harrisburg, 1875+

Secretary of State. *Reports of the United States Commissioners to the Paris Exposition 1867–'68*. WGPO, 1868
Reports of the United States Commissioners to the Paris Universal Exposition, 1878. WGPO, 1880

Secretary of Treasury. *Report ... on Commerce and Navigation of US*. WGPO, annual, 1821+

Tariff Commission. *Cutlery Products*. WGPO, 1938

Tariff Commission. *Pocket Cutlery*. WGPO, 1939

III: SECONDARY WORKS

(a) Trade periodicals, journals and newspapers

Allen, Edgar & Co. *The Edgar Allen News*. Sheffield, 1919+
American Cutler. New York, 1909–39
American Electrochemical Society. *Transactions*. South Bethlehem, Pa., 1902+
American Institute of Mining engineers. *Transactions*. New York, 1871+
American Iron and Steel Association. *Bulletin*. Philadelphia, 1866–1912
American Machinist. New York, 1877+
American Manufacturer and Trade of the West. Pittsburgh, 1872–1906
American Society of Mechanical Engineers. *Transactions*. New York, 1880+
American Society for Steel Treating (American Society for Metals). *Transactions*. Cleveland, Ohio, 1920+
Anglo-American Trade. 1918+
British Trade Journal. 1863+

Cassier's Magazine. New York, 1891–1913
Chronicle of the Early American Industries Association. Northampton, Mass., 1933+
Engineer. 1856+
Engineering. 1866–1901
Engineering and Mining Journal. New York, 1866–1913
Engineers' Society of Western Pennsylvania. *Proceedings.* Philadelphia, 1899+
Franklin Institute. *Journal.* Philadelphia, 1826+
Implement and Machinery Review. 1875+
Institution of Civil Engineers. *Minutes of Proceedings.* 1837+
Institution of Mechanical Engineers. *Proceedings.* 1847+
Iron Age. New York, 1873+
Iron and Coal Trades Review. 1869+
Iron Trade Review. Cleveland, Ohio, 1888+
Ironmonger. 1859+
Iron and Steel Institute. *Journal.* 1869+
Metal Progress. Cleveland, Ohio, 1930+
Midvale Steel Co. *Safety Bulletin,* 1914–23
Pittsburgh Gazette. Pittsburgh, 1833+
Quality see Sheffield Chamber of Commerce
Royal Society. *Obituary Notices* (later *Biographical Memoirs*) *of Fellows of the Royal Society.* 1932+
Royal Society for the Encouragement of Arts, Manufactures and Commerce. *Journal.* 1852+
Scientific American. New York, 1845+
Sheffield Chamber of Commerce. *Journal* (later *Quality*), 1918+
Sheffield Daily Telegraph. Sheffield, 1855+
Sheffield Independent. Sheffield, 1819+
Sheffield Iris. Sheffield, 1794–1856
Sheffield Technical School Metallurgical Society. *Journal.* Sheffield, 1891–2
Sheffield Times. Sheffield, 1846–74

(b) Articles

Adamson, Rolf. 'Swedish Iron Exports to the United States, 1783–1860', *Scandinavian Economic History Review* 17 (1969)
Armytage, W. H. G. 'A Sheffield Quaker in Philadelphia 1804–1806', *Pennsylvania History* 17 (July 1950)
'Science and Industry in Sheffield: Some Historical Notes', *Chemical Society. Anniversary Meetings. Sheffield, April 2–5, 1962*
Baldwin, George B. 'The Invention of the Modern Safety Razor: A Case Study of Industrial Innovation', *Explorations in Entrepreneurial History* 4 (1951–2)
Bardell, P. S. 'The Origins of Alloy Steels', in Norman Smith, ed., *History of Technology, 9th Annual Volume.* London: Mansell Publishing, 1984
Barraclough, Kenneth C. 'The Production of Steel in Britain by the Cementation and Crucible Processes', *Historical Metallurgy* 8 (1974)
'The Development of the Cementation Process for the Manufacture of Steel', *Post-Medieval Archaeology* 10 (1976)
'A Crucible Steel Melter's Logbook', *Historical Metallurgy* 12 (1978)
Barraclough, Kenneth C; and Kerr, J. A. 'Steel From 100 Years Ago', *Historical Metallurgy* 10 (1976)

'Metallographic Examination of Some Archive Samples of Steel', *JISI* 211 (July–December 1973)

Becker, W. H. 'American Wholesale Hardware Trade Associations, 1870–1900', *Business History Review* 45 (1971)

Bessemer, Sir Henry. 'On the Manufacture and Uses of Steel with Special reference to its Employment for Edge Tools.' Paper read at Cutlers' Company of London, December 1, 1880

Brooke, David. 'The Advent of the Steel Rail 1857–1914', *Journal of Transport History* 3rd. s., 7 (March 1986)

Burn, Duncan L. 'The Genesis of American Engineering Competition, 1850–1870', *Economic History* 2 (1931)

Cooper, Carolyn C. 'The Portsmouth System of Manufacture', *Technology and Culture* 25 (April 1984)

Cooper, C. C.; Gordon, R. B.; and Merrick, H. V. 'Archeological Evidence of Metallurgical Innovation at the Eli Whitney Armory', *I.A.: The Journal of the Society for Industrial Archeology* 8 (1982)

Daniels, Maygene. 'The Ingenious Pen: American Writing Implements from the Eighteenth Century to the Twentieth', *American Archivist* 43 (1980)

Darling, A. S. 'Metallurgical Developments Between 1900 and 1939', *Transactions of the Newcomen Society* 55 (1983–4)

David, Paul A. 'The Mechanisation of Reaping in the Antebellum Midwest', in Henry Rosovsky, ed., *Industrialization in Two Systems.* New York: John Wiley & Sons, 1966

Fleisher, Eric W. 'The Beginning of the Transatlantic Market for Swedish Iron', *Scandinavian Economic History Review* 1 (1953)

Flinn, M. W. 'The Travel-Diaries of Swedish Engineers of the Eighteenth Century as Sources of Technological History', *Transactions of the Newcomen Society* 31 (1958/9)

Flinn, M. W.; and Birch, Alan. 'The English Steel Industry Before 1856, with Special Reference to the Development of the Yorkshire Steel Industry', *Yorkshire Bulletin of Economic and Social Research* 6 (1954)

Gilmer, Harrison. 'Birth of the American Crucible Steel Industry', *Western Pennsylvania Historical Magazine* 36 (1953)

Gordon, Robert B. 'The Metallurgical Museum of Yale College and Nineteenth Century Ferrous Metallurgy in New England', *Journal of Metals* (July 1982)
'Materials for Manufacturing: The Response of the Connecticut Iron Industry to Technological Change and Limited Resources', *Technology and Culture* 24 (October 1983)
'Material Evidence of the Development of Metalworking Technology at the Collins Axe Factory', *I.A.: The Journal of the Society for Industrial Archeology* 9 (1983)

Harris, John R. 'Attempts to Transfer English Steel Techniques to France in the Eighteenth Century', in Sheila Marriner, ed., *Business and Businessmen.* Liverpool: Liverpool University Press, 1978
'First Thoughts on Files; *Tools & Trades* 3 (1985)

Hildebrand, K.–G. 'Foreign Markets for Swedish Iron in the 18th Century', *Scandinavian Economic History Review* 6 (1958)

Holderness, B. A. 'A Sheffield Commercial House in the Mid-Eighteenth Century: Messrs Oborne and Gunning around 1760', *Business History* 15 (1973)

Howard, Seymour. 'The Steel Pen and the Modern Line of Beauty', *Technology and Culture* 26 (October 1985)

Hulme, E. Wyndham. 'The Pedigree and Career of Benjamin Huntsman', *Transactions of the Newcomen Society* 24 (1943/5)

Hummel, Charles F. 'English Tools in America: The Evidence of the Dominys', *Winterthur Portfolio* 2 (1965)

Hunter, Louis C. 'Influence of the Market upon Technique in the Iron Industry in Western Pennsylvania up to 1860', *Journal of Economic and Business History* 1 (1928/9)

'Financial Problems of the Early Pittsburgh Iron Manufacturers', *Journal of Economic and Business History* 2 (May 1930)

Jenkins, Rhys. 'Notes on the Early History of Steel Making in England', *Transactions of the Newcomen Society* 3 (1922/3)

Keown, Samuel. 'Tool Steels and High-Speed Steels 1900–1950', *Historical Metallurgy* 19, No. 1 (1985)

'A History of Alloy Steels with Particular Reference to Sheffield Contributions', *Historical Metallurgy* 19, No. 1 (1985)

Kley, Ron. 'Researching Early Maine Craftsmen: John H. Hall and the Gunsmith's Trade', *Maine Historical Society Quarterly* 24 (Spring 1985)

Kouwenhoven, John A. 'The Designing of the Eads Bridge', *Technology and Culture* 23 (October 1982)

McClean, I. W. 'Anglo–American Engineering Competition, 1870–1914: Some Third Market Evidence', *Economic History Review* 29, 2nd s. (August 1976)

Musson, Albert E. 'Continental Influences on the Industrial Revolution in Great Britain', in Barrie M. Ratcliffe, ed., *Great Britain and Her World, 1750–1914: Essays in Honour of W. O. Henderson.* Manchester: Manchester University Press, 1975

Nicholas, Stephen J. 'The Overseas Marketing Performance of British Industry, 1870–1914', *Economic History Review* 37 (November 1984)

Nuttall, R. H. 'The First Microscope of Henry Clifton Sorby', *Technology and Culture* 22 (April 1981)

Pearce, Molly. 'Sheffield Penknives', Sheffield City Museums Information Sheet, No. 13 (1976)

Le Play, Frédéric. 'Mémoire sur la Fabrication de l'Acier en Yorkshire, et Comparison des Principaux Groupes d'Aciéres Européennes', *Annales des Mines* 4 Ser, Tome 3 (1843), pp. 583–714. Translated by K. C. Barraclough, *Historical Metallurgy Bulletin* 7 (Parts 1 & 2), *Historical Metallurgy Journal* 8 (Part 1)

Potter, Jim. 'Atlantic Economy, 1815–1860: The USA and the Industrial Revolution in Britain', in L. S. Pressnell, ed., *Studies in the Industrial Revolution: Essays Presented to T. S. Ashton.* Athlone Press, 1960

Rosenberg, Nathan. 'Technological Change in the Machine Tool Industry, 1840–1910', *Journal of Economic History* 23 (1963)

'Technological Interdependence in the American Economy', *Technology and Culture* 20 (1979)

Sanderson, Michael. 'The Professor as Industrial Consultant: Oliver Arnold and the British Steel Industry, 1900–14', *Economic History Review* 31, 2nd. s (November 1978)

Sawyer, John E. 'The Social Basis of the American System of Manufacturing', *Journal of Economic History* 14 (1954)

Sherlock, C. 'Cast Steel Bells', *Special Steels Review* No. 2 (Spring 1970)

Simons, Eric N. 'The Story of a Great Steel Firm', *Edgar Allen Magazine*, December 1953–October 1958

Smith, Cyril S. 'The Interaction of Science and Practice in the History of Metallurgy', *Technology and Culture* 2 (1961)
'The Discovery of Carbon in Steel', *Technology and Culture* 5 (1964)
Smith, Peter L. 'The Sheffield & South Yorkshire Navigation', *Transport History* 11 (1980)
Temin, Peter. 'The Composition of Iron and Steel Products, 1869–1909', *Journal of Economic History* 23 (1963)
'The Relative Decline of the British Steel Industry, 1880–1913', in Henry Rosovsky, ed., *Industrialization in Two Systems*. New York: John Wiley & Sons, 1966
Templeton, Joseph P. 'Jersey City: Early American Steel Center', *Proceedings of the New Jersey Historical Society* 79 (1961)
Timmins, John G. 'Concentration and Integration in the Sheffield Crucible Steel Industry', *Business History* 24 (March 1982)
Truman, J. 'The Initiation and Growth of High Alloy (Stainless) Steel Production', *Historical Metallurgy* 19, No. 1 (1985)
Tweedale, Geoffrey. 'Sheffield Steel and America: Aspects of the Atlantic Migration of Special Steelmaking Technology, 1850–1930', *Business History* 25 (November 1983)
'Sir Robert A. Hadfield, FRS (1858–1940), and the Discovery of Manganese Steel', *Notes and Records of the Royal Society* 40 (November 1985)
'Metallurgy and Technological Change: A Case Study of Sheffield Specialty Steel and America, 1830–1930', *Technology and Culture* 27 (April 1986)
'English *versus* American Hardware: British Marketing Techniques and Business Performance in the USA in the Nineteenth and Early Twentieth Centuries', in R. P. T. Davenport-Hines, ed., *Markets and Bagmen: Studies in Marketing and British Industrial Performance, 1830–1939*. Aldershot: Gower, 1986
'Transatlantic Speciality Steels: Sheffield High-Grade Steel Firms and the USA, 1860–ca. 1940', in Geoffrey Jones, ed., *British Multinationals, Origins, Management and Performance*. Aldershot: Gower, 1986
'Science, Innovation and the "Rule of Thumb": The Development of British Metallurgy to 1945', in Jonathan Liebenau, ed., *The Challenge of New Technology: Innovation in British Business*. Aldershot: Gower, 1987
'Business and Investment Strategies in the Interwar British Steel Industry: A Case Study of Hadfields Ltd, Sheffield, and Bean Cars', *Business History* (1987)
Uselding, Paul. 'Elisha K. Root, Forging and the "American System"', *Technology and Culture* 15 (October 1974)
Warren, Kenneth. 'The Sheffield Rail Trade, 1861–1930: An Episode in the Locational History of the British Steel Industry', *Institute of British Geographers Transactions* 34 (1964)
Welsh, Peter C. 'The Metallic Woodworking Plane: An American Contribution to Hand-Tool Design', *Technology and Culture* 7 (1966)
Williams, Michael. 'Clearing the United States Forests: Pivotal Years 1810–1860', *Journal of Historical Geography* 8 (1982)

(c) Books

Abels, Robert. *Classic Bowie Knives*. New York: Robert Abels Inc., 1967
Adams, Russell B. *King C. Gillette: The Man and His Wonderful Shaving Device*. Boston: Little Brown, 1978

Albion, Robert G. *The Rise of New York Port 1815–1860*. Hamden, Conn.: Archon Books, 1961

Allen, Thomas. *A New and Complete History of the County of York*. 3 vols. I. T. Hinton, 1828–31

Allen, Zachariah. *The Practical Tourist*. 2 vols. Providence, Rhode Island: A. S. Beckwith, 1832

Alling, George W. *Points for Buyers and Users of Tool Steel*. New York: D. Williams, 1903

American Axe & Tool Co. *Illustrated Catalogue 1894*. Repr. 1981 by Mid-West Tool Collectors Association and Early American Industries Association *Trade Catalogue*. Glassport, Pa.: 1907.

American Iron and Steel Institute. *Annual Statistical Report*. Philadelphia, 1913+ *Directory of Iron and Steel Works of the United States and Canada*. New York: American Iron and Steel Institute, 1873+ *Yearbook*. New York: American Iron and Steel Institute, 1911+

American Rolling Mill Company. *The First Twenty Years. A History of the Growth and Development of the American Rolling Mill Company, Middletown, Ohio, Beginning 1901, and Ending 1922*. Ohio, 1922

Anderson, George B. *One Hundred Booming Years: A History of Bucyrus-Erie Company 1880–1980*. South Milwaukee, Wisconsin: Bucyrus-Erie Co, 1980

Anderson, Joseph, ed. *The Town and City of Waterbury, Connecticut, From the Aboriginal Period to the Year Eighteen Hundred and Ninety-Five*. 3 vols. New Haven: Price & Lee Co, 1896

Andrews, Philip, W. S.; and Brunner, Elizabeth. *Capital Development in Steel: A Study of the United Steel Companies Ltd*. Oxford: Blackwell, 1951

Answer, Valerie. *Sheffield's Traditional Craftsmen*. Sheffield: Sheffield Educational Committee and Valerie Answer, 1980

Appleton's Cyclopaedia of American Biography. James G. Wilson and John Fiske, eds. 9 vols. New York: D. Appleton & Co, 1894–1922

Ardrey, Robert L. *American Agricultural Implements*. Chicago: The author, 1894

Arnold, John O. *British and German Steel Metallurgy*. Oxford University Press, 1915

Asher & Adams' Pictorial Album of American Industry 1876. repr. 1976, Glenn Porter, ed., New York: Rutledge Books

Ashton, Thomas S. *An Eighteenth Century Industrialist: Peter Stubs of Warrington, 1756–1806*. Manchester: Manchester University Press, 1939 *Iron and Steel in the Industrial Revolution*. Manchester: Manchester University Press, 2nd revised ed., 1951

Attman, Artur. *Fagerstabrukens Historia, Adertonhundratalet*. Uppsala: Almqvist & Wiksells Boktryckeri AB, 1958

Austin, John; and Ford, Malcolm. *Steel Town: Dronfield and Wilson Cammell 1873–1883*. Sheffield: Scarsdale Publications, 1983

Backert, Adolphus O., ed. *The ABC of Iron and Steel*. 1st edn., 1915. Cleveland, Ohio: Penton Publishing Co

Bailey, Chris H. *Two Hundred Years of American Clocks and Watches*. Englewood Cliffs, N. J.: Prentice-Hall, 1975

Bain, Edgar C. *Pioneering in Steel Research: A Personal Record*. Metals Park, Ohio: American Society for Metals, 1975

Baldwin–Lima–Hamilton Corp. *The Story of Standard Steel Works 1795–1945*. 1945

Baldwin Locomotive Co. *History of the Baldwin Locomotive Works 1831–1920.* Philadelphia, 1920

Baldwin Tool Co. *Illustrated Supplement to ... [Tools] Manufactured at the Arrowmammett Works, Middletown, Conn.* Middletown: Charles H. Pelton, 1857. Repr. 1976 by K. D. Roberts Publishing Co, Fitzwilliam, N. H.

Bale, Manfred P. *Woodworking Machinery: Its Rise, Progress and Construction.* C. Lockwood & Son, 3rd edn., 1913

Balfour, Arthur. *Hints to Practical Users of Tool Steel.* Sheffield, ca. 1920

Balfour, Arthur & Co. *A Centenary 1865–1965.* Nottingham, 1967

Barnard, Henry, ed. *Armsmear: The Home, The Arm, and the Armory of Samuel Colt. A Memorial.* 1866, n.p., repr. by Beinfield Publishing, 1976

Barraclough, Kenneth C. *Sheffield Steel.* Buxton: Moorland Publishing Co, 1976 *Steelmaking before Bessemer. Vol. 1, Blister Steel. Vol. 2, Crucible Steel.* Metals Society, 1984

Bathe, Dorothy and Greville. *Jacob Perkins. His Inventions, His Times & His Contemporaries.* Philadelphia: Historical Society of Pennsylvania, 1943

Bathe, Greville. *An Engineer's Note Book.* St Augustine, Fla: Allen, Lane & Scott, 1955

Bausman, Joseph H. *History of Beaver County Pennsylvania and its Centennial Celebration.* 2 vols. New York: Knickerbocker Press, 1904

Beach, Moses Yale. *The Wealth and Biography of the Wealthy Citizens of the City of New York.* New York: The Sun Office, 11th edn., 1846

Beauchamp, William M. *Past and Present of Syracuse and Onondaga County New York.* New York: S. J. Clarke Publishing Co, 1908

Becker, Otto M. *High-Speed Steel.* New York: McGraw-Hill, 1910

Bell, Alexander B., ed. *Peeps into the Past: Being Passages from the Diary of Asline Ward.* With an introduction and annotations by Robert E. Leader. Sheffield: Sir W. C. Leng & Co, 1909

Berdrow, William. *The Krupps: 150 Years Krupp History 1787–1937.* Translated by Fritz Homann. Berlin: Paul Schmidt, 1937

Berglund, Abraham; and Wright, Philip G. *The Tariff on Iron and Steel.* Washington, DC: The Brookings Institution, 1929

Bertoff, Rowland T. *British Immigrants in Industrial America, 1790–1950.* Cambridge, Mass.: Harvard University Press, 1953

Bessemer, Sir Henry. *Sir Henry Bessemer FRS: An Autobiography. With a Concluding Chapter (by his son, Henry Bessemer). Engineering,* 1905

Bexfield, Harold. *A Short History of Sheffield Cutlery and the House of Wostenholm.* Sheffield: Loxley Bros, 1945

Bining, Arthur C. *British Regulation of the Colonial Iron Industry.* Philadelphia: University of Pennsylvania Press, 1933 *Pennsylvania Iron Manufacture in the Eighteenth Century.* Harrisburg: Pennsylvania Historical Commission, 1938

Birch, Alan. *The Economic History of the British Iron and Steel Industry 1784–1879.* Frank Cass & Co, 1967

Bishop, John L. *A History of American Manufactures from 1608 to 1860.* Philadelphia: E. Young & Co, 3rd edn., 1868. Repr. New York: Augustus M. Kelley, 1966. With an introduction by Louis M. Hacker

Bland, Fred M. *Tramway Track, 1883 to 1923; or 40 Years of Tramway Practice.* Sheffield, 1923

Bolles, Albert S. *Industrial History of the United States.* Norwich, Conn.: Henry Bill Publishing Co, 1878

Bradbury, Frederick. *History of Old Sheffield Plate*. Macmillan & Co, 1912

Bradley-Smith, H. R. *Blacksmiths' and Farriers' Tools at the Shelburne Museum – A History of Their Development from Forge to Factory*. Shelburne, Vt.: Shelburne Museum, Pamphlet Series No. 7, 1966

Brailsford, Michael. *Lee Steel 1874–1974*. Sheffield, 1974

Brearley, Harry. *Knotted String: An Autobiography of a Steel-Maker*. Longmans, 1941

Stainless Steel: The Story of its Discovery. Repr. from the *Sheffield Daily Independent*, 2 February 1924

Steel-Makers. Longmans, 1933

Talks about Steel making. Cleveland, Ohio: American Society for Metals, 1946

Bridenbaugh, Carl. *The Colonial Craftsman*. New York: New York University Press, 1950

British Association Handbook & Guide to Sheffield. Sheffield: J. W. Northend, 1910

British Mechanic's and Labourer's Handbook, and True Guide to the United States. 1840

Brittain, Frederick. *Address … Before Council of the Sheffield Chamber of Commerce, 4 November, 1875, on the Results of Foreign Tariffs, especially with Reference to Sheffield*. Sheffield: *Daily Telegraph*, 1875

Broehl, Wayne G. *John Deere's Company: A History of Deere & Company and Its Times*. New York: Doubleday, 1984

Broling, Gustaf. *Anteckninar under en resa i England aren 1797, 1798 och 1799*. 3 vols. Stockholm: Tryckt hos J. P. Lindh, 1811–17

Bronson, Henry. *The History of Waterbury, Connecticut*. Waterbury: Bronson Bros, 1858

Brown Bayleys Ltd. *Brown Bayleys 1871–1971: A Centenary*. Sheffield, 1971

The Brown–Firth Research Laboratories. Sheffield, 1937

Brown, M. L. *Firearms in Colonial America*. Washington, DC: Smithsonian Institution Press, 1980

Bruce, Dwight H. *Memorial History of Syracuse, N.Y.* Syracuse: H. P. Smith & Co, 1891

Brumbach, Earl M. *Fifty Years of Progress 1889–1939: A Historical Sketch of the Carpenter Steel Co, Reading, Pa.* 1939

Buck, Norman S. *The Development of the Organisation of Anglo-American Trade, 1800–1850*. New Haven: Yale University Press, 1925

Buck Bros. *Trade Catalogue 1890*. Repr. Fitzwilliam, N. H.: Ken Roberts Publishing Co, 1976

Burn, Duncan L. *The Economic History of Steelmaking, 1867–1939: A Study in Competition*. Cambridge: Cambridge University Press, 1940

Burnham, Thomas H.; and Hoskins, George O. *Iron and Steel in Britain, 1870–1930*. Allen & Unwin, 1943

Cammell, Charles & Co. *Illustrated List of Files & Rasps, Saws, etc.* Sheffield: ca. 1860

Carnegie, David; and Gladwyn, Sidney G. *Liquid Steel: Its Manufacture and Cost*. Longmans, Green & Co, 1913

Carr, James C.; and Taplin, Walter. *A History of the British Steel Industry*. Oxford: Blackwell, 1962

Carter, Nathaniel H. *Letters from Europe*. 2 vols. New Yorks: G. & C. Carvill, 1827

Casterlin, Warren S. *Forty Years at Cast Steel and Tool Making*. Scranton, Pa.: 2nd edn., 1895

The Century's Progress. Yorkshire. London Printing & Engraving Co, 1893

Chandler, Alfred D. *The Visible Hand: The Managerial Revolution in American Business.* Cambridge, Mass.: Belknap Press of Harvard University Press, 1977

Chapman, Arthur W. *The Story of a Modern University: A History of the University of Sheffield.* Oxford University Press, 1955

Chase, Franklin H. *Syracuse and Its Environs: A History.* 3 vols. New York: Lewis Historical Publishing Co, 1924

Chesworth, Mary. *Nineteenth Century Sheffield Through its Billheads and Related Documents.* SCL: 1984

Chittenden, Russell H. *History of the Sheffield Scientific School of Yale University, 1846–1922.* 2 vols. New Haven: Yale University Press, 1928

Church, William C. *The Life of John Ericsson.* 2 vols. Sampson, Low & Co, 1890

Clark, Neil M. *John Deere: He Gave to the World the Steel Plow.* Moline, Ill.: 1937

Clark, Victor S. *History of Manufactures in the United States.* 3 vols. New York: McGraw-Hill, 1929

Clayton, W. Woodford. *History of Onondaga County, New York.* Syracuse: D. Mason & Co, 1880

Cobbett, William. *A Year's Residence in the United States of America.* New York: Clayton & Kingsland, 1818
Rural Rides. A. Cobbett, Strand, 1853

Cochran, Thomas C. *Frontiers of Change: Early Industrialism in America.* New York: Oxford University Press, 1981

Cochrane, Rexmond C. *Measures for Progress: A History of the National Bureau of Standards.* Washington, DC: National Bureau of Standards, 1966

Collins Co. *One Hundred Years.* Collinsville, Conn.: 1926

Colvin, William H. *Crucible Steel of America: 50 Years of Specialty Steelmaking in the USA.* New York: Newcomen Society in America, 1950

Company of Cutlers, Sheffield. *Extracts from the Records of the Company of Cutlers in Hallamshire in the County of York.* With an introduction by Sir Eric Mensforth. Sheffield: Scolar Press, 1972

Comparato, Frank E. *Chronicles of Genius and Folly: R. Hoe and Company and the Printing Press as a Service to Democracy.* Culver City, Calif.: Labyrinthos, 1979

Conway, William P. *Cast to Shape: A History of the Steel Castings Industry in the United States.* Steel Founders' Society of America, Ohio: Rocky River Press, 1977

Cooper, Thomas. *The Emporium of Arts and Sciences.* N.S. 1 (June–October 1813). Philadelphia: Kimber & Richardson, 1813–14

Copley, Frank B. *Frederick W. Taylor: Father of Scientific Management.* 2 vols. Taylor Society, New York: Plimpton Press, Mass., 1923

Coster, Ian. *The Sharpest Edge in the World: The Story of the Rise of a Great Industry.* Gillette Industries Ltd., 1948

Cox, John H. *Diary and Report of a Visit to Paris and the French Exhibition.* Sheffield: Clark & Greenup, 1878

Crescent Steel Co. *The Treatment of Steel. With A Chapter on the Hardening and Tempering of Steel by Geo. Ede.* Pittsburgh, 1884
Condensed Suggestions for Steel Workers. Pittsburgh, 1890

Crom, Theodore R. *Horological Shop Tools 1700 to 1900.* Melrose, Fla.: p.p., 1980

Crucible Steel Co. *50 Years of Fine Steelmaking.* 1951

Annual report. 1st–1900/1. Pittsburgh

Dane, E. Surrey. *Peter Stubs and the Lancashire Hand Tool Industry.* Altrincham: John Sherrat & Son, 1973

Danielsson, Erik. G. *Anteckningar om Norra Amerikas Fri–Staters Jerntillverkning Samt Handel Med Jern–Och Stalvaror.* Stockholm: P. A. Nordstedt & Soner, 1845

Defebaugh, James E. *History of the Lumber Industry of America.* 2 vols. Chicago: The American Lumberman, 1907

Desch, Cecil H. *The Steel Industry of South Yorkshire: A Regional Study.* Being a Paper read to the Sociological Society on 24 January 1922

Deyrup, Felicia J. *Arms Makers of the Connecticut Valley: A Regional Study of the Economic Development of the Small Arms Industry, 1798–1870.* Northampton, Mass.: Smith College Studies in History 33, 1948

Dictionary of American Biography. Allen Johnson and Dumas Malone, eds. 22 vols. New York: Charles Scribner's & Sons, 1928–44

Dictionary of Business Biography. David J. Jeremy, ed. 5 vols. Butterworths, 1984–6.

Dictionary of National Biography. Leslie Stephen and Sydney Lee, eds. 63 vols. Oxford University Press, 1885–1933

Disston, Henry & Sons. *Lumberman Handbook.* Philadelphia: 1912

The Saw in History. Philadelphia: 1915

The File in History. Philadelphia: 1920

Disston, Jacob S. *Henry Disston (1819–1878): Pioneer Industrialist, Inventor and Good Citizen.* New York: Newcomen Society in America, 1950

Doan, Gilbert E. *Bradley Stoughton.* Ohio: American Society for Metals, 1967

Dodd, George. *British Manufactures: Metals.* Vols 3 & 4. Charles Knight & Co, 1845

Doncaster, Daniel & Sons. *The Story of Four Generations, 1778–1938.* 1938

Daniel Doncaster & Sons Ltd 1778–1978. 1978

Edwards, William B. *Civil War Guns.* Harrisburg, Pa.: Stackpole Co, 1962

Eighty Years of Progress of the United States. 1864

Emerson, Wm. A. *History of the Town of Douglas (Massachusetts), From the Earliest Period to the Close of 1878.* Boston: Frank W. Bird, 1879

Erickson, Charlotte J. *American Industry and the European Immigrant 1860–1885.* Cambridge, Mass.: Harvard University Press, 1957

British Industrialists: Steel and Hosiery 1850–1950. Cambridge: At the University Press, 1959

Invisible Immigrants: The Adaptation of English and Scottish Immigrants in Nineteenth Century America. Weidenfeld & Nicolson, 1972

Firth–Brown Ltd. *100 Years in Steel.* Sheffield: 1937

Firth Sterling Steel Co. *Stainless Steel.* McKeesport, Pa.: 1923

Firth–Sterling Tool Steels. McKeesport, Pa.: 1925

Firth, Thomas & Sons. *The Development of Stainless Steel. Its Properties and Uses.* 1922

The Development of 'Staybrite' Steel. Its Properties and Uses. n.d., ca. 1925

Fischer, George Ltd. *The Metallurgist Johann Conrad Fischer 1773–1854 and His Relations with Britain.* Schaffhausen, Switzerland, 1947

Ford, Henry. *My Life and Work.* New York: Doubleday, Page & Co, 1924

Foster, Frank. *Engineering in the United States.* Manchester: At the University Press, 1906

Freedley, Edwin T. *Philadelphia and Its Manufactures.* Philadelphia: E. Young & Co, 1867

Fremont, Charles. *Files and Filing*. Translated by Geo. Taylor and dedicated to the Sheffield File Trades Technical Society. Isaac Pitman & Sons, 1920

French, Benjamin F. *History of the Rise and Progress of the Iron Trade of the United States*. New York: Wiley & Halsted, 1858

Furniss, Henry Sanderson (Lord Sanderson). *Memories of Sixty Years*. Methuen & Co, 1931

Gatty, Alfred. *Sheffield: Past and Present*. Sheffield: Thomas Rodgers, 1873

Gibb, George S. *The Whitesmiths of Taunton; A History of Reed and Barton 1824–1943*. Cambridge, Mass.: Harvard University Press, 1943

Gillette Safety Razor Co. *25th Anniversary*. 1926

Giolitti, Frederico. *The Cementation of Iron and Steel*. Translated from the Italian by Joseph W. Richards and Charles A. Rouiller. New York: McGraw-Hill, 1915

Goodman, William L. *The History of Woodworking Tools*. G. Bell & Sons, 1964
British Plane Makers From 1700. Needham Market, Suffolk: Arnold & Walker, 2nd. edn., 1978

Graeff, Arthur D., ed. *A History of Steel Casting*. Philadelphia: Steel Founders' Society of America, 1949

Grant, Allan. *Steel and Ships: The History of John Brown's*. Michael Joseph, 1950

Gray, Ralph D. *Alloys and Automobiles: The Life of Elwood Haynes*. Indianapolis: Indiana Historical Society, 1979
Stellite; A History of the Haynes Stellite Company, 1912–1972. Kokomo, Indiana: Cabot Corporation, 1974

Greeley, Horace; *et al*. *The Great Industries of the United States*. Hartford: J. B. Burr & Hyde, 1872

Green, Constance McL. *History of Naugatuck, Connecticut*. New Haven: Yale University Press, 1948

Greenwood, William H. *Steel and Iron*. Cassel & Co, 3rd edn., 1887

Gregg, James L. *The Alloys of Iron and Tungsten*. New York: McGraw-Hill, 1931

Griffith's Guide to the Iron Trade of Great Britain. Newton Abbot: David & Charles, 1967 repr. of 1873 edn., with an introduction by W. K. V. Gale

Grimshaw, Robert. *Saws: The History, Development, Action, Classification of Saws, etc.* Philadelphia: E. Claxton & Co, 1882

Griscom, John. *A Year in Europe*. 2 vols. New York: Collins & Co and E. Bliss & E. White, 1823

Grossmann, Marcus A.; and Bain, Edgar C. *High-Speed Steel*. New York: John Wiley & Sons, 1931

Habbakuk, H. John. *American and British Technology in the Nineteenth Century: The Search for Labour Saving Inventions*. Cambridge: At the Press, 1967

Hadfield, Robert A. *Faraday and His Metallurgical Researches*. Chapman & Hall, 1931
Metallurgy and Its Influence on Modern Progress with a Survey of Education and Research. Chapman & Hall, 1925
The Work and Position of the Metallurgical Chemist, also References to Sheffield and Its Place in Metallurgy. C. Griffin & Co. 1921

Hadfield's Steel Foundry Co Ltd. *Hadfield's Steel Foundry Company Ltd*. 1905

Hadfields Ltd. *Annual General Meetings*. 1919+
A Visit of HM the King to the East Hecla Works of Hadfields Ltd. 1915

A Short Description of Hadfields Ltd: Its History, Plant and Manufactures. 1938

The Hadfield System as Applied to War Material. Confidential booklet, n.d., in SCL

Halcomb Steel Co. *Catalogue and Hints on Steel.* Syracuse, New York: 1906

Hallam, Douglas J. *The First 200 Years. A Short History of Rabone Chesterman Limited.* Birmingham, 1984

Hammon, John W. *Men and Volts: The Story of General Electric.* Philadelphia: Lippincott & Co, 1941

Harbord, Frank W. *The Metallurgy of Steel.* C. Griffin & Co, 1904

Harper, Frank C. *Pittsburgh of Today, Its Resources and People.* 5 vols. New York: The American Historical Society, 1931

Hastings, G. W., ed. *Transactions of the National Association for the Promotion of Social Science. Sheffield Meeting, 1865.* Longmans, Green & Co, 1866

Hatch, Alden P. *Remington Arms in American History.* New York: Rinehart & Co, 1956

Hatch, Frederick H. *The Iron and Steel Industry of the UK under War Conditions.* P.p., 1919

Hatfield, John and Julia. *The Oldest Sheffield Plater.* Huddersfield: Advertiser Press, 1974

Hatfield, William H. *The Application of Science to the Steel Industry.* Cleveland, Ohio: American Society for Steel Treating, 1928

Sheffield Burns. Sheffield: J. W. Northend, 1943

Hayward, J. F. *English Cutlery.* HMSO: 1957

Henderson, William O. *Britain and Industrial Europe 1750–1870: Studies in British influence on the Industrial Revolution in Western Europe.* Liverpool: At the University Press, 1954

J.C. Fischer and His Diary of Industrial England 1814–51. Cass, 1966

Hershberg, Theodore, ed. *Philadelphia: Work, Space, Family, and Group Experience in the Nineteenth Century.* New York: Oxford University Press, 1981

Hey, David. *The Rural Metalworkers of the Sheffield Region.* Leicester University Press, 1972

Hibbard, Henry D. *Manufacture and Uses of Alloy Steels.* New York: John Wiley & Sons, 1919

Higham, Norman. *A Very Scientific Gentleman: The Major Achievements of Henry Clifton Sorby.* 1963

Himsworth, Joseph B. *The Story of Cutlery: From Flint to Stainless Steel.* Ernest Benn, 1953

Hindle, Brooke, ed. *America's Wooden Age: Aspects of Early Technology.* New York: Tarrytown, 1975

Histories of Famous Firms. 1957–8

History of Allegheny Co., Pennsylvania. Philadelphia: L. H. Everts & Co, 1876

History of Allegheny County, Pennsylvania. Chicago, Ill.: A. Warner & Co, 1889

Hoffman, Ross J. *Great Britain and the German Trade Rivalry.* Philadelphia: University of Pennsylvania Press, 1933

Hogan, William T. *Economic History of the Iron and Steel Industry in the United States.* 5 vols. Lexington, Mass.: D. C. Heath & Co, 1971

Holland, John. *The Picture of Sheffield or an Historical and Descriptive View of the Town of Sheffield in the County of York.* Sheffield: George Ridge, 1824

Holtzappfel, Charles. *Turning and Mechanical Manipulation.* 3 vols. London: P.p., 1843–50

Howard-White, F. B. *Nickel: An Historical Review.* 1963
Hounshell, David A. *From the American System to Mass Production 1800–1932: The Development of Manufacturing Technology in the United States.* Baltimore: Johns Hopkins University Press, 1984
Howe, Henry M. *The Metallurgy of Steel.* New York: Scientific Publishing Co, 1890
Howell, Kenneth T.; and Carlson, Einer W. *Men of Iron: Forbes & Adam.* Lakeville, Conn.: Pocketknife Press, 1980
Hoyt, Samuel L. *Men of Metals.* Ohio: American Society for Metals, 1979
Hummel, Charles F. *With Hammer in Hand: The Dominy Craftsmen of East Hampton, New York.* Charlottsville: University Press of Virginia, 1968
Hunt, Robert, ed. *Ure's Dictionary of Arts, Manufactures, and Mines Containing an Exposition of Their Principles and Practice.* 3 vols. Longmans, Green & Co, 6th edn., 1867
Hunter, Joseph. *Hallamshire: The History and Topography of the Parish of Sheffield in the County of York.* Revd. edn by Arthur Gatty. Sheffield : Pawson & Brailsford, 1869
Huntsman, Benjamin Ltd. *A Brief History of the Firm of B. Huntsman Ltd 1742–1930.* 1930
Hurt, R. Douglas. *American Farm Tools: From Hand-Power to Steam-Power.* Manhattan, Kans.: Sunflower University Press, 1982
Hussey, Wells & Co. *Steel Memorial, December 1, 1865.* Pittsburgh, 1865
Hutton, Robert S. *Recollections of a Technologist.* Isaac Pitman & Sons, 1964 *Supplement to His Recollections.* n.p., 1966
In Memoriam Calvin Wells. Philadelphia: J. B. Lippincott, 1910
Industries of Sheffield and District. Sheffield: Northern Caxton Publishing Co, 1905
International Exhibition of 1862. Reports by the Juries. W. Clowes & Sons, 1863
International Exhibition of 1862. The Illustrated Catalogue of the Industrial Department. British Division – Vol. II. Printed for H. M. Commissioners, 1862
The Iron and Steel Institute in America in 1890. Special Volume of 'Proceedings'. E. & F. N. Spon, 1892
Jeans, James Stephen. *American Industrial Conditions and Competition. Reports of the Commissioners Appointed by the British Iron Trade Association to Enquire into the Iron, Steel, and Allied Industries of the United States.* British Iron Trade Association, 1902
Steel: Its History, Manufacture, Properties and Uses. E. & F. N. Spon, 1880
Jennings, Russell Mfg. Co. *Price List of Russell Jennings Mfg. Co, c. 1899, with Supplementary Data by K. D. Roberts.* Fitzwilliam, N. H.: K. D. Roberts Publishing Co. 1981
Jeremy, David J. *Transatlantic Industrial Revolution: The Diffusion of Textile Technologies Between Britain and America, 1790–1830s.* Cambridge, Mass.: MIT Press, 1981
Jessop, William & Sons. *Visit to a Steelworks.* Sheffield, 1913
Jones, Peter d'A.; and Simons, Eric N. *The Story of the Saw.* Sheffield: Spear & Jackson Ltd., 1961
Jowitt, George. *George Jowitt & Sons Ltd. A History.* Sheffield: 1966
Kaempffert, Waldemar B., ed. *A Popular History of American Invention.* 2 vols. New York: C. Scribner's Sons, 1924

Kauffman, Henry J. *American Axes: A Survey of Their Development and Their Makers.* Vermont: S. Greene Press, 1972

Kebabien, Paul B. *American Woodworking Tools.* Boston: New York Graphic Society, 1978

Kebabien, Paul B. and Lipke, William C., eds. *Tools and Technologies: America's Wooden Age.* Burlington: University of Vermont, Robert H. Fleming Museum, 1979

Kelleter, Heinrich. *Geschichte der Familie. J. A. Henckels in Verbinding mit einer Geschichte der Solinger Industrie.* Solingen: J. A. Henckels, 1924

Kenyon, John & Co. *Bi-Centenary Celebration, 1710–1910. June 4th 1910.* Sheffield: Pawson & Brailsford, 1910

Kershaw, John B. C. *Electro-Metallurgy.* Constable & Co, 1908

Kingsbury, Benjamin. *A Treatise on Razors.* Simpkin & Marshall, 1797

Kohn, Ferdinand. *Iron and Steel Manufacture.* McKenzie, 1869

Kuniansky, Harry R. *A Business History of Atlantic Steel Company 1901–1968.* New York: Arno Press, 1976

Kuuse, Jan. *Interaction Between Agriculture and Industry: Case Studies of Farm Mechanization in Sweden and the United States 1830–1930.* Upsalla: Almqvist & Wiksell, 1974

Landes, David S. *Revolution in Time. Clocks and the Making of the Modern World.* Cambridge, Mass.: Belknap Press of Harvard University Press, 1983

Lardner, Dionysius. *The Cabinet Cyclopaedia. A Treatise on the Progressive Improvement and Present State of the Manufactures in Metal.* 3 vols. A. Spottiswoode, 1831–4

Lasansky, Jeannette. *To Draw, Upset, & Weld: The Work of the Pennsylvania Rural Blacksmith 1742–1935.* Lewisburg, Pa.: Oral Traditions Project of the Union County Historical Society, 1980

Leader, Robert E. *History of the Company of Cutlers in Hallamshire in the County of York.* 2 vols. Sheffield: Pawson & Brailsford, 1905–6
Sheffield in the Eighteenth Century. Sheffield: Sir W. C. Leng & Co Ltd, 2nd ed., 1905

Lee, Arthur & Sons Ltd. *Lee of Sheffield: A Family Enterprise.* Sheffield: 1962

Levine, Aaron L. *Industrial Retardation in Britain, 1880–1914.* Weidenfeld & Nicolson, 1967

Levine, Bernard. *Levine's Guide to Knives and Their Values.* Northbrook, Ill.: DBI Books, 1985

Lief, Alfred. *Camillus: The Story of an American Small Business.* New York: Columbia University, 1944

Lloyd, Godfrey I. H. *The Cutlery Trades: An Historical Essay in the Economics of Small-Scale Production.* Longmans, Green & Co, 1913

Local Register and Chronological Account of Occurrences and Facts Connected with the Town and Neighbourhood of Sheffield. Sheffield: Printed for John Thomas and Published by Robert Leader, 1830

Lyle, D. A. *Report on the Manufacture and Uses of Files and Rasps.* 1881

Lytle, Thomas G. *Harpoons and Other Whalecraft.* New Bedford, Mass.: Old Dartmouth Historical Society, 1984

McCloskey, Donald M. *Economic Maturity and Entrepreneurial Decline: British Iron and Steel, 1870–1913.* Cambridge, Mass.: Harvard University Press, 1973

McCullough, David. *The Great Bridge.* New York: Simon & Schuster, 1972

McHugh, Jeanne. *Alexander Holley and the Makers of Steel.* Baltimore: Johns Hopkins Press, 1980

MacKay, Donald. *The Lumberjacks*. Toronto : McGraw-Hill Ryerson, 1978

McMahon, A. Michal; and Morris, Stephanie A. *Technology in Industrial America: The Committee on Science and the Arts of the Franklin Institute, 1824–1900*. Wilmington, Del.: Scholarly Resources, 1977

Makins, G. H. *A Manual of Metallurgy, More Particularly of the Precious Metals, Including the Method of Assaying Them*. Philadelphia: H. C. Baird, 1865

Manchester Society of Engineers. Reports of Past Experimental Work on Cutting Tools, March 13, 1915

Manchester, William. *The Arms of Krupp 1587–1968*. London: Michael Joseph, 1964

Marples, Wm & Sons. *1909 Price List of American Tools*. Repr. Fitzwilliam, N. H.: Kenneth D. Roberts Publishing Co, 1980

Price List. 1907 Edition Repr. by Mid-west Tool Collectors Association, The Early American Industries Association & Arnold Walker, 1979

Marshall, A. C.; and Newbould, Herbert. *The History of Firth's (1842–1918)*. Sheffield: Thomas Firth & Sons, 1924

Mayr, Otto; and Post, Robert C., eds. *Yankee Enterprise: The Rise of the American System of Manufactures*. Washington, DC: Smithsonian Institution, 1981

Mechanical Engineers in America, Born Prior to 1861: A Biographical Dictionary. New York: American Society of Mechanical Engineers, 1980

Mehl, Robert F. *A Brief History of the Science of Metals*. New York: American Institute of Mining and Metallurgical Engineers, 1948

Men of the Period. Biographical Publishing Co, 1896

Merriam, Robert L.; *et al. The History of the John Russell Cutlery Company 1833–1936*. Greenfield, Mass.: Bete Press, 1976

Metcalf, William. *Steel: A Manual for Steel Users*. New York, 1911

Midvale Steel Co. *The Seventy-Fifth Anniversary of the Midvale Steel Company*. 1942

Miller, Henry R. *Fleming's Views of Old Pittsburgh: A Portfolio of the Past*. Pittsburgh: Crescent Press, 1932

Miller, William T. W. *Crushers for Stone and Ore: Their Development, Characteristics and Capabilities*. Mining Publications, 1935

Monypenny, John H. G. *Stainless Iron and Steel*. Chapman & Hall, 2nd edn., 1931

Moody, John A. *The American Cabinetmaker's Plow Plane. Its Design and Improvement 1700–1900*. Evansville, Ind.: 'The Tool Box', 1981

Morgan Crucible Co Ltd. *Battersea Works 1856–1956: The Morgan Crucible Company Ltd, Battersea, London*. 1956

Moriarty, Wilson H. *A Century of Steel Castings; A History of 100 Years of Steel Castings Service to American Industry*. New York: Newcomen Society in America, 1961

Mosely Industrial Commission to the United States of America, Oct.–Dec. 1902. Report of the Delegates. Manchester: Co-operative Printing Society, 1903

Moxon, Stanley. *A Fox Centenary: Umbrella Frames, 1848–1948*. Stocksbridge: The Company, 1948

Musson, Albert E.; and Robinson, Eric. *Science and Technology in the Industrial Revolution*. Manchester: Manchester University Press, 1969

Nalle, Richard T. *Midvale and Its Pioneers*. New York: Newcomen Society in America, 1948

National Cyclopaedia of American Biography. 34 vols. New York: White & Co, 1892–1947

National Federation of Iron and Steel Manufacturers (British Iron and Steel Federation). *Statistical Bulletin/Report* 1919–39

Navin, Thomas R. *The Whitin Machine Works Since 1831*. Cambridge, Mass.: Harvard University Press, 1950

Nelson, Daniel. *Frederick W. Taylor and the Rise of Scientific Management*. Madison: University of Wisconsin Press, 1980

Neumann, George C. *Swords and Blades of the American Revolution*. Newton Abbot: David & Charles, 1973

Nevins, Allan. *Selected Writings of Abram S. Hewitt*. New York: Columbia University Press, 1937

Nevins, Allan; and Hill, Frank E. *Ford*. 3 vols. New York: Scribner's Sons, 1954–63

Nicholson, John. *The Operative Mechanic and Practical Machinist*. 2 vols. 1st American edn. from 2nd London edn., Philadelphia: H. C. Carey & I. Lea, 1826

Nicholson File Co. *A Treatise on Files and Rasps*. Providence, R.I.: 1878

Odom, William. *Hallamshire Worthies: Characteristics and Work of Notable Sheffield Men and Women*. Sheffield: J. W. Northend, 1926

Osborn, Fred M. *The Story of the Mushets*. Thomas Nelson & Sons, 1952 *Tool Steel*. 1908

Osborn, Henry S. *The Metallurgy of Iron and Steel, Theoretical and Practical*. Philadelphia: H. C. Baird, 1869

Ouden, A. Den. *Electric Steelmaking up to 1930*. Nederland, 1981

Overman, Frederick. *The Manufacture of Steel: Containing the Practice and Principles of Working and Making Steel*. Philadelphia: A. Hart, 1851
A Treatise on Metallurgy; Comprising Mining, and General and Particular Metallurgical Operations. New York: D. Appleton, 1852

Pagé, Camille. *La Coutellerie Depuis L'Origine Jusqu'à Nos Jours*. 6 vols. Chatellerault: H. Rivière, 1896

Pankiewicz, Philip. *New England Cutlery*. Gilman, Conn.: Hollytree Publications, 1986

Parrish, H.; and Ross, T. J. *200th Anniversary 1742–1942: Taylor–Wharton Iron and Steel Company*. 1942

Parsons, John E., ed. *Saml. Colt's Own Record: Samuel Colt's Own Record of Transactions with Captain Walker and Eli Whitney, Jr. in 1847*. Connecticut Historical Society: Conn. Printers, 1949

Pawson and Brailsford's Illustrated Guide to Sheffield and Neighbourhood. Sheffield: 1862. Revd. 1879 by John Taylor

Payne, Peter L. *British Entrepreneurship in the Nineteenth Century*. The Macmillan Press, 1974

Peach, Lawrence Du Garde. *The Company of Cutlers in Hallamshire in the County of York 1906–1956*. Sheffield: Pawson & Brailsford, 1960

The Penny Cyclopaedia of the Society for the Diffusion of Useful Knowledge. 27 vols. Charles Knight, 1842

Percy, John. *Metallurgy: The Art of Extracting Metals From Their Ores, and Adapting Them to Various Purposes of Manufacture*. John Murray, 1864

Perspectives in Metallurgical Development. Proceedings of the Centenary Conference held from 16–18 July to Celebrate the Establishment of the University of Sheffield's Department of Metallurgy. Metals Society, 1984

Peterson, Harold L. *American Knives: The First History and Collectors' Guide*. New York: C. Scribner's Sons, 1958

Phillips, Sir John Arthur. *A Manual of Metallurgy, or Practical Treatise on the Chemistry of the Metals.* J. J. Griffin & Co, 1852

Pittsburgh, Its Industry and Commerce. 1870

Pittsburgh Chamber of Commerce. *The Mercantile, Manufacturing and Mining Interests of Pittsburgh, 1884.* Pittsburgh: W. G. Johnston, 1884

Platts, Harvey. *The Knifemakers Who Went West.* Longmont, Colo.: Longs Peak Press, 1978

Pollard, Sidney. *A History of Labour in Sheffield.* Liverpool: Liverpool University Press, 1959

Three Centuries of Sheffield Steel: The Story of a Family Business. Sheffield: Marsh Bros, 1954

The Sheffield Outrages. Bath: Adams & Dart, 1971

Porter, Glenn; and Livesay, Harold C. *Merchants and Manufacturers: Studies in the Changing Structure of Nineteenth Century Marketing.* Baltimore: Johns Hopkins Press, 1971

Post, Robert C., ed. *1876: A Centennial Exhibition.* Washington, DC: Smithsonian Institution, 1976

Pratt, Edwin A. *Trade Unionism and British Industry.* John Murray, 1904

Pring, John N. *The Electric Furnace.* Longmans, Green & Co, 1921

Professional and Industrial History of Suffolk County, Massachusetts. Boston: The Boston History Co, 1894

Pybus, Sylvia; and Elizabeth, Maria E.; et al. *Cutlery: A Bibliography.* Sheffield City Library, revd. edn., 1982

Ransom, James H. *Vanishing Iron Works of the Ramapos.* New Jersey: Rutgers University Press, 1966

Réaumur's Memoirs on Steel and Iron: A Translation of the Original Printed in 1722. By Anneliese Grunhaldt Sisco with an introduction and notes by Cyril S. Smith. Chicago: Chicago University Press, 1956

Reck, Franklin M. *Sand in Their Shoes: The Story of American Steel Foundries.* American Steel Foundries, 1952

Rees, Abraham, ed. *The Cyclopaedia; or Universal Dictionary of Arts, Sciences and Literature.* 45 vols. Longman et al., 1802–20: Published in America in Philadelphia by Samuel Bradford et al., 1810–24

Reports of Artisans Selected by a Committee Appointed by the Council of the Society of Arts to Visit the Paris Universal Exhibition 1867. Bell & Daldy, 1867.

Rhodes, Ebenezer. *Essay on the Manufacture, Choice, and Management of a Razor.* Sheffield: Montgomery, 1824

Richardson, Milton T. *Practical Blacksmithing.* 4 vols. New York: M. T. Richardson, 1889

Robert, G. A.; Hamaker, Jr., J. C.; and Johnson, A. R. *Tool Steels.* Ohio: American Society for Metals, 3rd edn., 1962

Roberts, Kenneth D. *Wooden Planes in Nineteenth Century America. Vol. II: The Union Factory, Pine Meadow, Connecticut, 1826–1929.* Fitzwilliam, N. H.: K. D. Roberts Publishing Co, 2nd edn., 1978, 1983

Some Nineteenth Century English Woodworking Tools, Edge and Joiner Tools and Bit Braces. Fitzwilliam, N. H.: K. D. Roberts Publishing Co, 1980

Roberts, Kenneth D.; and Roberts, Jane W. *Planemakers and Other Edge Tool Enterprises in New York State in the Nineteenth Century.* Cooperstown: New York Historical Association, Early American Industries Association, 1971

Robson, Charles, ed. *The Manufactories and Manufacturers of Pennsylvania in the Nineteenth Century.* Philadelphia: Galaxy Publishing Co, 1875

Roden-Hauser, W.; Schoenawa, J.; and Vom Baur, C. H. *Electric Furnaces in the Iron and Steel Industry*. New York: John Wiley & Sons, 2nd edn., 1913
Rodgers, Charles T. *American Superiority at the World's Fair*. Philadelphia: John J. Hawkins, 1852
Rodgers, Joseph & Sons Ltd. *Under Five Sovereigns*. 1911
A Royal Record. 1930
Rogin, Leo. *The Introduction of Farm Machinery in its Relation to the Productivity of Labor in the Agriculture of the United States During the Nineteenth Century*. University of California Publications in Economics No. 9, University of California Press, 1931
Rolt, Lionel T. C. *Tools for the Job: A Short History of Machine Tools*. Batsford, 1965
Rose, Joshua. *The Complete Practical Machinist*. Philadelphia: H. C. Baird & Co, 1890
Rosenberg, Nathan, ed. *The American System of Manufacturers: The Report of the Committee on the Machinery of the United States, 1855, and the Special Reports of George Wallis and Joseph Whitworth, 1854*. Edinburgh: Edinburgh University Press, 1969
Perspectives on Technology. Cambridge: Cambridge University Press, 1976
Rowe, Frank H. *History of the Iron and Steel Industry of Scioto County, Ohio*. Columbus, Ohio: 1938
Royal Society. *Lectures on the Results of the Great Exhibition of 1851*. D. Bogue, 1852
Russell, Carl P. *Firearms, Traps, and Tools of the Mountain Men*. New York: Alfred A Knopf, 1967
Ruttenber, Edward M.; and Clark, Lewis H., eds. *History of Orange County, New York, with Illustrations and Biographical Sketches of Many of its Pioneers and Prominent Men*. Philadelphia: Everts & Peck, 1881
Ryerson, Barry. *The Giants of Small Heath: The History of BSA*. Yeovil: G. T. Foulis & Haynes Publishing Group, 1980
Salaman, Raphael A. *Dictionary of Tools Used in the Woodworking and Allied Trades, c.1700–1970*. G. Allen & Unwin, 1975
Sanderson Bros & Newbould Ltd. *Hints on Steel*. 1917
Sanderson Kayser Ltd. *400 Years of Iron and Steel*. Repr. from *Sanderson Kayser Magazine*, 1969–71. Attributed to G. B. Callan
Saul, Samuel B, ed. *Technological Change: The United States and Britain in the Nineteenth Century*. Methuen, 1970
Sauveur, Albert. *Metallurgical Reminiscences and Dialogue*. Ohio: American Society for Metals, 1981
Scharf, John T.; and Westcott, Thompson. *History of Philadelphia*. Philadelphia: L. H. Everts & Co, 1884
Schib, Karl; and Gnade, Rudolf. *Johann Conrad Fischer 1773–1854*. Schauffhausen, Switzerland: George Fischer Ltd, 1954
Schmookler, Jacob. *Patents, Invention and Economic Change; Data and Selected Essays*. Eds., Z. Griliches & L. Hurwicz. Mass.: Harvard University Press, 1972
Scoffern, J.; et al. *The Useful Metals and Their Alloys . . . With their Applications to the Industrial Arts*. 1857
Scott, John D. *Vickers: A History*. Weidenfeld & Nicolson, 1962
Scott, Quinta; and Miller, Howard S. *The Eads Bridge*. Columbia: University of Missouri Press, 1979

Searle, Alfred B. _Refractory Materials: Their Manufacture and Uses._ C. Griffin, 3rd edn., 1950

Sears Roebuck Catalogue. _1887 Edition._ Fred L. Israel, ed., with an introduction by S. J. Perelman and Richard Rovere. New York: Chelsea House, 1968
1908 Edition. Joseph J. Schroeder, Jr., ed. Northfield, Ill.: DBI Books, 1971
1927 Edition. Alan Mirken, ed. New York: Bounty Books, 1970

Seebohm, Henry. _On the Manufacture of Crucible Cast Steel._ Sheffield: Pawson & Brailsford, 1884

Seed, Thomas A. _Pioneers for a Century, 1852–1952: A History of the Growth and Achievement of Samuel Osborn & Co Ltd._ Sheffield: 1952

Sellens, Alvin. _The Stanley Plane: A History and Descriptive Inventory._ Burlington, Vt.: The Early American Industries Association, 1975
Woodworking Planes. A Descriptive Register of Wooden Planes. P.p., 1978

Shadwell, Arthur. _Industrial Efficiency: A Comparative Study of Industrial Life in England, Germany and America._ 2 vols. Longmans & Co, 1906

Shaw, H. (Magnets) Ltd. _Magnets and Memories. A Celebration of the 200 Years of H. Shaw (Magnets) 1783–1983._ Sheffield: H. Shaw (Magnets), 1983

Sheffield and Neighbourhood: Comprising Accounts of the Early History and Progress of the Town, etc. Sheffield: Pawson & Brailsford, 1899

Sheffield and Rotherham 'Up-To-Date'. Robinson, Son & Co, 1897

Sheffield As It Is: Being an Historical and Descriptive Hand-book and Stranger's Guide, etc. Sheffield: J. Pearce, 1852

Sheffield. _Sheffield Development Department Town Hall 1922. The Metal Industries of Sheffield_

Sheffield. _Sheffield Lists._ Various dates

Sheffield Literary and Philosophical Society. _Portraits of Presidents._ Vol. 2. 1856–88. SCL

Sheldon, Joseph. _The Founders and Builders of Stocksbridge Works._ Stocksbridge: J. Sheldon, 1922

Simonds Manufacturing Co. _75 Years of Business Progress and Industrial Advance, 1832–1907._ Cambridge, Mass.: The University Press, 1907

Simons, Eric N. _Lockwood and Carlisle Ltd of Sheffield: A Chapter of Marine History._ n.d.

Sinclair, Bruce. _Philadelphia's Philosopher Mechanics: A History of the Franklin Institute._ Baltimore: Johns Hopkins University Press, 1974

Sisco, Frank T. _The Manufacture of Electric Steel._ New York: McGraw-Hill, 1924

Smiles, Samuel. _Industrial Biography: Iron Workers and Tool Makers._ John Murray, 1853. Repr. with an introduction by L. T. C. Rolt. Newton Abbot: David & Charles, 1967

Smith, Cyril S. _A History of Metallography: The Development of Ideas on the Structure of Metals Before 1890._ University of Chicago Press, 1960
ed. _The Sorby Centennial Symposium on the History of Metallurgy, Cleveland, 1963._ New York: Gordon & Breach Science Publishers, 1965
Sources for the History of the Science of Steel 1532–1786. Cambridge, Mass.: Society for the History of Technology and MIT Press, 1968
A Search for Structure: Selected Essays on Science, Art, and History. Cambridge, Mass.: MIT Press, 1981

Smith, H. Perry. _Syracuse and Its Surroundings._ 1878

Smith, J. Bucknall. _A Treatise Upon Wire. Engineering_ and New York: J. Wiley & Sons, 1891

Smith, Joseph. *Explanation or Key, to the Various Manufactories of Sheffield, With Engravings of Each Article.* John S. Kebabien, ed. Vermont: The Early American Industries Association, 1975

Smith, Roger K. *Patented Transitional & Metallic Planes in America 1827–1927.* Lancaster, Mass.: North Village Publishing Co, 1981

Spear & Jackson Ltd. *Continual Progress Since 1774.* n.d.

Spencer Clark Bi-Centenary. *200 Years of Metal Craftsmanship.* 1978

Stainton, James H. *The Making of Sheffield 1865–1914.* Sheffield: E. Weston & Sons, 1924

Stansfield, Alfred. *The Electric Furnace.* New York: McGraw-Hill, 1907
The Electric Furnace for Iron and Steel. New York: McGraw-Hill, 1923

Stansfield, Hazel. *Samuel Fox and Company Ltd 1842–1967.* Stocksbridge: 1967

Stones, Frank. *The British Ferrous Wire Industry 1882–1962.* Sheffield: J. W. Northend Ltd, 1977

Strassmann, W. Paul. *Risk and Technological Innovation: American Manufacturing During the Nineteenth Century.* Ithaca, New York: Cornell University Press, 1956

Sutcliff, Robert. *Travels in Some Parts of North America in the Years 1804, 1805, & 1806.* York: W. Alexander, 1815

Svedenstierna, Eric T. *Svedenstierna's Tour in Great Britain 1802–3: The Travel Diary of an Industrial Spy.* Translated by E. L. Dellow with an introduction by M. W. Flinn. Newton Abbot: David & Charles, 1973

Swank, James M. *History of the Manufacture of Iron in All Ages, and Particularly of the United States for Three Hundred Years, from 1585 to 1885.* Philadelphia: Published by the Author, 1884

Szymanowitz, Raymond. *Edward Goodrich Acheson.* New York: Vantage Press, 1971

Taber, Martha Van H. *A History of the Cutlery Industry in the Connecticut Valley.* Northampton, Mass.. Smith College Studies in History 41, 1955

Taylor, Frank H. *History of the Alan Wood Iron and Steel Company, 1792–1920.* n.d., published for private circulation

Taylor, Frederick W. *On the Art of Cutting Metals.* New York: American Society of Mechanical Engineers, 1907

Taylor–Wharton Iron & Steel Co. *Historically Speaking 1742–1917: 175th Anniversary.* 1917

Taylor, Wilmot. *The Sheffield Horn Industry.* Sheffield: J. W. Northend, 1927

Temin, Peter. *Iron and Steel in Nineteenth Century America: An Economic Inquiry.* Cambridge, Mass.: MIT Press, 1964

Thallner, Otto. *Tool Steel.* Philadelphia: H. C. Baird & Co, 1902

Thistlethwaite, Frank. *The Anglo-American Connection in the Early Nineteenth Century.* Philadelphia: University of Pennsylvania Press, 1959

Thorp, Raymond W. *Bowie-Knife.* Albuquerque: University of New Mexico, 1948

Thum, Ernest E., ed. *The Book of Stainless Steels.* Cleveland, Ohio: The American Society for Steel Treating, 2nd. edn., 1935

Thurston, George H. *Pittsburgh As It Is.* Pittsburgh: W. S. Haven, 1857
Pittsburgh and Allegheny in the Centennial Year. Pittsburgh: A. A. Anderson & Co, 1876
Pittsburgh's Progress, Industries and Resources. Pittsburgh: A. A. Anderson & Co, 1886

Timmins, John Geoffrey, ed. *Workers in Metal Since 1784. A History of W. & G. Sissons Ltd*. Sheffield: 1984

Timmins, Samuel. *The Resources, Products, and Industrial History of Birmingham and the Midland Hardware District*. Robert Hardwicke, 1866

Tomlinson, Charles. *The Useful Arts and Manufactures of Great Britain. First and Second Series*. Christian Knowledge Society, 1861
ed. *Cyclopaedia of Useful Arts, Mechanical and Chemical, Manufactures, Mining, and Engineering*. 3 vols. Virtue & Co, 1866

Tooker, Elva. *Nathan Trotter, Philadelphia Merchant, 1783–1853*. Cambridge, Mass.: Harvard University Press, 1955

Torrey, Julia W. *Old Sheffield Plate*. Boston and New York: Houghton & Mifflin Co, 1918

Trebilcock, Clive. *The Vickers Brothers: Armaments and Enterprise, 1854–1914*. Europa, 1977

Trumbull, Levi R. *A History of Industrial Paterson*. Paterson, N. J.: Carleton M. Herrick, 1882

Turner, C. A. *A Sheffield Heritage: An Anthology of Photographs and Words of the Cutlery Craftsmen*. Division of Continuing Education. University of Sheffield and Sheffield Trades Historical Society, 1978

Turner, Henry. *The Manufacture of Files, and the Material From Which They Are Made; With Remarks on Machine-Cut Files and Unions*. Sheffield: 2nd edn., 1862

Turner, Thos. & Co and Wingfield Rowbotham. *Handicrafts That Survive. Centenary Souvenir 1802–1902*. Sheffield: 1902

Tweedale, Geoffrey. *Giants of Sheffield Steel: The Men Who Made Sheffield the Steel Capital of the World*. Sheffield: SCL, 1986

Tylecote, Ronald F. *A History of Metallurgy*. Metals Society, 1976

Tyzack, Wm Sons & Turner Ltd. *Centenary Souvenir 1812–1912*. Sheffield: 1912

US Centennial Commission. *International Exhibition 1876: Reports and Awards. Group I*. Philadelphia: J. B. Lippincott & Co, 1878

Vickers, Sons & Maxim Ltd. *Their Works and Manufactures*. Repr. from *Engineering*, 1902

Wagoner, Harless D. *The US Machine Tool Industry from 1900 to 1950*. Cambridge, Mass.: MIT Press, 1966

Warner, Ken, ed. *Knives '86*. 6th annual edn. Northbrook, Ill.: DBI Books, 1985

Warren, Kenneth. *The American Steel Industry, 1850–1970: A Geographical Interpretation*. Oxford: Clarendon Press, 1973

Washer, Richard. *The Sheffield Bowie and Pocket-Knife Makers 1825–1925*. Nottingham: T. A. Vinall, 1974

Wertime, Theodore. *The Coming of the Age of Steel*. Leiden: University of Chicago Press, 1962

Wheeler, Madden & Bakewell. *Illustrated Price List 1860*. Repr. 1976 by the Early American Industries Association, South Burlington, Vt.

White, John H. *American Locomotives: An Engineering History, 1830–1880*. Baltimore: Johns Hopkins Press, 1968
The American Railroad Passenger Car. Baltimore: Johns Hopkins University Press, 1978

Willey, Francis V.; and Locock, Guy. *Report on a Visit to the USA*. Federation of British Industries, 1925

Williams, Richard R. *The American Hardware Store: A Manual of Approved*

Methods of Arranging and Displaying Hardware. New York: D. Williams & Co, 1897

Williamson, Harold F. *Winchester. The Gun that Won the West*. Washington, DC: Combat Forces Press, 1952

Williamson, Harold F.; and Myers, Kenneth H. *Designed for Digging; the First 75 Years of Bucyrus-Erie Company*. Evanston, Ill.: Northwestern University Press, 1955

Williamson, William R. *I*XL Means I EXCEL: A Short History of the Bowie Knife*. Robert E. P. Cherry, 1974

Wilson, Erasmus. *Standard History of Pittsburgh, Pennsylvania*. Chicago: H. R. Cornell & Co, 1898

Wilson, Ronald E. *200 Precious Metal Years: A History of the Sheffield Smelting Company Ltd 1760–1960*. Ernest Benn, 1960

Wiss, J. & Sons. *A Story of Shears and Scissors 1848–1948*. Newark, N.J.: 1948

Woodward, Calvin M. *A History of the St. Louis Bridge*. St Louis: G. I. Jones & Co, 1881

The Working Man: A Weekly Record of Social and Industrial Progress. 2 vols. Cassell, Petter & Galpin, 1866

Worssam, W. Samuel. *History of the Bandsaw*. Manchester: Emmott & Co, 1892

Wostenholm, George & Son. *Trade Catalogue 1885*. Repr. Louisville: Americana/Reed, 1975

Wright, Carroll D. *Comparative Wages and Prices: 1860–1883. Massachusetts and Great Britain*. [*From the Sixteenth Annual Report of the Massachusetts Bureau of Statistics and Labor*]. Boston: Wright & Potter, 1885

Wright, Frazer. *Stanley 1936–1986*. Sheffield, 1986

Young, Arthur. *A Six Months Tour Through the North of England*. 4 vols. W. Strahan, 1770

Young, Edward. *Labor in Europe and America*. Washington, DC: Government Printing Office, 1875

Zapffe, Carl A. *Stainless Steels*. Cleveland, Ohio: 1949

INDEX